REF

57
537
1986.

REFERENCE USE ONLY

THE ENCYCLOPAEDIA OF FASHION

Frontispiece: Parisian eveningwear
from *La Gazette du bon ton*,
1925.

GEORGINA O'HARA

THE ENCYCLOPAEDIA OF FASHION

Introduction by Carrie Donovan

Harry N. Abrams, Inc., Publishers, New York

SEP 8 1987

DOUGLAS COLLEGE LIBRARY

Acknowledgments

The compilation of a book of this kind is not possible without the advice, criticism, encouragement, help, and support of many people. The author would like to thank the following for their efforts with some or all of the above, and, in particular, for their time: Hardy Amies, Gunnel Andresen (Scandinavia), Cindy Cathcart at the Condé Nast Library in New York, Meredith Etherington-Smith for information on Patou and Lucile and for some helpful suggestions, Claude Fillet (Switzerland), Peter Hope Lumley for supplying many missing links, Janice Phillips for her help with typing and collating, and Holly Warner in Paris, who helped get the ball rolling at the very beginning. In addition, this book could not have been produced without the support of my family and Steven Callan.

Library of Congress Cataloging-in-Publication Data

O'Hara, Georgina.
   The encyclopaedia of fashion.

   Bibliography: p.
   1. Fashion—Dictionaries.   2. Costume—History—19th century—Dictionaries.   3. Costume—History—20th century—Dictionaries.   I. Title.
GT507.053   1986   391'.003'21   86–3542
ISBN 0–8109–0882–4

Copyright © 1986 Georgina O'Hara
Introduction copyright © 1986 Carrie Donovan

Published in 1986 by Harry N. Abrams, Incorporated, New York. All rights reserved. No part of the contents of this book may be reproduced without the written permission of the publishers

Times Mirror Books

Printed and bound in Great Britain

CONTENTS

A 1901 evening gown designed by Jacques **Doucet** for the actress Rosa Bruck.

INTRODUCTION

THE ASSUMPTION that anything fashionable is frivolous makes the author of this encyclopaedia see magenta.

Georgina O'Hara, who has compiled an impressive reference work of seemingly everything and everyone connected with the subject of fashion, states unequivocally her passionate belief that people should take fashion more seriously than they do. For Ms. O'Hara, the study of fashion can be at once "a history lesson, a geography lesson, an economics lesson, and a mathematics lesson." She sees particular aspects of fashion as sensitive recorders of the times in which they exist. No one should dispute her beliefs; fashion really is all about change.

If something is fashionable, it is current, the latest trend. Ironically, however, no sooner does something become fashionable than it begins a downward cycle. First the fashion becomes widely popular, and quickly thereafter achieves "mass" popularity, then it fades into the background, superseded by the newest trend. In the past this scenario was cut and dried, but in recent decades residues of one fashionable movement have hung on and been incorporated into the next. In addition, the setters of recent fashion trends have purposely delved into historical times in order to find things to reincarnate. Yet the results accurately reflect the multilayered and varied climate of our times. All this further bears out the author's theory of fashion as a mirror of the moment.

This encyclopaedia carefully and thoroughly covers all the variegated aspects of fashion and will prove invaluable to students and cognoscenti of the subject. There are succinct summations of such things as leg warmers, zoot suits, accordion pleats, gaucho pants, mob caps, and moiré. It is also particularly satisfying to discover that certain superb artists and illustrators who captured the essence of a particular moment of fashion—such as Bernard Boutet de Monvel and Count René Bouët-Willaumez—have not been forgotten. They are included along with the late great Eric and the still very active René Gruau (who, amusingly enough, finds himself noted directly before a description of the G-string).

Ms. O'Hara's inquisitive, probing research has also resulted in a volume that should interest and fascinate an audience beyond the realm of students and scholars. In recording the broad panorama of fashion, she reveals facts about many other personalities who have pushed or at least nudged fashion in one way or another. There are, of course, brief discourses on designers and manufacturers (crisply up-to-date with the inclusion of New York's latest star, Donna Karan, and Paris's Azzedine Alaia), but also on the often quite controversial "private" persons whose own styles and points of views have set off trends or put a personal stamp on a period of fashion. These include such past and present supermedia stars as Jacqueline Kennedy Onassis, Brigitte Bardot, Katharine Hepburn, and Greta Garbo.

Also of note to a general audience interested less in the precise than the encyclopaedic aspects of fashion is the author's incisive inclusion of many of the publications editors, art directors, and photographers that have invented, recorded, and perhaps manipulated fashion in their own way. Here one finds the American *Vogue*'s art director, Dr. Agha, who was followed by the brilliant painter and sculptor—now Condé Nast's editorial director—Alexander Liberman; the incomparable Diana Vreeland; and John Fairchild, the remarkable "éminence grise" of *Women's Wear Daily*, *W*, and *M* publications.

To be sure, some readers are certain to find omissions, but these will be few and minor, for this book is truly impressive in its scope. Georgina O'Hara has gone a long way towards establishing her conviction that "people should take fashion seriously." With *The Encyclopaedia of Fashion*, she also proves that fashion makes for highly entertaining browsing and reading.

CARRIE DONOVAN
Fashion Editor, *New York Times Magazine*

PREFACE

FASHION IS A mobile, changing reflection of the way we are and the times in which we live. Dress has always been used as a social tool to display wealth and position, just as the deliberate rejection of status symbols relays other messages. Clothes can reveal our priorities, our aspirations, our liberalism or conservatism. They go a long way toward satisfying simple or complex emotional needs, and they can be used consciously or unconsciously to convey subtle or overt sexual messages. Clothes contribute tone and hue to our environment and give form to our feelings. They are the first and last words of the language that is fashion.

The Encyclopaedia of Fashion covers this multifarious subject in many of its guises, from around 1840—when the sewing machine came into use, setting the cornerstone of the ready-to-wear industry—until the 1980s. It concentrates on the five major fashion capitals of the nineteenth and twentieth centuries: Paris, London, New York, Rome and, latterly, Milan. From these five cities the main thrust of fashion direction emerged, and it was to these cities that creative individuals were drawn, though of course other centers, such as Hollywood, have also made their contribution.

Biographies of designers—the innovators, creators, and interpreters, even those whose contribution was no greater or smaller than producing good work during a specific period of time—form an important component of this book. The first designer of consequence was Charles Worth, an Englishman in Paris, who deserves the title "king of *haute couture*" in more ways than one. In him we can see the beginnings of the modern-day fashion designer, a celebrity in his own right whose marketing and publicity stunts, coupled with indisputable talent, extended his influence far beyond the wardrobe of the well-dressed. Worth led the way for other great fashion names: Doucet, Paquin, Poiret, Lucile . . .

Travel, communications, and the middle classes spread the word. Patou brought mannequins from America to show his clothes in Paris; these models of sporty American women suited to perfection the jaunty clothes of the 1920s. But the reins were to pass out of male hands during the 1920s and 1930s and into the hands of the two undisputed queens of fashion: Chanel and Schiaparelli. Chanel's ideas are still alive today: her look was as casual, unstructured, and uncomplicated as she herself was complicated. But she was also a great stylist, who knew the impact of a strategically placed bow or brooch.

It was Schiaparelli who brought humor to fashion, with her irreverent clothes that poked fun at everyone but the wearer. Through her, fashion and art fused. She took from the art world its most avant-garde ideas and used them in her designs. Some of her experiments are only today being put into practice.

During World War II America fell out of touch with Paris and began to go her own way. In the French capital itself fashion marked time until 1947, when Dior arrested everyone's attention. Although as early as 1939, and certainly through the war years, many Parisian designers had been working toward a new shape which was to become known in 1947 as the New Look, it was Dior who launched it, and it is with Dior's name that it will be irrevocably linked.

The *haute couture* of Balmain and Balenciaga dominated in the 1950s but that was to change in the following decade when Saint Laurent showed street fashion on the runway and Mary Quant became the heroine of the 1960s. What has been called the "sober seventies" saw the establishment in the US of two highly influential designers, Ralph Lauren and Calvin Klein. The other fashion capitals resorted, in general, to a modernization of classic looks or, at the other extreme, to theme dressing, disco dressing, ethnic fashion, and "executive dress" for women. At the end of the decade the Japanese held court: Miyake, Kawakubo, and Kansai Yamamoto built a bridge not only from the East to the West but also from the 1970s to the 1980s. They introduced layer dressing and with it an entirely new attitude to clothing.

Fashion has also been influenced by cinema costume designers, especially in the early part of the 20th century. The influence of television has been more general, but the power of many of its images—spacemen in bodysuits, armies in battle fatigues, hippies, even little known African tribes—has helped to spread, or even start, a trend.

Illustrators are also included, for their pens and brushes reproduced with their own particular flair and imagination many aspects of fashion and society in an era when the two were firmly linked. At the turn of the century there were more than one hundred fashion periodicals published in Paris. The artists of the *Gazette du Bon Ton* created their own. Bakst's theater designs influenced pre-World War I fashions while Barbier and Lepape epitomized the female of the period as Eric was to do thirty years later. Photography then became the dominant visual form. Steichen, Hoyningen-Huene, and Horst followed by Avedon, Penn, Parkinson and, later, Bailey brought their own interpretations of mood and style, of life through a camera lens.

Twentieth-century fashion would be meaningless without the publishers and editors whose eyes selected the styles of tomorrow and whose hands signed up the talent and skill of the day to the avatars of fashion, the magazines. Condé Nast, John Fairchild, Edna Woolman Chase, Diana Vreeland, Carmel Snow—their names are as revered today as the designers they featured in the pages of *Harper's Bazaar*, *Vogue*, and the trade bible, *Women's Wear Daily*. Artists are also listed: Christian (Bébé) Bérard, who worked with Schiaparelli; Raoul Dufy, who designed fabric for Bianchini-Férier; Mondrian, whose paintings inspired Saint Laurent; and Bridget Riley, of Op Art fame.

There are those who march with—and sometimes lead—fashion, whose names could not be excluded: Cartier, Schlumberger, and

Kenneth Jay Lane, for example, in the world of jewelry; Ferragamo, Frizon, and Blahnik in shoes; Paulette, Reboux, Daché, Fox, and Shilling as milliners; Hermès and Gucci for accessories. The reader will also find Jackie Kennedy Onassis, Brigitte Bardot, Jawaharlal Nehru, and Dwight D. Eisenhower, for these are among the people who have influenced fashion or given their name (often unintentionally) to a fashion garment or style.

Clothes, accessories, and fabrics are also listed alphabetically—A-line, bobby socks, cameo, duster, ethnic, fan, gamine, hobble skirt, ikat, jumper, knitting, loden, mink, negligée, obi, page boy, reticule, Sloane Ranger, tabard, umbrella, veil, worsted, zouave—and help make up the more than 1,000 entries.

Fashion is also the result of designers and brilliant commercial minds interacting together. For inasmuch as art and society affect fashion, so too do industry, commerce, and science. Furthermore, to write about fashion over the last 140 years it is also necessary to take into account factors that have not changed fashion itself but have altered our attitudes toward it. Fashion and the Women's Movement, for example, are firmly linked, sometimes as allies, sometimes as opponents. Designers flirted with male fashion for women in the late nineteenth century, and in the early twentieth century the more assertive designers tackled the subject head on. Chanel got to the bones of male garments and cut women's along the same lines. By the 1960s social attitudes had changed to such an extent that designers felt free to make skirts so short that women showed their underwear, or to create suits that were indistinguishable from a man's. Men, for their part, decked themselves out in flowered shirts and pants and grew their hair long.

Other battles, besides the battle of the sexes, have also contributed to fashion. In the early 1860s Garibaldi's "red shirts" had an impact far from the Italian shoreline. The great wars of the twentieth century put many women into men's jobs—and into their clothes: pants, siren suits, battle jackets. When fabric was rationed, skirts became shorter. Colonization—the British in India—introduced calico, madras, and jodphurs.

Travel, too, provided tremendous scope for fashion. The early motor car brought with it long duster coats and veiled hats; cruises demanded chic cruisewear; and the hunt for a fashionable tan came hand-in-hand with resortwear.

A healthy interest in sport popularized Fair Isle sweaters, plus-fours, long divided skirts, and Patou's tennis dresses for Suzanne Lenglen. The vogue has continued with exercisewear and dancewear. Swimsuits have a history all of their own and in the 1980s are beginning to resemble pieces of sculpture wrapped around the body.

Developments in exercisewear are directly related to progress in the manufacture of fibers and fabrics. Early swimsuits, made of knitted fibers—mostly wool—emerged from the water completely shapeless. The more flexible, chemically produced fibers of recent years have enabled designers to produce garments which are sturdier and longer-lasting, and which are acceptable on the beach, at the exercise class, or at the dinner party.

The advancement of textiles has also been significant in the field of underwear. The cumbersome, clumsy, woolen items of the nineteenth century were replaced by lighter and far more luxurious pieces some forty years later. More than one item of underwear has become outerwear over the last 140 years; the peignoir became a tea gown and eventually a day dress; the bra and panties became a bikini; the corset prepared the way for the swimsuit; and the chemise, earlier worn as a nightshirt or under a corset, became a dress shape. The flounced and flowing skirts of the 1960s resembled petticoats of the previous century.

In the first half of the twentieth century the fashion illustrator Marcel Vertès wrote: "Time was when dresses were like monuments, made from precious materials brought from distant lands. They were put together one after the other—constructed as an architect constructs a house, slowly and with infinite care. Not merely to dazzle the eye—they were meant to outlast the generation which conceived them." Since the demise of *haute couture* in the late 1950s and early 1960s, fashion has been more democratic, in theory available to everyone, easily accessible, and competitively priced. Yet if clothes aim for the middle ground, they will never satisfy all our demands on them. A timeless fashion never looks old but it also never looks new. How can we laugh at ourselves, poke fun at each other, and fulfill our craving for novelty and change if fashion remains more or less the same? In recent years, we have enjoyed the fruits of easily available ready-to-wear—the same clothes can be found in stores from Liverpool to Austin, Texas—but we yearn for something more. We want clothes that speak of the future or tell of the past, clothes that give us the chance to wear something we might have missed and clothes that reflect many mirrored messages. Fashion is the embodiment of all these things.

Note to the reader:
Alphabetization of entries in this encyclopaedia is by the word-by-word method: thus "bra" is followed by "bra slip" rather than by "braces." Cross-references are indicated by SMALL CAPITALS, with the exception of the names of fabrics and furs, which occur too frequently to be usefully cross-referenced. Cross-references to black and white illustrations are denoted by an asterisk; those to color plates by the abbreviation "col. pl."

A

Abraham Textile manufactory founded in Switzerland in the 19th century. In 1943 it became a limited company with headquarters in Zürich. Principally known for the manufacture and distribution of silks to the international *haute couture* and ready-to-wear industries, Abraham also produces plain and print cottons, wools, rayons, jacquard, and jersey. A major supplier to France, Abraham manufactured SAINT LAURENT's popular SHAWLS during the 1970s.

accordion pleats Fine, narrow, regular pleating created by sewing or pressing minute DARTS into the fabric of dresses and skirts, usually from the waistband towards the hem. Accordion pleating was used in the construction of BALL GOWNS during the late 19th century. By the turn of the century it was an integral part of many styles and became especially popular during the 1920s and 1950s. *See also* BOX PLEATS *and* SUNRAY PLEATS.

acetate Man-made cellulose acetate fabric or yarn created in Germany in 1869. Work on the fiber was continued by Swiss chemists Camille and Henri Dreyfus of Basle in the 1900s, but their research was interrupted by the outbreak of World War I when acetate was used to make waterproof varnishes for French and British fabric-covered airplanes. In 1920 British Celanese Ltd made a commercially viable acetate fiber using the Dreyfus method. Acetate has since been used to make lingerie, blouses, dresses, and knitwear as well as other garments requiring lightweight, silky fabrics. Amcel, Dicel, and Tricel are all acetate fiber fabrics.

acrylic Synthetic fiber often used as a substitute for wool. It was first launched commercially in 1947 but not produced in any great volume until the 1950s. Acrylic is a strong, warm fabric that drapes well. It is often used to make SWEATERS and TRACKSUITS, and is also made into linings for BOOTS, gloves, jackets, and slippers. Common tradenames for acrylic are Acrilan and ORLON.

Adolfo *c.*1930–. Milliner, designer. Born Adolfo Sardiña in Havana, Cuba. Adolfo was encouraged in his adolescent ambition to become a dress designer and was sent to Paris where he worked in BALENCIAGA's hat salon. In 1948 he moved to New York and was employed by the milliner Bragaard, and at the department store Bergdorf Goodman. Shortly afterward, he became chief designer at Emme, a wholesale millinery company. During the 1950s, Adolfo was recognized for his technique of shaping hats by stitching, without the use of wiring or inner stuffing. In 1962, he started his own business and was patronized by Gloria Vanderbilt and other US society women. Adolfo's innovations include jersey visor caps, hats with removable goggles, huge fur BERETS, and flower braided pigtails that were dyed to match the wearer's hair color. In the 1960s he also showed a "Panama Planter's Hat" made of straw and trimmed with striped ribbon or jersey, shaggy COSSACK hats made of velour or fur, and variations on BOWLERS and PILLBOX HATS. His evening creations included feathered headdresses. At millinery shows Adolfo dressed the mannequins in garments he had designed and customer demand for these persuaded him to produce a ready-to-wear collection. In 1966 he showed a long melton officer's coat with EPAULETS and trimmed with gold buttons. He followed this with gingham DIRNDL skirts and lacy cotton blouses, jersey JUMPSUITS, organdy JUMPERS, GIBSON GIRL blouses, and PATCHWORK skirts. During the 1970s Adolfo abandoned the theatrical design elements that had been his hallmark in the previous decade, basing his collections instead on clean, straight lines and showing knitted suits and tailored crochet dresses. For many years Adolfo has been noted as a clothes designer for the wives of US political leaders.

Adri *c*.1930–. Designer. Born Adrienne Steckling in St. Joseph, Missouri, USA. Adri attended the School of Fine Arts at Washington University in St. Louis, Missouri, and in the summer of 1955 she became guest editor for *Mademoiselle*'s college issue. The following year she studied at Parsons School of Design in New York, where she was strongly influenced by designer Claire MCCARDELL, then a lecturer at the school. Adri worked for the wholesale house of B. H. Wragge for many years and for Anne FOGARTY. In 1972 she began producing her own line of clothes, including accessories. Her clothes are functional, practical, and easy to wear. She believes in building a wardrobe piece by piece with interchangeable separates—a style of dressing that has remained popular for several decades.

Adrian 1903–59. Costume designer. Born Gilbert Adrian in Naugatuck, Connecticut, USA. Adrian studied at the School of Fine and Applied Arts, New York, and in Paris. He designed costumes for Broadway shows until 1925, when he went to Hollywood to make clothes for Rudolph Valentino. From 1926 to 1928 Adrian worked for De Mille Studios, but shortly afterward he joined Metro-Goldwyn-Mayer, where he designed costumes for Greta GARBO, Joan Crawford, Jean Harlow, and Norma Shearer, among others. For Garbo in *A Woman of Affairs* (1929), he created a SLOUCH HAT that influenced fashion for at least ten years. In *Romance* (1930) he dressed her in an ostrich-feather-trimmed hat which partially obscured one eye. This hat became known as the "Eugénie" and was widely copied. The PILLBOX hat for Garbo in *As You Desire Me* (1932) was another trendsetter, as was the SNOOD created for Hedy Lamarr in *I Take This Woman* (1939). For actress Joan Crawford in *Letty Lynton* (1932), Adrian made a wide-shouldered white organdy dress with ruffled sleeves and a narrow waist. The "Letty Lynton" dress was widely copied throughout the USA; Macy's department store in New York reported selling 500,000 similar styles. Adrian gave Crawford her visual hallmark: wide, padded shoulders that made her hips look smaller. For Jean Harlow he produced slinky, figure-hugging dresses, cut on the BIAS. His designs were characterized by bold silhouettes and patterns, DOLMAN and KIMONO sleeves, long tapering waistlines, and diagonal fastenings. Adrian favored asymmetric lines. He frequently used black crêpe for slim, bias-cut evening gowns. In 1942 Adrian retired from the cinema and opened a shop in Beverly Hills, California. His designs were mass-produced, though he continued to make original garments for films on a freelance basis until his death.

Aertex Cotton cellular fabric introduced in England during the late 19th century by Lewis Haslam, one-time Member of Parliament for Newport, Monmouthshire, England, and two doctors: Sir Benjamin Ward Richardson and Richard Greene. In 1888 the three men formed the Aertex Company. By 1891 the company was manufacturing women's underwear in Aertex fabric. Aertex has always been popular for undergarments and sportswear. Since the 1970s, it has also been made into shirts, blouses, and skirts for summer wear.

Aesthetic Dress Dress associated with the Aesthetic Movement of the 1880s to the 1900s, which took inspiration from the garments depicted in the work of Millais, Holman Hunt, Rossetti, and other Pre-Raphaelite painters. The Aesthetic Movement applied to painting, graphics, and the decorative arts. Aesthetic dress consisted of medieval-like robes—loose, unstructured, and with little detail and few accessories or trimmings. The aim of the movement was to encourage women to adopt a more natural style than the tiny waists and full bosoms decreed by the fashions of the period. Women who wore Aesthetic Dress loosened their corsets (some abandoned them altogether) and wore garments that created a smoother, more fluid, outline. The style appealed to intellectuals and those involved in the art world and it was linked to the general movement for women's emancipation. The Irish playwright and wit, Oscar Wilde, was a spokesman for the Aesthetic Movement. Wilde practiced what he preached, dressed in a velvet jacket, knee breeches, and black silk stockings—an outfit that was considered flamboyant and un-masculine by his contemporaries. See also RATIONAL DRESS

This example of **Aesthetic Dress**, advertised in Liberty's catalog c. 1909, harmonizes well with the Art Nouveau furnishings.

15

Thousands copied the **Afro** hairstyle of leading black American militant, Angela Davis, photographed in 1971.

Afro Naturally grown, bushy hairstyle popular among black Americans since the 1960s. Created by artificial methods, the style is also worn by whites.

Agha, Dr. Mehemet Fehmy *c*.1896–1950. Art director. Born in Kiev, Russia. Agha studied at the Ecole des Beaux Arts in Paris during the 1920s and later gained a doctorate in political science. He worked in Paris as a studio chief for the Dorland Advertising Agency before joining German VOGUE in Berlin, where he was discovered by Condé NAST. In 1929 Agha moved to *Vogue* in New York. He altered the visual style of the magazine by introducing sans-serif typefaces and by revolutionizing layouts and front covers. He was responsible for presenting the work of the photographers BEATON, HORST, HOYNINGEN-HUENE, and STEICHEN. Agha also contributed written features to the magazine. In 1943 Alexander LIBERMAN, his heir-apparent, took over.

Agnès B *c*.1943–. Designer. Born in Paris, France. Agnès B joined *Elle* magazine as a junior editor at the age of seventeen. Two years later she moved to DOROTHEE BIS as a designer but left in 1964 to work freelance, designing for Pierre d'Alby and several other manufacturing companies. In 1975 she opened her first shop in Paris where she sold inexpensive, simply constructed clothes. Her fair prices and casual styles had attracted an international audience by 1980. Agnès B specializes in individual separates. Their charm often lies in the fact that they have an already-worn look: baggy SHETLAND and ARAN SWEATERS, DUNGAREES, painter's shirts, and generously cut T-SHIRTS produced in unusual shades.

aigrette Tall FEATHER, often from the osprey or egret, which adorned the CHIGNON hairstyle or trimmed a hat in the late 19th century. Aigrette plumes were worn on hats until the 1940s.

Alaia, Azzedine dates unknown. Designer. Born in Tunisia. Alaia studied at the Ecole des Beaux Arts in Tunis. Moving to Paris, he worked for DIOR, LAROCHE, and MUGLER until the late 1970s when the attention paid to his work and the demand for it from private clients persuaded him to launch his own collections. Alaia's early designs concentrated on body-hugging, curvaceous forms in soft glove leather, jersey, and silk. His first show was held at New York department store Bergdorf Goodman in 1982 and featured a modern-day HOUR GLASS look. Zippers were used in his early collections, positioned so as to accentuate body shape. Studded, black leather GAUNTLETS were also shown. A designer with an international audience, Alaia is justly famous for his LITTLE BLACK DRESSES, swathed cashmere outfits, and figure-hugging knitwear.

Albini, Walter 1941–83. Designer. Born in Busto Arsizio, Italy. Albini studied fashion illustration and design in Italy before moving to France where he worked as an illustrator for Italian magazines. He returned to Italy in 1960 and joined KRIZIA for three years. Albini also produced several ready-to-wear collections for BASILE before opening his own business in 1965. Inspired by the glamorous clothes of the movies of the 1930s and 1940s, Albini successfully translated these ideas into subtle, cleverly cut garments which achieved considerable acclaim in Europe. He often worked with silk and handled other luxurious fabrics in a sensitive manner. Albini's influence was cut short by an early death.

Aldrich, Larry *See* OP ART.

Alençon lace Alençon is a town in Normandy, France, famous for its needlepoint lacemaking from the mid-17th century until the end of the 19th century. Needlepoint LACE originated in Venice, and early Alençon versions were classically designed with carefully arranged swags and flowers on a fine net background outlined with a heavy, raised outer edge.

The jewelry of the British Royal Family, worn by the Duchess of Fife (*left*), Queen **Alexandra** (*center*), and Princess Victoria (*right*).

Alexandra, Queen 1844–1925. Born Alexandra Caroline Charlotte Louisa Julia, daughter of Christian IX, in Copenhagen, Denmark. In 1863 Alexandra married the Prince of Wales, who later became Edward VII. As the Princess of Wales, she was responsible for several fashion innovations. She wore a full-length, double-breasted PELISSE which buttoned to the hem. This practical coat was widely copied. She also initiated a vogue for wearing a CHOKER of jewels. Her famous "dog collar," as it was sometimes known, consisted of rows of PEARLS from the neck to low on the BODICE. She also wore round her neck a wide band of velvet onto which a brooch or clasp was pinned. During the late 19th century, a PETTICOAT—the Alexandra—was named after the Princess.

Alice faces the Red Queen, her hair drawn back demurely in an **Alice band**.

Alexandre 1922–. Hairdresser. Born Alexandre Louis de Raimon in Saint-Tropez, France. Alexandre trained in Cannes at one of the salons belonging to master hairdresser ANTOINE. He joined Antoine's principal salon in Paris in 1939 and shortly after World War II became its artistic director. He formed his own company in 1952. Over the following twenty-five years, Alexandre created more than five hundred hairstyles. He is credited with the revival of wigs during the 1960s and he influenced fashions for CHIGNONS, short back-combed hair, and BEEHIVES. Alexandre is also known for his technique of decorating intricate styles with ribbons and jewels. His clients have included Greta GARBO, Elizabeth Taylor, Sophia Loren, and Maria Callas. For many years he was personal hairdresser to Princess Grace of Monaco. Alexandre collaborates with numerous couture houses in Paris, including BALMAIN, CHANEL, GIVENCHY, LANVIN, PATOU, SAINT LAURENT, UNGARO, and VALENTINO, creating hairstyles for their seasonal collections.

Alice band Band of material, often ribbon or velvet, worn across the top of the head to keep hair off the forehead. It is named after the heroine of Lewis Carroll's book *Through the Looking-Glass* (1872), who is shown in the book's illustrations to be wearing a narrow band in her hair. Alice bands have been popular since the end of the 19th century, mostly for girls and young women.

A-line Dress shape dating from *c.* 1955. The A-line dress or skirt flares from the bust or waist to form two sides of a triangular "A." The hem is the third side. *See* DIOR.

Alix *See* GRÈS.

aloha shirt *See* HAWAIIAN SHIRT.

alpaca Wool of the alpaca, a member of the camel family native to the Andes mountain regions of South America. In 1836 Sir Titus Salt introduced alpaca cloth, which at that time was a blend of alpaca and silk. Cheaper than pure silk, alpaca had many of the lustrous qualities of the heavy types of silk available during the 19th century. Alpaca was popular during the 1840s when the health cult of that period created an upsurge of interest in woolen materials. It was used to make outer garments and to line coats. From the late 19th century, alpaca was blended with cotton. During the 1900s the cloth was made into dresses and suits. In the second half of the 20th century, the word alpaca refers to a rayon crêpe fabric with a wiry texture, which is mainly used for outerwear.

Amies, Hardy (Edwin) 1909–. Designer. Born in London, England. Amies left England at the age of eighteen to work in France and Germany. He returned to London in 1930 as the representative of a British weighing machine company. Four years later he was introduced to the fashion house of LACHASSE, where he became managing director and designer. The house specialized in tweed suits for women and in 1937 Amies created a suit called "Panic" which attracted a great deal of attention because of its fine tailoring and fit. During World War II, he contributed to the UTILITY SCHEME operated by the British Board of Trade. In 1945 Amies opened his own house selling couture and ready-to-wear clothes, particularly classically tailored suits and dresses which were often made of tweed and woolen fabrics. He designed day dresses for the Queen (then Princess Elizabeth) and was awarded a Royal Warrant in 1955.

A-line suit from Christian Dior, for Spring 1955.

Amies is also known for his PUFF-SLEEVED evening dresses and lavish BALL GOWNS. In 1962 he became the first women's couturier to design for men. He has an international reputation as both a womenswear and menswear designer. *See* *LINTON TWEEDS.

Andrevie, France *c*.1950–84. Designer. Born in Montauban, France. In 1971 Andrevie was working as a designer for the Belgian firm Laurent Vinci. She moved from Belgium to St. Tropez in 1976 and there launched her own line in a BOUTIQUE. The following year she was hailed as an innovative new designer by the French and the Americans. Andrevie cleverly mixed textiles in large, bold shapes. Her clothes were classic in style but modern in manner. She was particularly known for her unusual color combinations.

angora Hair of the Angora goat, which originates in Turkey. Angora is also the hair of the Angora rabbit, which is native to the island of Madeira and now farmed in the USA, Europe, and Japan. In both cases, angora is characterized by long, smooth, soft fibers. It is mixed with rayon and wool for dresses, knitwear, and SWEATERS. *See also* MOHAIR.

aniline dye Dyestuff produced from indigo by Sir William Perkin in England in 1856. Mauve was the first color to be discovered, in 1858, followed by bright purple, green, and magenta. Until this time, animal and vegetable dyes had been used to color fabrics.

ankle socks During World War II, when clothes were rationed and nylon STOCKINGS in short supply in the UK, British women wore lisle stockings or went bare-legged. British VOGUE promoted the use of ankle socks, which were usually white and made of cotton or wool. Some styles were made in tweed to match suits. *See also* BOBBY SOCKS.

ankle straps Worn by women for many centuries both as decoration and as a means of securing the foot inside the shoe, ankle straps have been popular at some point in almost every decade, on both high-heeled and flat shoes.

Anna Karenina 1. The heroine of Tolstoy's novel of the same name which was published in 1876. Several films based on the book were made: in 1927, US title *Love* (costumes by Gilbert Clark); in 1935 (costumes by ADRIAN); and in 1947 (costumes by Cecil BEATON). Anna Karenina became a term, loosely used, for various dress styles that were glamorous, romantic, and fur-trimmed. 2. In the mid-1960s a coat style, known as the Anna Karenina coat, became popular. Cut to any length, it was decorated with FROGGING and had a circlet of fur on the neckline.

Annie Hall Style of dress popularized by American actress Diane Keaton in the film *Annie Hall* (1977), for which Ralph LAUREN designed the costumes. Keaton dressed in oversize garments, notably baggy pants, an extra-large man's shirt, and a man's pinstriped WAISTCOAT. A TIE and floppy hat completed the outfit. Other interpretations of the style included mixing expensive designer-label garments with second-hand clothes from an earlier period.

anorak Hip-length, hooded garment worn by Eskimos. The word is believed to come from the Aleutian Islands. The anorak was originally made of sealskin. In the second half of the 20th century it is

Classic Hardy **Amies** tweed suit from his 1953/54 collection.

Antoine's famous blond or platinum streak on a dark head of hair in a style for 1931.

usually made of nylon and insulated with other man-made fibers. The anorak is zipped or buttoned from hip to neck and worn for sporting activities and casual attire. *See also* PARKA *and* WINDCHEATER.

Antoine 1884–1976. Hairdresser. Born Antek Cierplikowski in Sieradz, Poland. At fourteen Antoine was apprenticed to a barber and after qualifying went to work for Pawel Lewandowski, the leading Polish hairdresser. Between 1902 and 1906 Antoine worked for salons in Biarritz, Cannes, Deauville, Nice, Paris, and London. He then settled in Paris and became a private hairdresser who paid house calls on his clients. Some years later he opened a salon which was patronized by many socialites and actresses, including Sarah Bernhardt. He bobbed the hair of French actress Eve Lavallière in 1910, cutting it short in a style normally worn by children. This fashion was not widely adopted in Europe until 1912. During World War I, Antoine introduced brightly colored wigs. He experimented with hair dyes in non-natural colors and in 1924 dyed Lady Elsie Mendl's gray hair blue, creating a popular trend. From 1925 until 1939 he commuted between Paris and New York, where he ran a beauty establishment for Saks Fifth Avenue's Manhattan store. Antoine is credited with the SHINGLE cut of the late 1920s, the upswept hairstyles of the 1930s, the design of both Greta GARBO's long bob and Claudette Colbert's bangs (fringe), and the introduction of a blonde or white lock on an otherwise dark head of hair.

Antonio 1943–. Illustrator. Born Antonio Lopez in Puerto Rico. Antonio moved to New York as a child. He studied at the High School of Industrial Art and the Fashion Institute of Technology. In the early 1960s he worked as a sketch artist on SEVENTH AVENUE, until in 1964 he met the designer Charles JAMES, who was to be an enormous influence on him. Antonio worked with James, drawing all the designer's clothes, for a number of years. In the early 1970s Antonio moved to Paris where he established himself as the foremost fashion illustrator on both sides of the Atlantic. His clever drawings of sculptured women are positive, vital, and modern. His style is highly distinct: bold, sweeping brush strokes show both garments and accessories in clear, attentive detail. This close attention in no way slows down the pace of the illustration. It can be said of Antonio that his work helped create a return to the almost forgotten art of fashion illustration in magazines. He continues to influence many younger artists.

appliqué Appliqué takes the form of ornamental pieces of fabric sewn or glued on to another piece of fabric or garment. Petal, leaf, and flower designs or animal motifs are commonly applied to cotton, lace, and satin. Appliqué was popular during the 1950s, when simple felt motifs adorned CIRCLE SKIRTS, and in the 1970s, when more elaborate designs were sewn on to padded satin jackets.

apron Traditionally, a small frilled piece of fabric worn in front to protect clothes, which ties with strings of the same fabric behind the back at waist level. During the latter part of the 19th century, aprons made of silk and trimmed with lace were part of fashionable dress. Since that time, aprons have not been worn as fashion garments. In the 1950s long and short versions appeared in highly patterned cotton. These were popular as household garments, but were not worn outside the home. *See also* PINAFORE.

Aquascutum The firm of Aquascutum (from the Latin, literally "water-shield") was established in 1851 as a tailor's shop in London, England. Aquascutum coats were some of the first showerproof coats to be made from wool and were worn by British soldiers in the trenches during World War I. These ankle-length TRENCHCOATS had a military appearance, emphasized with EPAULETS and brass rings on the belt, a style which remained popular into the 1980s. In World War II Aquascutum provided coats for the British Royal Air Force and Navy as well as for the Army. Between the wars, the company also sold fashionable showerproof coats for women, who required suitable attire for their more active, outdoor lives. In the early 1950s Aquascutum RAINCOATS were made exclusively from Wyncol D.711, a cotton and nylon poplin. In 1955, a cotton gabardine in iridescent shades was introduced. Up to this point, rainwear had been made chiefly in gray, blue, and beige. These new coats were lined with satin and woven fabrics. In the same year, the company broke with tradition and shortened the raincoat to the knees. Aquascutum claims to have been the first company, in 1958, to blend wool and mohair in the production of evening coats, initially manufactured for men. The need for reproofing raincoats after dry cleaning was eliminated in 1959 with a process, introduced by the company, named Aqua 5. During the 1976–77 season, the "Club Check" was launched as a lining for men's raincoats. This pattern was subsequently used for accessories and in the 1980s for a clothing range for both men and women.

It is hard to believe that there are 60 years between these two raincoats from **Aquascutum**. Both have their origins in the trenchcoat.

WEATHERPROOF SPECIALISTS SINCE 1851

Aquascutum Field Coat.

Waterproof and Windproof. Essentially a Sports and Country weather-shield. Adapted from the impenetrable Aquascutum Trench Coat. Also made in pure new wool and weatherproof Aquascutum cloth.

AQUASCUTUM Ltd. 100 Regent Street, LONDON, W.

Eight

Traditional **Aran** sweater.

Aran Style of knitting associated with the people of the Aran Islands off the west coast of Ireland. Coarse, handspun wool, usually in its natural, off-white color, is knitted in cables, twists, and bobbles into a center front and two side panels, creating an embossed effect. Aran knitting was traditionally used for SWEATERS but since the mid-20th century has also been used for CARDIGANS, coats, scarves, TAM O'SHANTERS, and MITTENS. It is always associated with casual attire.

Argentan lace Lace produced in the town of Argentan in Normandy, France, from the mid-16th century until the late 19th century. It resembles ALENCON LACE but has a larger hexagonal net background and characteristic variety in the corded threads which connect the lace patterns.

Argyle Multicolored diamond pattern—an approximation of the TARTAN of the Scottish clan Argyle—formerly hand-knitted in Britain but now machine-made throughout the world. The Argyle pattern is most often seen on socks, scarves, and SWEATERS.

Armani, Giorgio 1935–. Designer. Born in Piacenza, Italy. Armani studied medicine at Milan University. After military service he joined the Italian department store chain La Rinascente as a window dresser. His first work as a designer was with menswear manufacturer Nino CERRUTI in 1961. From then until 1975, when he set himself up as a fashion consultant, Armani worked for several designers, including Emanuel UNGARO. After establishing his own company he rose swiftly to become one of Italy's most highly acclaimed ready-to-wear designers for both men and women. One of the few designers to move from the field of menswear to womenswear, Armani maintains an understated style. His clothes for women follow many of the principles of male dress, with exaggerated but controlled proportions. Large, loose BLAZER jackets, well-cut pants and SHORTS, and tailoring based on generous, supple lines are his hallmarks. He made considerable impact in 1982 with his brief CULOTTES. Armani is also noted for his leather designs, especially jackets, for both sexes. His men's suits are famous worldwide for their clear, uncluttered look and fine textures.

army surplus Ex-forces surplus gear, such as DUFFLE COATS, flying jackets, pants, and boots, were made available to the public during the 1950s. They became part of the fashion scene in the 1960s.

Arrow collars and shirts The detachable, starched collar on men's shirts is believed to have been invented in the USA in the 1820s. Forty years later these collars were in great demand. A manufacturing plant was established around this time by Messrs. Maullin and Blanchard in Troy, New York. The company merged with Coon & Company in 1889 and shortly after launched the Arrow trademark. In 1913 the company became Cluett, Peabody & Co., Inc. Artist J. C. LEYENDECKER was engaged to illustrate Arrow shirt collars for advertisements. At the end of World War I, Arrow were manufacturing over four hundred different kinds of shirt collars. In the following years, as the demand for detachable collars declined, Arrow produced a shirt with the collar as an integral part, which was preshrunk and tailored to fit the lines of the body. After World War II, Arrow helped popularize colored shirts. Designers have adapted men's shirts to womenswear since the early part of the 20th century, closely following fashionable alterations in cut and fit. Arrow shirts are typical of the styles imitated.

Armani for men in 1977.

Art, goût, beauté French, high-fashion, monthly magazine published between 1920 and 1933. It became *Voici la Mode: art, goût, beauté* until 1936. It was mostly printed by the *pochoir* method, which produced a high standard of color reproduction. Contributing artists to the magazine were, notably, Georges BARBIER, Paul IRIBE, Georges LEPAPE, Charles MARTIN, and André MARTY.

artificial silk Term used between 1890 and the 1920s to describe fabrics made of rayon fibers. In 1889, a Frenchman, Comte Hilaire de Chardonnet, exhibited an artificial silk based on cellulose. Commercial production began in France in 1891 and the fabric was used in the manufacture of underwear, and later, in the 20th century, for blouses and dresses. *See also* RAYON.

Men such as these touched the hearts of American women in the late 19th and early 20th centuries. Joseph Leyendecker's drawings and paintings for the **Arrow** shirt company provoked the kind of fan mail a pop star might receive today. Although Arrow were specialists in men's shirts, it is easy to see how women's blouses evolved.

Artificial silk outfits shown at Holland Park Hall in London in 1926. On the left is an accordion-pleated cape, in the center a pajama style, and on the right a dress and bloomers, presumably beachwear.

Art Nouveau velveteen fabric, printed in England c.1899, designed by Alphonse Mucha.

Art Nouveau Decorative art form which spread across Europe during the 1890s. It took its name from L'Art Nouveau, a shop opened in Paris in 1895 by Siegfried Bing. Other proponents of the movement were Meier-Graefe, also in Paris, and Arthur Lasenby LIBERTY in London. Although Art Nouveau was mainly expressed in architecture, interior decoration, and furniture design, it also found its way into the design of jewelry and fabrics. It is distinguished by graceful, if exaggerated, lines, elongated strokes ending in curlicues, and flower and leaf motifs. Art Nouveau textiles were revived by Liberty in the 1960s. *See also* KLIMT and MUCHA.

ascot Man's mid-19th-century CRAVAT with wide ends, worn around the neck and looped under the chin. Part of formal dress, it was usually made of a plain fabric, often silk, and unfringed. The loop, or double knot, was sometimes held in place by a jeweled pin. In the 1980s the ascot is mainly worn by women.

Ashley, Laura 1925–1985. Designer and manufacturer. Born Laura Mountney in Merthyr Tydfil, Wales. In 1944 she joined the Women's Royal Naval Service and later worked at the National Federation of Women's Institutes. She married Bernard Ashley in 1949 and four years later they formed a company for the production of printed headscarves and tea towels. In 1969 Laura Ashley designed a shortsleeved SMOCK top, based on a gardener's smock, which was made of 100 percent cotton. During the 1960s she designed voluminous dresses with PATCH POCKETS and, toward the end of that decade, ankle-length printed cotton dresses. Her long JUMPER dresses were worn over high-necked blouses. In the early 1970s, Laura Ashley created EDWARDIAN-style dresses, many with high, frilly collars and LEG-OF-MUTTON sleeves, or SCOOP NECKS and short PUFF SLEEVES. Most of her fabrics were printed with simple floral motifs based on 18th- and 19th-century patterns: tiny geometric prints, flowers, trailing sprigs, and fine spots and stripes. Until the early 1980s the company designed and manufactured garments in cotton only. Recent collections have included clothes in cotton mixtures and jersey fabrics.

astrakhan Originally the fleece of the karakul lamb which is found in the Soviet Union. It was popular until the late 19th century, used as a trimming on the collars and cuffs of coats and made into hats. In the 20th century it is the name given both to the fleece itself and to a heavy fabric, knitted or woven, with a deep-pile surface of curled loops which imitates the fleece. Also known as persian lamb.

Augustabernard dates unknown. Designer. Born Augusta Bernard in Provence, France. Augustabernard opened her house in 1919. She made tasteful, well-cut garments on elegant lines and was highly successful until 1934, when she retired.

Avedon, Richard 1923–. Photographer. Born in New York, USA. Avedon studied philosophy at Columbia University from 1941 to 1942. During World War II he was assigned for two years to the US Merchant Marine's photography branch where he took pictures of personnel. In 1944, back in civilian life, Avedon began to study photography at New York's New School for Social Research. In the same year he also persuaded the New York branch of the department store Bonwit Teller to lend him some high-fashion apparel. The photographs from this session earned Avedon commissions from the store. In 1945 Alexey BRODOVITCH, art director of HARPER'S BAZAAR, hired Avedon as staff photographer to take pictures of celebrities and cover the fashion scene. Twenty years later Avedon moved to VOGUE. Famous for his fashion photographs and celebrity portraits, Avedon used a wide-angle lens, exaggerated camera angles, and strobe lighting to capture the unusual, often disassociated expressions on the faces of his subjects. In his early fashion pictures he chose unfamiliar settings, such as zoos, a circus, the NASA launch pads at Cape Kennedy, and junk yards, and he encouraged his models to move about while he took the shots. The resulting pictures were original and dramatic. In the late 1950s and 1960s, Avedon concentrated the majority of his work in a studio.

Azagury, Jacques 1958–. Designer. Born in Casablanca, Morocco. Azagury went to England at an early age. He left school early to work in a clothing factory in London's East End and then spent two years at the London College of Fashion and one year at St. Martin's School of Art in London. *Harper's & Queen* magazine featured his diploma show, in 1978, and orders for Azagury's garments soon followed. His knitted three-piece outfit—a strapless short tube worn with a long pleated skirt and a long sleeveless coat with a draped back—was a great success. The following year he established his own business. Azagury specializes in glamorous evening clothes, well-tailored and cut, which he sells worldwide.

B

Baby doll nightdress of 1963.

Josephine **Baker** shocked and enthralled the world with her exotic dancing and various states of undress. She could be seen at the Folies-Bergère in outfits such as this ostrich feather dress.

David **Bailey**'s photograph of top model Jean Shrimpton, taken in 1965.

babushka From the Russian for grandmother, a babushka is a triangular headscarf, usually made of cotton, which is worn as both protective and decorative headgear by women all over the world. Traditionally a rural garment, it became briefly fashionable as part of the FOLKLORIC and PEASANT trends of the 1970s.

baby doll Nightwear introduced during the late 1950s, popularized by the film *Baby Doll* (1956). Often short and trimmed with synthetic lace, bows, and tiny ribbons, baby-doll garments are reminiscent of 19th-century children's underwear.

bagheera Fine, uncut pile velvet used for evening gowns until the early part of the 20th century. In later years imitation bagheera was made from rayon crêpe.

Bailey, David 1938–. Photographer. Born in London, England. After leaving school Bailey spent a brief period in the RAF before taking up photography. He worked as an assistant to John FRENCH in 1959. The following year he began his career as a fashion photographer, working for numerous magazines, including VOGUE, *Elle*, and GLAMOUR, and for many British newspapers. Bailey was hailed as one of the most innovative photographers of the 1960s. His lively, fresh style successfully captured the prevailing youthful outlook of the decade. He worked consistently with one model, in the 1960s Jean Shrimpton and later Marie Helvin, concentrating on the relationship between the girl and the clothes, emphasizing the freedom of fashion with clear, striking, uncomplicated pictures. During the 1970s he began directing films and since then has produced several books of his photographs. *See also* *QUANT.

Baker, Josephine 1906–75. Music-hall artist. Born in St. Louis, Missouri, USA. Baker was attracted to the theater and to music and dance from an early age and left home at sixteen to join a touring theatrical troupe from Philadelphia. After appearing in the choruses of shows in Boston and on Broadway in the early 1920s, she joined the *Revue Nègre*, with which she traveled to London and Paris. During the late 1920s she worked in Paris at the Folies-Bergère and the Casino de Paris. Baker made black skin fashionable and promoted beads, necklets, bracelets, anklets, brightly dyed gloves, bangs (fringes) and colorful costumes. She often appeared on stage naked or wearing only a feathered loincloth. A MAILLOT of tulle, decorated with DIAMANTE, was designed for one of her performances. Baker became a French citizen during World War II.

Bakst, Léon (Nikolaevich) 1866–1924. Artist. Born Lev Rosenberg in St. Petersburg, Russia. Bakst attended the Imperial Academy of Arts in St. Petersburg and worked for many years in that fashionable city as both a court painter and a costume and scenery designer. In 1906 he went to Paris to prepare the Russian section of the artists' Salon d'Automne. He returned to France two years later with Sergei DIAGHILEV as a scenery painter and costume designer for the *BALLETS RUSSES. Working between two cities, Bakst founded a liberal school of painting in St. Petersburg and produced plays for

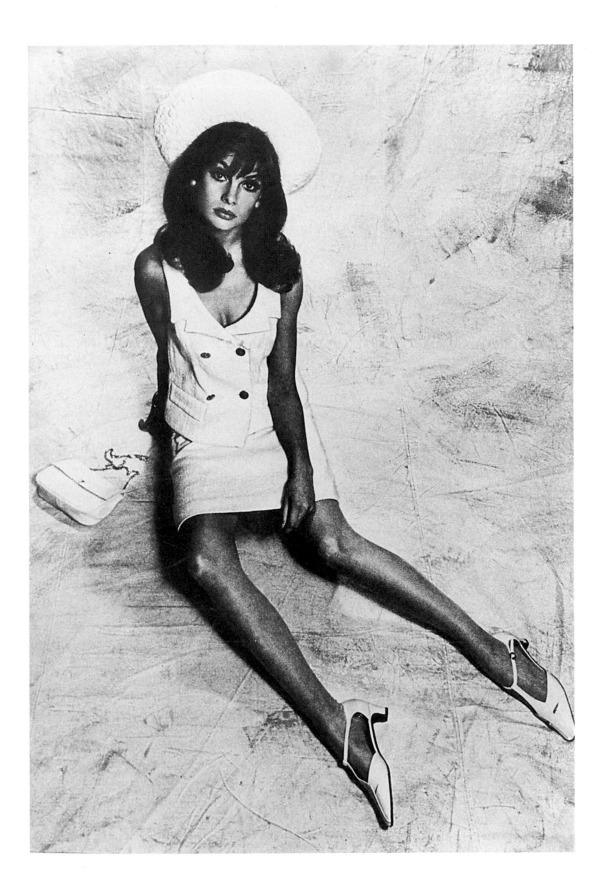

The unmistakably dramatic lines of a **Balenciaga** suit, *c.* 1950.

the Paris Opéra. His contribution to fashion comes through his association with the Ballets Russes, for which he designed vivid, brilliantly colored sets and costumes which directly influenced clothing of the period.

balaclava Helmet-like head covering, either knitted or crocheted, named after a village in the Crimea that was the scene of the Charge of the Light Brigade in 1854. For soldiers in the two world wars, British and US women knitted balaclavas in khaki, a color used for camouflage. The cuff around the neck of a balaclava may be drawn up over the chin and mouth. The balaclava was seen as a fashion item on the runways of Paris during the 1960s.

Balenciaga, Cristobal 1895–1972. Couturier. Born in Guetaria, near San Sebastian, Spain. Balenciaga's talents revealed themselves early. By the age of fourteen he was already able to copy couturier clothes. He trained as a tailor and in 1916 opened a dressmaking and tailoring establishment in San Sebastian. By the early 1930s he had earned a reputation as Spain's leading couturier. Balenciaga moved to Paris between 1936 and 1937. His tailoring background enabled him to design, cut, put together, and sew a gown. Balenciaga was not an advocate of popular trends; his clothes were often formal: uncluttered, balanced, and restrained. He frequently used somber colors, such as shades of dark brown, though he later gained a reputation as a colorist and in a collection of the late 1950s showed lambswool that had been dyed bright yellow and pink. Balenciaga emphasized the stark elegance of his designs by using blocks of white against darker tones. In 1939 he introduced a dropped shoulder line with a nipped-in waist and rounded hips, a style that prefigured the 1947 NEW LOOK. After the war he showed jackets with more natural waistlines and large sleeves. In 1946 PILLBOX HATS featured in his collections. Ten years later Balenciaga created a distinctive line by raising the hemlines of his dresses and coats at the front and dropping them sharply at the back. In the same year, 1956, he presented a loose CHEMISE dress, known as the SACK. During the 1960s he showed loose, full jackets with DOLMAN SLEEVES. Models at his 1963 shows wore harlequin TIGHTS and he was one of the first designers to put his models into BODYSTOCKINGS. His name is still associated with large buttons and a collar which, raised on a band, stands away from the throat and neck. Considered to be purist and classicist, Balenciaga made garments that were instantly identifiable. He retired in 1968.

Balkan blouse Low-waisted blouse with full sleeves which became fashionable in Europe after the Balkan Wars (1912–13).

ball gown Traditionally a full-skirted gown reaching at least to the ankles, made of a luxurious fabric, delicately and exotically trimmed. Most versions are cut off the shoulder with DECOLLETE necklines. The ball gown has changed little in shape since the mid-19th century. Although man-made fabrics are now sometimes used, the most common fabrics are satin, silk, taffeta, and velvet with trimmings of lace, pearls, sequins, EMBROIDERY, ruffles, and ruching. *See* *BALLERINA SKIRT *and* *CRINOLINE.

ballerina skirt Full skirt that reaches to just above the ankles. A popular style during the 1950s.

ballet shoes Flat slippers with a well-boxed toe to support the feet in point-dancing. Some styles have a thread that can be pulled to create

Ballerina skirts have been a consistently popular length for ball gowns, especially for young women.

gathers around the toe area. Ribbons are often sewn to the slipper and wound criss-cross around the ankle. Ballet shoes, without ribbons or a reinforced toe, were popular as bedroom slippers during the 1940s. *See also* PUMPS.

Ballets Russes Series of ballets devised by Sergei DIAGHILEV in Russia in the early years of the 20th century. For the first time the décor, costumes, and music were integral parts of the dance itself, which relied on mime. The colors, fabrics, and designs of the costumes strongly influenced fashion. Inspired by the Orient, the costumes were unrestrained, fluid, and brightly colored, in contrast to the rigidly constructed shapes and pale, delicate hues of the late 19th century. Many designs were painted on to linen, or appliqué was used on various cloths, particularly velvet. Trends were created for richly embroidered satins and silks, HAREM PANTS, AIGRETTES, TURBANS, and brilliant jewels. The Ballets Russes first appeared in Paris in 1909, one year later in London. Many ballets were produced, including *Firebird* (1910); *Schéhérazade* (1910) in which Nijinsky, painted black, danced the role of a slave; *Daphnis and Chloe* (1912); *L'Après-midi d'un faune* (1912); and *Jeux* (1913). *See also* BAKST *and* POIRET.

balloon skirt Skirt introduced after World War II. It was gathered at the waist and seamed to curve in toward the knees where it was held in place by a circular band on the hem. *See also* CARDIN.

balloon sleeve Nineteenth-century sleeve shape that was full over the upper arm and narrowed from elbow to wrist.

balmacaan Loose-fitting, calf-length, tweed overcoat with RAGLAN sleeves. Balmacaans were worn by men in the 19th century and had been adapted to womenswear by the end of the century.

Program for the **Ballets Russes**, designed by Léon Bakst.

Balmain, Pierre (Alexandre) 1914–82. Designer. Born in St. Jean de Maurienne, France. Balmain's family owned a wholesale drapery business. Balmain studied architecture at the Ecole des Beaux Arts in Paris but did not complete his studies. He worked for MOLYNEUX between 1934 and 1939 and then spent two years at LELONG, where he met DIOR. Balmain opened his own house in 1945. In that year he showed long, bellshaped skirts with small waists—a line that became popular in 1947 as part of Dior's NEW LOOK. In 1951 he opened branches in the USA selling ready-to-wear clothes. Balmain's success in the USA is attributed to the fact that he was able to translate French fashion into clothes for the American woman's generally larger frame, without compromising style. Balmain designed many sportswear collections for this ready-to-wear market. His talent as a designer lay in his ability to make simple, tailored suits as well as grand evening gowns, in the same slender, supple, and elegant lines. His clothes were not fussy but fun—elegant fun. During the 1950s he popularized the STOLE for day as well as evening wear and created a vogue for SHEATH DRESSES beneath jackets. His coats were generously cut to give a full back and were sometimes half-belted. In the same period, his COSSACK-like wraps and CAPES were trendsetters. Balmain was noted as a designer for the international set.

Balmoral boot In the mid-19th century Queen Victoria's devotion to her Scottish estate at Balmoral helped popularize in the UK fashions for TARTAN and garments named after Scottish towns. The Balmoral boot covered the ankle, had a thick sole, and was suitable for walking. Made of leather, it was decorated with brass eyelet holes and elaborate stitching.

Balmoral petticoat White or gray horsehair PETTICOAT worn instead of a cage CRINOLINE from the mid-19th century. *See also* BALMORAL BOOT.

bandanna Probably from the Hindu "bandhnu," a primitive method of tie-dyeing. The name was given to the large, brightly colored handkerchiefs produced by this process. The bandannas used by cowboys in the American West were often quite simple pieces of cloth dyed one color which could be worn around the neck or pulled up over the chin, mouth, and nose as protection against dust or as a means of concealing identity. Bandannas were worn, tucked into denim shirts, during the 1950s and 1960s, particularly in the USA, when COWBOY clothes were popular. *See also* TIE-DYE.

bandeau 1. From the French for "band." In the 20th century the word is used to describe a headband worn around the forehead to keep hair out of the eyes during sporting activities. This type of bandeau was popularized by Suzanne *LENGLEN in the 1920s, by HIPPIES of the 1960s, and by US tennis player John McEnroe in the late 1970s. 2. A piece of fabric, often elasticated, which is worn around the bust, as in a BIKINI. A bandeau-style dress is one with a horizontal band across the bust.

Banks, Jeff 1943–. Designer. Born in Ebbw Vale, Wales. Banks studied textile and interior design at Camberwell School of Art, London, from 1959 to 1962. In 1964 he opened a shop called Clobber, in London, where he sold both his own designs and those of others. In 1974 he became involved with the establishment of the Warehouse Utility chain of shops which provides inexpensive

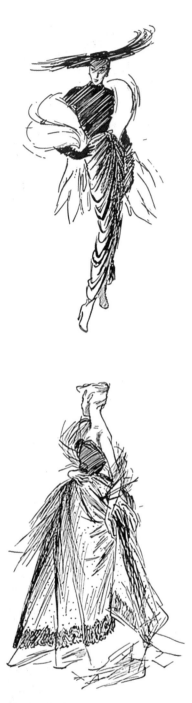

The kind of creations that made **Balmain** famous. Women loved the designer for his tailoring, uncluttered ball gowns, and fine taste. Drawings by René Gruau.

fashions in bold colors for a predominantly young market. He has also worked freelance for a number of companies, including LIBERTY of London. Throughout the 1970s Banks was completely in tune with contemporary fashions. With an imaginative use of inexpensive fabrics he was able to provide young women with access to fashion without compromising taste. He continues to do this through the Warehouse chain in the 1980s.

Banlon Tradename of the US firm Joseph Bancroft & Sons for a process that texturalizes yarn, adding crimp and stretch to synthetic fabrics. Banlon fiber was popular in the 1960s, made up into socks, SWEATERS, and dresses.

Banton, Travis 1894–1958. Costume designer. Born in Waco, Texas, USA. Banton was educated at Columbia University and the Art Students League, New York. His early design career took place in New York with a dress manufacturer and he did not go to Hollywood until his thirtieth year, in 1924. Paramount Pictures employed Banton as a costume designer for the film *The Dressmaker From Paris* (1925) which starred Leatrice Joy. During the 1920s Banton created costumes for many actresses, including Bebe Daniels, Pola Negri, and Clara Bow. In the 1930s he designed for other Paramount stars—Claudette Colbert, Marlene Dietrich, Kay Francis, Greta GARBO, Carole Lombard, and Mae West—and set the Paramount hallmark of elegant, sensuous clothes, which were often cut on the BIAS. Banton joined 20th Century Fox in 1939 and stayed for several years. He worked for Universal Studios from 1945 to 1948. During his film career, Banton designed costumes for over two hundred productions. In the 1950s he returned to the retail trade.

barathea Worsted or woolen fabric used in the 19th century for outer garments. In the 20th century it is used for making suits.

Barbier, Georges 1882–1932. Illustrator, costume designer. Born in Nantes, France. Barbier studied at the Ecole des Beaux Arts in Paris from 1908 to 1910. He spent many years designing theatrical costumes and sets and worked as an illustrator for LA GAZETTE DU BON TON, LE JOURNAL DES DAMES ET DES MODES, FEUILLETS D'ART, FEMINA, and VOGUE. He was interested in both 18th-century art and ART NOUVEAU and the strong influence of the latter can be seen in the curlicues and flowing shapes of his supple, fashionable women. Barbier also illustrated albums of ballet dancers and made wood engravings. *See* *FEMINA *and* col. pl.

Bardot, Brigitte 1934–. Actress. Born in Paris, France. Bardot modeled for *Elle* and JARDIN DES MODES until 1952, when she became an actress. In 1956 she was photographed wearing a gingham BIKINI decorated with frills. At her second wedding in 1959, she wore a pink gingham dress trimmed with lace. It had a SCOOP NECK, nipped-in waist, full skirt, and three-quarter-length sleeves. This dress, with a more modest neckline, was widely copied in Europe and the USA.

barège 1. Lightweight, semi-transparent dress fabric made of silk and wool, with an open-mesh weave. Barège was most often used as a veil or headdress during the 19th century. It was first produced in the valley of the same name in France, although Paris later became the center of production. 2. A printed shawl which was popular in France during the mid-19th century.

The Warehouse chain under the influence of Jeff **Banks** brought inexpensive fashion to the streets of London during the 1970s. This Fall 1984 photograph shows the fashionable waistcoat worn over long loose shirts. Note the vogue for the creased look.

Travis **Banton**'s seductive gown for Tallulah Bankhead in *Thunder Below* (1932).

The **basque** is gathered on to the hem of a bodice.

Barnett, Sheridan 1951–. Designer. Born in Bradford, England. Barnett studied at Hornsey College of Art and Chelsea College of Art, London, from 1969 to 1973. He worked freelance for several manufacturers, including Quorum, before forming a company with Sheilagh Brown in 1976. The firm closed in 1980 and Barnett taught for several years before turning once more to design, first for Salvador and then for Reldan. His designs are unfussy, clearly planned, and classic.

barrel shape Skirt shape created by banding fabric from the waist into a narrowed hem. First seen in the HOBBLE SKIRTS of the early 1900s and later, in a much shorter version, in skirts of the early 1960s. *See* CARDIN *and* POIRET.

Barthet, Jean *c.*1930–. Milliner. Born in the Pyrenees, France. Barthet arrived in Paris in 1947 and launched his first collection of hats in 1949. By 1965 he was established as one of France's most prominent milliners, providing MONTANA, RYKIEL, and UNGARO with hats for their collections. Although Barthet's hats are structured shapes, his signature hat is a man's FEDORA, scaled down for women. As well as custom-made items—mainly for actresses and socialites—Barthet designs millinery lines.

Basile Company founded in Milan, Italy, in 1969 by businessman Aldo Ferrante, who had previously been employed by KRIZIA and MISSONI. Basile started as a small company manufacturing menswear. In Ferrante's hands it became known for its luxury sportswear and eveningwear, tailored suits, and jackets, which are both retailed and wholesaled. ALBINI, TARLAZZI, and VERSACE are just three designers who have worked at Basile.

basque Short skirt addition sewn on to the BODICE of a dress or jacket. The basque is pleated or gathered onto the hem of the bodice. In the 20th century it is also known as a peplum.

Bass Weejuns Slipper type MOCCASIN made by the G. H. Bass Company, which was founded in Wilton, Maine, USA, in 1876. Bass Weejuns have been popular for casual wear since 1936. Also known as a penny loafer.

bateau neckline Shallow, boat-shaped neckline which runs from one shoulder to the other and is the same depth front and back. A popular style for dresses and blouses since the early 1920s.

Bates, John *c.*1935–. Designer. Born in Ponteland, Northumberland, England. Bates left the War Office in London in the 1950s and went to work alongside Gérard PIPART at the design house of Herbert Siddon on Sloane Street in Chelsea. Two years later he became a freelance fashion illustrator and sold many of his sketches to Belinda BELLVILLE. After a brief period with a wholesale design company he was invited in 1964 to form the company Jean Varon. Under this name Bates contributed a wide range of youthful designs to the 1960s and 1970s fashion picture. He introduced some of the shortest MINI-dresses in the early 1960s; PANTS SUITS in 1962; STRING-VEST dresses in 1963; a bridal CATSUIT, striped tube dresses, and stockings with matching dresses in 1964. Bates also designed costumes for Diana Rigg in the role of Emma Peel in the British television series *The Avengers*. By 1965 copies of these clothes were on sale; the leather outfits and the white vinyl coat were enormously

John **Bates**'s famous backless evening dress of 1973.

From *Les Modes*, April 1912, an illustration by Georges **Barbier** of two
of Paul Poiret's designs. The Egyptian influence is clearly shown in the
model on the left. Note also the turbans and aigrettes.

A 1950s favorite: Givenchy's **Bettina blouse**, named after Bettina Graziani, one of the designer's favorite models.

Youthful 1980s designs in black and white from the London firm of **Body Map**.

popular. In the same year Bates showed broderie anglaise eveningwear and RESORTWEAR and SEE-THROUGH mini dresses. Although he experimented widely with daring OP ART print fabrics and bold shapes, he adhered to a clear, simple silhouette and acquired a reputation for EMPIRE-LINE evening dresses which were often elaborately embroidered and beaded. In the 1970s he produced extra-long MAXI coats and his designs in general became more fluid and sophisticated. In 1973 he designed a white Banlon dress with a plunging back and a long inverted V from the heels to the knees. In 1980 Bates formed his own company. Eveningwear plays a major part in his collections.

bathing suit The late-19th-century bathing suit was composed of two pieces: a long TUNIC and knickers which together almost completely covered the body. It was usually made of serge or wool and therefore unsuitable for bathing. Around the turn of the century, the cumbersome tunic and knickers began to be replaced by one-piece garments. These were popularized by the swimmer Annette KELLERMAN, who competed against men in swimming events held in the River Thames in London, the Seine in Paris, and the English Channel. The first rib-knit, elasticized, one-piece bathing suit was made in the US in 1920 by the Jantzen company and in 1924 Jean PATOU introduced bathing suits with Cubist inspired designs. CHANEL was also instrumental in promoting bathing suits. In the 1920s most bathing suits were designed for beachwear, rather than for swimming. In the following decade backless costumes became popular. After World War II, the invention of fast-drying, lightweight fabrics helped further to popularize swimwear. By the mid-20th century, "bathing suit," "swimsuit," and "bathing costume" were interchangeable names for the same garment. Swimsuits in the 1950s were often boned and corseted to emphasize the bust and minimize the waist, and they resembled foundation garments of the period. Briefer costumes began to appear during the 1960s, cut away around the tops of the thighs and around the arms and shoulders. This trend continued throughout the 1970s and at the end of that decade the one-piece swimsuit was back in fashion. Swimsuits in the 1980s are often sculpted around the lines of the body. *See also* BIKINI, *BRIGANCE, *GERNREICH, *and* LASTEX.

batik East Indian method of wax printing where wax is applied to certain areas of a fabric to prevent those areas from being dyed. A popular form of printing fabrics for dresses, blouses, and men's shirts during the 1960s and 1970s. *See also* ETHNIC.

batiste Originally a sheer, finely woven cloth of cotton or linen which was named after an 18th-century French linen weaver, Jean Baptiste. It has become the generic name for a sheer, fine, mercerized cotton which is used for blouses, dresses, and lingerie; a fine wool which is lighter than challis; a sheer silk; and a polyester, rayon, or cotton blend fabric.

Battelle, Kenneth 1927–. Hairdresser. Born in Syracuse, New York, USA. After being discharged from the US Army at the end of World War II, Battelle studied liberal arts at the University of Syracuse. He subsequently attended the Wanamaker Academy of Beauty Culture in New York and then returned to Syracuse where he worked as a hairdresser for four years. After a brief period in Miami, Florida, he joined the Helena Rubinstein salon in New York during the mid-1950s. Battelle's fame came in the early 1960s when he moved to the

An elaborate **batik** design.

Cecil **Beaton**'s sketch for *My Fair Lady* (1964), in which the cartwheel hat and S-bend shape capture the spirit of another age.

New York beauty establishment set up by milliner Lilly DACHE and started to create fashionable hairstyles for prominent American women, notably Jacqueline Kennedy (ONASSIS). Battelle gained a reputation both for expertly cut GAMINE styles and for his work with wigs.

battle jacket Waist-length, single-breasted jacket used by the US Army during World War II. It was adapted to civilian use by both sexes after the war. A battle jacket is generously cut, especially over the shoulders, with long sleeves and pockets. It is fastened with buttons or zips up the front. *See also* BOMBER JACKET *and* EISENHOWER JACKET.

batwing sleeve *See* DOLMAN SLEEVE.

beach coat Short, hip-length jacket made of terry cloth which was popular as beach attire during the 1950s.

beanie Small, round skullcap, once known as a calotte, which originated in Ancient Greece. It later became an ecclesiastical headdress. During the 1930s it was a briefly popular hat style for women.

Beaton, (Sir) **Cecil** (Walter Hardy) 1904–80. Photographer, designer, illustrator, writer. Born in London, England. Beaton was educated at Harrow and at St. John's College, Cambridge. He went to London in 1925 to work as a clerk and typist, teaching himself photography in his spare time. His photographic experiments and designs for theater sets soon led to commissions. When Beaton sailed for New York in 1929, he was already a successful society and fashion photographer. He worked for British and American VOGUE until 1936. The particular style of photography for which Beaton was noted involved the use of artificial backdrops of mirrors, cellophane, and ruched silver fabrics, against which he would pose his subjects as if they were part of an elaborate tableau. In the mid-1930s Beaton moved to Hollywood, where he took portraits of actresses and designed scenery and costumes for the theater. A prolific illustrator, Beaton contributed to numerous magazines in England and the USA. He published several books of observations on fashion and fashionable people, some of which were illustrated with photographic studies and caricatures. After World War II, Beaton worked mostly on theater, film, and opera design. He created the costumes for thirteen films, notably *Anna Karenina* (1947), *Gigi* (1958), and *My Fair Lady* (1964). He was knighted in 1972. *See* *JAMES.

beaver Light-brown fur of a water rodent previously found all over Europe but now existing predominantly in Canada and the USA. The fur is thick, soft, warm, and hard-wearing. Beaver coats were fashionable during the late 19th century. In the 20th century they are considered practical rather than glamorous.

bed jacket Rib-length jacket of 19th-century origin worn in bed over a nightgown. Usually made of lightweight synthetic fabrics.

beehive Hairstyle popular during the 1950s. The hair was back-combed to achieve a tall dome shape on top of the head. *See* ALEXANDRE.

A Patons **bedjacket** design for home-knitters, using 3-ply, non-shrink vest wool, late 1940s.

beehive hat Exaggerated hat shape, popular between 1910 and 1915. The high dome extended low on to the forehead, where the fabric was sometimes turned up in a brim.

Beene, Geoffrey 1927–. Designer. Born in Haynesville, Louisiana, USA. Beene left Tulane Medical School in New Orleans before taking a degree and started work in the display department of the Los Angeles branch of the clothing store chain I. MAGNIN. In the mid-1940s he moved to New York and studied at the Traphagen School of Fashion. Beene spent 1946 and 1947 in Paris, attending the Académie Julian and the tailoring studio of Maison MOLYNEUX. The following year he returned to New York and worked for several ready-to-wear companies before leaving the last one, Harmay, in 1958 to join major manufacturer Teal Traina. In 1963 Beene set up his own company. During the 1960s he gained a reputation for high-waisted, braid-edged EMPIRE dresses, simple SHIFTS, and dresses produced on a T-line. Beene stressed the simplicity of this last shape by adorning the collars and cuffs with detail. One of the first US ready-to-wear designers to show short skirts with long jackets, Beene also attracted considerable attention in 1967 with a long black evening dress that was constructed like a cassock and worn with a curé's hat. In another collection he showed long, sequined evening dresses resembling oversize football SWEATERS, complete with numbers on the back. Beene's clothes are structured but never rigid, and rely on the craftsmanship of careful detail. Many of his designs contain an element of fantasy. He has a casual approach to opulent fabrics, successfully blending them with less expensive materials, for example flannel trimmed with RHINESTONES, quilted ticking and chiffon, jersey and taffeta. His less expensive line is called Beene Bag.

Beer House opened by a German designer in Paris in 1905. It was a popular house for dresses and underwear until the outbreak of World War I.

bell bottoms Traditionally, sailors' pants which were cut into a bell shape from knee to ankle. In the 1960s a version of bell bottoms, with the fabric clinging tightly to the thigh and flaring out from the knee, were popular with both men and women. The HIPSTER PANTS of the same period were similarly styled.

Bellville, Belinda dates unknown. Designer. Born in London, England. Bellville's grandmother, Cuckoo Leith, was a famous London dressmaker. As a debutante Bellville worked as an administrative assistant for various magazines and photographers. In 1953 she opened her own ready-to-wear and couture business. She hired David SASSOON in 1958. *See* BELLVILLE SASSOON.

Bellville Sassoon Company founded in London in 1953 by Belinda BELLVILLE. David SASSOON became a partner in 1958. Bellville Sassoon specializes in softly fashioned, discreet clothes which are popular among actresses and London society. It is well known for chiffon, organdy, and tulle evening dresses and designs a large number of wedding outfits. DIANA, PRINCESS OF WALES (then Lady Diana Spencer) promoted the company's SAILOR COLLAR in 1981. *See* *CRINOLINE.

belt The belt has its origins in a military girdle or band which was worn around the waist to support clothes or hold weapons. In

Reversible organdy and quilted charmeuse evening jacket of 1984, cut on a basic T-shape, shows Geoffrey **Beene**'s skill at geometry and at balancing different weights of fabrics.

37

women's fashion, the popularity of the belt has always been dependent on the positioning of the waistline and on the style of dress. The belt did not feature prominently until the 1850s, when it was often made in the same fabric as the dress or skirt. Later in the century, influenced by the ART NOUVEAU movement, belts with decorative buckles became popular. In the 1920s, as the waistline dropped, belts disappeared from fashion, but a decade later their popularity was restored and self-fabric belts were again common. After World War II belts became noticeably wider, to focus attention on the narrow waist and full hips of the New Look, and this trend extended well into the 1950s. In the 1960s leather, plastic, and gilt chain belts were often seen and there was a brief trend for a version of the wide-buckled cowboy belt. In the 1970s musculine style belts were worn, usually of leather, in different widths and styles, and brightly colored belts were especially popular. Toward the end of the 1970s the Japanese influence on fashion created a trend for extra-long belts which wrapped around the body several times. From 1960 to the 1980s, belts have been made from rubber, plastic, suede, metal, leather, and fabric. *See* CUMMERBUND, OBI, *and* SASH.

Bender, Lee 1939–. Designer. Born in London, England. Bender attended St. Martin's School of Art in London from 1955 to 1957 and then spent a year at the London College of Fashion. After her graduation, she and her husband opened Bus Stop, a London BOUTIQUE. The store's success enabled them to open other UK branches. Bender sold inexpensive, young, casual clothes until the late 1970s, when she closed down.

Benetton Family firm established in North Italy in the early 1960s by Luciano Benetton which specializes in inexpensive but fashionable knitwear. Benetton has used wool, lambswool, shetland, and a wool and angora mix for casual, simply designed SWEATERS and CARDIGANS in a wide spectrum of colors. Benetton also sells T-SHIRTS, JEANS, and pants in cotton and cotton mix fabrics. The company's worldwide chain of stores is distinguished by eye-catching colors, low cost garments, and fashion-conscious knitwear. Luciano Benetton's two brothers, Gilberto and Carlo, and his sister Guiliana joined the firm in the late 1960s.

Benito, Edouard 1892–? Illustrator. Born Eduardo García Benito in Spain. At the age of twelve Benito entered the atelier of Mignon, a painter who had been a pupil of Vierge. Seven years later he moved to Paris and established himself as a portrait painter, decorative artist, and illustrator. Benito worked for numerous magazines and periodicals, including LA GAZETTE DU BON TON, LE GOUT DU JOUR, LA GUIRLANDE, and LES FEUILLETS D'ART. During the 1920s he illustrated for VOGUE, producing many stylish and memorable covers. His strokes were strong, simple, and economical but very supple. With swift lines he captured the taut, smooth women who were the epitome of the 1920s.

Bérard, Christian 1902–49. Artist, illustrator. Born in Paris, France. Fascinated by the theater and ballet as a child, Bérard compiled albums of costume and scenery designs. By the end of the 1920s, he was an influence on and inspiration to several designers, notably DIOR and SCHIAPARELLI. Although painting was Bérard's first love, he concentrated during the 1930s on fabric and interior design, and book and fashion illustration. His work appeared in HARPER'S BAZAAR and later in VOGUE and was instantly recognizable by his free, elliptical style, indicating elegant shape and form without severe delineation. Bérard was an adventurous colorist. His use of light/dark combinations was initially considered avant-garde, but subsequently became acceptable and even fashionable.

beret Soft, circular cap of ancient Greek or Roman origin. The two most common beret styles are the Basque beret, often worn with the band showing, and the Modelaine, which has no band. The tiny spike on the top of the beret was originally sewn on to cover the eye of the weave. Berets were fashionable in the 1880s, trimmed with flowers, FEATHERS, and ribbons. Since that date, they have mostly remained unadorned. Berets were popular during both World War I and World War II when elastic for millinery purposes was scarce. The most noted revival of berets occurred during the late 1960s and 1970s prompted, in part, by the actress Faye Dunaway's beret in the film *Bonnie and Clyde* (1967). *See* KANGOL.

Beretta, Anne-Marie 1937–. Designer. Born in Beziers, France. Beretta showed her early designs to Roger Bauer at Jacques GRIFFE and he encouraged her to pursue a career in fashion. In the 1950s Beretta studied fashion in Paris before starting to work for Jacques Esterel and Antonio CASTILLO, designing for the theater in spare moments. In 1965 she joined manufacturer Pierre d'Alby and launched a highly successful line of brown linen garments. A brief period at Georges Edelman was followed by work for Ramosport, who in the 1980s manufactured her rainwear designs. She designed freelance for a number of other companies, notably Bercher, where she produced leather lines. In 1974 she established her own business. Beretta has a serious, somber style. She sees her clothes as mobile sculptures. Cleverly proportioned and confidently executed, her coat designs are famous for their huge collars and asymmetrical lines. She produced a successful collection of three-quarter-length pants in 1979. One of her favorite fabrics is linen, which she uses in clean summer lines. Beretta also designs skiwear and contributes to the stylishly tailored separates of the Italian firm Maxmara.

bergère Straw hat with a low crown and wide brim, first popular during the 18th century and revived during the 1860s. It was associated with the shepherdess fashions of the late 19th century.

Berhanyer, Elio 1931–. Designer. Born in Córdoba, Spain. At the age of seventeen, Berhanyer left home for Madrid to seek work as a manual laborer. Ten years later he was employed by the fashion magazine *La Moda* and in fashion shops, painting in his spare time. In 1959 he opened his own salon. In the years that followed Berhanyer grew to be one of Spain's leading designers, a self-taught specialist in tailoring. He created smartly cut black dresses, which he teamed with BOLEROS and ruffled blouses in the traditional Spanish manner. He also made coats, suits, and stately evening gowns. Berhanyer's handling of fabric and seaming imparted a formal, somewhat austere, line to some of his creations. He is also noted for his menswear.

Berlei Berlei was founded in 1907 as Grover & Company, a corsetry business in Sydney, Australia, by a Mrs. Grover and a Miss Mobberly. In 1910 Fred R. Burley acquired shares in the company and two years later bought the entire stock. The trademark "Berlei" was registered in 1917. The company specialized in making CORSETS and BRASSIERES for the wholesale trade and from 1926 based its

A fashion perennial, the **beret** has been worn by everyone from gangster's molls in the 1930s to English schoolgirls of the 1970s. This one, the traditional "Modelaine," is by the British firm Kangol, whose name has been synonymous with berets since World War II.

Elio **Berhanyer**'s confident black wool crêpe pants suit for 1970, inspired by the Spanish toreador.

This lace **bertha** of *c.* 1843 emphasizes the bust and narrows the waist. The elaborate jewels add focus, against the background of a completely bare neck and a deceptively simple-looking hairstyle.

designs for underwear on statistics and information from an anthropometric survey conducted by Sydney University. In 1934 a branch of the company was established in London. Since 1968 it has been a subsidiary of Dunlop Australia Ltd. Berlei maintains an international reputation and leading brand status for its retail and wholesale foundationwear.

Bermuda shorts During the 1930s and 1940s Bermuda became a popular holiday resort. Since local laws did not allow women to reveal their legs, a fashion developed for shorts which reached almost to the knee. Bermuda shorts have since become popular with both sexes as summerwear. Some versions are cuffed.

bertha Mid-19th century cape-like collar, usually made of lace.

Bettina blouse Introduced by GIVENCHY in 1952, the Bettina blouse was named after Bettina Graziani, one of Paris's top models, who worked exclusively for Givenchy in the 1950s. The blouse was made of shirting, with a wide, open neck and full, ruffled broderie anglaise sleeves. It was popular for several years and widely copied in Europe and the USA. *See* col. pl.

Biagiotti, Laura 1943–. Designer. Born in Rome, Italy. Biagiotti graduated from Rome University with a degree in archaeology. She first joined her mother's small clothing company but left in 1972 to set up a design business in Florence. Biagiotti is celebrated in Italy as a classic knitwear designer, specializing in cashmere and wools. Her designs are restrained, soft, and fluid, the main interest provided by the detail and fabric. Biagiotti also creates sportswear, day, and evening ranges.

Bianchini-Férier Firm established in Lyons, France, by Charles Bianchini, an Italian textile manufacturer who settled in Paris in the 1890s. At the turn of the century Bianchini joined forces with a Monsieur Férier to form the company Bianchini-Férier. The firm produces its own fabrics, mainly silks, but it also purchases fabrics from other companies and sells them under its own name. In the

A fabric design for **Bianchini-Férier** by Raoul Dufy.

early 1900s Bianchini-Férier launched a crêpe georgette which became very popular. *See also* DUFY *and* POIRET.

bias cut A cut across the grain of a fabric, which causes the material to fall into a smooth, vertical drape and allows it to be easily manipulated into clinging folds by the designer. Bias-cut dresses were worn during the 1920s and 1930s, frequently featuring in films of that era. *See* ADRIAN *and* VIONNET.

Biba *See* HULANICKI.

big-shirt Over-sized shirt for women, often cut along the lines of men's casual shirts. These have been popular since the 1950s, and became known as big-shirts in the 1980s, at which time they were accepted as a fashion garment shape for day and evening as well as casual wear.

bikini Abbreviated two-piece BATHING SUIT. The bikini was launched simultaneously in France in 1946 by a little-known designer, Louis Réard, and a designer with a greater reputation, Jacques HEIM. Heim called his bikini the *atome*, but when in the same year the USA conducted atomic bomb tests on a site called Bikini Atoll, the garment was renamed the "bikini." Early bikinis were trimmed and decorated with animal motifs and artificial flowers or were made of crochet. The bikini was already popular in France by the 1950s but was not accepted in the USA until *c.*1965. In the 1970s a very brief version—the string—appeared. Two minuscule triangles of fabric were held together by ties at either hip, and the bra-like top was attached by ties around the neck and back. *See* BARDOT.

biretta Originally ecclesiastical headgear, a biretta is a square cap with three or four projections radiating from the center. It was first seen as a fashion item for women after World War II and enjoyed a brief vogue.

bishop sleeve Long sleeve on a dress or blouse which is full below the elbow and gathered or left loose at the wrist. Popular since the mid-19th century, it faded from the fashion scene in the early 1970s.

Blahnik, Manolo 1943–. Shoe designer. Born in Santa Cruz, Canary Islands. Blahnik studied literature at the University of Geneva and then moved to Paris where he spent 1968 studying art at the Ecole du Louvre. After a short period in London in 1970 he went in the following year to New York. When a portfolio of his sketches was brought to the attention of US fashion editors, he was put in touch with an Italian shoe manufacturer and the meeting resulted in Blahnik's first shoe collection. In 1971 he moved to London and later that decade sold his shoes through his Manolo Blahnik shop. Blahnik has designed shoes for Ossie CLARK, Perry ELLIS, Calvin KLEIN, Jean MUIR, Zandra RHODES, and Yves SAINT LAURENT, and in the 1980s he designs for Rifat Ozbeck and Jasper CONRAN, among others. In the 1980s he opened a shop in New York under his own name. Blahnik is noted for his use of colored leather, often decorated with graceful, fluid designs. He is an influential shoe designer with an international reputation.

The "string" **bikini** of the mid-1970s.

Blass, Bill (William Ralph) 1922–. Designer. Born in Fort Wayne, Indiana, USA. Blass went to New York in 1941 and sketched for David Crystal, a SPORTSWEAR manufacturer, before being drafted into the army. After World War II, he worked for Anna Miller & Co. When Miller merged with manufacturers Maurice RENTNER Ltd in 1959, Blass stayed on and, in 1962, became vice president. In 1967 he bought the company, renaming it Bill Blass in 1970. Blass is best known as a designer of American sportswear. He takes traditional garments, such as the HACKING JACKET, and by softening the lines creates a more fluid, less severe, design. His suits are tailored but consciously curved to emulate the female body. Even his most structured garments are softened by gentle bends at the hem, lapels, or fastenings. Blass uses tweeds and shirtings, and often designs his garments with a discreet splash of color, such as a bright frill of lace or a fur trim. His use of ruffles has been particularly effective. His simple summer dress of 1963, which had a small ruff at the neck and hem, was a bestseller. In 1968 model Jean Shrimpton appeared in an advertisement wearing a beige, chantilly lace dress of Bill Blass design, with ruffled collar and cuffs. Public demand for this dress was so great that Maurice Rentner Ltd put the design into mass production. Blass showed a PEA JACKET made of white mink in 1966. He is also an established eveningwear designer, creating dresses which, like his daywear, trace sinuous lines but tend toward exaggeration. Blass has successfully mixed tailored jackets and flounces for eveningwear.

Bill **Blass** from the 1960s to the 1980s: (*anticlockwise*) a lace trimmed mini-dress of 1968; a summer evening gown in green organza trimmed with ribbon and white lace, 1968; a mixture of tailored cut and exaggerated ruffles for 1982; and (*opposite*) unusual hemlines for wool gabardine jackets and coats for Spring 1984.

Right: Mrs. Amelia **Bloomer**, *c.* 1850, wearing the outfit that she advocated for all sensible women.

Far right: **Bloomers** in action: the complete cycling outfit with boater, jacket and bloomers, and flat shoes.

blazer Loose-fitting, lightweight sports jacket worn by men at the turn of the 20th century. It was originally made of flannel with either bold regimental stripes of solid color or thin stripes. During the 1920s, the blazer was appropriated by women and worn with pleated skirts, shirts, and ties. The naval-style blazer with gilt buttons has also been interpreted as a fashion garment. The classic length for a blazer is to the top of the thigh. Shorter versions form part of school uniform. Blazers were popular with women during the 1970s, when they became an important ingredient of female EXECUTIVE dress, teamed with a tailored skirt and a blouse or man's shirt. *See* *KLEIN, CALVIN.

Bloomer, Amelia Jenks 1818–94. In the mid-1850s Dexter Bloomer, proprietor and editor of a New York weekly journal, *The Seneca County Courier*, published an article suggesting that the short skirts and ankle-length trousers worn by Turkish women were far more practical than the voluminous long-skirts and PETTICOATS of their European and American counterparts. Mr. Bloomer's wife, Amelia, took up the theme and printed an article in her own feminist paper, *The Lily*, calling for functional clothing for women. Several women thereupon abandoned the KNICKERBOCKERS and NORFOLK JACKET worn at the time for sporting activities and dressed instead in an outfit consisting of a fitted BODICE; a full, knee-length skirt; and TURKISH TROUSERS, or BLOOMERS, which reached to the ankle, where they were frilled and gathered. In England this outfit was known as the Camilla costume. It was not adopted by significant numbers of women until the 1880s and 1890s, when cycling became popular. The wearing of bloomers was initially the object of public outrage, amusement, and ridicule.

bloomers Since the late 19th century, the word bloomers describes any loose, full, trouser-like garment which is gathered at some point between the knee and ankle and worn under long skirts. *See* BLOOMER.

blouson *1.* Hip-length outer jacket with a drawstring through the bottom hem which, when pulled, creates soft gathers around the hips. The garment's shape originated in the ANORAK worn by Eskimos and in the water- and wind-proof clothing of Arctic explorers. During the second half of the 20th century, the blouson shape is generally associated with casual attire for both sexes. 2. Blouse of lightweight fabric, which is gathered to fall in soft folds on a band about the hips.

Blumenfeld, Erwin 1897–1969. Photographer. Born in Berlin, Germany. After World War I, Blumenfeld moved to Holland where he worked for seventeen years as a bookseller, art dealer, and leather goods merchant, while teaching himself photography. In 1936 he set himself up in Paris as a professional photographer. Two years later he received commissions from VOGUE, shortly followed by a contract with HARPER'S BAZAAR. Blumenfeld spent several of the World War II years interned in a prisoner-of-war camp and after the war went to New York, where he took US nationality. He continued to work freelance for French and American *Vogue*, *Harper's Bazaar*, and numerous other magazines. Blumenfeld's early work was distinguished by surreal images. He experimented with solarization, double-exposure, and optical distortion. His use of damp cloth to drape and swathe the female form was widely copied by younger photographers. During the 1950s, Blumenfeld successfully adapted his technique to color photography and produced many bold, striking, often slightly erotic, pictures.

boa Long, fluffy, tubular scarf made of FEATHERS or fur. During the late 19th and early 20th centuries, feather boas, particularly those made from ostrich feathers, were very popular. Boas were revived during the 1930s and 1960s.

boat neck *See* BATEAU NECKLINE.

boater Circular straw hat with a flat top and straight brim. The crown is trimmed with a band of ribbon. Boaters are so named

The **boater**, shown here in 1893 worn by both sexes, was considered suitable for churchgoing as well as for boating.

During the 1860s the **bodice** was a fitted top section of a dress, treated as a fashion item in itself. It was only during the 20th century that the word began to refer to the top section of a garment, shown here with darts.

because, teamed with striped BLAZERS and flannel trousers, they made up the male uniform for the summer sport of boating from the late 19th century until *c.* 1940. They were popular with women during the 1920s and have featured as part of summer uniform in many British girls' schools.

bobbin lace *See* LACE.

bobby socks Short, usually white, socks worn since the mid-1940s by US teenagers. They were particularly popular in the 1950s, teamed either with flat or high-heeled shoes, CIRCLE SKIRTS over layers of PETTICOATS, and tight SWEATERS, or with flat BROGUES and long KILTS. *See also* ANKLE SOCKS.

bodice *1.* Portion of a dress or coat between the shoulders and waist. During the 15th century the bodice was a close-fitting garment made of two layers of linen which were sewn or pasted together for greater stiffness. In the 16th century WHALEBONE was used to create a severe, rigid, front panel. By the 19th century, the bodice was tight-fitting and boned. Bodices have varied in length depending on the position of the waistline at any particular period in history. *2.* In the 20th century, the bodice is a dressmaker's term for the top front and back section of a garment which is joined at a high waistline to a skirt section. *See* BUST BODICE *and* CORSET.

Body Map Company formed in London in 1982 by David HOLAH and Stevie STEWART, specializing in unstructured, layered clothes for a young market. The two designers work frequently with black, cream, and white, redefining traditional body shapes by layering different textures and prints on top of each other. *See* col. pl.

bodystocking The bodystocking has its origins in the LEOTARD and the early-19th-century MAILLOT. It was introduced in the 1960s to wear under the semi-transparent dresses then in vogue. The bodystocking is a fine, knitted garment, usually flesh colored, with a low neck, no back, and narrow shoulder straps. For complete body cover, it can be teamed with matching TIGHTS or made in one piece. It is designed without buttons or bows in order to follow smoothly the line of the body.

Bohan, Marc (Roger Maurice Louis) 1926–. Born in Paris, France. Bohan's mother was a milliner. Bohan obtained a certificate in art and philosophy from the Lycée Lakanal in Paris. He gained his early design experience between the years 1945 and 1958 working for three houses in succession: PIGUET, MOLYNEUX, and PATOU. During these years he was also briefly employed by Madeleine DE RAUCH and worked as a freelance designer for a New York wholesale clothing company. In 1958 the house of DIOR sent Bohan to London as director of its English operation. He was recalled two years later to take on the position of chief designer and artistic director of Dior, succeeding SAINT LAURENT. During his first decade at Dior, Bohan gained a reputation as a designer who could turn pop fashion into haute couture without sacrificing the youthful spirit of the clothes. In 1961 he presented a narrow silhouette with long, slim BODICES and narrow skirts. Bohan's most widely influential collection, in 1966, featured garments based on the film *Doctor Zhivago* (1965). He showed full, fur-trimmed, and belted coats, swirling calf-length dresses, and BOOTS. Famous for his eveningwear, Bohan designs elegant BALL GOWNS and evening dresses in exotic fabrics. Many

The classic lacy **bodystocking** of the 1960s.

styles have bows, like BUSTLES, attached to the back. He has successfully carried the house of Dior through two decades.

boilersuit Once worn by men employed in manual labour, boilersuits became compulsory wear in munitions factories during World War II. Made of heavy cotton or denim, the boilersuit is an all-in-one garment with long sleeves, a long BODICE section that is zipped or buttoned from the navel to the collar, pants, and pockets. *See also* SIREN SUIT *and* col. pl.

bolero Open, sleeveless, BODICE-like jacket, reaching almost to the waist, of Spanish origin. In the early 20th century boleros were worn with high-necked frilly blouses and sweeping skirts. During the 1960s and 1970s they were revived and worn with either skirts or pants. For eveningwear, boleros in black velvet were popular. Boleros for daytime wear have been made of many fabrics, including various cottons, brocade, felt, denim, and leather. Some versions are trimmed with BRAID.

bombazine Fine, plain or twilled weave fabric of silk warp and worsted weft, usually black. First produced in ancient China and later in Europe, bombazine was used for MOURNING DRESS from the 16th until the late 19th century.

bomber jacket Waist-length woolen garment adapted from the jackets worn by fighter pilots in the British Royal Air Force during World War II. It is generously cut with wide but fitted sleeves which are gathered or elasticated at the wrist. A zipper fastens the jacket at the front from the waist to the neck, where the collar can be turned up. Since World War II bomber jackets have been worn as casual attire by both sexes and can be made of almost any fabric. *See also* BATTLE JACKET *and* EISENHOWER JACKET.

bonnet Headgear with or without a front brim, which covered the top, sides, and back of the head and tied under the chin. In the 19th century bonnets were usually made of straw and trimmed with crêpe, lace, satin, silk, or velvet. Some styles exposed the face while others concealed it. At least one variation formed an oval frame around the face with the curved brim pulled down over the ears.

Despite the immensely elaborate hairstyles of the 19th century, **bonnets** were essential dress accessories. Round or oval, bonnets generally concealed the profile. They were decorated with ribbons and lace.

The walking **boot** of the late 19th century, a version of which became the popular "granny boot" of the 1960s.

Ties, usually ribbon, were attached to the brim or sewn to the insides of the bonnet. By the early 20th century bonnets were rarely worn as fashion items.

boots In the 19th century women wore boots with daywear in both summer and winter. They were usually low-heeled, made of leather or finer materials, and laced or buttoned to reach the lower calf. In the first half of the 20th century boots became mainly utilitarian items—worn during wartime and also in bad weather. Fashion boots, designed purely for effect, emerged during the 1960s. They were shown in all lengths, from the ankle to high on the thigh. Materials ranged from plastic and vinyl to leather. In the 1970s fashion boots constructed to encase the foot and leg to the knee became popular winter attire in a range of colors. In the same decade other styles also became popular, such as small, cuffed ankle boots or leather COWBOY boots with elaborate tooling. *See* COURREGES BOOT *and* *GERNREICH.

botany Fine wool originally obtained from the MERINO sheep of Botany Bay, New South Wales. In the 19th century botany wool was made up into outer garments but during the 20th century its use has been mainly limited to SWEATERS.

Bouché, René 1906–63. Artist, illustrator. Born in France. A successful painter and portraitist, Bouché contributed to VOGUE throughout the 1940s as a fashion illustrator and observer of fashionable society. He worked in pen and ink or crayon, skilfully blending the character of the dress with that of the wearer. His drawings of women were elegant, vibrant, and often amusing, though he was able to vary his style to produce a less defined, more abstract, form.

bouclé From the French *boucler*, "to curl." Bouclé fabric is woven or knitted from looped yarn which gives it a highly napped surface. Jackets and SWEATERS made from bouclé fabric have been popular since the 1950s. Bouclé is also the name of a knitting yarn.

boudoir cap Nineteenth-century cap, worn to protect the coiffure when dressing, which was made redundant by the 20th century's short hairstyles. Made of muslin or cambric, it was threaded with ribbons that could be pulled and tied to encircle the head and keep the cap in place. The boudoir cap was sometimes shirred and often had a lace border.

Bouët-Willaumez, (Count) **René** dates unknown. Illustrator. Born in Brittany, France. Bouët-Willaumez was a frequent contributor to VOGUE during the 1930s and 1940s. His style was soft and fluid, usually pen and ink drawings of fashions and fashionable women. He was considered to be a rival of the illustrator ERIC.

Bourdin, Guy 1935–. Photographer. Born in France. After being demobilized from military service in France, Bourdin spent time with Man RAY. During the 1960s he established himself as an artist and photographer but his rise to popularity came toward the end of the decade. In the 1970s he frequently worked for French VOGUE. Bourdin's pictures are hard, distant, and distinctly cold. Sex, violence, and surrealism are integral parts of his work. He became famous in 1976 when he produced a provocative catalog of lingerie, "Sighs and Whispers," for the New York department store Bloomingdales. His surreal photographs for Charles JOURDAN shoes are equally well known.

Boutet de Monvel, Bernard 1881–1949. Painter, illustrator. Born in Paris. Fellow Zouave officer of Jean PATOU, Boutet de Monvel was a talented painter and illustrator. Lucien VOGEL commissioned him to work on the GAZETTE DU BON TON until the publication folded in 1915. After World War I, Boutet de Monvel contributed fashion illustrations to FEMINA, VOGUE, and HARPER'S BAZAAR. His economic, controlled style was in great demand and he was responsible for the design of many of Patou's advertisements.

boutique Boutiques started in the 1920s as small shops within couture houses. They sold the by-products of couture—a sportswear line at PATOU, jewelry at CHANEL. During the 1930s other designers followed suit: Lucien LELONG opened a boutique to sell his "editions" (less expensive versions of model clothes requiring only one fitting or none at all). After World War II, boutiques opened throughout the world showing a selection of merchandise from various designers or an exclusive designer label. During the 1960s, boutiques specializing in young, inexpensive fashions or second-hand clothes proliferated, the most famous being those in London's Carnaby Street, King's Road, and Kensington. *See also* SCHIAPARELLI.

bow tie Man's necktie in the shape of a stiff bow often made of grosgrain ribbon or velvet and usually part of formal dress. A popular accessory with women at the time of the vogue for UNISEX clothing in the 1960s.

bowler Also known in the USA as a derby. A hard hat with a round crown and a brim well curved at the sides, worn by men during the latter part of the 19th century. After World War I, bowler hats became acceptable formal wear in Britain, replacing top hats. Until

An English polka-dotted **bow tie** designed during the 1960s.

Bowlers (also known as derbies) were in general use on many occasions right up to World War II.

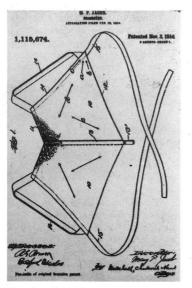

The first **bra**: the original patent granted to Mary Phelps Jacob in 1914.

the 1950s and 1960s they were associated with London businessmen who worked in the city. They are rarely seen today. Women wore bowlers during the 1960s when the UNISEX trend encouraged the swapping of items of dress between the sexes, but they have never been a major fashion item for women.

box pleat Pleat made of two flat folds turned inward toward each other.

bra, brassière Brassières date from the early 1900s. A design for a brassière made from two handkerchiefs and narrow ribbon was patented in the USA in 1914 by Mary Phelps JACOB (Caresse Crosby). Until the mid-1920s brassières were boneless and were designed to flatten the bust and push it downward. They were widely adopted during the 1920s when fashionable at-home dresses and, later, COCKTAIL DRESSES were often made of revealing, semi-transparent fabrics. By 1925, brassières had adjustable front straps and a division between the breasts in the BANDEAU front. During the late 1920s the Kestos Company of America produced a brassière made of two triangular pieces of fabric secured to elastic that was pulled over the shoulders, crossed at the back, and buttoned at the front under a darted "cup." During the late 1920s and 1930s corsetry companies began manufacturing brassières which were boned and stitched into different cup sizes. A boned strapless brassière appeared in the late 1930s and it was during this decade that the word bra came into popular usage. In the 1940s the use of foam pads gave additional shape to many bras. Their outline was most exaggerated during the 1950s, when bras were both wired and stitched in circular patterns to further stiffen the fabric. The strapless bra was popular during the 1950s, when it was worn under off-the-shoulder, strapless dresses. In the same decade, manufacturers began producing bras for teenagers.

The Kestos **bra**, from a 1935 advertisement.

A SUPPLEMENT OF FASHION BY DARLING'S OF EDINBURGH

KESTOS BRASSIÈRE-
ACCENTUATES FEMININE BEAUTY

Unnoticeably, but not unnoticed, the Kestos Brassière is a cunning wisp of loveliness that subtly enhances feminine curves. It is the only brassière that gives scientific and correct support in the most *natural* way . . . because it is fashioned to conform with the principles of Nature.

In many materials for day or evening wear. In a popular range of prices from 3/11

Sent free on approval

DARLING & COMPANY
124 Princes Street, Edinburgh

Above Women putting on make-up at a Royal
Ordinance Factory in the UK during World War II,
before going back to the business of shell
production. They have been provided with **boilersuits**
of fire-resistant serge and fireproof turbans.

Below A selection of **buttons** from the 1930s.

Four shoes from the master shoe designer,
Ferragamo.

Ferragamo's famous "invisible" shoe of 1947 created
with nylon threads set a vogue which has been
observed in almost every decade since, particularly in
the 1970s. The kid-covered heel is known as the "F"
shape.

Sandal with upper of two bands of gold and silver
kid with wedge sole covered in luxurious bead-
embroidered red velvet. 1938.

Sandal with upper of padded gold kid straps and
platform sole and heel in cork layers covered with
various colored suedes. 1938.

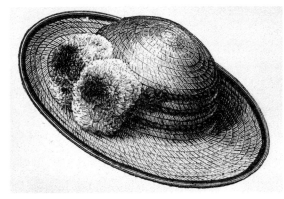

The **breton** hat of 1880, trimmed with pompons and silk cord.

The 1960s saw greater flexibility of design and further liberation and comfort for women through the introduction of fabrics containing LYCRA. Since the 1970s, moldings of thermoplastic fibers at high temperatures have produced one-piece seamless bras. *See* BERLEI, GERNREICH, *and* WARNERS.

bra slip Bra section with narrow straps which is attached to a waist slip below the bust. A form of bra slip was first seen in the 1930s but it was not until the 1960s, when changes taking place in fashion created a need for lingerie to be more functional and less obtrusive, that the garment became popular. Underwear sets of bra, panties, and waist slip were produced, and the bra slip further reduced the number of undergarments needed by women.

braces *See* SUSPENDERS.

braid Narrow band of fabric created by weaving or braiding threads together. Commonly used on uniforms, braid became fashionable in the 1930s, when CHANEL used it to trim the edges of suits.

Braque, Georges 1882–1963. Artist. Born in Argenteuil, France. Braque trained as a decorator before studying painting in Paris in the early 1900s. He was part of the Fauvist movement until he met PICASSO in 1907. The two painters developed the art form that came to be known as CUBISM. Braque's work influenced textile designers of the 1920s and 1930s. *See* FAUVISM.

breton Hat, originally worn by peasants in France, with a brim that rolls up all the way around. The breton has been popular throughout the 20th century.

Brigance, Tom 1913–. Designer. Born in Waco, Texas, USA. Brigance studied at Parsons School of Design in New York from 1931 to 1934 and later attended the Sorbonne in Paris. From 1939 until 1941, when he joined the US Army, Brigance was employed as a designer at New York department store Lord & Taylor. After his demobilization in 1944, Brigance worked as a freelance designer. In 1949 he established his own business. He is known as a specialist beachwear designer.

Bri-nylon Tradename of ICI Fibres Ltd for a nylon fabric.

British Warm Name given to an overcoat worn by British officers during World War I which became popular for civilian use in

A nylon knitted jacquard swimsuit for 1970 designed by Tom **Brigance**. Bandannas and over-size sunglasses were popular accessories of the period.

postwar years. The British Warm was made of a heavy cloth—camel, cashmere, melton, or wool—and slightly shaped to fit the body. It was knee-length or longer, single- or double-breasted, with large pockets, deep REVERS, and leather buttons. Various styles existed until the 1950s.

broadcloth Generic term for a variety of cloth. Originally, broadcloth was a woolen shirting fabric cut wider than any other cloth. It is also a closely woven wool suiting cloth with a smooth nap and lustrous appearance, or a tightly woven cotton cloth with a fine crosswise rib.

brocade Rich, jacquard-weave fabric which has a raised design, usually flowers or figures, woven into it, often in silk, gold, or silver threads. Brocade has been associated with eveningwear since the mid-19th century.

broderie anglaise Also known as Swiss or Madeira embroidery, broderie anglaise is a form of embroidery initially created with a needle and thread. It is characterized by a white thread on a white background (usually cotton) into which a pattern of round or oval holes is pierced. The edges of the holes are then overcast with stitches. Known in Europe since the 16th century, broderie anglaise was particularly popular from 1840 to 1880, when it was made up into nightwear and underwear, most often for children. From the 1870s a Swiss machine successfully copied the styles. During the 20th century, broderie anglaise has been used for dress trimmings and summer attire and is still in use for underwear.

Brodovitch, Alexey 1898–1971. Photographer, art director, teacher. Born in St. Petersburg, Russia. Brodovitch was educated in St. Petersburg. He went to Paris as a refugee around 1918, and in the early 1920s he painted scenery for DIAGHILEV'S BALLETS RUSSES, as well as designing fabrics, posters, books, and magazines. Brodovitch worked for a French advertising agency from 1926 to 1928 and then served briefly as art director of the Trois Quartiers department store. In 1930 he emigrated to the USA where he became director of the Philadelphia Museum School of Industrial Art, opening a small Design Laboratory six years later to maintain close contact with students. In 1934 Brodovitch was appointed art director of HARPER'S BAZAAR and for twenty-four years his ideas dominated the visual side of the magazine. He encouraged young photographers and used the magazine as a platform for new ideas in fashion photography and graphic design. Throughout his career Brodovitch was involved as a consultant, lecturer, and tutor on numerous design teams at US colleges and universities. After the closure of the Laboratory at the Philadelphia Museum in 1938, he opened in 1941 the Brodovitch Design Laboratory at the New School for Social Research in New York and taught there until 1949. Brodovitch resigned from *Harper's Bazaar* in 1958 but continued teaching and lecturing until 1967, when he retired to France.

brogue Stout shoe that originated in Scotland and Ireland as a single piece of untanned leather held together by a tie lace. The 20th-century brogue is a laced, flat-heeled, stitched leather shoe decorated with a perforated design. The word brogue also describes an OXFORD shoe that has been punched and stitched in the same manner.

Man's black calf **brogue**, *c.* 1900.

brooch clip *See* DRESS CLIP.

Brooks Brothers Established in New York in 1818 as Brooks Clothing Company, Brooks Brothers was a pioneer of ready-to-wear clothes for men. In 1896 a Brooks Brothers representative was impressed by the button-down shirt collars worn by polo players in England, and four years later the store introduced the button-down shirt to the USA. It was one of several Brooks Brothers specialties, many of which originated in England. Others include the foulard tie, madras fabric for shirts (originally designed for British officers in India), Harris tweed (imported from Scotland), SHETLAND sweaters, and the POLO COAT, which was originally white with pearl buttons and a full belt but later made in camel and gray with various belt styles. These fashions were introduced between the 1890s and the outbreak of World War I. In 1949, Brooks Brothers began selling pink cotton button-down shirts for women. Cashmere polo shirts, introduced in the 1950s, were also appropriated by women.

The **Brooks Brothers** button-down shirt collar, still one of the most popular shirt styles in the USA today.

Brooks, Donald 1928–. Costume and fashion designer. Born in New York City, USA. Brooks was educated in New Haven, Connecticut, and studied art and English literature at the Fine Arts School of Syracuse University, New York, from 1947 to 1949. He briefly attended Parsons School of Design, leaving to work for the first of many ready-to-wear companies. By 1958 Townley Frocks, manufacturers of sportswear designed by Claire MCCARDELL, gave Brooks his own label. In the mid-1960s Brooks was one of the first designers to include luxurious evening pants and voluminous PAJAMAS in his collections. He used cotton a great deal, often reversing traditional seasonal colors. In 1959 he began working as a costume designer. His plays include *Barefoot in the Park* (1962), and his films *The Cardinal* (1963) and *Star!* (1968). Brooks is recognized for his promotion of the CHEMISE, and the creation of simple, unadorned dresses, trimmed coats, and STOLES.

Brunelleschi, Umberto 1879–1949. Illustrator and costume designer. Born in Montemurio, near Pistoia, Italy. Brunelleschi studied at the Accademia delle Belle Arti in Florence. In 1900 he moved to Paris where he worked as a caricaturist and illustrator, often under the name Harun-al-Rashid. In 1902 he collaborated with illustrator Paul IRIBE on *L'Assiette au beurre*, a successful illustrated paper, for a special issue which satirized fashionable painters of the time. Brunelleschi was a painter himself and contributed to the Paris Salons from 1903 to 1910. By 1912 he was illustrating books, designing posters, and working for both the JOURNAL DES DAMES ET DES MODES and FEMINA. He also worked as a costume designer. In 1914 Brunelleschi went to Italy to illustrate Italian magazines. He returned to Paris after World War I. In the following two decades his costumes were seen at the Roxy Theater in New York, at La Scala in Milan, and at the Folies-Bergère in Paris. He created many costumes for Josephine BAKER's revues. In his early years Brunelleschi's work was recognizable by its clearly executed, delicate lines and fanciful flourishes. During the late 1920s his colors became stronger, in some cases more somber, and later still his subjects lost the element of fantasy that had been his early hallmark.

The classic **Brooks Brothers** coat, restrained and balanced—a style that has hardly changed in 40 years.

Brussels lace Needlepoint LACE, famous since the 17th century, which reached the peak of its popularity in the 19th century. Made in several Belgian towns, Brussels lace characteristically incorporates ornate designs of leaves and flowers.

WHEN YOU TRAVEL
BY AIR...

Practically every type of overcoating is either made by or confined to Burberrys, and include none but the best as regards qualities, colours and patterns.

At Burberrys there are overcoats and overcoatings of gossamer textures right through all grades to those which generate generous warmth, not by weight but by rich thickly woven wools.

BURBERRY   OVERCOATS

The double-breasted **Burberry** overcoat went everywhere.

bubble cut Hairstyle of short, curly hair, usually achieved by permanent waving. It is so named because the curls resemble bubbles. Bubble cuts were popular from the late 1950s until the 1970s.

bubble dress In 1957, French designer Pierre CARDIN introduced short-skirted, bubble-shaped dresses and skirts, produced by BIAS cutting over a stiffened base.

buckle Attachment or device for fastening belts, straps, and garments. Buckles can be both functional and decorative. They vary in shape and size according to fashion trends.

Burberry *See* BURBERRY, Thomas.

Burberry, Thomas 1835–1926. Storeowner. Born in Dorking, Surrey, England. Burberry trained as an apprentice to a draper. In 1856 he opened his own drapery business, T. Burberry & Sons, in Basingstoke, Hampshire. In collaboration with the owner of a cotton mill, he produced a waterproof coat based on the close weave and loose style of an agricultural SMOCK. The cotton cloth, called "GABARDINE," was proofed in the yarn before weaving, then closely woven and proofed again. In 1891 Burberry established a wholesale business in London. He specialized in making gabardine clothes for active leisure pursuits and for the sports field. Most popular was the smock-like "Walking Burberry," cut on straight, easy-fitting lines with a fly-front fastening and RAGLAN sleeves. In 1902 Burberry established "Gabardine" as a trademark. Seven years later "The Burberry" was registered as a trademark for the company's coats.

During World War I Burberry designed coats for the British Royal Flying Corps (later the RAF). The military style model of the Burberry became the TRENCHCOAT of that war. It had a deep back YOKE, EPAULETS, buckled cuff straps, a button-down storm flap on one shoulder, and storm pockets. Metal D rings on belts were intended for the attachment of military accouterments. After the war, the trenchcoat was absorbed into civilian life. Known as a "Burberry," it has been copied worldwide.

burnous Full, hooded cloak of Arab origin which was often embroidered and trimmed with tassels. The burnous shape formed the basis of the 19th-century MANTLE.

Burrows, Stephen (Gerald) 1943–. Designer. Born in Newark, New Jersey, USA. Burrows studied at the Philadelphia Museum College of Art from 1961 to 1962 and the Fashion Institute of Technology, New York, from 1964 to 1966. In 1968 he opened a boutique with designer Roz Rubenstein. Shortly after, Burrows and Rubenstein went to work for the New York department store Henri Bendel, leaving in 1973 to open their own design house. At the beginning of his career, Burrows was noted for his adventurous approach to clothing design and construction. He created garments in leather, notably a nail-studded black jacket and PATCHWORK pants. His hallmark was the highly visible use of machine-made stitching, often zigzags, which he used on the hemlines of skirts, creating a fluted, crinkled effect that was often described as a lettuce-edge. He top-stitched in contrast colors and inlaid patches of color. Burrows is also known for comfortable, supple leisure clothes and for his contributions to the bright, body-conscious garments of the DISCO scene. Matte jersey in hot shades is a favorite fabric.

bush jacket Jacket traditionally worn in the African bush or on safari, made of water-repellent corduroy, heavy cotton, or linen, often suede-finished and waterproofed. Based on the style of a man's loose shirt, it reached to below the hips, and featured breast pockets, shell pockets, and pleated hand pockets. It was often belted. *See* SAFARI JACKET *and* SAINT LAURENT.

busk Strip of WHALEBONE or shell which was inserted in a CORSET or STAYS during the late 19th century to create the S-BEND SILHOUETTE of the period. Shaped like a long paper knife, thicker at the top than at the bottom, the busk was held in place by laces. It extended from the bust to the waist or hips.

bust bodice Undergarment popular until the 1920s. Based on the CAMISOLE, it was heavily boned, padded, and taped to give a full, bow-fronted, rounded appearance to the bust. It either fitted around the bust or was slightly longer, reaching to the waist. The bust bodice was replaced by the BRA.

buster brown collar Broad, round, starched collar first worn by small boys in the early 20th century. It was named after "Buster Brown"—hero of a US comic strip popular from c.1909—who wore a tweed suit of knee-length pants and double-breasted belted jacket, with a round-collared shirt. This style of collar has been adapted to womenswear by various designers.

bustier Item of underwear known in various forms from the early 19th century. It is a deep, waisted garment based on a BRA and

The **burnous** at Liberty of London in 1908.

57

A 1973 snakeskin version of the **butcher's boy cap.**

CAMISOLE which embraces the ribs and hip bones. The shoulder straps are set far apart to enable the bustier to be worn with BATEAU NECKLINES. It was popular in the 1950s and emerged in the 1980s in exotic fabrics as outerwear for evening.

bustle Pad of cork, down, or other type of stuffing worn under a skirt, which is attached to the back below waist level and which serves as a base over which the skirt's material is pleated or looped. The bustle was the prevailing skirt shape during the 1860s and 1870s. A wood, steel, or WHALEBONE basket which tied at the waist and curved down to the hips was also worn under skirts. Some bustles were made of spring metal bands. *See also* CRINOLINE *and* *WORTH.

Busvine House founded in London in 1863 by a Mr. Busvine, who had trained under Henry CREED the Younger. Busvine supplied riding outfits and other tailored garments to members of the British Royal Family. By the turn of the century, Busvine had become a household word among the aristocracy. Branches were established in Paris and Berlin. In the 1920s Richard Busvine, grandson of the founder, opened a branch in New York. He became chief designer of the London branch in the 1930s. In 1939 Busvine merged with REDFERN.

butcher's boy cap Large cap with a broad brim, based on a 19th-century tradesman's cap. The butcher's boy cap was popular during the 1960s, made of tartan, velvet, vinyl, and other fabrics.

Butterick, Ebenezer New England tailor who, in 1863, made paper patterns of a gingham dress designed by his wife. He graded the

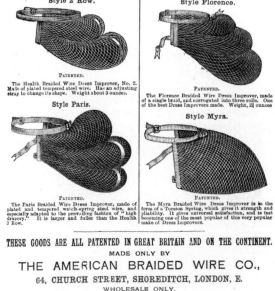

Known as dress improvers, late-19th-century **bustles** were designed in all manner of shapes.

Schiaparelli's acrobat **buttons** on her Circus jacket of 1938.

patterns so that dresses of different sizes could be made. Shortly after, Butterick began making shirt patterns and by the 1880s he had several thousand agencies in the USA and Canada selling his patterns. First established in New York, he set up in London's Regent Street in 1873 and published his patterns for men's, women's, and children's fashions in reviews and magazines. He also founded a publishing empire of more than thirty magazines.

button Buttons have been used as decorative items of dress since the 14th century, although their prominence is entirely dependent on fashion trends. By the early 19th century, machine-made fabric buttons and buttons of ceramics, glass, and papier-mâché were in existence but they were not strongly featured in fashions of the period. From the mid-19th century, shell, mother-of-pearl, black glass, stamped steel and brass, and molded horn were often used for buttons, which by this time had become integral parts of fashion design. Dresses and blouses were made with many tiny buttons. In the 1880s there was a revival in the use of enamel (previously popular in the 18th century), and buttons were also made of glass or porcelain, or covered with embroidery. These trends continued until World War I, when there was a marked decline in the number of buttons used. The Art Deco movement of the 1920s brought buttons once more into fashion's focus and this interest continued throughout the 1930s and stimulated the production of buttons made from wood, cork, plexiglass, and synthetic plastics. Novelty buttons enjoyed a fashion vogue in this decade. Used as strategic parts of clothing designs, they often resembled baskets of fruit or cigarette packs. MAINBOCHER presented silver clasp buttons, ROCHAS showed buttons in the shape of open books, and PATOU adorned his outfits with flower pots, foxes, mermaids, and snake buttons. SCHIAPARELLI also used unusual buttons in her designs, notably the acrobat buttons of her Circus jacket. After World War II, buttons became less decorative and more functional. *See* col. pl.

Ocelot coat with sleeves of blue fox by **Calman Links,** *c.* 1935.

cable knit Raised decorative pattern resembling twisted cables, used in knitted SWEATERS. In the 20th century, cable knit sweaters are worn for casual attire and sports.

Cacharel, Jean (Louis Henri Bousquet) 1932–. Designer. Born in Nîmes, France. Cacharel began his design career as an apprentice tailor. In 1956 he moved to Paris and two years later opened a small atelier where he made men's shirts. This venture was soon abandoned and Cacharel started a company designing for women. In the early 1960s he introduced a highly successful *chemisier crêpon* based on a man's shirt and made up in a fabric usually associated with nightwear. During the 1960s Cacharel became famous for his fitted blouses and shirts—often made in LIBERTY print/floral cottons—CULOTTE skirts, and gaberdine MINI skirts with three pleats at either side. Both types of skirts were worn with short, tight, brightly colored SHETLAND sweaters over delicately printed shirts and blouses which often featured embroidery on the collars. This style of dressing was widely copied. During the 1970s, Cacharel introduced to his ready-to-wear designs bolder, more colorful patterns, many of which were inspired by the prints and weaves of Africa and the Far East. Emanuelle KHANH worked with him from 1962 until 1967. Since 1968, Cacharel has employed photographer Sara MOON to create the company's distinctive marketing image.

caftan Believed to have originated in ancient Mesopotamia. Loosely cut, ankle-length garment, open at the front, with long, wide sleeves, which was usually bound with a sash and made from silk or cotton. In the 1950s DIOR showed versions of the caftan, without the sash, worn over floor-length evening dresses. During the 1960s HALSTON and SAINT LAURENT were just two designers who utilized this basic shape. In the 1970s caftans became popular as eveningwear and, cut in generous proportions, as at-home gowns. Some versions were zipped from neck to ankle. Most were worn without a sash. The caftan shape is also used in nightgowns. Caftans can be made from almost any fabric. Synthetic fabrics which trace the body's lines are frequently chosen, as are satin and heavily embroidered fabrics.

calico Ancient fabric first made in Calicut in southwest Madras, India. Calico is a durable, coarse cotton cloth which is usually dyed. Often used as household cloth, in the 20th century it has been made up into casual summer attire.

Callot Soeurs Couture house founded in Paris in 1895 by the three daughters of a Parisian antique dealer, who specialized in the sale of lace. The sisters began by selling ribbons and lingerie. They then used old velvet and lace to construct elaborate day dresses which were often adorned with tiers of beads and more lace. For eveningwear Callot Soeurs designed heavy satin gowns and were among the first designers to promote lamé dresses. Their designs were popular with actresses and international hostesses. Callot Soeurs closed in 1937.

Calman Links Company founded in London in 1893 by Hungarian-born Calman Links (1868–1925). The company specialized in producing high quality *FUR garments. Father was succeeded by son, Joseph G. Links (b. 1904), who in the 1930s developed production methods aimed at reducing the cost of high-grade furs without sacrificing style. The company's attempts to produce fur garments designed with young people in mind were halted by World War II. After the war, Calman Links worked with BALMAIN, DIOR, AMIES, CAVANAGH, and LACHASSE. In 1955 the company was appointed Furriers to the Queen. From 1972 Calman Links has placed increasing emphasis on ready-to-wear designs for the international market.

cambric Closely woven white cotton fabric, first made in Cambrai, France, which is finished with a slight gloss on one side. It was used in the 19th century for making simple blouses and SHIFTS.

camel hair Used in the 19th century to make outer garments for men and women, camel hair, also known as camel hair wool, is the short, soft undercoat of the camel. In its natural color it was a popular fiber for coats. During the 19th century a cloth known as camel hair—a blend of cashmere and wool—became popular. It was dyed the same color as natural camel hair. Camel hair coats, both real and imitation, have maintained their popularity throughout the 20th century.

cameo Hard stone, usually agate, onyx, or sardonyx, into which a design is cut in relief. Cameos were popular in Greece during the Hellenistic period. During the 1st century BC, cameo cutting was centered in Rome. Throughout the 18th and 19th centuries, copies of ancient cameos were the most fashionable form of jewelry, pinned to blouses and dresses or worn on a band around the throat.

camiknickers Item of underwear combining a CAMISOLE and a pair of knickers that often buttoned between the legs. At the turn of the century many varieties of camiknickers existed. Some fastened with buttons at the side or in the front; some voluminous versions did not have fastenings but were drawn about the waist by ribbons or elastic. The camisole top usually had thin straps, often made of ribbon, and was trimmed with lace or embroidery. The knicker length varied from the knee to the top of the thigh. Over the years, camiknickers have been adapted according to the prevailing styles in clothes. During the 1920s and 1930s slim-line garments required lightweight, unobtrusive underwear. At this time, camiknickers were called "step ins"—a reference to the method of putting them on. In the 1980s camiknickers are invariably brief and cut very short. Originally made of cotton, lawn, satin, or silk, camiknickers have since the 1970s been made mostly in easycare synthetic fabrics.

Camilla costume *See* BLOOMER.

camisole Item of underwear introduced during the early 19th century which is based on a loose, sleeveless BODICE or CHEMISE. Originally, it was worn between the CORSET and dress as a protective layer. It covers the body from the bust to the waist and has fine shoulder straps. In the early part of this century, when many women discarded their corsets, the camisole was worn next to the skin. It was originally made of cotton or lawn, with more elegant versions trimmed with lace. Satin and silk were popular fabrics during the

This classic Jaeger **camel-hair** coat, still a great cold weather favorite today, worn here in 1920 with the inevitable cloche pulled down toward the eyes.

Cameo dating from the 1850s.

The **cap**—or flat hat—worn by men at all levels of society since the turn of the century.

1930s. The gradual introduction of synthetic, easycare fibers has increased the appeal of the camisole. *See* *NAINSOOK.

camp shirt US term for a generously cut blouse with breast pockets and wide sleeves that reach almost to the elbow. The camp shirt buttons down the front and is made up in both inexpensive and luxurious fabrics.

canvas Strong, plain-woven cloth, used in both its heavy and light weights for footwear and sportswear. It featured strongly in post World War II summer fashions. *See* CASHIN.

cap Brimless covering for the head, with a stiff peak over the forehead, originally worn by workmen. During the 1960s, very large, brightly colored versions, often made of leather or PVC, became popular.

cap sleeve Small, triangular sleeve which sits on the shoulders, either forming a stiff cap or falling on to the arms to provide minimal coverage. The cap sleeve has been used on dresses and blouses throughout the 20th century. It is especially popular for summer wear.

cape Full outer garment, traditionally a shorter version of the CLOAK but without slits for the arms. Capes were fashionable during the late 19th century and from the 1950s to the mid-1970s, in varying lengths and fabrics. *See* BALMAIN *and* TRIGERE.

Capezio US company founded in 1887 to make BALLET SHOES. In 1944 Claire MCCARDELL persuaded Capezio to make PUMPS based on ballet shoes. These became widely popular.

capri pants During the 1950s fairly loose pants, tapered to the midcalf, became fashionable summer attire. They were named after the Italian island of Capri, which was a popular holiday resort at the time.

Capucci, Roberto 1929–. Designer. Born in Rome, Italy. Capucci studied at the Accademia delle Belle Arti in Rome. He worked for designer Emilio Schuberth before opening his own house at the age of twenty-one. Acclaimed in Italy, Capucci went to Paris in 1962, only to return to Rome seven years later. He cuts and drapes fabric into extraordinary, extravagant, magnificent, and daring clothes that give the impression of being created for a woman whose presence is rarely felt; she is there only to display Capucci's mastery of line and cut.

car coat Woolen outdoor garment which originated in the USA in the 1950s. Styled to be convenient for driving, it is a a hip-length semi-fitted jacket, often double-breasted.

caracul *See* KARACUL.

cardigan Long-sleeved military jacket of knitted worsted, trimmed with fur or BRAID and buttoned down the front. It was worn by British Army officers during the Crimean War and named after the 7th Earl of Cardigan, James Thomas Brudenell (1797–1868), who led the Charge of the Light Brigade. In the 20th century the style, minus the collar, was adapted for sportswear. The cardigan became

In 1957 **Capucci** created this unusual evening dress with two large panniers attached to the bodice above the belted waist.

a popular garment with home knitters, and knitwear manufacturers produced a variety of styles and designs based on a woolen (or wool mix) garment which buttons down the front and has long sleeves. CHANEL helped to popularize the cardigan during the 1920s and 1930s as part of a two-piece outfit of cardigan-jacket and skirt or a three-piece outfit of cardigan-jacket, SWEATER, and skirt. During the 1950s there was a brief vogue for wearing cardigans back to front. *See* *PRINGLE *and* TWINSET.

Cardin, Pierre 1922–. Designer. Born in San Biagio Di Callalta, near Venice, to French parents. Cardin was brought up in St. Etienne in the Loire region of France. He left home at seventeen to work for a tailor in Vichy, where he began making suits for women. In 1944, after the Liberation of France, Cardin went to Paris where, one year later, he found work with PAQUIN and SCHIAPARELLI. He met Christian BERARD and Jean COCTEAU and made the costumes for Cocteau's film *Beauty and the Beast* (1947). Cardin also worked for DIOR. In 1949 he began producing theatrical costumes. Over the following seven years Cardin gained a reputation as both a maker of men's suits and a designer of extravagant and fantastic costumes. During this period he took over a small shop for his own menswear and womenswear. In 1957 Cardin produced his first women's collection, followed six years later by a ready-to-wear line. During the 1950s he designed coats with draped hemlines and loose back panels, BUBBLE skirts, and unstructured CHEMISES. In the 1960s he introduced colored wigs made by the Carita sisters. His CUT-OUT dresses; coats that flared from curved, stitched collars; and large, APPLIQUE pockets were widely influential. Cardin's 1964 collection was labelled *"SPACE AGE." It comprised knitted CATSUITS, tight leather pants, close-fitting HELMETS, and BATWING JUMPSUITS. In the same decade he raised skirts to four inches above the knee and plunged necklines, back and front, to the navel. Cardin is associated with the use of supple, knitted fabrics made up into BODYSTOCKINGS, catsuits, tubular dresses, TABARD tops over LEGGINGS, and TIGHTS. He has frequently used the BIAS CUT to produce spiral dresses and is fond of COWL draping. During the 1960s and 1970s Cardin's creations revealed a strong, forceful designer, in whose work the shape of the body sometimes took second place to the line of his clothes. His designs were unfussy and bold, often with irregular outlines. Cardin is a conceptual designer, able to carry an idea through a complete collection. The clear, coherent aspects of his work have been copied and translated into styling details by numerous other designers and manufacturers.

Carnaby Street Street in the West End of London which became famous in the 1960s for its many BOUTIQUES selling fashionable, inexpensive clothes, such as T-SHIRTS, MINI skirts, BELL BOTTOMS, and HIPSTERS, as well as trendy accessories. The name is now synonymous with the youth cult of the "swinging sixties." *See also* KING'S ROAD.

Carnegie, Hattie 1889–1956. Designer, manufacturer. Born Henrietta Kanengeiser in Vienna, Austria. The family moved to the USA and changed their name to Carnegie. At fifteen, Carnegie began work in Macy's New York department store, dressing hats. In 1909 she opened a hat shop with a partner who made dresses. Carnegie bought out her partner four years later and took over the clothing design. Although she was unable to sew or draw, Carnegie's talent lay in being able to communicate her ideas to others who carried

The classic **cardigan**, shown here in 1918.

Carrickmacross lace of the 19th century, worked in floral patterns.

them out. She launched her first collection in 1918, followed by a ready-to-wear collection ten years later. During the 1930s and 1940s Carnegie's name was synonymous with smart but conventional suits and dresses. Her tailored suits in grey worsted with straight skirts, tidy collars, and jeweled buttons, and her neat black dresses became status symbols for US women. Carnegie was inspired by *haute couture* but avoided any theatricality or extravagance in her designs. She visited Paris frequently and her success has much to do with the fact that she was able to adapt Paris fashion to US taste.

Carosa Italian firm founded in Rome in 1947 by Princess Giovanna Caracciolo. The house produced high quality fashions in good fabrics. It closed in 1974.

Carrickmacross lace Muslin lace with APPLIQUE motifs, originating in the town of Carrickmacross in the Republic of Ireland. This fine, gauzy lace was first made in 1820 and its popularity endured for one hundred years.

Cartier Company manufacturing jewels and bijouterie founded in Paris in 1847 by Louis-François Cartier (1819–1904). Alfred Cartier (1841–1925), son of the founder, moved the company to its luxurious premises on Paris's Rue de la Paix in 1898. In the same year, Alfred Cartier's son Louis-Joseph (1875–1942) entered the business. By the turn of the century, Cartier was a well-established jewelry company, suppliers to royal houses around the world. In 1902, Alfred Cartier's second son, Pierre (1878–1964), opened a branch in London. In 1909 a branch was opened in New York. Cartier is not only famous for its jewelry but also for its development of the wristwatch, including in 1907 a design for the famous Brazilian aviator, Alberto Santos-Dumont, and in 1931 the production of a luxury waterproof watch.

cartwheel hat Hat with a very large, often straight but occasionally downward curving brim of even width. It has a shallow crown and is usually made of straw. The cartwheel hat was popular before and after World War II until the late 1950s. *See* *BEATON.

Cartier stomacher of 1913. The diamonds are set in platinum and the pendant section is detachable.

Carven House founded in Paris in 1937 by Carven Mallet, a dressmaker who specialized in designing for the petite woman and who adjusted the proportions of accessories accordingly. Carven sells *haute couture* and ready-to-wear formal and informal clothes.

Cashin, Bonnie 1915–. Designer. Born in Oakland, California, USA. Cashin's mother was a dressmaker. After graduating from high school, Cashin joined a ballet company in Los Angeles. She went with the company to New York where she designed costumes for the Roxy Theater's dance chorus. In 1937 she produced a sportswear collection for manufacturers Adler & Adler, subsequently working for that company full-time. In 1943 she moved to 20th Century Fox in Hollywood and in six years created costumes for more than thirty major films. She returned to New York in 1949 and opened a business four years later. Cashin's fashion philosophy was evident from her clean, uncomplicated designs; her clothes were designed to be loose-fitting and functional, and were often worn in layers which could be discarded according to climate or temperature. One of the great US designers of the 20th century, many of Cashin's designs are still relevant in the 1980s. She was skilled at mixing fabrics and worked frequently with canvas, leather, poplin, suede, and tweed. During the 1950s and 1960s—her most creative years—she produced, among numerous other garments: Chinese-style jackets over dresses, canvas and poplin RAINCOATS, fringed suede dresses, wool TABARDS, KIMONO coats piped with leather, long dinner jackets made of upholstery fabric, and hooded jersey dresses. She is most often associated with the introduction and popularization of the PONCHO as a fashion garment and with long, fringed at-home skirts made from plaid mohair.

From Bonnie **Cashin**: (*below*) the 1961 poncho in mohair and wool; (*above*) the 1962 "Noh" classic coat in mohair edged with suede; and (*left*) a 1963 3-piece layered outfit with leather shell.

cashmere Rare natural fiber combed from the fleece of the kashmir goat, which is found in Inner Mongolia, the People's Republic of China, Iran, Iraq, Turkey, and Afghanistan. Known since the 14th century, cashmere has been used extensively in Europe since the 19th century, when it was often made up into children's dresses and blended with other fibers to make women's outer garments. In the 20th century, cashmere is used for coats, dresses, scarves, and SWEATERS. As it is an expensive fabric to produce, it is often mixed with other fibers, such as wool. A garment made of cashmere alone is considered a luxury item. *See also* PRINGLE *and* TWINSET.

Cassini, Oleg (Loiewski) 1913–. Designer. Born in Paris, France, of Russian parents. Cassini was educated in Florence at the English Catholic School and graduated from the Accademia delle Belle Arti in 1934. His mother ran a dress shop in Florence and after working with her Cassini opened a small salon making one-off designs. In 1936 he went to New York, where he was employed by various manufacturers on SEVENTH AVENUE until 1940, when he joined 20th Century Fox in Hollywood. After World War II, Cassini became head of the wardrobe department at Eagle-Lion Studios. By 1950 he was back on Seventh Avenue. During the 1950s the name Cassini was associated with glamorous, ready-to-wear SHEATH DRESSES, knitted suits, jackets, and COCKTAIL DRESSES. He also designed extensively for musicals and television. In 1961 Jacqueline Kennedy (ONASSIS) appointed him official designer for her wardrobe. He worked closely with her in the evolution of her personal clothing style, creating many widely copied garments. These included a high-necked, silk ottoman evening gown and a fawn-colored, semi-fitted wool coat with a removable circular collar of Russian sable, which was worn over a matching wool dress.

Castelbajac, Jean-Charles de 1950–. Designer. Born in Casablanca, Morocco. Castelbajac moved to France with his family in the mid-1950s. In 1968 he began designing for his mother, who had her own clothing business. Shortly afterward he designed several lines for Paris manufacturer Pierre d'Alby before opening his own business in 1975. Castelbajac achieved fame in the mid-1970s with his functional, modernist, high-tech clothing. As a foil to the clearly defined structure of his designs, he uses natural fabrics and fibers. He is famous for his chic yet rugged sportswear and also for his hand-painted fabrics which did much to influence the "wearable art" garments popular during the early 1980s.

Castillo, Antonio 1908–. Designer. Born Antonio Canovas del Castillo del Rey in Madrid, Spain. Castillo studied at the Colegio del Pilar in Madrid, the University of Madrid, and at El Sacro Monte in Granada. He designed dresses, jewelry, and hats for the houses of PAQUIN and PIGUET from 1936 until 1944, when Elizabeth Arden persuaded him to join her salon in New York. Castillo worked with Arden from 1945 to 1950 and produced collections based on natural shoulder lines and slim silhouettes topped with small hats. He was also in demand as a costume designer for the New York Metropolitan Opera and Broadway. In 1950 he returned to Paris and joined LANVIN. In one of his first collections for this house, in 1951, he showed white satin evening gowns trimmed with mink. Castillo continued to produce designs based on Lanvin's original ROBES DE STYLE, with close-fitting BODICES and long, flowing skirts. He employed soft fabrics for his coats and dresses, which were often draped at the hip or panneled at the side. Between 1956 and 1960,

Above left: Oleg **Cassini**'s sketch for one of Jacqueline Kennedy's most famous outfits: the pillbox hat; the Chanel-like beads at the neck; the short, slightly tailored two-piece; the three-quarter-length sleeves on the jacket, and the long gloves. This outfit was widely copied throughout the USA. It is shown (*top*) worn by Jacqueline Kennedy in June 1961, on President Kennedy's state visit to Paris. *Above right:* Jackie Kennedy's dinner dress—another success for Oleg **Cassini** in the 1960s. Based on the Empire line, its focus was the eye-catching decoration pinned to the front.

CAPES featured often in his collections, fringed and triple-tiered in 1956, hip or floor length by 1960. In 1962 Castillo left Lanvin and two years later opened his own business. He continued to create elegant clothes and elaborate costumes for private clients, the theater, and the movies, notably for the film *Nicholas and Alexandra* (1971).

Castle, Irene 1893–1969. Dancer. Born Irene Foote in New Rochelle, New York, USA. In the 1910s, Irene Castle and her husband, Vernon Blythe Castle, became a popular dance team, working first at the Café de Paris in Paris, but traveling often to the USA and other parts of Europe. Irene Castle adapted her clothes for dancing by shortening them, using soft, flowing fabrics, and either slitting her skirts or adding extra fullness. Her buckled shoes, narrow velvet HEADBAND trimmed with pearls, and her habit of wearing men's coats and CAPS were widely copied. She also bobbed her hair and helped to popularize the boyish silhouette of the 1910s and 1920s.

catsuit All-in-one garment, usually with long sleeves, which is either zipped or buttoned at the front from the navel to the neck. The catsuit was popular in the 1960s and owed its name to the fact that it was made from slinky, clinging fabrics. Catsuits were often worn with BOOTS. *See* CARDIN.

Caumont, Jean-Baptiste 1932–. Designer. Born in Béarn, France. Caumont studied art in Paris. He worked briefly for BALMAIN and illustrated fashion for VOGUE and *Marie-Claire*. Toward the end of the 1950s he began to work for the Italian department store chain La Rinascente in Milan and in 1965 he established his own ready-to-wear label in that city. Caumont is well known for his knitwear designs. His menswear range, "Caumont Monsieur," dates from 1970.

Cavanagh, John (Bryan) 1914–. Designer. Born in Ireland. Cavanagh trained at MOLYNEUX in London and Paris during the 1930s. After World War II, he studied fashion in the USA for several years and in 1947 joined BALMAIN in Paris. Four years later Cavanagh returned to London where, in 1952, he opened his own house. Successful from the start, Cavanagh approached his work as a couturier with a keen eye for cut and line. He promoted full-skirted, round-shouldered looks as effectively as lean, long lines. His designs in the 1950s anticipated the SACK or CHEMISE dress. Cavanagh's success continued throughout the 1960s with the production of wholesale and ready-to-wear lines. He retired in 1974. *See* *KLEIN, BERNAT.

Celanese Trademark of the Celanese Corporation of America. The company produces fashion fabrics from acetate and rayon.

Cerruti, Nino (Antonio) 1930–. Designer. Born in Biella, Italy. The Cerruti family textile business was established in 1881 by three brothers. Centered around an old mill, the company specialized in producing high quality woolen fabrics. At the age of twenty, Nino Cerruti, eldest grandson of one of the three brothers, left university and took over the firm. During the 1950s, as a means of promotion, he commissioned four plays for which he designed the costumes. In 1963 he launched a knitwear line. His first men's ready-to-wear venture was established in 1967, the same year in which he set up his

Irene **Castle**, the epitome of the modern woman, danced her way into the limelight. She created a vogue for short haircuts and for clothes that did not restrict movement.

Cerruti's 1980/81 collection included these classic examples of suits for both sexes.

studio in Paris. Nine years later, Cerruti launched a womenswear line. His clothes for men and women, usually sportswear, are classically tailored, elegant, and made of high quality fabrics. In the field of menswear Cerruti is an acknowledged leader in suits.

challis Lightweight plain woven fabric originally made from silk and wool and printed with a delicate floral pattern. The word is believed to derive from the Anglo-Indian "shalee," which means soft. Twentieth-century challis is made from wool mixed with cotton and rayon and is mostly used as a dress fabric.

Chambre Syndicale de la Haute Couture In 1868 the Syndicale de la Couture Parisienne was established as a craftsmen's guild. In the 1880s, under the leadership of Gaston WORTH, it became the Chambre Syndicale de la Couture Française and began to monitor the work of its members. Its name was again changed in 1911, to the Chambre Syndicale de la Couture Parisienne, and at this time its membership became limited. Designs lodged with the Syndicale were protected by copyright. The Syndicale presented group showings of couturiers' work, notably in San Francisco in 1945. It established strict rules for overseas buyers and laid down guidelines, still in existence today, for the running of a couture house.

Chanel, Coco 1883–1971. Designer. Born Gabrielle Bonheur Chanel in Saumur, France. Although many questions surround Chanel's early life, it is generally believed that she had acquired some experience in dressmaking and millinery before she moved to Deauville in 1910 to work in a hat shop. Between 1912 and 1914 she started two shops, one in Paris and one in Deauville, where she made and sold hats, simple loose blouses, and CHEMISES. Chanel's clothes were designed to be worn without CORSETS and were constructed with fewer linings to make them lighter and less rigid. As early as 1914 she was showing a simple chemise dress. In 1916 she began to make garments from jersey, a cheap fabric previously used only for underwear. Later, demand for this fabric and for a specially woven knit called kasha persuaded Chanel to manufacture them. In 1918 Chanel was producing CARDIGANS and TWINSETS. She adapted men's SWEATERS and showed them worn over plain, straight skirts. In 1920 she introduced wide-legged pants for women, based on sailor's BELL-BOTTOMS, which she called "yachting pants." These were followed two years later by wide, generously cut beach PAJAMAS. Chanel's personal life brought her into the public eye and increased her influence on fashion during the post-World War I years. She herself wore the clothes she had adapted from traditional menswear: belted RAINCOATS, plain open-neck shirts, BLAZERS, cardigans, pants, and soft BERETS. Gray and navy-blue were her favorite colors but she also created a vogue for beige. She became a celebrated figure, the archetypal GARCONNE—flat-chested, slender, wearing loose, comfortable clothes and sporting a short, boyish haircut. Throughout the 1920s Chanel introduced one fashion idea after another. She teamed tweed skirts with sweaters and strings of pearls, transformed PEA JACKETS and raincoats into fashionable attire, and popularized the LITTLE BLACK DRESS. Her collarless cardigan jacket was braid-trimmed, accessorized with PATCH POCKETS, and worn with knee-length tweed skirts. Her simple chemise dresses had round, straight, or BOAT NECKS, hung loosely to the mid- or lower calf and were worn with waist- or hip-length belts. Her other innovations of the period included oversized flat black bows, gilt buttons on blazers, SLING-BACK sandals, and PURSES/handbags with

Left: **Chanel** evening dress in black mousseline de soie, 1925.

Right: **Chanel**'s neatly styled dress and bolero.

The unmistakable flat-chested, slender figure of Coco **Chanel**, sketched here by her friend and colleague Jean Cocteau. Chanel's own-design evening dress for 1937 features many of the fashion touches that made her famous: the collarless, elegant dress, the obvious jewelry trimmings, and the large bow in her hair.

en 1937 - Robe du soir

Jean Cocteau
1937

Coco **Chanel**, sporting her famous knitted three-piece cardigan suit, ropes of pearls, and two-tone shoes.

Parasol cover in **Chantilly lace,**
1850s.

gilt chains. She had a particularly strong influence on jewelry, showing smart tweed suits worn with rows of artificial pearls or gilt chains. During the 1930s she commissioned Duc Fulco DE VERDURA to design elaborate COSTUME JEWELRY using fake and semi-precious stones in ostentatious settings. In 1929 Chanel opened a boutique in her Paris salon to sell accessories: bags, BELTS, scarves, and jewelry. The following year she went to Hollywood to design clothes for several United Artists films. Back in France in the mid-1930s, Chanel focused much of her attention on manufacturing. She closed her salon in 1939. In 1954, at the age of seventy-one, she reopened and showed once more the neat suits that had been her hallmark before World War II. The fashion world was shocked to see revamped prewar fashions but more women than ever took to wearing the Chanel suit, and by the 1960s it had become a symbol of traditional elegance, worn (as in the 1920s) with a gilt chain purse and a string of pearls. The look endures today, particularly in the USA.

Chantilly lace Bobbin LACE woven in many European towns, including Grammont in Belgium, and Chantilly and Bayeux in France. It is usually black with swags of flowers and scattered dots on a fine background. The Chantilly shawl, in black or white, was popular during the late 19th century.

Charles, Caroline 1942–. Designer. Born in Cairo, Egypt, of English parents. Charles attended Swindon School of Art, Wiltshire, until 1960, when she became an apprentice to Michael Sherard. She spent almost two years working with Mary QUANT before setting up on her own in late 1963. During the 1960s Charles proved to be a popular designer of young, fashionable clothing. She created MINI dresses

British designer Caroline **Charles**'s cotton voile top and skirt reflect the gypsy vogue of the 1970s.

and skirts in pure cotton and flannel. From the TUNICS and pants of the late 1960s Charles moved with ease to the long, flowing fashion lines that predominated in the early 1970s. Using beautiful, often luxurious, prints and patterns, she established herself as a designer of more sophisticated clothes, a reputation she carried into the 1980s. Her collections are essentially practical, based on the idea of a cohesive working wardrobe. Charles acts as design consultant for several large manufacturing companies and has created collections for J. C. Penney's, the US retail and mail order company.

Charleston An American dance of the 1920s. Its energetic side-kicks from the knees made shorter dresses for women essential. The hems of these mostly simple, tubular dresses were often fringed to give the appearance of length without impeding movement.

charmeuse Trade name of a lustrous, lightweight cotton, rayon, or silk fabric of satin weave, developed in the 20th century.

Chase, Edna Woolman 1877–1957. Editor. Born Edna Alloway in New Jersey, USA. Chase started her career in the circulation department at VOGUE in the late 1890s. She became a reporter, then managing editor, and in 1914 was appointed editor. In that year she persuaded a US manufacturer to put on a fashion show using live models in the Parisian manner. Rather than attempt to depend on Paris during the World War I years, Chase encouraged US manufacturers to provide fashion for the many rather than the few, and championed a "more taste than money theme" in *Vogue*. As *Vogue*'s editor-in-chief, she fashioned the American woman's taste for nearly forty years. In 1933 she went to London, where her efforts prevented the closure of British *Vogue*. Chase returned to New York to retire nineteen years later, in 1952.

chatelaines Created in the 17th century to carry watches and seals, chatelaines were long chains, usually of silver, which wound round the waist and hung down over the skirt. They were revived in the 1830s. From 1849 chatelaines made of steel were used to hold an increasing number of practical objects—scissors, thimble, keys, etc. Chatelaines were rarely seen after the 1880s.

check Checks were developed by landowners in Scotland during the 19th century as an alternative to TARTAN, which was considered unsuitable for everyday wear or workwear. They were adapted from local weaves, based on tartan patterns and colors. It was also common to issue checks as commemorative patterns. During the 20th century checks were first used for men's suits and coats but quickly became popular for women, made up into suits, coats, dresses, skirts, and, in the 1960s, pants.

cheesecloth Thin, loosely woven, plain weave cotton which originated in India. Cheesecloth has mainly been used as a household fabric and for interlining garments. During the late 1960s and 1970s it was developed as a fashion fabric, dyed in bright colors and embroidered. Many of the cheesecloth dresses, skirts, and PEASANT-style blouses popular at the time were imported from India.

Chelsea Area of London which has been synonymous with fashion since the 17th century, when it became a popular habitat for artists.

In the 20th century the "Chelsea look" has taken many forms, too various to itemize. The last distinctive style is associated with the 1960s when BOUTIQUES and shops sprang up in Chelsea's main street, the KING'S ROAD, which attracted customers of all ages. The shops specialized in inexpensive, ready-to-wear clothes, many directly from designers. The 1960s "Chelsea look"consisted of MINI skirts, thigh-high leather BOOTS, and tight, SKINNY-RIB sweaters. *See* JOHN, AUGUSTUS; *and* QUANT.

The **chemise**, a 19th-century undergarment from which most 20th-century dress styles evolved.

chemise One of the simplest of garments, the chemise has existed in one form or another for thousands of years. Usually constructed from two rectangular pieces of fabric sewn at the shoulders and sides, it can be collarless and sleeveless. Chemises are made of cotton, linen, lawn, or silk, and the more luxurious of these fabrics are often decorated. Before the 19th century the chemise was also known as a SMOCK and was worn as an undergarment, either on its own or between the body and a CORSET or STAYS. Most chemises were drawn on over the head and had back fastening buttons or ties. During the 19th century, the chemise became a shirt-like blouse. *See* CHEMISE DRESS.

chemise dress In the early 20th century the CHEMISE shape was adapted by many designers. CHANEL was one of the first to create chemise dresses; simple, loose garments with long sleeves and a belt that tied under the bust, around the waist, or at the hips. LANVIN, PAQUIN, and WORTH also designed chemise dresses. In the 1950s a loose dress, based on the chemise, appeared at BALENCIAGA's collections. *See also* DIOR *and* SACK.

chenille Fabric with a fur-like texture created by weaving the warp threads in groups, originating in France during the 17th century. Chenille can be made from cotton, silk, rayon, or wool. In the late 19th century it was used for making evening gowns.

cheongsam Close-fitting SHIFT dress originally worn in the Far East. It usually has a MANDARIN collar, long sleeves, and a slit at both sides of the skirt to permit walking. It was briefly popular in the late 1950s and 1960s as evening attire.

Cheruit, Madeleine dates unknown. Designer. Born in France. Cheruit trained with the couture house of Raudnitz in Paris. Around 1906 she opened her own house and became well known in 1914 for her walking suits and afternoon dresses. After World War I she designed cinema capes and full evening skirts. In 1925 she created hand-painted Cubist-inspired dresses. Many of Cheruit's gowns were heavily ornamented and embroidered and started to lose their appeal in the mid-1920s when less complicated attire became fashionable. The house closed in 1935.

The turn-of-the-century **chesterfield**, with velvet collar and cuffs.

chesterfield The chesterfield was named in the 1830s after Philip Dormer Stanhope, 4th Earl of Chesterfield. The 19th-century chesterfield was a man's gray wool overcoat with a fitted waist and velvet collar. (In the previous century black velvet strips had been sewn on to coat collars of the French nobility as a sign of mourning for the death in 1793 of Louis XVI of France.) After World War I the long-line chesterfield with black velvet collar was copied for young women. Variations of the style—double-breasted with pockets—appeared throughout the 19th and 20th centuries.

chiffon Light, gossamer-sheer fabric created by tightly twisted yarns. Chiffon is made of silk, wool, or synthetics. It has been used almost exclusively for eveningwear. Chiffon scarves were popular during the 1950s and 1960s as fashion accessories.

chignon Hairstyle created by coiling long hair into a loose, but carefully pinned, bun-shape at the back of the head. It was a common style from the 19th century until the 1920s, often adorned or decorated. The chignon was popular during the late 1960s and early 1970s as part of the revival of EDWARDIAN-style fashions.

chinchilla Long, dense, soft fur of a rodent which originates in the Andes mountain range of South America. The fur is usually pale gray and a black streak runs along the length of the tail. Chinchilla was a fashionable fur at the turn of the century for trimming coats and cloaks. Since around 1900, most chinchilla has been ranched.

The **chignon** in 1922, soon to be threatened by the fashionable short haircuts of the mid-1920s.

chintz From the Hindu, *chint*, "a printed cloth." Chintz is a cotton cloth that is glazed by starch. It usually features designs of flowers, fruits, and birds and has been popular as a furnishing fabric since the 1600s. Most chintz was originally imported from India but as production in the UK increased, the British began to export chintz to Europe. In the early 1980s chintz was used to make fashion garments.

chiton Garment originating from ancient Greece. Although various versions are recorded, the chiton was generally made from a large, rectangular piece of cloth which was wrapped around the body, secured at one shoulder, and belted under or over the waist. Alternatively, it was constructed by fastening the top edges of two pieces with a series of clasps along both arms, which created sleeves, and tying the garment under the bust. The chiton has been adapted to numerous cuts and styles throughout the ages. FORTUNY used the chiton shape for his "Delphos gowns."

Chloé Ready-to-wear company based in France. Karl LAGERFELD designed for Chloé from 1965 to 1983, reinforcing the company's image of high quality ready-to-wear designed with a nod in the direction of couture.

choker Collar of pearls, or a band of fabric, often velvet, worn closely around the throat and decorated with jewels. Used in the 19th century for evening wear, the choker was in vogue again in the late 1960s and early 1970s. Also known as a dog collar.

Chong, Monica 1957–. Designer. Born in Hong Kong. Chong was educated in Hong Kong and Australia. In the early 1970s she moved to England, where she studied fashion design at Chelsea College of Art in London from 1974 to 1977. After leaving college Chong worked for the London store Browns before producing in 1978 a first collection composed of twelve pieces for a young market. Since then Chong has moved steadily from strength to strength and in the 1980s she designs day and eveningwear for the Tricoville group, among others.

circle skirt Cut from one or two pieces of fabric, the circle skirt was

Circle skirt for fashionable teenagers in 1953, advertised by Sears, Roebuck.

all the rage during the 1950s when it was often worn with layers of PETTICOATS. It is closely associated with the rock 'n' roll era.

ciré French for "wax." Process whereby wax, heat, and pressure are applied to fabrics such as satin, producing a smooth, lustrous effect. Ciré fabrics have been popular throughout the 20th century, notably during the 1920s, 1930s, and 1960s.

Claiborne, Liz 1929–. Designer. Born in Brussels, Belgium. Claiborne studied at the Fine Arts School and Painter's Studio in Belgium, and also in France and the USA. In 1949 she won a HARPER'S BAZAAR Jacques HEIM design contest which entitled her to travel and sketch in Europe. Upon her return to New York she joined Tina LESER and then, shortly after, Omar KIAM. In 1960 she began to design for the Youth Guild Inc. In the following year she was one of many designers who helped promote the idea of removing the strict classifications of clothes for specific occasions by designing complete wardrobes of mix-and-match separates. In 1976, Claiborne opened her own company. She continues to produce predominantly youthful, fashion-conscious clothes.

Clark, Ossie 1942–. Designer. Born Raymond Clark in Liverpool, England. Clark attended Manchester College of Art from 1957 to 1961 and then spent three years at the Royal College of Art in London. While at the RCA, Clark began designing for Quorum, a company dating from the early 1960s. Quorum became one of the most popular BOUTIQUES in CHELSEA, and Clark joined the firm full-time in 1966. During the late 1960s and early 1970s he was responsible for introducing and popularizing a variety of trends. His large-collared, leather motor cycle jacket, cut very short and zipped on one side at the front, became a widely copied high-fashion garment. He produced HOT PANTS, MAXI coats, and GYPSY dresses with HANDKERCHIEF POINTS. In the late 1960s Clark used metallic leather and snakeskin as fabrics, but his skill is mainly associated with the use of crêpe, satin, jersey, and chiffon. Many of his dress fabrics were designed by his wife, Celia Birtwell. Soft ruching, plunging necklines, and tiny waists were the hallmarks of Clark's body-conscious clothes. In the early 1970s his crêpe, ankle-length, large-sleeved, WRAP-AROUND DRESSES, which fitted at the back

Ossie Clark's blouse from the Edwardian revival of 1970.

leaving a triangle of bare skin, attracted enormous attention and demand. Later, in 1975, Clark worked for the London dress manufacturer Radley, where his crêpe and chiffon ready-to-wear evening dresses were produced. He left after a few years but rejoined the firm in 1983.

Collection of **cloaks** from Maison Gagelin, once Charles Frederick Worth's employer. This illustration comes from an 1850s issue of the *Petit Courier des Dames*.

Clive 1933–. Designer. Born Clive Evans in London, England. After completing his National Service, Clive attended Canterbury Art School. He then moved to London where he worked for John CAVANAGH, MICHAEL, and LACHASSE. In 1961 Clive opened his own *haute couture* and ready-to-wear business. His daywear—youthful, yet well-tailored and smart—was very popular throughout the 1960s. Clive closed the firm in 1971.

cloak Generic term for a loose outer garment, with or without sleeves, which covers the body from the shoulders to hips, knees, or ankles. It can be collarless, but is often made with either a high, stiff collar or a flat collar that sits on the shoulders. Cloaks were popular in the late 19th century and during the 20th century, particularly in the 1960s. *See* BALMAIN, CAPE, *and* TRIGERE.

cloche Woman's hat worn from *c.*1915 until the mid-1930s, achieving greatest popularity during the 1920s. The cloche is a tight-fitting hat covering the head from the back of the neck and worn pulled down low over the forehead. It is either brimmed or brimless. In the 1920s cloches were often decorated with grosgrain ribbon.

clutch purse Known in the 1920s and 1930s as a *pochette*, a clutch purse is a handbag without straps. It has been popular throughout the 20th century in various shapes and sizes, from the small beaded evening bag to the large ENVELOPE bag.

The **cloche hat** of the 1920s was worn pulled down low onto the forehead. Note the elaborate bow encircling the head and drawing attention to the eyes.

coat dress *See* COAT FROCK.

coat frock A fashion innovation dating from World War I, the coat frock is a one-piece, long-sleeved garent tailored along the lines of a coat but trimmed in the manner of a dress. During the second half of the 20th century, it became known as a coat dress.

cocktail dress Cocktails—a US invention—became popular in the early 1920s. Along with the cocktail hour came the need for appropriate clothing. The cocktail dress, which could also be worn for dinner, banished the TEA GOWN or afternoon dress once and for all. It was short (to the knee or below), usually made of lightweight wool, satin, silk, velvet, and other luxurious fabrics, embroidered or decoratively trimmed, and often cut to reveal the shoulders and arms. The cocktail dress has remained fashionable throughout the 20th century. *See* *GIVENCHY *and* *LELONG.

Cocteau, Jean 1889–1963. Artist, stage designer, illustrator, poet, playwright. Born in Maisons-Lafitte, France. Cocteau was closely associated with the world of fashion through both the theater and his friendship with Elsa *SCHIAPARELLI. He designed for DIAGHILEV's ballets and worked closely with Schiaparelli, who encouraged his nonconformist attitudes and applied his surreal themes to her fashion accessories. Cocteau also designed covers for a number of magazines, notably HARPER'S BAZAAR. *See* *CHANEL.

Comme des Garçons *See* KAWAKUBO.

Complice *See* GENNY.

Connolly, Sybil *c.* 1921–. Designer. Born in Dublin, Ireland. Connolly was educated in Waterford. In 1938 she went to London to study dress design at Bradley's dressmaking establishment in London but returned to Dublin at the outbreak of World War II. Connolly joined the Irish fashion house of Richard Alan and was made a director at the age of 22. She opened her own couture business ten years later. During the early 1950s Connolly attracted a great deal of attention with her method of hand-pleating fine handkerchief linen, which she made up into delicate blouses and dresses. She specialized in adapting traditional textiles—such as Irish crochet and linens, Carrickmacross lace, and Donegal tweeds—to fashion garments. Throughout the 1950s and 1960s Connolly helped popularize handwoven woolens, tweeds, and mohairs as fashion fabrics. She also developed an international reputation for her work as an interior designer.

Conran, Jasper 1959–. Designer. Born in London, England. Son of Sir Terence Conran, who has influenced British and European home furnishing design since the 1960s. Conran attended Parsons School of Art and Design in New York from 1975 to 1977. He spent a brief period as a designer at FIORUCCI before returning to London where he created a womenswear collection for the New York department store Henri Bendel. In 1977 he joined the British firm of Wallis as a consultant. His first collection under his own name was shown one year later. Conran rarely strays from the style set by this early collection. He retains a simplicity of approach which produces an easy, soft fit that suits many women. He uses quality fabrics, cut into comfortable garments which do not impose on the wearer.

Conway, Gordon 1894–1956. Illustrator, costume designer. Born in Clairborne, Texas, USA. Conway was educated in the USA and Italy. Around 1915 she took her first sketches to Heyworth Campbell, art editor of Condé NAST publications, and as a result began working for VOGUE, VANITY FAIR, and HARPER'S BAZAAR. Her soft, colorist style was strongly influenced by BARBIER, ERTE, and LEPAPE. In 1920 Conway arrived in London. She continued submitting illustrations to US magazines while working for British

Ireland's most famous designer, Sybil **Connolly**, produced evening and day wear. This dress dates from the early 1960s.

and French publications. In 1930 she began to design costumes for British films and theater. She retired to Carbin, Virginia, in 1936.

coolie hat Southeast Asian hat made of bamboo leaves or straw, traditionally worn by laborers to provide protection from sun and rain. Generally made in one piece, the coolie hat is cone shaped and slopes downward on a steep, straight slant which completely covers the head. It was popular during the 1930s and 1950s.

corduroy Perhaps from the French *corde du roi*, "cloth of the king." Corduroy is a durable cotton or rayon velvet cut-pile fabric which has wide or narrow whales, cords, or ribs. Up to the 19th century, it was associated with livery and was also used for the work clothes of agricultural laborers. During the 19th century corduroy was made into breeches, coats, and hunting attire. In the 20th century it has become popular for casual dress, mainly jackets, skirts, and pants.

co-respondent shoe *See* SPECTATOR.

Corfam Trade name for a chemically made leather substitute, developed by DU PONT in the USA, which was soft, supple, and porous, allowing the feet to breathe. Corfam was introduced during the 1960s and was used by the British shoe manufacturers RAYNE to make women's COURT shoes. Mary QUANT used it for ankle boots.

Corolle line The Corolle line, called so because of the huge skirts which spread like flowers from fitted BODICES and tiny waists, was introduced in 1947 by Christian DIOR. It was immediately nicknamed the NEW LOOK. Skirts often used fifteen or even twenty-five yards of material, which was then lined with tulle to increase the swollen shape. Dress bodices were tightly constructed to emphasize the bust and minimize the waist.

corsage Small bouquet of flowers worn at the waist or bosom of evening gowns during the 19th century and popular until the early 20th century.

corset The 19th-century corset, used to achieve the fashionable small waist of the period, was a descendant of the 15th-century BODICE, which was stiffened by two pieces of linen pasted together. Worn under a dress but often over a thin cotton or muslin SHIFT, corsets were usually constructed of WHALEBONE pieces inserted as paneling into a fabric shape. They laced tightly at the front or back of the waist and were the subject of great controversy from around 1850, when reform groups on both sides of the Atlantic protested at the physical damage caused by tight lacing. Despite these protests, the late 19th century produced the most elaborate shapes achieved by corsetry. The S-BEND SILHOUETTE became popular, created by corsets which reached down over the hips and thrust the bust forward. In the early 1900s POIRET claimed to have freed women from corsets, as did LUCILE and VIONNET. At this time the boned corset was replaced by woven ELASTIC material which flattened the waist rather than drawing it in. Undergarments in the 1920s heralded the approach of the ROLL ON and GIRDLE of the 1930s. In 1947 the WASPIE emerged to create the tiny waists of the NEW LOOK. Corsets have always been made in different colors, the most popular of which are black, white, gray, and pink. *See also* STAYS.

In 1901 readers of *The Ladies' Field* were introduced to the "Specialité **Corset**," made of "real whalebone," and promising "an additional elegance of form."

From *La Vie Parisienne* of June 1924, a cartoon of a woman being laced into her **corset**.

Cossack Word describing the inhabitants of southeastern Russia. In the early 20th century the term Cossack was associated with Russian soldiers, who wore dark-colored overcoats with flared sleeves and full skirts, leather boots, and ASTRAKHAN hats. In the late 1960s Yves SAINT LAURENT was just one designer who delved into Russian costume history to produce a "Cossack" collection composed of baggy pants tucked into tall boots; full, flowing skirts; dresses and coats which were often tied with bold SASHES; and large, fur hats.

costume jewelry Jewelry made either of gemstones which resemble precious stones or of imitation stones which meet periodic fashion trends. Costume jewelry was developed in the 18th century, mainly for the emerging middle classes and the wealthy who, for reasons of security, wore valueless jewelry while traveling. It continued to be popular throughout the 19th century. In the 1920s costume jewelry developed into an accessory in its own right rather than mere imitation. In the hands of CHANEL and SCHIAPARELLI it became witty and ostentatious. Following this period, new design approaches to costume jewelry produced fashionable pieces which were no longer thought of as second rate. This trend has continued and high prices can now be commanded for jewelry that is an integral part of the fashion scene. See *LANE *and* RADANNE.

cotton The cotton plant, which grows to a height of between three and five feet, produces a fiber-covered seed pod. The cotton is picked by hand or machine and the fibers are removed by a gin, invented in 1792 in the American South by Eli Whitney. Cotton has been used for every kind of fashion garment, though it is particularly suited to underwear and lightweight summer attire.

This 1965 outfit from **Courrèges**, the "Space Age" designer, is typically stark and futuristic.

Courrèges, André 1923–. Designer. Born in Pau, France. Courrèges studied to be a civil engineer but after a brief period he abandoned this career and went to Paris to work in a small fashion house. In 1949 he joined BALENCIAGA, where he remained until he opened his own house in 1961. During the early 1960s Courrèges introduced very short skirts; MINI dresses with pants and PANTS SUITS in white and silver; tube shaped pants and pants cut on the BIAS; white dresses trimmed with beige and vice-versa; mid-calf white BOOTS; and goggles. His clothes were sharp, angular, and subject to a highly disciplined design. Simple, stark, TRAPEZE-shaped dresses and coats were boldly piped in contrast colors. During the late 1960s Courrèges produced ready-to-wear lines. He softened the austerity of his clothes—which by this time had begun to give the impression of a uniform—by using curves, and showed cosmonaut suits, knitted CATSUITS, coats with circle welt seams around the armholes and over the ribs, and SEE-THROUGH and CUT-OUT DRESSES. His all-white collections were trimmed with bright orange, navy, pink, and blue. He became known as the "SPACE AGE" designer because of his functional, uncluttered, futuristic designs. He closed his business in 1965 only to reopen the following year for several couture clients and to create inexpensive ready-to-wear lines. His 1970s collections featured clothes made of softer fabrics and colors, many trimmed with ruffles. Pastel shades predominate in Courrèges' clothes, which are sporty, clearly defined, and well-tailored.

Courrèges boot Made of white kid, calf or patent leather, this widely copied boot was introduced during the 1960s by André COURRÈGES. It was designed to reach the mid-calf with open slots at the top and a bow or tassel in front.

Courtauld's artificial silk, stockinette, and crêpe-de-chine was made up into underwear in the early part of the 20th century.

Navy **court shoe**, tapered to almost a stiletto heel, and trimmed with a red bow, from the Rayne Spring/Summer 1964 collection.

court shoe Introduced in the mid-19th century, the court shoe is an enclosed shoe with a low or medium heel and a line which narrows toward the toe. It has been popular since its introduction, though fashion dictates the heel type and height in every decade.

Courtauld In 1809 George Courtauld set up a silk mill in Essex, England. His son, Samuel Courtauld III (1793–1881), extended the family business from 1816. By 1850 Samuel Courtauld & Company were the largest manufacturers of silk mourning crape in England. Considerable quantities were exported abroad until the general vogue for mourning fashions declined in the mid-1880s. In 1904 the company bought the exclusive British rights to the viscose process of making artificial silk, which was later known as rayon. By 1914 Courtauld's had established a monopoly of viscose yarn production in Great Britain and the USA. Throughout the 20th century, Courtauld's has been a giant of the synthetic fiber manufacturing industry. It produced Britain's first acrylic fiber, Courtelle, in the 1950s.

Courtelle Courtauld's (UK) trade name for its acrylic fiber.

couture Abbreviation of HAUTE COUTURE. The term couture refers to individually created, rather than mass-produced, clothes. In the 1980s, it also covers limited editions of clothing.

Coveri, Enrico 1952–. Designer. Born in Florence, Italy. Coveri studied at the Accademia delle Belle Arti in Florence. In 1973 he began working freelance for several companies, creating knitwear and SPORTSWEAR lines under the name Touche, among others. He moved to Paris in 1978 to work at the Espace Cardin. Shortly after, he returned to Italy where he established his own company. Coveri is a bold designer of young, fun-loving fashions. He blends strong colors into striking, clever designs of knitted tops and pants that have a broad appeal. Coveri is also well known for his habit of including comic characters and pop art designs in his clothes.

cowboy Fashion based on the working clothes of American cowboys and early American pioneers, which included CHECK cotton shirts, BANDANNAS, JEANS or GAUCHOS, and thick-heeled BOOTS decorated with tooled leather. PONCHOS and fringed leather jackets were also worn. Cowboy fashions were popular in the late 1960s and 1970s.

cowl Piece of material attached to a garment at the neck, which can be used as a hood or left draped at the back or front. In the 20th century cowl-neck SWEATERS and dresses became popular, cut so that the drape fell in soft folds around the neck on to the chest.

Crahay, Jules François 1917–. Designer. Born in Liège, Belgium. Crahay attended schools in Paris during his teenage years. He worked in his mother's dressmaking shop in Liège and as a salesman for the house of Jane Regny in Paris. In 1952 he joined Nina RICCI in Paris, where he became chief designer. Crahay's 1959 collection, which featured low, plunging necklines, anticipated the GYPSY style popular in the early 1960s. Throughout his career at Ricci, Crahay achieved a reputation as an accomplished eveningwear designer. In 1963 he moved to LANVIN, succeeding Antonio del CASTILLO.

crape 1. Crêpe. 2. Thin worsted fabric used for clerical gowns and MOURNING attire in the 19th century.

Crawford, Joan *See* ADRIAN.

Creed, Charles 1909–66. Designer. Born in Paris, France, of English parents. Creed was educated at Stowe school in England before being sent to Vienna, Austria, to study tailoring and art. On his return to England he joined LINTON TWEEDS in Carlisle to learn about weaving. This was followed by a spell with New York department store Bergdorf Goodman. In the 1930s Creed joined his family's tailoring firm in Paris. During the World War II years he managed to design while on leave from the army and became involved in the UTILITY SCHEME. After the war he opened his own house in London which was noted for its classically tailored and refined suits. He worked in London and New York during the remainder of the 1940s, creating lines for US SPORTSWEAR manufacturers. He was not a fashion innovator but, like his father and grandfather, he produced woolen and tweed suits of careful and cautious distinction. *See* CREED, HENRY (THE ELDER); *and* CREED, HENRY (THE YOUNGER).

Creed, Henry (the elder) dates unknown. Born in England. The first Creed firm of tailors was established in London at the beginning of the 18th century. Henry Creed opened a branch in Paris during the 1850s. *See* CREED, CHARLES; *and* CREED, HENRY (THE YOUNGER).

A **crinoline** ball gown of 1982 by Bellville Sassoon.

Right: In the days of the **crinoline** it was impossible to get dressed alone; many pairs of hands were needed for the complicated and time-consuming process.

Creed, Henry (the younger) 1863–? Designer. Born in Paris, France, of English parents. The son of a tailor who had established a business in Paris, Creed made riding habits for the British Royal Family. He became famous for his tailored suits (TAILLEURS), which he produced for women in the early 1900s and which became immensely popular. The suits were cut with a BASQUE jacket and full skirt flaring over the hips. Creed promoted the use of tweed in his suits. *See* CREED, CHARLES; *and* CREED, HENRY (THE ELDER).

crêpe Word describing a variety of fabrics, natural and synthetic, which have been given a crinkled texture by the use of heat and a crêpe weave.

crêpe de chine Crêpe made from raw silk. Popular since the 19th century for lightweight garments, such as lingerie and blouses.

crêpe georgette Sheer, highly crêped fabric, usually made of silk, silk and cotton, silk and rayon, or other mixtures. During the 20th century it has been used for lightweight blouses and eveningwear.

crêpon Generic term for a crinkle-weave fabric which resembles crêpe. In the second half of the 20th century it has been used for dresses, blouses, underwear, and nightwear. In the early 1960s CACHAREL designed a crêpon shirt for women.

crew neck sweater Sweater with a high, flat neckline that sits close to the neck. Popular for men and women during the 20th century.

crinoline In the 1840s, the crinoline was a small BUSTLE made of horsehair (from the French *crin*, "horsehair"). During the 1850s the cage frame crinoline, made of steel hoops, was introduced. This produced skirts of extraordinary width. The style was promoted in Paris by the Empress EUGENIE, and women in Europe followed her lead. In *c.* 1865 the shape altered to flatten the skirts in front, while producing a fullness at the back. *See also* *WINTERHALTER.

crochet Decorative craftwork created by looping yarn or thread with a specially hooked needle. Often used for SHAWLS and blankets. Crochet dresses were briefly popular during the 1960s.

Cromwell buckle Cut steel buckle, often decorated with PASTE stones or beads, worn on the front of a shoe from the 1860s. A shoe with such a buckle was known as a Cromwell or Molière shoe.

Crosby, Caresse *See* JACOB.

Cruz, Miguel 1944–. Designer. Born in Cuba. Cruz trained at the CHAMBRE SYNDICALE DE LA HAUTE COUTURE in Paris and then worked for CASTILLO and BALENCIAGA. In 1963 he moved to Italy where he designed freelance before opening his own ready-to-wear business in Rome. Cruz is noted for his leather, suede and knitwear designs. He produces his own lines in addition to designing for other companies.

Cuban heels The gauchos of South America wore boots with short, straight, rather thick heels which supported their feet in stirrups. The heels, known as "Cuban heels," became popular on BOOTS and shoes for men in the 1950s and 1960s. There was a vogue in the 1970s for women to wear cuban-heeled boots with pants tucked into them, or to team them with long, flared, denim skirts.

Cubism Abstract art movement dating from the early 20th century, spearheaded by Georges BRAQUE and Pablo PICASSO. The artists superimposed several viewpoints of the subject, broken down and recomposed in geometric components. Artists such as Sonia *DELAUNAY-TERK and designer Jean PATOU took inspiration from Cubism to create bold geometric shapes and patterns in textile design. The influence of Cubism was widespread, affecting not only clothes, but also accessories, particularly PURSES/handbags, compact cases, jewelry, and shoes. *See* col. pl. PATOU.

culottes Originally French workmen's trousers, culottes (UK: divided skirts or trousers) are wide pants. In the 19th century, they were worn for cycling. The word has come to mean a skirt of varying lengths that is divided into two sections to cover each leg. In the 1930s culottes were very full, making the division less obvious. Since that time they have been popular for casual wear in both summer and winter. In the 1960s and 1970s, calf-length versions of culottes, called GAUCHOS, were popular.

cummerbund From the Hindi and Persian *kamarband*, "loincloth." Wide cloth band worn as a waist SASH, part of traditional male dress in India, Persia, and South America. During the late 19th century the cummerbund was adopted by European men, in silk, satin, or faille, and worn in place of a WAISTCOAT for evening attire. Women adopted the cummerbund for day and eveningwear in a variety of fabrics during the 20th century.

cut-out dress Dress with large circles cut out at either side and/or in the center back and front. André COURREGES was one of the first designers to introduce cut-out dresses and TUNICS in the early 1960s.

Culottes in 1937.

D

Wendy **Dagworthy**'s feeling for fabric was revealed in her 1985 collection.

Daché, Lilly *c.* 1907–. Milliner. Born in Bègles, France. While still a teenager, Daché was apprenticed to a Bordeaux milliner. Several years later she moved to Paris and worked for Caroline REBOUX. In 1924 Daché joined Macy's store in New York as a sales assistant in the millinery department. She moved in the same year to a New York milliner's and shortly after bought out the stock. Success came swiftly. Daché was famous for her draped TURBANS, close-fitting brimmed CLOCHE HATS that were molded to fit the head, SNOODS, and CAPS. For almost three decades, she was one of the foremost milliners in the USA. In 1949 she began designing dresses and accessories. *See* *PARNIS.

Dacron Tradename for a man-made fiber manufactured by DU PONT in the USA during the early 1950s. It was a popular choice for ruffled blouses of the mid-1950s. *See* POLYESTER.

Dagworthy, Wendy 1950–. Designer. Born in Gravesend, Kent, England. Dagworthy attended Medway College of Art from 1966 to 1968 and studied art and design at Middlesex Polytechnic from 1968 to 1971. She then joined wholesale manufacturer Radley, before opening her own business in London in 1973. Dagworthy specialized in loose, easy, ready-to-wear shapes in natural fibers, employing resourceful features such as double pockets and detachable hoods. Her clothes for both men and women are designed to be practical and flexible, embracing all occasions and seasons. She enjoys mixing patterns and textures.

Dahl-Wolfe, Louise (Emma Augusta) 1895–. Photographer. Born in San Francisco, California, USA. In 1914 Dahl-Wolfe attended the San Francisco Institute of Art. For the next twenty years she studied, worked as an interior decorator, and traveled. It was not until the mid-1930s that she turned her attention seriously to a lifelong interest—photography. Her first job as a fashion photographer was with Saks Fifth Avenue store in New York. In 1936 she joined *Harper's Bazaar*, to which she contributed regularly until she retired. Dahl-Wolfe is noted for her painterly use of color.

Dali, Salvador 1904–. Painter. Born in Figueras, Spain. Originally a Cubist, Dali became a Surrealist in 1929. His wild, fantastic imagery was meticulously carried out in the detail of his work. He designed fabrics for *SCHIAPARELLI and contributed many ideas to jewelry and fashion design. *See* SURREALISM.

damask Originally a richly decorated silk fabric brought to the West in the 12th century via Damascus in Syria, where it was also produced. The fabric has a figured pattern which is part of the weave and is self-colored. Damask was a popular dress fabric during the 19th century but in the 20th century has become associated with home furnishing.

Danskin In 1882 Joel and Benson Goodman established a dry goods business in Manhattan, New York, selling hosiery, leatherware, and women's and children's clothes. In 1923 the Goodman sons took over and created Triumph Hosiery Mills in Philadelphia,

Pennsylvania. During the 1930s the company specialized in producing theatrical stockings and cotton and silk hosiery in hard-to-fit sizes. The name Danskin was created in the 1950s, at the same time that the firm produced its first LEOTARDS, as well as the first dance TIGHTS to make a serious attempt to deal with the problem of the baggy knee and ankle. In the following decade Danskin introduced a fashionable range of children's nylon sportswear, SWEATERS, seamless exercise and dance tights, and PANTIEHOSE. A snap-crotch bodysuit was introduced in 1970. Throughout the 1970s, in response to the upsurge of international interest in gymnastics and dance, Danskin created numerous leotard and swimsuit designs in shiny nylon and Spandex blends. The company's up-to-date attitude to dance and exercise clothes helped to move dancewear from the exercise studio onto the streets. The leotard became popular wear at DISCOS and often replaced the swimsuit on the beach. In turn, leotards helped to regenerate interest in one-piece swimsuits. Danskin uses cotton and wool blends and Antron and Spandex fibers. Two designers have made their names with the company: Bonnie August, who left in 1983, and her successor, Yvonne Sanchez.

dart Pointed tuck sewn on the reverse of a garment to shape it to the lines of the body. *See* *BODICE.

David, Jules 1808–92. Illustrator. Prolific and accomplished illustrator, working in Paris, who contributed to numerous magazines, including *Journal des jeunes personnes*, *Nouveautes*, *Gazette rose*, *Cendrillon*, *Nouveautes parisiennes*, *Moniteur de la mode*, *Messager des modes*, *Moniteur des demoiselles*, *Moniteur des dames et des demoiselles*, and various English and German publications. He had a precise, clear style and used color in a more adventurous manner than did his contemporaries. David's models were also more animated than the traditional, stiff fashion plate models of the mid- and late 19th century. *See* *PRINCESS LINE.

de Castelbajac *See* CASTELBAJAC.

de la Renta, Oscar 1932–. Designer. Born in Santo Domingo, Dominican Republic. De la Renta studied at the University of Santo Domingo and the Academia de San Fernando in Madrid, Spain. Although he intended to become an abstract painter, he took the first step towards a career in fashion when he designed a gown for the debutante daughter of the US ambassador to Spain which was featured on the cover of *Life*. Shortly after, de la Renta joined BALENCIAGA's couture house in Madrid. In 1961 he went to Paris as an assistant to Antonio del CASTILLO at the house of Lanvin-Castillo. Two years later he followed Castillo to Elizabeth Arden's couture and ready-to-wear salon in New York. In 1965, de la Renta moved to Jane DERBY and on her retirement that same year he established his own business. During the 1960s he swiftly developed a reputation as a designer of extravagant, opulent, yet tasteful clothes. He created a variety of theme collections based on fashions of the *belle époque*, abstract art prints, Orientally inspired evening clothes, and exotic flamenco dresses. His 1967 GYPSY collection attracted a great deal of attention. Over the following years de la Renta established himself as a couture and ready-to-wear designer of positive, vibrant dresses, coats, suits, and daywear, created with a bold yet controlled use of color. He is famous for his eveningwear: COCKTAIL DRESSES and formal gowns, many of which are elaborately trimmed with embroidery, frills, and ruffles.

Oscar **de la Renta** uses dramatic frills and an oversize bow for part of his eveningwear collection, 1984.

Fulco **de Verdura**'s exquisite seashell and bird.

de Luca, Jean-Claude 1947–. Designer. Born in Paris, France. De Luca studied law in Switzerland and Italy. He worked for GIVENCHY for one year before leaving to join DOROTHEE BIS in 1972. Shortly after, he turned to freelance designing. De Luca has designed under his own name since 1976. He produces glamorous, sophisticated, and traditional clothing along fluid lines.

de Meyer, Baron Adolphe 1868–1949. Photographer. Born in Paris, France. De Meyer was brought up in Saxony, studied in Paris, and moved to London in 1895. In 1901, after his marriage, he became Baron de Meyer, ennobled by the King of Saxony. In 1913 De Meyer moved to New York and began working for Condé NAST at VOGUE. He produced romantic, soft-focus pictures, which relied heavily on back-lighting, of society women in fashionable clothes. He was not a portraitist—his subjects were only one part of the picture—but a pictorialist. His work concentrated on the sparkle of white and silver, on shiny surfaces, and on the suggestion of ethereal beauty and nonchalance. In 1918 De Meyer returned to Paris on a contract from HARPER'S BAZAAR and he remained with the magazine until 1932. During his reign at *Vogue* and the early years at *Harper's Bazaar* De Meyer's work was widely imitated but by the early 1930s his style had gone out of fashion and his influence had waned.

de Rauch, Madeleine dates unknown. Designer. Born in France. De Rauch designed her own clothes before opening a couture house with her two sisters in 1928. The house was well known for its sporty day clothes. It closed in 1973.

de Ribes, Jacqueline 1930s–. Born Jacqueline de Beaumont in France. An internationally famous society hostess, de Ribes launched a line of clothes in 1983. She is noted mainly for her elegant, stately day- and eveningwear.

de Verdura, Fulco 1898–1978. Jeweler. Born Fulco Santostefano della Cerda, duke of Verdura, in Palermo, Sicily. De Verdura went to Paris in 1927 and worked as a textile and jewelry designer for CHANEL. In 1937 he moved to New York, where he was employed by the jeweler Paul Flato, who soon put him in charge of his Californian branch. In 1939 De Verdura opened his own shop in New York. He became associated with the revival of gold mounts, rather than platinum, and the promotion of baked enamel jewelry. He often worked in gold and produced a collection of small boxes. His great skill lay in mixing semi-precious and precious pieces in the same setting, the ideas for which he took from nature: shells, feathers, wings, and leaves, for example. De Verdura also used classical motifs, such as tassels from coats of arms and mariners' knots. His twisted baroque pearls and his gold chains were highly prized. A widely influential jeweler whose timeless designs have been a source of inspiration to others, De Verdura sold his business in 1973.

décolleté Low-necklined BODICE of a blouse or dress. The Victorian version was cut low on the shoulders. The décolleté neckline is a traditional component of evening dresses and BALL GOWNS.

deerstalker Man's traditional tweed hunting cap. The deerstalker has back and front peaks, and some versions have earflaps. In the 20th century it has also been worn by women.

Delaunay-Terk, Sonia 1884–1979. Artist. Born Sonia Terk in

Worth's tasteful **décolleté** line for the Comtesse de Greffulhe's evening dress of 1896.

Sonia **Delaunay-Terk**'s textile designs in 1920 show a strong Cubist influence.

Odessa, Russia. Delaunay-Terk was brought up in St. Petersburg, where she studied painting. In 1905 she moved to Paris to further her studies and married the artist Robert Delaunay in 1910. Delaunay-Terk painted bold, abstract canvases dominated by curves, triangles, and squares. In 1925 she worked with the textile company BIANCHINI-FERIER and created printed geometric designs in contrast colors. In the same year she produced PATCHWORK designs which Jacques HEIM made into coats. Her influence can be noted in the work of PATOU, SCHIAPARELLI, and other designers of the 1920s and 1930s.

Delineator, The In New York in the early 1870s, Ebenezer BUTTERICK produced a magazine, *The Ladies Quarterly Review of Broadway Fashions*, to promote the sale of his paper patterns. In 1877 he merged the magazine with *Metropolitan*, which subsequently, as *The Delineator*, became one of the top selling women's journals. Until 1894, when the base of the magazine was broadened to include general features on the home, *The Delineator* was devoted entirely to fashion. Later, it also included fiction. By 1920 it had achieved a circulation of one million and had several overseas editions. In 1928 the Butterick Publishing Company merged *The Designer* with *The Delineator*. In turn, *The Delineator* was absorbed by *The Pictorial Review* in 1937.

Dell' Olio, Louis 1948–. Designer. Born in New York, USA. Dell' Olio graduated from Parsons School of Design in 1969. He worked with Teal Traina and other wholesale companies until 1974 when he joined Anne KLEIN. With Donna KARAN, Dell' Olio has consistently interpreted the original sportswear styles of the company into relevant, contemporary clothes cut on clean lines.

Delman Leading US shoe manufacturer with interests throughout the world. *See* DELMAN, Herman B.

Delman, Herman B. 1895–1955. Shoe manufacturer. Born in Portersville, California, USA. Delman was educated in Portland, Oregon, where his family owned a small shoe store. After service in the US Marine Corps during World War I, Delman opened a shoe store in Hollywood, followed by a branch on New York's Madison Avenue. He promoted young shoe designers, whom he hired to make shoes in the windows of his stores. In 1938 Delman signed up Roger VIVIER, and though this association was interrupted by World War II, their agreement was renewed in 1945, and Delman manufactured Vivier's shoes and represented Vivier worldwide for several years. *See also* RAYNE.

denim Cotton twill weave fabric of white and blue threads which originates from the French town of Nîmes, hence the origin of the word—*serge de Nîmes*. In the 20th century denim has been used for workwear, as it is strong, durable, and washable. By the 1940s, it was being made into fashion dresses, skirts, jackets, and pants. Denim reached the height of its popularity in the 1970s with the mass manufacture of JEANS, often with designer labels. *See also* STRAUSS.

department stores Until the early 19th century, clothes and accessories were sold in stores alongside other utilities. In 1838 the Englishman Emerson Muschamp Bainbridge opened a store in Newcastle upon Tyne with a draper, William Dunn, and by 1849 they had divided the store into thirty-two departments. Monsieur and Madame Boucicauts started the Paris department store Au Bon

Marché in 1852. Department stores increased in popularity during the second half of the 19th century and during the 20th century they played an important part in the promotion of fashion. The New York store Bloomingdales was one of the first to organize small fashion departments that enabled designers to show a small selection of clothes in a BOUTIQUE environment to a large number of people.

derby *See* BOWLER.

derby Shoe style similar to an OXFORD which ties with eyelets and laces. It has quarters and facings stitched on to the vamp.

Derby, Jane 1895–1965. Designer. Born Jeanette Barr in Rockymount, Virginia, USA. Award-winning designer of dresses for the petite woman, Derby was owner and president of Jane Derby Inc., a ready-to-wear company on New York's SEVENTH AVENUE. Inspired by the simplicity of CHANEL's dresses, Derby specialized in producing day and afternoon dresses in rich tweed and black crêpe, often trimmed with chiffon and net.

Dessès, Jean 1904–70. Designer. Born Jean Dimitre Verginie in Alexandria, Egypt, of Greek parents. In 1925 Dessès abandoned the legal studies that were preparing him for a career in diplomacy and began working for a couture house, Maison Jane, in Paris. He opened his own establishment in 1937. After World War II Dessès returned to Egypt and Greece. His designs in the 1940s and 1950s reflected the influences of his travels. He specialized in creating draped evening gowns in chiffon and mousseline based on early Greek and Egyptian robes; embroidered dresses; and SHEATH DRESSES with tight jackets and flowing evening skirts. Dessès was a popular designer with European royalty and movie stars. In 1949 he began producing ready-to-wear lines for the US market.

di Camarino, Roberta 1920–. Designer. Born in Venice, Italy. Finding refuge in Switzerland during World War II, di Camarino began making PURSES/handbags. In 1945 she returned to Venice where she started a firm, "Roberta." From striped velvet satchels and carved leather bags, di Camarino progressed to scarves, umbrellas, belts, shoes, and gloves. She has also designed and produced fabrics and garments which are sold throughout the world under the "Roberta" label. Her innovative design ideas put the spotlight on fashion accessories in the post World War II years.

Diaghilev, Sergei (Pavlovich) 1872–1929. Ballet impresario. Born in Novgorod, Russia. After completing his studies in St. Petersburg, Diaghilev founded a magazine entitled *Mir Iskusstra* ("The World of Art"). The preparation and organization of an exhibition of Russian art at the Salon d'Automne took him to Paris in 1906. In 1909 Diaghilev returned to Paris with the BALLETS RUSSES. Over the following years he introduced to Europe the dancers Nijinsky, Pavlova, and Rubinstein; the music of Stravinsky, Ravel, and Prokofiev; the stage sets, designs, and costumes of PICASSO, Derain, de Chirico, Matisse, and BAKST; and the choreography of Balanchine.

diamanté Decoration on clothes, accessories, and textiles consisting of diamond-like, glittering stones. Throughout the 20th century diamanté has been popular for eveningwear.

Above: Long lapels, breast pockets, gathered waistband and belt, and a basque-like hem on this jacket in **Dior**'s 1949/50 collection. The sleeves are extraordinary, but their smooth lines and the straight skirt are required to support the highly detailed and otherwise top-heavy jacket.

Center: Very tall, knife-pleated skirt in **Dior**'s 1951/52 collection. Note the controlled collar shape and the long darts that emphasize the bust and narrow the waist. A large hat balances the width of the skirt.

Right: The positioning of the buttons, and the trimming on collar and pockets add further crispness to the classic, streamlined look of this perfectly proportioned suit from **Dior**'s 1949 collection. There is a contrasting softness in the curves of the hat.

Diana, Princess of Wales 1961–. Born Lady Diana Spencer in Northamptonshire, England. In 1981 Lady Diana married the Prince of Wales and became the focus of world attention. Before her engagement she favored ruffled blouses and simple dresses and skirts in plain or small floral prints. With her marriage came a new elegance. The Princess of Wales is responsible for promoting low-heeled PUMPS, SAILOR COLLARS and ruffled collars, strapless evening gowns, and hats. Her style of dress is widely copied. *See* *EMANUEL.

Dicel Tradename for the cellulose acetate fiber produced by British Celanese Ltd. It was introduced during the 1950s and made up into a variety of garments.

Dior, Christian 1905–57. Designer. Born in Granville, Normandy, France. Dior abandoned his political science studies to take up music but instead spent his time running an art gallery and traveling, until 1935, when he began earning a living in Paris selling fashion sketches to newspapers. In 1938 he joined Robert PIGUET. He moved in 1942 to LELONG, where he worked alongside Pierre BALMAIN until cotton magnate Marcel Boussac offered him the opportunity to open his own couture house. Dior's first collection, in 1947, originally called the COROLLE LINE, was nicknamed the NEW LOOK. New Look dresses had huge skirts which blossomed out from tiny waists, and stiffened, boned BODICES. Skirts were longer than in previous years, pleated, gathered, draped, and paneled, often lined with tulle to create fullness. Hats were worn on the side of the head and often accompanied by a choker necklace. In Dior's 1948 collection, ENVOL, skirts were scooped up at the back, worn with jackets that were cut with loose, fly-away backs and stand-up collars. The following year Dior showed slim skirts with a pleat at the back, strapless evening dresses, and bloused bodices and jackets. In 1950 skirts were shorter and jackets were large and box-shaped, some with HORSESHOE COLLARS. Over the following seven years Dior introduced his version of the COOLIE HAT, which was worn low over the eyes and trimmed with bows; and a popular PRINCESS LINE which gave the illusion of a high waist by employing curved shoulder lines on short jackets and by placing belts high on the back of coats and jackets. His three-piece of 1952—CARDIGAN jacket, simple top worn outside, and soft skirt made of crêpe in pastel shades—influenced fashions

Christian **Dior**'s New Look that
surprised the world in 1947. Most
women delighted in the
exaggerated female form, but
some deplored the extravagant use
of fabric and the artificial
construction of the outline.

for many years. Many of his collections featured three-quarter-length sleeves and STOLES which remained popular throughout the 1950s. In 1953 he raised skirts again to a couple of inches below the knee and showed them with top-heavy BARREL-shaped coats and jackets. Dior spearheaded a revival of men's suiting in 1954, naming his collection that year the H-LINE. Hats were either closely cropped or huge CARTWHEELS. He made a white handkerchief lawn jacket, softly pleated and bloused, the neckline filled in with white beads. The H-line was particularly suited to eveningwear. The A-LINE and the Y-LINE, featuring large, V-shaped collars and giant stoles, followed in 1955. Many Orientally inspired clothes became fashionable that year, including Dior's version of the CAFTAN and CHEONGSAM. He also achieved considerable success with a high-waisted, spaghetti-strapped chiffon dress and a long-length SHEATH. Dior's last collection, in 1957, was based on the VAREUSE, a garment with a stand-away collar, cut to hang loosely on to the hips. He also showed khaki BUSH JACKETS with button-down flap pockets, a belted vareuse, Oriental TUNIC dresses, and a beltless CHEMISE DRESS with standaway collar and PATCH POCKETS. Dior favored black, navy blue, and white. He accessorized his clothes by pinning brooches to the neck, shoulder, and waist. Ropes of pearls wound around the neck have been an extensively copied fashion since Dior introduced them in the 1950s. His undisputed elegance of line and sculptured structures have influenced decades of women and designers.

directoire Popular term for a high-waisted line. The *style directoire* is associated with the French directory period (1795–99), when French designers revived early Greek and Roman dress. The *directoire* dress has a long straight skirt, an exaggeratedly high waistline, low DECOLLETE, and small, tight PUFF SLEEVES. It was popular in the 1880s and 1900s and again in the 1960s. *See* EMPIRE LINE, MCCARDELL, *and* POIRET.

dirndl Full skirt loosely gathered into the waistband to create soft pleats. Originally part of PEASANT costume, dirndl skirts are thought to have originated in the Austrian TYROL. The style has been popular since the 1940s.

disco The emergence of discothèques in the 1960s prompted many extremes of style, but by the 1970s disco fashions had become acceptable for day as well as eveningwear. US designers, such as Stephen BURROWS, Betsey JOHNSON, and Norma KAMALI, produced clothes which adapted to, or were designed for, disco dancing. These included LEOTARDS, T-SHIRTS, SHORTS, and stretch JEANS, all of which allowed ease of movement. The US firm of DANSKIN sold numerous leotards with matching tights and contrast-color WRAP-AROUND SKIRTS as discowear. Fabrics for dance clothes ranged from cotton, corduroy, and denim, to suede and velvet. The addition of Spandex fiber to many fabrics increased their stretch capabilities. Eye-catching metallic accessories, RHINESTONES, and SEQUINS were popular, as were tropical print patterns, imitation snakeskin, football SWEATERS, and bright silk shirts. The discothèques of the 1970s were showcases for extravagant, exotic fashions.

divided skirt *See* CULOTTES *and* GAUCHOS.

djellabah Hooded cloak of Moroccan origin with long, wide sleeves, worn open at the neck and reaching to the knee or longer. It was originally made of cotton or wool and often trimmed with

braid. During the 1960s and 1970s the djellabah shape was used by many designers as inspiration for coat and dress styles.

Doeuillet Couture house founded in Paris in 1900 which remained popular throughout the 1900s but became less prominent during the 1920s. In 1929 it merged with DOUCET.

dog collar *See* CHOKER.

Dolly Varden Style of dress popular from *c.* 1870, named after the heroine of Charles Dickens's novel *Barnaby Rudge* (1841). The costume consisted of a flower-sprigged dress with a tight BODICE, panniered overskirt, and BUSTLE, worn over a differently colored underskirt. A large, drooping, flower-trimmed hat completed the outfit. *See also* WATTEAU.

Dolly Varden hat Flower-trimmed BONNET-style hat with a small crown and wide front brim. Ribbons, attached to the crown, are tied under the chin. *See* DOLLY VARDEN.

dolman 1. Man's long, coat-like garment originating in Turkey. The dolman was first adapted to a male fashion garment in the 18th century as a loose-sleeved robe. In the following century it was introduced in various forms for women. Worn as an outer garment, the dolman was often three-quarter-length, loose-sleeved, and fastened at the neck. It was straight in the front and fitted over the BUSTLE at the back. 2. In the 20th century the word dolman describes any ankle-length wrap with long, generous sleeves, which is trimmed with lace, fringed, and ruched. The dolman shape has been imitated as a coat, often made of cashmere, velvet, wool, and PAISLEY-patterned fabrics.

dolman sleeve Cut as an extension of the BODICE of a dress, blouse, or jacket, the dolman sleeve is designed without a socket for the shoulder, thus creating a deep, wide armhole that reaches from the waist to a narrowed wrist. This type of sleeve was popular during the 1930s. Also called a batwing sleeve.

Donegal tweed Handspun tweed that originated from County Donegal in Ireland. In the 20th century the name applies to a variety of machine-made tweeds which have colored slubs woven into the fabric.

donkey jacket Originally a workman's jacket, the donkey jacket is hip-length and cut with wide shoulders and long sleeves. Made of melton, serge, or wool, it was first adapted to casual wear during the 1920s and became popular again in the 1950s. Some versions have leather patches sewn over the elbows and across the shoulders.

Donovan, Terence 1936–. Photographer. Born in London, England. Donovan worked from the age of fifteen for several photographic printers and photographers before taking a job as a military photographer from 1954 to 1956. He then spent a year with photographers John FRENCH and John Adrian. In 1957 Donovan opened his own studio. Over the following years his name became a familiar byline on the fashion pages and covers of many magazines, including *Elle* and *Marie-Claire* in France, and *Cosmopolitan* and VOGUE in Britain. *See* *QUANT.

Dorothée Bis Chain of stores opened by Elie and Jacqueline Jacobson in Paris and later in the USA. In the late 1950s Jacqueline Jacobson ran a children's wear BOUTIQUE. In 1962 her husband, Elie, closed his wholesale furriers and the two embarked on a joint business venture—a boutique selling adult versions of young girls' clothes: knee socks, peaked CAPS, CUT-OUT DRESSES, and PANTS SUITS. Jacqueline Jacobson also designed knitwear. The shop became known for ribbed POOR BOYS, crochet SWEATERS, and dresses that looked like very long, handknitted sweaters. Most of the knitwear was teamed with woolen TIGHTS, crochet scarves, and CLOCHE HATS. In the 1980s clothes from Dorothée Bis achieved more sophistication in both cut and color. The knitwear, however, retained its distinctive long, body-hugging lines. *See also* KHANH.

dorothy bag PURSE/handbag named after a character of the same name in A. J. Munby's play, *Dorothy*, which was popular in England during the 1880s. A dorothy bag is a rectangular piece of fabric with a drawstring ribbon or chain at the neck which, when pulled, closes the bag, making a small frill. A popular style between the 1880s and 1920s.

Doucet, Jacques 1853–1929. Designer. Born in Paris, France. Doucet inherited a lingerie shop from his grandparents before he was twenty. In 1875 he opened a couture house where he created extravagant gowns made of lace, mousseline, satin, and silk. His TEA GOWNS, tailored suits, and fur-lined coats were extremely popular. He was one of the best known and most highly respected couturiers of the late 19th and early 20th centuries. Actresses, socialites, and royalty chose Doucet's salon both for his taste in fabrics and for the quality and workmanship of his clothes. He became famous for his delicate treatment of pastel colors and fabrics—particularly iridescent silks—and for his way of using fur as if it were a lighter,

Drainpipe trousers, worn with pumps and sweaters, served as casual dress in the UK in 1960.

softer fabric. He took 17th- and 18th-century paintings, of which he was an avid collector, as inspiration for dresses and BALL GOWNS. In the early part of the 20th century, Doucet embraced the movement to oust the rigid CORSET, but retained the quality and classical treatment of fabric in many of the models he produced. After Doucet's death the house merged with DOEUILLET.

drainpipe trousers Tight, narrow pants which were first popular for men in the UK in the 1950s. Similar pants were worn by women in the 1960s.

drawers Long, baggy knickers, originally on view below skirts, which by the early 19th century had become general items of underwear. Many styles opened at the back, others fastened at both front and back as almost separate sections. In most cases, the legs were loose fitting. Drawers were usually made of cotton and linen. As slimmer silhouettes became fashionable in the early 1900s, drawers were replaced by less voluminous garments, such as CAMIKNICKERS.

Drécoll The house of Drécoll was originally founded by Christopher Drécoll in Vienna, Austria. In the early 20th century the name was bought by a Belgian businessman, who opened in Paris in 1905. The house was known for elaborate and detailed TEA GOWNS, promenade gowns, and evening dresses. Drécoll closed in 1929.

dress clip Fashion item which first appeared around 1930. It consisted of two jeweled clips attached to either side of a dress or blouse, just below the shoulders. Often made of DIAMANTE, the dress clip remained an important accessory throughout the 1930s and 1940s, worn mostly on evening and COCKTAIL DRESSES.

dressing gown Garment which evolved from the PEIGNOIR in the early 19th century. The dressing gown—literally, a robe to put on between changes of dress or before dressing—was a loose, long-sleeved, coat-like gown, usually made of lightweight, luxurious fabric. In the course of the 20th century, dressing gowns were designed to be suitable for wear around the house, rather than just in the bedroom, and were made of heavier fabrics. Each decade produced designs in sympathy with prevailing trends, though the basic shape—ankle-length and long-sleeved—has rarely altered. A dressing gown wraps or ties at the waist or is buttoned from the neck to the knee or ankle. *See also* HOUSECOAT, KIMONO, *and* TEA GOWN.

Drian, Etienne dates unknown. Artist working in Paris between 1910 and the mid-1920s whose highly distinctive style illustrated the exclusive pages of the GAZETTE DU BON TON and other magazines. Drian's figures are easily recognized by their extreme fluidity of movement.

drill Strong cotton fabric, similar to denim. Traditionally used in the USA as a fabric for workwear, it has been in use since the 1940s as a fashion fabric for summer attire.

dry cleaning Process invented in 1849 by a French tailor, Monsieur Jolly-Bollin, who discovered the stain-removing qualities of turpentine. By the late 19th century, it was possible to clean complete garments rather than unpick and later resew stained sections, a method used by early dry cleaners.

Dress clips were important accessories during the 1930s.

Etienne **Drian**, an illustrator whose skill at depicting fashionable women in motion resulted in many commissions. This one, for *Fémina* in 1911, is accompanied by text extolling hand kissing, popular in France.

Dryden, Helen 1887–? Illustrator. Born in Baltimore, Maryland, USA. Dryden studied at the Pennsylvania Academy of Fine Arts. She became well known in the early 1920s as a designer of magazine covers and articles, especially for VOGUE.

Du Pont Firm founded in 1802 by Eleuthère Irénée du Pont de Nemours (1771–1834) in Wilmington, Delaware, USA, to manufacture gunpowder. Du Pont's sons added a woolen mill and so began a textile business that was to pass through generations of the same family until the 1970s. In the 1920s the company acquired from France the license to produce cellophane. This was followed by the acquisition of a further French invention, rayon. The American based company has been extensively involved in the production of synthetic fibers since the early 20th century. *See also* CORFAM *and* NYLON.

Once military garments, **duffle coats** became popular in the post-World War II years.

duffle bag Sturdy, cylindrical canvas bag originally used by servicemen for carrying kit. Stout cord is threaded through metal eyelets and drawn together to seal the top. The duffle bag shape was used in shoulder bags, made of various fabrics, during the 1970s.

duffle coat Short coat, with or without a hood, worn during World War II by men of the British Royal Navy. Cut to hip or knee length, the coat was made of a heavy woolen material and fastened with rod-shaped wooden toggles that passed through rope or leather loops. Surplus duffle coats were sold to the public after World War II and became popular winter garments for both men and women.

Dufy, Raoul (Joseph) 1877–1953. Artist. Born in Le Havre, France. Dufy left school at fourteen to work in a coffee importing company. In 1895 he started evening classes in drawing and painting at the Ecole Municipale des Beaux Arts in Le Havre. In 1900, after a year's military service, he moved to the Beaux Arts in Paris. Somewhat later Dufy came into contact with the Fauves, a group of artists who were developing a new painting style characterized by bold handling of strong colors. He held his first one-man show in 1906. During the following years Dufy's tone and use of color became more subdued. Dufy worked closely with the decorative arts throughout his life. In 1911, with Paul POIRET, he became involved in the development of dye techniques and color printing. Shortly after, he joined the French textile company *BIANCHINI-FERIER as artistic director. Dufy designed silks and brocades in bold, often crude, lines and strong colors. Many women who took no interest in his paintings wore clothes made from fabrics of his design or decorated their homes with his furnishing textiles. Dufy also designed décor for the theater, opera, and ballet. *See* FAUVISM.

Duncan, Isadora 1878–1927. Dancer, choreographer. Born in San Francisco, California, USA. Duncan was interested in music, poetry, and dance from an early age. In San Francisco, New York, and Chicago, she scandalized audiences with her loose, flowing, and often revealing robes and her improvised ballet pieces which she danced barefoot. In the early 1900s she left the USA for Europe and was eventually acclaimed in London, Paris, and other European cities. Duncan established a school of dance near Berlin in 1904 and another in Moscow in 1921. Her constant travels brought her and her Grecian-style robes into public view throughout Europe and helped popularize a general trend toward less restrictive clothing.

dungarees From the Hindi *dungri*, a coarse calico material. Dungarees were used by workmen in the early 20th century and adopted by women during both world wars. In the late 1940s and early 1950s denim dungarees became fashionable. Dungarees consist of pants and a bib panel with shoulder straps. Various pockets and flaps have at one time or another adorned dungarees, notably during the 1960s.

duster Long, lightweight coat, made of gabardine or wool, introduced during the late 19th century for motoring. The duster had long sleeves and a high collar and enveloped the body from the neck to the ankles.

dyes Until the mid-1850s dyes were obtained from natural sources: purple was extracted from varieties of shellfish; yellows and oranges came from saffron, turmeric, henna, and safflower; blue was the product of indigo and woad; red (cochineal) came from the dried bodies of the Mexican Coccus insect. Manmade dyes came into popular use during the late 19th century. *See* ANILINE DYES.

Dynasty American television soap opera about the private lives of members of wealthy US oil families, which has been internationally successful since its introduction to American television audiences in 1983. The women in the series wear costly silk and satin tailored clothes, often styled in the manner of Hollywood costumes of the 1930s, though in keeping with 1980s fashion trends. Designed by Nolan Miller, these clothes have created fashions for smart separates, two-piece suits, and elaborate COCKTAIL and at-home dresses. The series has also popularized opulent COSTUME JEWELRY.

The **duster** protected clothes from the ill-effects of motoring in the early 20th century.

Kees van Dongen captures the spirit of Isadora **Duncan** in a Parisian poster of the early 20th century.

E

Edina and Lena *See* RONAY.

Edward VIII (Albert Christian George Andrew Patrick David) 1894–1972. Born in Richmond, Surrey, England. Edward was Prince of Wales from 1910 until 1936, when he became King Edward VIII. He abdicated the same year to marry in 1937 Mrs. Wallis Simpson, and was given the title of Duke of Windsor. As a young man, the Prince of Wales was responsible for many male fashions. During the 1920s he promoted the wearing of suede shoes, PLUS FOURS, PANAMA HATS, and FAIR ISLE sweaters. Trips he made to Paris in the 1930s inspired French designers to use the Prince's suiting material for womenswear. *See also* *SAILOR SUIT.

Edwardian The so-called Edwardian style of dress is associated with the period between the 1890s and 1910. Its silhouette is high-collared and long sleeved, with an ample bosom, and a tightly fitted and boned waistline curving onto full hips where the bulk of the skirts are gathered onto the buttocks and flow behind and in front to reach the ankles. Skirts were enlarged with GODETS, and BUSTLES were worn to increase fullness. Some dresses, especially evening gowns, were worn off the shoulder. Hats were either small, floral affairs or large, plumed versions the size of tea trays. A PARASOL or small PURSE was carried. The well-to-do Edwardian woman of the period was required to make many changes of dress during the day. Most of her clothes were made of sumptuous fabrics and heavily trimmed with lace and ribbons. Elaborate hatpins and jewelry, often PARURES, were also worn. In the 1970s a major revival of Edwardian fashion took place. Lacy blouses with high, frilly necklines were worn with long, full skirts and laced BOOTS. CHOKERS and PASTE jewelry of the period were also popular, particularly the brooch pinned at the base of the throat. Laura ASHLEY was an exponent of this style of dressing. *See* ALEXANDRA, QUEEN; BLOOMERS; GIBSON GIRL; MERRY WIDOW; *and* S-BEND.

Egyptian fashions Excavations in Egypt during the 1890s prompted a fashion for imitations of Egyptian dress, particularly headdresses and jewelry. The discovery in 1922 of Tutankhamun's tomb caused an escalation in fashions for draped, flowing dresses, bangs (fringes), HEADBANDS, and pyramid and scarab motifs.

Eisenhower jacket Garment introduced during World War II and named after American Dwight Eisenhower who in 1943 became Supreme Allied Commander in Western Europe and organized the D-Day invasion of France and the Allied landing in Normandy. The Eisenhower jacket was waist-length, belted, with a turn-down collar and sleeves that buttoned at the cuffs. The style has been popular for casual attire for both sexes since the 1940s. *See also* BATTLE JACKET *and* BOMBER JACKET.

elastic Fabric made from interwoven threads of indiarubber. By 1830 elastic panels had replaced the spiral metal bands which had earlier been used for CORSETS and underwear. Because of its flexibility, elastic has been used extensively in the manufacture of

Edward VIII, shown in Sir William Orpen's portrait wearing a Fair Isle sweater, plus-fours, brogues, and cap—all of which he helped to popularize.

Elegant **Edwardian** women at an art gallery, 1902.

Perry **Ellis**, adapting the man's suit to the female figure of the 1980s.

underwear, swimwear, and exercise garments since the 19th century.

Ellis, Perry (Edwin) 1940–. Designer. Born in Portsmouth, Virginia, USA. Ellis gained a BA in business studies at the College of William and Mary and then took an MA course in retailing at New York University. From 1963 to 1967 he worked as a buyer for the Miller and Rhoads department store in Richmond, Virginia. In 1968 he joined John Meyer of Norwich, New York, as design director. After six years he left to become sportswear designer for the Vera companies, where, in 1978, he was given his own label. Ellis started his own company in 1980. His contemporary, classic menswear designs were already widely acclaimed in the USA, and he swiftly gained a reputation for crisply stylish women's coats, pants, and knitwear. Ellis's designs for women are spirited and graceful. Many of the clothes are cut on mannish lines which he skilfully adapts for the female figure. He frequently uses textured wools and tweeds.

Emanuel, David and **Elizabeth** Designers. David Emanuel 1953–. Born in Bridgend, Glamorgan, Wales. Emanuel attended Cardiff School of Art from 1971 to 1972 before transferring to the Harrow School of Art in 1973. Elizabeth Weiner 1953–. Born in London,

England. From 1972 to 1975 Weiner attended Harrow School of Art, where she met and married Emanuel. The Emanuels were accepted at the Royal College of Art in 1975 and in 1977 they showed their final year collection. Demand for their designs was sufficient for them to open a salon in London immediately after leaving college. The Emanuels specialized in off-the-shoulder, bouffant-style eveningwear for the wholesale market. In 1979 they began designing couture clothes for well known women from all over the world plus a ready-to-wear line. They became famous for their very feminine dresses and for their luxurious evening attire, particularly BALL GOWNS, which were generally full-skirted and made of lace, silk, taffeta, tulle, and velvet. In 1981 DIANA, Princess of Wales (then Lady Diana Spencer), commissioned the Emanuels to design her wedding dress. *See also* *SAILOR COLLAR.

embroidery Ornamental needlework of colored designs worked on to fabric. Embroidery has been used to decorate many items of womenswear for centuries. It was created by hand until the 20th century. *See also* FOLKLORIC.

Empire line Low-cut dress gathered underneath the bust, popularized by Empress Josephine during the French Napoleonic Empire (1804–14). The style is also known as the DIRECTOIRE or the *RECAMIER.

The **Emanuels'** wedding dress design for Diana, Princess of Wales, 1981.

An exhibition in London in 1985 stimulated a great deal of renewed interest in the clothes of **Fortuny**, worn here in a contemporary, off-the-shoulder style.

Gold pendant designed in 1899 by Georges **Fouquet**, who worked mainly in the Art Nouveau style. Fouquet's jewelry often included colored gemstones, such as these cabochon rubies and pendant cabochon sapphires.

One of the most evocative symbols of "swinging London" of the 1960s
and early 1970s: the interior of Barbara **Hulanicki**'s famous Biba
department store, decorated in a nostalgic 1930s style that was copied
throughout the world in homes and stores.

engageantes Washable half-sleeves that could be tied to the arm inside a bell-shaped or PAGODA sleeve. They ended at the wrist in closed cuffs or open frills. Engageantes were worn from the mid- to the late 19th century.

envelope bag Rectangular PURSE/handbag of various sizes with a fastening panel shaped like an envelope flap. Like the CLUTCH PURSE, it is strapless. A fashionable handbag shape during the 20th century.

Envol Name, meaning "flight" or "winged," given by Christian DIOR to his 1948 collection. Skirts were scooped at the back like a bustle, or to one side, and worn with short jackets which had deep cuffs and standaway collars. Other jackets were flared into full shapes at the back and worn with straight, tubular skirts.

Engageantes under bell shaped sleeves of the 1880s.

epaulet 1. Shoulder strap on a military jacket or coat used as a means of keeping military accouterments in place. It was also employed as decoration. Popular in the late 19th century, the epaulet also appeared on military-style jackets and coats throughout the 20th century, notably in the 1930s and 1960s. 2. Shoulder decoration which evolved from the full sleeves of the mid- to late 19th century.

éponge From the French for "sponge," the term éponge refers to a group of fabrics that are spongy, porous, and soft. Fabrics in this group, many of which are made of cotton, have been popular for beachwear and summerwear since the 1930s.

Eric 1891–1958. Illustrator. Born Carl Oscar August Erickson in Joliet, Illinois, USA, of Swedish parents. Eric attended Chicago's Academy of Art for two years. He left around 1909 and worked for several years as a commercial artist and sign painter before moving to New York in 1914. In 1916 his first illustrations appeared in VOGUE and by 1925 he was a regular artist on the magazine, specializing in drawings of people in fashionable settings. Eric's illustrations were lively, fluid, and confident, in contrast with the flat, linear styles of the 1920s. In his fashion sketches, he stressed the importance of detail. He continued working for *Vogue* until the 1950s.

ermine Silky fur of a weasel found in Canada and Eastern Europe. The ermine's fur is brown in summer but turns white in winter. The white fur is traditionally used for trimming ecclesiastical and legal robes. Ermine is rarely used in fashion.

Erté 1892–. Illustrator, designer. Born Romain de Tirtoff in St. Petersburg, Russia. Erté (adapted from the French pronunciation of his initials, R. T.) studied painting in Russia before leaving for Paris in 1911. He was employed by Paul POIRET from 1913 to 1914 and also worked briefly with DIAGHILEV on theater and ballet décor. From 1916 to 1926 he produced numerous covers for American HARPER'S BAZAAR and in the 1920s he worked in Paris and New York designing sets for the Folies-Bergère and the Ziegfeld Follies. He also created many costumes for Josephine BAKER. On a visit to Hollywood in 1925, he worked as a designer on several films. Erté's style was strongly influenced by 16th-century Persian and Indian miniatures. His drawings of the female form were curvilinear, expressive, and highly stylized: elegant, often decadent, women,

Once used on military garments, the **epaulet** adorns a man's coat by the 1930s.

103

DOUGLAS COLLEGE LIBRARY

In 1977 Sears advertised the 4-piece vested suit, ideal for the **executive** woman.

The 4-pc. Vested Suit
Ours is wool and polyester handsomely man-tailored in two combinations of checks and solids. The shaped hacking-pocket jacket and fitted watch-pocket vest are lined for comfort. The tailored fly-front zipped pants and back-zipped skirt are elasticized in back for fine fit.
a fashion essential and only $64.99 misses' sizes

(1 and 2) FABRIC: Woven of wool and polyester. Jacket and vest lining plus vest back and vest belt of acetate taffeta.
DETAILING:
Jacket . . . 2-button. Tab trim on bodice; flap trim below. Two flapped hacking-style pockets. Fully lined.
Vest . . . 5-button closing. V-neck-line. Two set-in pockets. Adjustable back belt. Front lined.
Pants . . . zipper fly front; elasticized back waist. Slightly flared legs.
Skirt . . . back zipper closing; elasticized back waist. Front pleat. Length: about 25½ inches; Tall Misses' sizes about 27½ inches.
Suit made in Columbia.
The blouse and sweater shown are not included.
CARE: Use professional dry cleaning.
SIZES, COLORS, ORDERING INFO:
Misses' sizes 8, 10, 12, 14, 16, 18. (Fit 5 ft. 3 in. to 5 ft. 6½ in.) *State size.*
(1) N 17 G 3000KF—Beige jacket and pants; checked vest and skirt in beige and deep taupe
(2) N 17 G 3001KF—Checked jacket and skirt in beige and deep taupe; beige vest and pants
Shpg. wt. 3 lbs. 6 oz. $64.99
Tall Misses' sizes 12T, 14T, 16T, 18T, 20T. (Fit 5 ft. 7 in. to 5 ft. 11 in.) *State correct size.*
(1) N 17 G 3010KF—Beige jacket and pants; checked vest and skirt in beige and deep taupe
(2) N 17 G 3011KF—Checked jacket and skirt in beige and deep taupe; beige vest and pants
Shpg. wt. 3 lbs. 6 oz. $67.99

The Accessories
Berets sold on pages 19 and 83; blouse on page 14; sweater, page 12; shirt, page 41; hosiery, pages 49 and 93; oxford shoe on page 27; pin, page 12

70 Sears

trailing furs, jewels, and accessories, were subject to idiosyncratic motifs and precise detail. After World War II Erté continued to design costumes and décor for the opera, theater, and ballet.

espadrille Braided, corded, or rope-soled shoe with a canvas upper which originates in Mediterranean countries, where it was mainly worn by fishermen. It became a popular summer shoe for women during the second half of the 20th century.

Estevez, Luis 1930–. Designer. Born in Havana, Cuba. Estevez was educated in the USA and then studied architecture in Havana. A summer job at the New York department store Lord & Taylor stimulated him to make a career in the fashion world. He attended the Traphagen School of Fashion in New York before leaving for Paris to work for two years for PATOU. In 1955 Estevez opened his own business in New York. He moved to California in 1968 and established himself as a designer of glamorous eveningwear, especially for the Eva Gabor collection. A line was produced under Estevez's own name in 1974. Since 1977 he has, once again, run his own company, specializing in an elegant, smooth, restrained style that epitomizes the West Coast.

ethnic Term used by fashion designers and writers to describe garments inspired by clothes indigenous to South America, Africa, the Middle and Far East, the Orient, the Pacific, and countries with large peasant communities. Ethnic clothes are nearly always simple and functional. Some are crudely patterned and coarsely woven while others are skilfully made and elaborately decorated. During the 1970s ethnic clothes were highly popular mixed with fashionable, designer label clothes.

Eton crop Short, straight haircut for women, resembling that of the pupils of Eton College, the English boy's school. The hair was cut well above the ears. A popular style in the 1920s and 1930s. In later years a curl was extended onto the cheek.

Eton jacket Short, square BLAZER worn by boys at Eton College in England from the mid-19th until the early 20th century.

Eugénie, Empress 1826–1920. Born Eugenia Maria del Montijo in Granada, Spain. On her marriage to Napoleon III in 1853 Eugénie became Empress of the French. In 1870 she was exiled to England. A fashion leader throughout her reign, she is generally associated with the popularization of the CRINOLINE in the 1850s. From 1860 WORTH created many of her gowns and these were eagerly copied by ladies of her own court and others throughout Europe. ADRIAN designed a hat, the "Eugénie," named after the versions worn by the Empress. *See* *WINTERHALTER.

Eugénie hat *See* ADRIAN *and* EUGÉNIE, EMPRESS.

Excelsior Modes Quarterly magazine published in Paris from 1929 to 1939 and featuring black and white illustrations and photographs.

executive During the 1970s, as more women took on highly paid jobs traditionally held by men, "executive" dress for women became part of the general fashion picture, not restricted to working women. It consisted of tailored suits—skirts and jackets—often in pinstripe fabric, worn either with a man's shirt and TIE or with a blouse and BOW TIE or knotted silk scarf at the neck. BLAZERS became popular for both day and eveningwear, worn not only as part of a tailored silhouette but also with full skirts or casual pants.

Fabergé, (Peter) Carl 1838–1920. Born Karl Gustavovich Fabergé in St. Petersburg, Russia. Fabergé was educated in Germany, Italy, France, and England and in 1870 took over his father's successful jewelry business in St. Petersburg. Fabergé's floral designs of precious and semi-precious stones were popular with European royalty and aristocracy. His fascination with the Louis XV period influenced many of his designs. Fabergé is also remembered for a collection of jeweled eggs, made for the Russian royal family and other European monarchs.

Fabiani's long evening culottes for 1968.

Fabiani, Alberto dates unknown. Designer. Born in Tivoli, Italy. Fabiani went to Paris as an apprentice tailor at the age of eighteen, returning to Rome three years later to work in his family's retail clothing business. After five years he took over the business. During the 1950s Fabiani achieved international acclaim for his uncompromising but imaginative tailored suits and dresses. In 1953 he married rival designer SIMONETTA and during the 1960s they opened a house together in Paris. Fabiani returned after several years to Rome, where he resumed his career as a leading couturier and accessory designer until his retirement in the early 1970s.

Fabrice, Simon dates unknown. Designer. Born in Haiti. Fabrice moved to New York with his family at the age of fourteen. After studying at the Fashion Institute of Technology, he became a fabric designer and in 1975 he opened his own business. Fabrice quickly gained a reputation as a competent designer of luxurious and sexy eveningwear. His signature dresses are hand-painted and frequently beaded.

faconné Faconné, the French for figured, describes certain fabrics that have scattered motifs or patterns woven into the cloth.

faggoting Criss-crossed stitch used to make an open, decorative join between two edges of fabric, often the seam of a garment. *See* VIONNET.

faille Light, soft, glossy silk or rayon cloth fabric with a cross-wise rib effect. Similar to grosgrain, but much softer, faille has been used since the mid-19th century for many women's garments, especially coats and dresses.

Fair Isle Multicolored geometric design, named after Fair Isle, one of the Scottish Shetland Isles where it originated. On a SWEATER, the Fair Isle design is usually confined to a band across the upper chest which often drapes around the neck from shoulder to shoulder. During the 1920s the Prince of Wales helped to popularize the Fair Isle sweater, which he wore to play golf. *See* *EDWARD VIII *and* *RONAY.

Fairchild, John (Burr) 1927–. Publisher. Born in Newark, New Jersey, USA. After graduating from Princeton in 1949, Fairchild worked for two years in a research company before joining Fairchild Publications, founded by his grandfather Edmund Fairchild. He became a reporter for the clothing trade newspaper, WOMEN'S WEAR DAILY, in New York. In 1954 he was sent to Paris as head of the newspaper's French bureau. Once there, Fairchild broke with traditional fashion journalism by filing gossip pieces along with fashion news, ignoring embargoes set by couture houses in order to publish sketches ahead of the preset deadlines, and presenting his articles in a lively, informal, and irreverent style. In 1960, Fairchild returned to New York and took over as publisher of *Women's Wear Daily*. He immediately gave space to first rate fashion illustrators and continued to report both useful, factual trade stories and society news of charity events and parties. In 1965 he became chief executive of Fairchild Publications, resuming the role of publisher of *WWD* in 1971. In 1970 he launched a new paper, *W*, and later *M*, for the men and women he had christened "The Beautiful People."

fan From the Latin *vannus*, "winnowing-fan," the folding fan came to Europe through Eastern trade in the late 15th or early 16th centuries. It reached the height of its popularity and elegance in the 18th century, when many fans were hand-painted and depicted mythological and biblical figures as well as birds, animals, and flowers in pastoral scenes. Printing superseded painting in the 19th century and many comemorative fans were issued. Fans waned in popularity after the turn of the 20th century. They have been made from sandalwood, ivory, mother-of-pearl, and TORTOISE SHELL, and their sticks have been covered with FEATHERS, animal skins, silk, paper, and lace. Fans were used both during the day and in the evening, though in the second half of the 19th century they were more common in the evening.

Commemorative **fan** from the 1850s and (*above*) a charming design by Georges Barbier.

A 1926 **fedora**—a popular hat style that has remained unchanged throughout the 20th century.

Fath, Jacques 1912–54. Designer. Born in Maison-Lafitte, France. Fath worked as a bookkeeper and broker at the Paris Bourse (Stock Exchange). In the early 1930s, after a year's military service, he spent several years in private study of costume and fashion design. In 1937 he opened a salon and swiftly gained a reputation as a leader of French fashion, though it was not until after World War II that his name became known worldwide. Fath was famous for his hourglass shapes, plunging necklines, tiny waists, and full skirts. To some extent an unsung hero of fashion, Fath anticipated in 1939 the style of dress which in 1947 became known as the NEW LOOK. In 1948 he visited the USA and designed a ready-to-wear line. Throughout his career, Fath was a popular designer in the USA, where his lighthearted and witty clothes were welcomed. His garments were almost without exception created on soft lines with curving, simple, structured shapes. Credit is also given to Fath for introducing stockings with Chantilly lace tops. *See* *GRUAU.

Fauvism Art movement of the early 1900s, generally associated with the 1905 Salon d'Automne in Paris and the work of a group of artists including Henri Matisse and André Derain. Their brightly colored distorted shapes in flat, two-dimensional patterns prompted a critic to name them *Les Fauves* (the wild beasts). Fauvist use of color had a considerable impact on both fashion and textile design.

feathers The widespread use of feathers in late-19th-century fashion created a worldwide demand. In London, in 1906, for example, 37,000 ounces of feathers were sold at auction. Other main sales centers were Paris and New York. Many species became extinct as plumage hunters plundered sources in the USA, Burma, Malaya, Indonesia, China, Australia, and Europe. The American Ornithologists' Union, which was founded in 1883, estimated that 5 million birds were killed each year to supply feathers for fashion items such as FANS, hats, and MUFFS. The most popular feathers came from the egret. These were used extensively for AIGRETTES and in millinery.

fedora Soft, felt hat from the Austrian Tyrol which has a tapered crown with a center crease. It was named after *Fédora*, a play by the French dramatist Victorien Sardou shown in Paris in 1882. Women began to wear fedoras toward the end of the 19th century, especially for sporting activities. Fedoras were popular for men from the same period until the 1950s. *See also* HOMBURG.

felt Nonwoven fabric made by matting or bonding fibers such as cotton, fur, rayon, and wool. Traditionally used to make hats and as a lining during the 19th century, felt became popular in the 1950s when it was made up into coats and CIRCLE SKIRTS, which were often decorated with APPLIQUE motifs.

Fémina Bimonthly fashion review started in 1901. At various periods it was published monthly, and occasionally three times a month. In 1917 it became *Fémina et vie heureuse réunis*, reverting four years later to its original title until publication ceased in 1956. Some of the most celebrated artists, illustrators, and, in the years following World War II, photographers, contributed to the magazine.

Fendi Company founded in 1918 by Adele Fendi (1897–1978) which has been run since 1954 by her five daughters, their husbands, and their children. The sisters are Paola (born 1931), Anna (born 1933),

Cover of the May 1921 issue of
Fémina, drawn by Georges
Barbier.

Franca (born 1935), Carla (born 1937), and Alda (born 1940). The company produced soft leather PURSES/handbags and summer bags of woven strips of binding canvas. In 1962 Karl LAGERFELD was employed to design furs and four years later Fendi began showing fur collections to international buyers. The company's major contribution to fashion lies in its pioneering techniques of fur cutting. Backed by Lagerfeld's design skill, Fendi has dominated the fur market with its use of dyed furs and high quality workmanship.

Fendi, Adele *See* FENDI.

Feraud, Louis (Eduard) 1920–. Designer. Born in Gagnières, France. In 1949 Feraud established a house in Cannes which was patronized by many movie stars visiting the festival. He subsequently became a costume designer before moving in 1960 to Paris, where he opened a ready-to-wear business. A practising painter, Feraud has been inspired by the art of other cultures, notably those of South America. There is a sensitive use of color in his designs which, since the 1960s, have become increasing classical.

Ferragamo, Salvatore 1898–1960. Shoe designer. Born in Bonito, near Naples, Italy. Ferragamo began working in a shoemaker's at a very early age. When he was sixteen he joined his brothers in California, where he made shoes by hand for the American Film Company. This work led to private commissions from actors and actresses. During the 1920s he designed roman sandals with laces which tied around the ankles. In 1923 he went to Hollywood to work for the film studios of Universal, Warner Bros, and Metro-Goldwyn-Mayer. Ferragamo returned to Italy in 1927 and set up a workshop in Florence with about sixty workers—the first large-scale production of hand-made shoes. Clients from all over the world came to Ferragamo. He claimed to have originated the WEDGE heel in 1938, PLATFORM SOLES, and metal support in high heels. He experimented with cork, lace, needlework, raffia, snailshells, raw silk, webbing, taffeta, manila hemp, and nylon. In 1947 he invented the "invisible shoe," made with uppers of clear nylon and a black suede heel. Though he was no slave to fashion, Ferragamo's innovations and designs were well in advance of contemporary styles. By 1957 he had created over 20,000 styles and registered 350 patents. *See* col. pls.

Ferre, Gianfranco 1944–. Designer. Born in Legnano, Italy. Ferre qualified as an architect in Milan in 1967, but turned instead to designing jewelry for Walter ALBINI. His designs for other accessories soon made him famous. Established as a freelance designer since 1970, Ferre completed jewelry commissions for LAGERFELD and FIORUCCI. By the mid-1970s he was designing sportswear and outerwear. Since the establishment of his own house in 1978, he has emerged as one of the most talented Italian creators of ready-to-wear clothes. His garments are usually graphically created in strong shapes and bright colors. Highly sensitive to form and outline, Ferre shows collections that bear the hallmarks of one whose early training was in the careful study of detail, in analysis, and in planning. Ferre's intellectual approach to design produces powerful and controlled clothes which are often folded and layered to create his precise statements.

Feuillets d'art, Les Luxurious arts review published from 1919 to 1922. Although it was planned as a twice-monthly publication, its appearance was irregular. It consisted of a wallet containing plates covering fashion and the arts. Contributors included BARBIER, Robert Bonfils, DRIAN, MARTY, and LEPAPE.

fichu Small scarf or SHAWL worn draped around the shoulders and fastened with a brooch at the breast. A fichu can also mean a ruffle or piece of fabric, often lace, which is sewn across the bosom of a blouse or dress.

Fiorucci, Elio 1935–. Designer. Born in Milan, Italy. Fiorucci inherited a shoe store from his father in 1962. In the mid-1960s he began traveling to London to bring MINI skirts and other fashionable garments back to his store in Milan. In 1967 he opened a larger store, selling clothes from London's youth-oriented designers. Fiorucci became world famous in the mid-1970s. A constant traveler, he collected ideas and items which he passed on to a team of designers. The garments in Fiorucci stores were fresh, new, and often amusing: plastic GALOSHES in bright colors, electronic accessories, computer graffiti T-SHIRTS, and FLUORESCENT socks and scarves. Fiorucci captured the spirit of the moment for a predominantly young market, recycling old ideas in new ways. His tightly cut, streamlined JEANS of the 1970s were in great demand.

Fichu in tulle and cream-colored lace, fastened with a flower brooch. From *La Mode universelle*, 16 June 1876.

Fisher, Harrison 1875–1934. Illustrator. Born in New York, USA. Fisher was taught by his father, landscape painter Hugh Antoine Fisher. The family moved to San Francisco, California, when Fisher was still a child. He studied at the Mark Hopkins Institute of Art in San Francisco and by the age of sixteen was already selling illustrations to the *San Francisco Call* and the *Examiner*. Fisher became well known for his graceful illustrations of mobile and animated young women, notably on the covers of the fashion magazine *Cosmopolitan*.

fishnet Large, open-weave knit associated in the 20th century with STOCKINGS and PANTIEHOSE.

flannel Generic term which covers many woolen fabrics woven in different weights of worsted. The term includes man-made fibers. Flannel is usually soft and made of a plain or twilled weave slightly napped on one side. In the 19th century it was often used to make PETTICOATS. During the 20th century assorted weights of flannel have been used for underwear, outerwear, jackets, dresses, skirts, and pants.

flannelette Soft cotton fabric which is slightly napped on one side. It has been used since the late 19th century for underwear, nightwear, and children's clothes.

flapper Term used in the early 1900s to describe a young girl who had yet to become a debutante. By the 1920s it meant any young woman who cut her hair short, wore CLOCHE HATS and later BERETS, a short skirt and blouse, stockings rolled at the knees, and heeled—usually T-bar—shoes. She was commonly thought of then, as now, as a rather dizzy young thing who spent her time dancing the Charleston.

flea market clothes Clothes bought at flea markets are invariably old and usually inexpensive compared to new ready-to-wear garments, though the recent vogue for antique items has increased prices. Shopping at flea markets for clothes of the 1900s to 1940s and, more recently, of the 1950s, became popular in Europe and the USA during the early 1970s when prevailing fashions included an EDWARDIAN revival and many styles based on ETHNIC and FOLKLORIC costumes.

flounce Strip of material which is gathered and sewn on to the hem of a garment, usually a skirt. The flounce can be of the same fabric as the garment or of a different material. Flounces have adorned dresses and skirts, particularly eveningwear, throughout the 19th and 20th centuries.

flying suit *See* JUMPSUIT.

Foale, Marion 1939–. Designer. Born in London, England. Foale studied at Walthamstow School of Art and the Royal College of Art in London, graduating in 1961. The following year she set up a partnership with fellow student Sally Tuffin. Woollands, a popular London store, bought many Tuffin & Foale clothes, which were geared to the young, ready-to-wear market. As 1960s designers they incorporated both nostalgic and modernist ideas into their garments. The partnership was dissolved in 1972.

Fogarty, Anne 1919–81. Designer. Born Anne Whitney in Pittsburgh, Pennsylvania, USA. In 1936 Fogarty attended Allegheny College in Pennsylvania before transferring one year later to the Carnegie Institute of Technology, where she studied drama. In 1939 she took courses at the East Hartman School of Design. Shortly afterward, Fogarty went to New York and in the early 1940s worked as a model for design houses Harvey Berin and Sheila Lynn. She then spent a brief period at Dorland International Advertising Agency before becoming, in 1948, designer for a teenage dress manufacturer, Youth Guild Inc. In 1950 she created ballet length cotton dresses with stiffened PETTICOATS, a silhouette which became extremely popular with teenagers. Fogarty joined Margot Dresses Inc. in the same year and designed coats, hats, shoes, jewelry, and lingerie. In 1957 she went to Saks Fifth Avenue where, several years later, she launched the "Paper Doll," a high-waisted, low-necked, short-sleeved, shirred BODICE dress with a full skirt. Fogarty created youthful, pretty clothes. She was one of the first US designers to produce BIKINIS.

folkloric Style of dress associated with PEASANT costume. By the end of World War I, large numbers of Russian emigrés had settled in Paris, but the influence of Russian costume on fashion was attributed to peasants rather than aristocrats. Russian and Bulgarian embroidery patterns were used to decorate garments. In the 1930s DIRNDL SKIRTS became popular and East European embroidery—usually simple, bright shapes of flowers, plants, and leaves—enjoyed a revival. In the 1960s and 1970s peasant inspired fashions became popular once more. They merged with the ETHNIC trends of those decades and were adapted to garments and decoration. *See* RUSSIAN, SAINT LAURENT, and TYROLEAN.

Fontana *Haute couture* house founded in Parma, Italy, in 1907. The three daughters of the founder took over the business and moved to Rome in 1936. In the 1950s their high quality dresses, evening gowns, and suits were worn by movie stars, socialites, and the wives of US presidents.

Cardinal's outfit for Ava Gardner from **Fontana**, with a black and white collar, red buttons, hat and crucifix, 1956.

Fortuny, Mariano 1871–1949. Textile and dress designer. Born Mariano Fortuny y Madrazo in Granada, Spain. Fortuny studied painting and drawing in Spain before spending periods in France and also in Germany, where he learned about chemistry and dyes. In 1889 he settled in Venice, taking photographs, painting, sculpting, and making etchings and drawings. Fascinated by the effects of diffused light, he created stage sets for the theater and opera. In the late 1890s, Fortuny began to print textiles. Inspired by the velvet and brocades of the Italian 15th and 16th centuries, tapestries from the East, and Grecian robes, Fortuny created pleated gowns and cloaks which he dyed with vegetable dyes. Although made of silk, they resembled rich velvets. Between 1901 and 1934 he registered more than twenty inventions in Paris for stage lighting systems and textile printing processes. His "Knossos" scarf of 1906 was inspired by Cycladic art. It was a rectangular silk veil which could be used in a number of ways, tied around the body or worn as a decoration with the "Delphos" gown, a cylindrically shaped, loose-fitting silk satin garment which undulated with rich color, created by a special pleating process which Fortuny patented in 1909. The Delphos dress was sleeveless or had DOLMAN SLEEVES, and could be tied about the waist with a silk cord. All Fortuny's dresses emphasized the female form in movement. Isadora DUNCAN was one of his most famous clients. Fortuny adapted most forms of ethnic dress into lavish, exotic garments: the Japanese KIMONO, North African BURNOUS and DJELLABAH, Indian SARI, and Turkish DOLMAN. Fortuny was famous for his printed patterns. Vegetables were often taken as motifs. Many of Fortuny's gowns and VEILS were weighted with delicate beads, which also served as trimming, made on the Italian island of Murano. After his death, the Fortuny process was bought by Countess Gozzi, who, as Elsie McNeill, had earlier helped Fortuny to market his furnishing fabric in the USA. A mixture of artist and couturier, Fortuny had an enlightened view of dress design, combining color and texture with cut in a unique manner that has earned him one of the crowns of fashion. *See* col. pl.

Fouquet, Georges 1862–1957. Born in Paris, France. Son of a French jeweler, Alphonse Fouquet (1828–1911), Fouquet joined his father's firm in 1891. He specialized in ART NOUVEAU jewelry, particularly pieces designed by Alphonse MUCHA. Fouquet also created some neoclassical pieces. *See* col. pl.

fourreau style *See* PRINCESS LINE.

fox Soft, glossy, luxuriant, long fur of an animal found in most cool climates in the world, particularly Scandinavia and Canada. In the 20th century most fox is ranched. Fox is distinguished by its long underfur. It can be beige, blue, brown, red, silver, or white. Different colors have been popular at different times, but the fur itself is seldom out of fashion.

Fox, Frederick 1931–. Milliner. Born in New South Wales, Australia. Fox trained as a milliner for nine years in Sydney before leaving in 1958 for London. He secured a position at the milliners Longee in Brook Street and worked there until he opened his own business in the mid-1960s. Fox became the favorite milliner of a number of designers, including Hardy AMIES and John BATES. He has an international clientele and has created hats for Queen Elizabeth and other members of the British Royal Family.

Gina **Fratini**'s bridal design for 1978.

Fratini, Gina 1934–. Designer. Born Georgina Caroline Butler in Kobe, Japan, of English parents. Fratini was brought up in England, Burma, and India. She joined the Royal College of Art Fashion School in London in 1950. After graduation she spent two years traveling with the Katherine Dunham dance company of California, designing scenery and costumes. Back in England, Fratini established her own business and produced her first collection in 1966. A widely influential designer at the start of her career, she set her own style and remained faithful to it. Some of her first garments were SMOCKS and long, velvet JUMPERS. She followed these with gauze and chiffon dresses, all totally in keeping with the 1970s. Her instantly recognizable label is the floating, frilly tulle, silk, and lace dress. She designs romantic evening gowns and lighthearted, easy daywear.

French, John 1907–66. Photographer. Born in London, England. French attended Hornsey School of Art from 1926 to 1927 and then spent a brief period with a block-making firm and in a commercial art studio before leaving London in 1930 to study painting in Italy. He returned after six years and found employment as a freelance illustrator for the English newspaper, the *Daily Express*. In the same year he began work as an art director for a photographic studio, Carlton Artists. After World War II French returned to Carlton Artists, only to establish his own company and photographic studio in London two years later. He worked for major newspapers, magazines, designers, and advertising agencies throughout the 1950s. French became famous for his clear, stylish, uncluttered black and white photographs taken against clean backgrounds. He strongly influenced many younger photographers who worked with him.

frill Narrow ruffle gathered to the edge of a neckline, armhole, cuff, or hem.

John **French** photographed this model in a cowl-neck sweater and fur coat in 1964.

Frissell, Toni 1907–. Photographer. Born Antoinette Wood Montgomery Frissell in New York, USA. Working as a caption writer on American VOGUE in 1930, Frissell was encouraged by Editor Carmel SNOW to experiment with photography. A year later Frissell's fashion pictures began to appear in magazines including *Vogue* and *Town and Country*, and she was soon placed under contract at *Vogue* to cover the fashion pages and take on general assignments. In 1947 she moved to HARPER'S BAZAAR. Frissell's casual, lively pictures reflected her own active, sporty life. She shot fashion outdoors in natural settings—an avant-garde approach at a time when models were usually carefully posed in a studio. Frissell was also an avid traveler, a war correspondent, and a portrait photographer specializing in children. *See* PUCCI.

Frizon, Maud 1941–. Shoe designer. Born in Paris, France. Frizon worked for many years as a model in Paris and was a particular favorite of COURRÈGES. In 1970 she launched her first shoe collection in which each pair of shoes was hand-cut and finished. She was an overnight success. Frizon designs elegant, highly sophisticated, and often witty shoes in unusual combinations: lizard and snake, suede and satin, canvas and crocodile. Her name is associated with the promotion of the cone heel. She has designed shoes for ALAIA, MISSONI, MONTANA, MUGLER, and RYKIEL.

frock coat The 19th-century frock coat was adapted from a military coat, and became formal dress for men. It appeared in various forms but was basically a long-sleeved, knee-length garment with tails, collars, REVERS, buttoning, and back vents. It was full-skirted for brief periods during the 19th century. The basic coat has been used as a foundation for many styles of women's coats in the 20th century.

frogging Decorative BRAID fastening which loops over buttons or a braid toggle. Originally worn on military uniforms, frogging fastenings have adorned women's coats and jackets since the 19th century. *See* ANNA KARENINA.

fun fur Since the 1960s, imitation fur coats have become the fashionable alternative to the real thing. They are made from a variety of fibers that often include mixtures of acrylic, modacrylic, and polyester. Imitation fur has two advantages over real fur: it can easily be dyed bold, brilliant "fun" colors, and it is relatively inexpensive.

Paco Rabanne's synthetic **fun fur** for 1972–73.

fur Fur became fashionable in the 19th century, reaching the peak of its popularity in the 1890s and early 1900s. Sealskin was the first popular fur and was used for CAPES and fitted jackets and later for coats. Many other furs have been used over the years, depending on availability and fashion trends. Fur has been used for coats, jackets, hats, MUFFS, STOLES, TIPPETS, and for trimming on dresses and evening gowns. *See also* ASTRAKHAN, CHINCHILLA, ERMINE, FOX, KARACUL, MINK, RACCOON, SABLE, SEAL, *and* SQUIRREL.

furbelow Term dating from the 19th century which describes a trimming, usually at the hem of a skirt.

Models disembarking prior to a **fur** fashion show by Calman Links, 1966.

G

gabardine *1.* Clear-surfaced, twill weave fabric with a fine diagonal rib effect. Gabardine can be made in a variety of weights from natural and synthetic fibers. It has been used since the 19th century for suits, coats, dresses, skirts, and pants. 2. A registered tradename. *See* BURBERRY.

Galanos, James 1924–. Designer. Born in Philadelphia, Pennsylvania, USA, of Greek parents. After graduating from the Traphagen School of Fashion in New York, Galanos sold fashion sketches to several New York designers. In 1944 he moved to Columbia Studios in California as an assistant to Jean LOUIS. He left in 1947 to take up a one-year apprenticeship in Paris with PIGUET. Galanos then returned to New York as a ready-to-wear designer. In 1951 he was back in California and three years later showed his first collection in Los Angeles. He swiftly gained a reputation among US women for his precisely executed and clever clothes. Galanos was acclaimed for the cut of his dresses, suits, and coats, made up in European fabrics, but he was patronized mostly for his eveningwear and COCKTAIL DRESSES. In the 1950s he was one of the first designers to show the HORSESHOE NECKLINE on suits and to pioneer bold prints for after-six garments. During the 1960s and 1970s he created slimline, classically draped evening dresses with billowing sleeves. Galanos frequently works with chiffon, printed silks, velvets, brocades, and hand-painted silks and laces. He has also used wool for eveningwear and is known for low-backed, black wool crêpe dresses. Many prominent US women buy his clothes.

Galitzine, Princess Irene *c.*1916–. Designer. Born in Tiflis, Russia. The Princess's family fled to Rome during the Russian Revolution. After studying languages and art, Princess Galitzine joined the FONTANA sisters, for whom she worked for three years. Toward the end of the 1940s she opened her own house. Her first collection was shown in 1959 but it was not until the following year that she achieved her greatest success with the launch of her "Palazzo Pajamas"—wide-legged evening pajamas made of soft silk. Some versions were beaded and fringed. Evening pajamas such as these became a firm fixture of the fashion scene during the 1960s. The Princess was also noted for her eveningwear, especially dinner suits and open-sided gowns. The house closed in 1968 but Princess Galitzine continued to design on a freelance basis.

galoshes Protective rubber overshoes, first worn by men in the mid-19th century. They were adopted by women in the early part of the 20th century.

gamine French for tomboy or street urchin. In fashion parlance the word gamine has two meanings. The gamine look is exemplified by Audrey HEPBURN and Zizi JEANMAIRE. Both have short haircuts that frame their elfin faces. The gamine style of dress is understood to mean an outfit of a sleeveless PULLOVER, CARDIGAN, KNICKERBOCKERS, tweed CAP, and long muffler or scarf. François Truffaut's film *Jules et Jim* (1962) created a vogue for this style.

The 1964 version of Princess **Galitzine**'s famous palazzo pajamas.

Garbo, Greta 1905–. Actress. Born Greta Gustafsson in Stockholm, Sweden. Garbo attended the Royal Dramatic Theater training school in Stockholm. She made several films in 1923 and 1924 before moving in the following year to the USA, where she was engaged by Louis B. Mayer for the Metro-Goldwyn-Mayer studios. Between then and 1941, when she renounced the cinema, Garbo starred in many films, including *The Temptress* (1926), *Love* (1927), *Flesh and the Devil* (1927), *Mata Hari* (1930), *Grand Hotel* (1932), *Queen Christina* (1933), *The Painted Veil* (1934), *Anna Karenina* (1935), *Camille* (1937), *Ninotchka* (1939), and *Two Faced Woman* (1941). Her shoulder-length hairstyle was widely copied and she created a fashion for SLOUCH HATS and TRENCHCOATS. *See* ADRIAN.

garçonne *La Garçonne* was the title of a novel by Victor Margueritte, published in 1922. It was considered extremely risqué, describing as it did the relaxed sexual mores of a Sorbonne student who had an illegitimate child. The heroine, who cut her hair short and wore a shirt, TIE, jacket, and other mannish clothes, became a symbol of the liberated, active modern woman. The garçonne style came to be identified with a boyish silhouette, short hair, and little makeup.

garibaldi Shirt/blouse worn by women in the early 1860s, named after the Italian soldier and patriot Guiseppe Garibaldi. The garibaldi was a scarlet blouse made of merino or muslin and worn with a black silk skirt. Black BRAID was sewn to the narrow collar. Some versions had full sleeves that were gathered at the wrist; other "red shirts," as they were known, were worn beneath the dress BODICE, revealing only the sleeves. It was fashionable to complete the look by banding the hem of a skirt with scarlet fabric. *See also* ZOUAVE JACKET.

garter Band of decorated ELASTIC worn around the thigh which holds STOCKINGS in position. The introduction in the 1880s of the garter belt (UK: suspender belt) signaled the decline of the garter, though it continued to be worn until the 1930s.

gather Fabric drawn together by threads to create fullness.

gaucho pants Pants adapted from the wide-bottomed, mid-calf divided skirts worn by the South American cowboy. SAINT LAURENT popularized gauchos in the 1960s, when they were worn with BOOTS, shirts, and wide belts with large silver buckles.

Gaultier, Jean-Paul 1952–. Designer. Born in Paris, France. Gaultier first sketched ideas for collections at the age of fourteen. When he was seventeen he dispatched his sketches to several major designers and was invited by Pierre CARDIN to join his company for one year. Gaultier then worked for Jacques Esterel, Jean PATOU, and, in 1974, for Cardin's manufacturing operation in the Phillipines before starting his own firm in 1977. Since that time he has become one of the most influential young French ready-to-wear designers. His clothes are humorous, showy, and extremely clever—a mixture of tomboy zest and film star glamor. Gaultier successfully mixes old and new in fabrics and cuts. He has produced SWEATSHIRTS trimmed with lace and satin, upside-down Eiffel Towers as heels for shoes, and bracelets which resemble tin cans. Fun-loving and witty, Gaultier's designs challenge many ideas of dress without offending. In the early 1980s he had several strong seasons, showing various

Garters were often ornate in design. This 1930s example was made of metal.

Jean-Paul **Gaultier** slashed away shoulders to reveal more layers beneath—a style dating from 1983.

PLAIDS worn together and cut-away T-SHIRTS, worn loosely over each other, leaving parts of the arms and shoulders exposed. Both these and other Gaultier looks have their origins in the London street clothes of the late 1970s.

gauntlets Gloves with close-fitting hands and long, wide arms reaching almost to the elbow. Medieval-style gauntlets, made in soft suede and leather that fell in folds over the wrists, were popular during the 1920s and 1930s.

gauze Thin, open-weave, transparent fabric which has been used for trimming since the 19th century.

Gazette du bon ton, La Witty arts and fashion magazine founded in 1912 by Lucien VOGEL. It contained fashion illustrations printed by the *pochoir* method, a time-consuming and expensive process in which the images were created by building up hand-painted gouaches with metal stencils. The results were brilliant color reproductions. The magazine was published monthly until 1915, and then irregularly until 1925, when it was bought by Condé NAST and merged with VOGUE. *La Gazette du bon ton* attracted some of the best artists of the time: BARBIER, BAKST, BENITO, Pierre Bonfils, BOUTET DE MONVEL, Pierre Brissaud, DRIAN, IRIBE, MARTY, MARTIN, Pierre Morgue, and Ferdnand Siméon, all of whom illustrated articles and produced clear, stylish fashion plates of garments in anecdotal settings in keeping with the style of the magazine.

Genny Italian fashion house established in 1961. In 1975 Gianni VERSACE produced the classically styled Complice line for the company. Versace went on to design the younger Byblos line until 1977, when he was replaced by Guy PAULIN. In 1981 Keith VARTY took over. Since 1980, Claude MONTANA has been responsible for designing the Complice line, as well as other Montana/Genny labels, such as Montana Donna.

georgette Silk or rayon fabric, similar to chiffon, which is used for eveningwear. A crêpe version has a dull-textured surface.

Gernreich, Rudi (Rudolph) 1922–85. Designer. Born in Vienna, Austria. Gernreich's father was a hosiery manufacturer and his aunt kept a dress shop in which Gernreich worked as a teenager. In 1938, with numerous other refugees, Gernreich fled to California. He attended the Los Angeles City College from 1938 to 1941 and then spent a year at the Los Angeles Art Center School. For the next six years Gernreich worked with a dance troupe as a dancer and costume designer. In 1948 he became a freelance fashion designer until, in 1951, he formed a partnership with manufacturer Walter Bass to supply clothes to Jax, a Los Angeles BOUTIQUE. Some years later he opened his own company, G. R. Designs Inc., which became Rudi Gernreich Inc. in 1964. In the 1960s Gernreich proved to be a competent and innovative designer of separates and SPORTSWEAR for a predominantly young market. He made SHIRTWAIST dresses in luxurious fabrics, reversible CAPE coats, and swimsuits without inner foundations. His best known fashion contributions are the TOPLESS BATHING SUIT, with straps from a high waistband at the front to the back, which was introduced in 1964 to a scandalized world; the "no-bra bra," made of molded nylon cups attached to shoulder straps and a narrow ELASTIC band encircling the rib cage; the "no-sides bra," which was cut low in front with deep armholes

Bathing suit designed by Rudi **Gernreich** in 1965, worn with a visor and thigh-high ciré boots.

Kenzo's use of vivid color and his mastery of draping are combined in this eye-catching evening dress from a 1979 collection.

A 1921 design by Jeanne **Lanvin**.

Lucile was best known for her turn-of-th[e]
gowns in predominantly pastel shades.

to be worn with deep DECOLLETE evening dresses; the "no-front bra," with a sculptured front for dresses which were slit to the waist; and the "no-back bra," anchored about the waist instead of the rib cage. In 1964 corset manufacturers WARNERS commissioned him to design a BODYSTOCKING which was made up in flesh-colored stretch nylon. Other Gernreich innovations included patterned hosiery and knitted tank suits that resembled gym tunics.

ghillie Originally a Scottish heeled dancing shoe popularized by EDWARD VIII when he was Prince of Wales. It had laces which criss-crossed through loops of leather on the vamp. During the 1950s, the name was given to flat sandals with criss-cross laces which were worn in hot weather as casual footwear.

Gibb, Bill 1943–. Designer. Born in Fraserburgh, Scotland. Gibb joined St. Martin's School of Art in London in 1962, transferring to the Royal College of Art in 1966. He sold an early collection to Bendel's New York department store and left the RCA in 1968 before completing his course. After working for Baccarat for three years he struck out on his own in 1972 and opened a retail business three years later. Gibb was a highly acclaimed designer in the 1970s, famous particularly for his eveningwear: fantastic, floating chiffon dresses and supple jersey dresses adorned with APPLIQUE and EMBROIDERY. In 1974 he produced a knitwear collection which became highly successful. Despite his considerable design talents and his skill in handling lavish and exotic fabrics, Gibb was forced for financial reasons to close his firm in the late 1970s. His 1980s freelance designs still carry the sensitive yet exotic Gibb hallmark, often with his personal motif, a small bee.

Gibson, Charles Dana 1867–1944. Illustrator. Born in Roxbury, Massachusetts, USA. Gibson studied at the Art Students League in New York from 1884 to 1885. He worked first with silhouettes before turning to pen and ink drawings which he sold in 1886 to the humorous weekly *Life*. Five years later Gibson's drawings were the paper's star attraction. From 1886 to 1889 Gibson worked for the weekly *Tid-Bits* (which became *Time*), *Collier's Weekly*, *Harper's Monthly*, HARPER'S BAZAR, *Scribner's*, and many other publications. In 1889 he went to London and then to Paris, where he spent two months studying at the Académie Julian. Returning to New York in 1890, Gibson settled down to chronicle the lives of his fellow Americans through his patriotic, romantic, and often satirical, drawings. He became famous for his GIBSON GIRL, a poised, independent, self-reliant woman, who remained the ideal symbol of American womanhood for twenty years.

Gibson Girl Character created by Charles Dana GIBSON, which appeared in his pen and ink drawings from 1890 until 1910. The "Gibson Girl" was tall, slender, and poised, her hair piled into a CHIGNON or tucked under a plumed hat. She wore a starched blouse and long flowing skirts over a small BUSTLE. She represented the modern, active woman and was shown in some illustrations wearing shorter skirts, especially when she was cycling or engaged in other sporting activities. The Gibson Girl image was appropriated by manufacturers of CORSETS, skirts, shoes, and household items. She inspired the song "Why Do They Call Me a Gibson Girl?," from the musical *The Belle of Mayfair* (1906), and the revue *The Gibson Bathing Girl*, which was performed by the Ziegfeld Follies (1907). In Britain she was personified by American actress Camille Clifford,

Dots and squiggles tied up in knots for Bill **Gibb**'s ultra-feminine dress for 1977.

The famous **Gibson Girl**, created by Charles Dana Gibson in 1890.

who first appeared on the London stage in 1904, and in the US by Irene Langhorne, a debutante from Virginia, who married Gibson in 1895.

gigot sleeve *See* LEG-OF-MUTTON SLEEVE.

gilet Sleeveless garment with a blouse, shirt, or BODICE front, worn over blouses and dresses since the 19th century. *See* WAISTCOAT.

gingham From the Malayan word *ginggang*, "striped," a light- or medium-weight fabric originally made of linen and later of COTTON. It is woven from predyed yarns into checks of various sizes. Gingham was a popular fabric for summer dresses during the 19th century and became fashionable in the 1940s and 1950s for dresses, blouses, skirts, PLAYSUITS, and BIKINIS. *See* BARDOT.

Girbaud, François and **Marithé** Designers. Girbaud, François 1945–. Born in Mazamet, France. Bachellerie, Marithé 1942–. Born in Lyon, France. The couple met in Paris in the mid-1960s and in 1969 opened a BOUTIQUE selling American style *JEANS of their own design. In 1970 they sold BELL-BOTTOMS made of denim, and in the 1970s set a style for both stone-washed jeans and baggy jeans. Many of their ideas found their way into the hands of other designers. Since 1975 the Girbaud team have developed over fourteen lines, including a leather range and children's wear. Their clothes are sold world-wide. One of their most popular lines in the 1980s was a PEDAL PUSHER, made up in denim.

girdle Boneless, lightweight, elastic CORSET introduced during the 1920s. It encased the hips and stomach, often with elastic side panels, supporting STOCKINGS with a garter belt (UK: suspender belt). The girdle became progressively lighter in weight, especially during the 1930s. During the second half of the 20th century, the girdle was largely replaced by the ROLL-ON, as women rejected rigid corsetry which could not be worn under pants. Since the late 1970s women have favored a more natural look, which has in its turn made the roll-on unfashionable.

Givenchy, Hubert (James Marcel Taffin) **de** 1927–. Designer. Born in Beauvais, France. Givenchy attended the Ecole des Beaux Arts in Paris and briefly studied law. He worked for FATH from 1945 to 1946, PIGUET from 1946 to 1948, and LELONG from 1948 to 1949. He was then employed by SCHIAPARELLI until he opened his own business in 1952. Givenchy's collection contained many garments made in shirting and included the BETTINA BLOUSE. He is considered by many to have taken on BALENCIAGA's mantle in producing elegant, often formal, clothes and high-style BALL GOWNS and evening dresses. During the 1950s he exaggerated the CHEMISE (SACK) shape into a kite outline that was wide at the top and tapered towards the hem. Givenchy is the favorite designer of many film actresses and internationally prominent women. His name is linked with Jacqueline ONASSIS and also with Audrey HEPBURN, whose clothes he designed for the film *Breakfast at Tiffany's* (1961).

Glamour Originally *Glamour of Hollywood*, a monthly magazine that offered patterns to its readers when it was first published in 1939 by Condé NAST. It became *Glamour* during the 1940s and the patterns were dropped. *Glamour* caters to the twenty-five to forty-

Cocktail dresses from **Givenchy**: *center*, 1958; *left* and *right*, 1957.

five age group and covers fashion, beauty, the home, travel, and general features of interest to women.

gloves Since early times gloves have been made from pliable fabrics to follow the contours of the hand. During the 19th century gloves were worn for both day and evening and were an essential part of dress. Numerous styles were popular, including fingerless MITTENS, short and long leather and kid gloves, and gloves with leather hands and lace arms. Gloves were also made from embroidered silk, cotton, net, and knitted silk, and were fastened by tiny buttons at the wrist. In the 20th century, with the exception of long evening gloves, gloves became utilitarian items. By the end of the 1950s they were rarely seen except in cold weather or as high fashion accessories and had ceased to be a symbol of status and wealth. Fingerless mittens became fashionable in the late 1970s and early 1980s.

godet Piece of fabric of triangular shape, wider at the bottom than at the top, which is sewn into a skirt, dress, or coat to increase fullness. Godets have been used in dressmaking since the 19th century.

Goma, Michel 1932–. Designer. Born in Montpellier, France. Goma studied dressmaking and art. At the age of nineteen he moved to Paris where he sold his fashion sketches. From 1950 to 1958 he worked for Lafaurie and eventually bought the company, renaming it Michel Goma. He closed down in 1963 and joined PATOU, where he stayed for ten years.

Gordon, Lady Duff See LUCILE.

gore Flared panel sewn into skirts to increase their width. Gored skirts were popular during the 19th century. Exaggerated gores, with pointed ends near the waist and fullness at the hem, became fashionable during the 1930s.

Goût du jour, Le Fashion and arts review published in Paris from 1920 to 1922. It contained the work of notable illustrators of the period, including BENITO, Pierre Brissaud, Robert Bonfils, MARTY, and Ferdnand Siméon.

granny style Style of dress popular during the late 1960s and early 1970s. "Granny clothes" included collarless "grandfather" shirts; *SHAWLS; long, full skirts; small round-rimmed spectacles; and either thick-heeled, round-toed shoes or high, laced *BOOTS.

Gréco, Juliette 1927–. Singer. Born in Montpellier, France. Gréco has been involved with the French theater as both singer and dramatist since 1942. She became known to the fashion world in the 1940s when she created a vogue for long, straight hair, black clothes, and a loosely tied RAINCOAT worn with the collar turned up.

Greenaway, Kate (Catherine) 1846–1903. Born in England. Book illustrator, painter. Greenaway illustrated children's books from the 1870s to the 1890s, notably *Under the Window* (1878). The clothes in her illustrations were reminiscent of 18th-century costume. The picturesque manner in which Greenaway detailed garments, such as BONNETS, SMOCKS, and EMPIRE-LINE dresses with frilled necks and sleeves, inspired many designers and fashion trends in the late 19th century.

Greer, Howard 1886–1974. Costume designer. Born in Nebraska, USA. Greer left the University of Nebraska in 1916 and joined the fashion house of LUCILE in New York. After World War I he worked for Lucile, MOLYNEUX, and POIRET in Paris. He returned to New York in 1921 and designed costumes for the Greenwich Village Follies. In 1923 he joined Paramount Pictures in Hollywood. Over the next five years Greer created costumes for many films, dressing

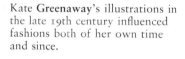

Kate **Greenaway**'s illustrations in the late 19th century influenced fashions both of her own time and since.

actresses such as Pola Negri and Bebe Daniels. In 1927 he opened a couture shop but continued to work freelance for various film companies. He was known for his glamorous, sophisticated evening gowns and dresses which were worn by actresses both on and off the film set. He retired in 1962.

Grès, (Madame) Alix 1899–. Designer. Born in Paris, France. Frustrated in her ambition to become a sculptor, Grès began her design career by making "toiles," muslin couture designs, which she sold to major Paris fashion houses. In 1934 she opened her own house as Alix Barton. The house closed during World War II but reopened afterward under the name Grès. Grès' designs have always been individual and uncompromising and have made her internationally recognized as a classicist. She drapes and molds jersey, silk, and wool—her favorite fabrics—until the dresses resemble classical Greek sculptures. Many of her loose coats and simple dresses are constructed with deceptive detail. Her famous evening gowns are often the result of hours of work, pleating fabric into precise configurations to achieve an elegant simplicity. Although she has influenced many designers, no one has equaled her particular mastery of fabric. Grès has often used asymmetric shapes, BIAS CUTS, and DOLMAN SLEEVES in her creations. Her clothes excel in independence and quality. *See* PREMET.

gretchen neckline Low-cut, round, gathered neckline based on a PEASANT blouse, introduced during the 1920s. It was a popular style on both dresses and blouses.

Griffe, Jacques 1917–. Designer. Born in Carcassonne, France. Griffe trained with a tailor for several years in his home town and while still a teenager he went to Toulouse to extend his apprenticeship with a couturier. In 1936, after completing his military service, he joined VIONNET in Paris. Here he learned to drape and cut material on small wooden dummies in the Vionnet tradition. After World War II Griffe worked briefly for MOLYNEUX before opening his own couture and ready-to-wear business in 1946. A craftsman at cutting and draping, his clothes were fluid and soft. Griffe retired in the 1960s.

Grima, Andrew 1921–. Jewelry designer. Born in Rome, Italy. In 1946 Grima established a company in London to manufacture traditional pieces of jewelry. In the 1960s he began to design contemporary jewelry and in 1966 opened a shop in Jermyn Street, London, where he specialized in creating gold pieces adorned with quartz, tourmaline, and citrine stones. In 1970 Grima received a Royal Warrant.

Grimm, Gerd 1911–. Illustrator. Born in Baden, Germany. Grimm was educated at the arts school in Karlsruhe and at an industrial arts school in Nüremberg. In the 1920s he published his first advertising work and shortly after was asked to join the staff of the magazine *Die Dame*. Throughout the Nazi régime, Grimm lived in France and Italy. In 1950 he emigrated to the USA, where he worked for *Esquire* and the Lord & Taylor department store, among others. He returned to Baden in the 1960s. Grimm's work as a prominent advertising and editorial illustrator spans many years. His unusual perspectives, set in eye-catching color and arrangement, reflect a joyous sensitivity to fashion.

A large, square-cut citrine is surrounded by gold and diamonds in one of Andrew **Grima**'s designs.

Andrew **Grima**'s tourmaline and diamond clip of yellow gold.

This René **Gruau** illustration of a Jacques Fath design shows a dress being worn, rather than modeled.

grosgrain Closely woven, heavily ribbed fabric, usually made of silk, which originated in the Middle Ages. It has been used since the 1920s for millinery.

Gruau, René 1908–. Illustrator. Born Renato de Zavagli in Venice, Italy. While still a teenager, Gruau made fashion sketches which were accepted by German, French, and Italian magazines. Professional by the age of eighteen, he moved to Paris where he worked for the following twenty years. From 1946 Gruau illustrated advertisements for DIOR perfumes. His bold, rhythmic, colorful drawings of modish women are still relevant and contemporary to the 1980s. His style ranges from open-faced, friendly women who look as if they enjoy wearing fashionable clothes to elegant, seductive creatures who wear their garments with an air of mystery. Gruau is one of the few artists whose design career has successfully spanned five decades.

G-string 1. Single strip of cloth worn between the legs which is kept on by means of a cord around the waist or hips. 2. The scantiest version of the BIKINI, first seen in Europe during the 1950s.

Gucci When the family millinery business failed in 1906, Guccio Gucci started a saddlery shop in Florence, Italy. He was succeeded by his sons and grandsons. Taking traditional leather accessories, the company redesigned them with equestrian motifs. A successful duffle bag was launched in 1925. In 1932 the famous MOCCASIN shoe with the tongue caught in a gilt bit became popular. From the mid-1960s Gucci became increasingly involved in the sale of PURSES/handbags, BELTS, and shoes, many bearing stirrup or bit designs.

guêpière *See* WASPIE.

guernsey Believed to be derived from "gansey," a worsted yarn used to make a shirt-like garment worn by fishermen in the Channel Islands. During the late 19th century the word guernsey came to be identified with a crew neck SWEATER worn by fishermen on Guernsey and Jersey. Usually made of dark blue wool, the guernsey has become associated with casual wear during the second half of the 20th century.

Guirlande, La Fashion, art, and literary review published monthly in Paris from 1919 to 1920. It contained illustrations by artists such as Georges BARBIER and Umberto BRUNELLESCHI.

gusset Small, triangular or diamond-shaped piece of fabric which is inserted in the seams of a garment to increase strength and facilitate movement.

gym tunic Sleeveless garment with a flat YOKE over the bust, which hangs to a knee- or calf-length hem by deep, inverted pleats. Since the early 1900s it has been associated with exercise attire for women. It is also known as a gym slip and worn in the 20th century by British schoolgirls.

Gucci accessories in the 1980s, with the famous initials for the status conscious.

gypsy Style of dress comprising full, flounced skirts and blouses with low-cut, often elasticated, necklines, usually made of lightweight and brightly colored fabrics. Scarves wound around the neck or waist are another dominant feature of gypsy-style dress. In 1959 Jules François CRAHAY produced a gypsy collection and in the early 1970s Thea *PORTER and Caroline *CHARLES created dresses and two-piece outfits based on gypsy costume.

H

hacking jacket Fitted, single-breasted jacket which is flared from the waist and has a single back vent. It has been worn since the 19th century for horse riding and was adapted as a fashion garment during the latter half of the 20th century.

Halston's silk jersey halter-neck jumpsuit and suede jacket from 1972.

Halston 1932–. Designer. Born Roy Halston Frowick in Des Moines, Iowa, USA. Halston attended the University of Indiana and the Chicago Institute. In 1953 he opened a millinery salon in a Chicago hotel and included among his clients Gloria Swanson and Deborah Kerr. In 1958, Halston joined Lilly DACHÉ in New York. He moved shortly after to the millinery salon of Bergdorf Goodman's New York department store. Halston designed many hats for Jacqueline Kennedy (ONASSIS), including a beige felt PILLBOX HAT which was widely copied. In 1966 he began designing ready-to-wear garments, leaving Bergdorf Goodman to open his own business. During the late 1960s and 1970s Halston established a reputation as a designer of knitwear, SWEATERS and wide-legged jersey pants, TURTLENECKS, long slinky HALTER-NECK dresses, cashmere dresses for day and evening, sweater sets, and boxy, square jackets and coats. He also tie-dyed chiffon and used matte jersey in many of his collections. In 1972 he made a SHIRTWAIST of ultrasuede, which was widely copied. Halston has designed costumes for the Dance Theatre of Harlem and for Martha Graham. American socialites patronize him as an eveningwear designer.

halter neck High panel on the front of a dress or blouse which is tied around the back of the neck, leaving the back and shoulders exposed. The halter neck was very popular during the 1930s for evening and beach attire. *See* *HALSTON.

Hamnett, Katharine 1948–. Designer. Born in Gravesend, Kent, England. Hamnett attended Cheltenham Ladies College and St. Martins School of Art in London. She graduated in 1970 and increased her freelance design commissions working for British, French, Italian, and Hong Kong firms. In 1979 she established her own business and has subsequently become a popular and innovative designer, notably on the British and Italian markets. Many of her garments are based on the workwear of different countries which she adapts to fashionable clothing. A supporter of the peace movement, she produced in 1984 over-size T-SHIRTS printed with anti-war slogans.

handbag *See* PURSE.

handkerchief A highly fashionable accessory during the 19th century, the handkerchief was an embroidered, lace-edged square of cambric, linen, muslin, or silk. In the 20th century, the handkerchief generally has a purely functional purpose, though there are vogues in almost every decade for a decorative handkerchief tucked into a breast pocket of a coat or jacket.

handkerchief dress Tunic dress composed of large square pieces of fabric with deep borders, trimmed to match the main dress. A style briefly popular during the 1880s.

handkerchief points Zigzag hem of a skirt or dress composed of deep V points similar to one of the corners of a handkerchief. A periodically popular style during the 20th century, notably in the late 1960s and early 1970s.

Handley-Seymour, Mrs. Dressmaker who founded a business in London shortly before World War I. She received a Royal Warrant and was extremely popular during the 1920s and 1930s. Queen Mary was her most famous client.

haori Loose, knee-length, long-sleeved coat originating in Japan. The shape has been adapted to fashion trends during the 20th century.

Hardwick, Cathy 1933–. Designer. Born Kasuk Surh in Seoul, Korea. Hardwick studied music in Japan before moving in the 1960s to the USA, where she opened a BOUTIQUE in San Francisco. She later moved to New York and started a firm in 1972. Hardwick designs adventurous, middle-range, ready-to-wear clothing under her own name. She is especially noted for her creative handling of silk.

harem pants Full, ankle-length divided skirt or pants based upon the trousers worn by Turkish women. They are pleated or gathered into a band at the ankle. Harem pants first became popular when the BALLETS RUSSES appeared in Europe in the early 1900s. They were worn as eveningwear in the early 20th century, reaching the height of their popularity in the 1930s.

harem skirt *See* HAREM PANTS.

Haring, Keith 1962–. Artist. Born in Kutztown, Pennsylvania. Haring spent two years at Manhattan's School of Visual Arts. In December 1980 he started to draw groups of small white figures on billboards in Manhattan subway stations. The figures, which resembled the outlines of cookie-cutters, attracted so much attention that in the early 1980s Haring began to use them on T-SHIRTS, buttons, and garments. Clothes painted with Haring's figures soon became collectors' items.

Harp, Holly 1939–. Designer. Born in Buffalo, New York, USA. Harp studied art and costume design at North Texas State University and after graduating opened a BOUTIQUE in Los Angeles in 1968. Her collections were sold at the New York department store Henri Bendel in 1972. The following year Harp began manufacturing her own clothes. She is known for her theatrical, nostalgic creations of hand-printed silk and matte jersey, and her ultra-soft fabrics. Many of her designs have a flowing, romantic appeal.

Perfect for the tango, deep bordered **handkerchief dresses** of *c.* 1910 like this one allowed women to move freely without showing too much leg.

Harem pants in the 1930s, with cuffed and buttoned ankle.

Harper's Bazaar In 1867 Fletcher Harper of the US publishers Harper Brothers launched *Harper's Bazar*, a women's magazine covering the home and fashion. It was published weekly until 1901, when it became monthly. In 1913 *Harper's Bazar* was bought by the Hearst publishing empire and in 1929 the second "a" was added to "Bazar." A widely influential magazine, never more so than when under the editorship of Carmel SNOW, *Harper's Bazaar* promoted fashion design, photography, and illustration. It was in direct competition with American VOGUE for most of the 20th century.

Harris tweed Soft, thick, tweed originally handloomed from woolen yarns dyed with vegetable dye by the inhabitants of the Scottish Outer Hebrides Islands of Barra, Harris, Lewis, and Uist. The tweed was exported to the mainland during the 1840s and since that time has been used to make coats, jackets, and suits for men and women.

Hartnell, (Sir) **Norman** (Bishop) 1901–79. Designer. Born in London, England. After leaving Cambridge University without a degree, Hartnell began designing clothes. In 1923 he worked briefly with LUCILE before opening his own premises in London. He showed his first collection in Paris in 1927, followed by a second, highly acclaimed, collection in 1930. He was appointed dressmaker to the British Royal Family in 1938 and designed gowns for their overseas visits. Hartnell made clothes for the Queen Mother as well as Queen Elizabeth II's wedding and going-away dress and, in 1953, her Coronation gown. He also created dresses for many actresses.

Norman **Hartnell**'s historic coronation dress for Queen Elizabeth II, embroidered with the emblems of Great Britain and the Commonwealth.

Hartnell gained a reputation for his imaginative use of satin, tulle, EMBROIDERY, and trimmings on evening gowns, BALL GOWNS, and wedding dresses. He was also known for his tailored suits, coats, and woolen tweed garments. From 1942, Hartnell produced ready-to-wear lines and he designed for Berketex from the late 1940s. He was knighted in 1977.

haute couture The French word *couture* means sewing or needlework. *Haute couture* is high quality fashion design and construction. The designer or *couturier* (*couturière*) creates models from a *toile*, made in fine linen or muslin, which bears his or her name. Garments based on the *toile* are then made up. The Syndicat de la Couture Parisienne (now the CHAMBRE SYNDICALE DE LA HAUTE COUTURE) was a union of dress designers founded in Paris in 1868 to prevent designs being plagiarized. *Haute couture* relies heavily on a large group of specialists, who make buttons, gloves, costume jewelry, millinery, and trimmings to a high level of workmanship. *Haute couture* is labor-intensive and costly. By the end of the 1950s many couture houses had closed, making way for inexpensive ready-to-wear lines from manufacturers. In the second half of the 20th century some couturiers have licensed manufacturers to use their names on cosmetics, perfume bottles, jewelry, stockings, and general fashion and household accessories. The extent of a couturier's design input and fee or royalties depends on each individual contract.

Hawaiian shirt Man's oversized shirt printed with brightly colored designs of fruit, flowers, exotic birds, and dancing girls. Hawaiian shirts were made popular by US tourists returning from Hawaii in the 1950s. Also known as aloha shirt.

Hawes, Elizabeth 1903–71. Designer. Born in New Jersey, USA. Hawes studied at Vassar College and at Parsons School of Design in New York City. In 1925 she went to Paris where she worked for several years as a sketcher at fashion shows. Macy's and Lord & Taylor, the New York department stores, appointed her their Paris based stylist. In 1928 she returned to New York and opened her own business. Hawes's clothes were simple and soft, and followed natural proportions. She became well known with the publication of her first book, *Fashion is Spinach* (1938).

Head, Edith 1899–1981. Costume designer. Born in Los Angeles, California, USA. Head graduated from Stanford University and the University of California, and then continued her studies at the Otis Institute and Chouinard Art School in Los Angeles. In 1923 she worked for Howard GREER at Paramount Pictures in Hollywood. After a spell as Travis BANTON's assistant in 1927, she was made head designer of the studio in 1938, a position she held until 1967. In the late 1960s she worked for Universal Films. During her time at Paramount, Head also designed for films made by Metro-Goldwyn-Mayer, Columbia, 20th Century Fox, and Warner Bros. She has over one thousand screen credits to her name. Mae West, Marlene Dietrich, Elizabeth Taylor, and Grace Kelly are among the actresses for whom she designed. In 1936 Head's *SARONG for Dorothy Lamour in *The Jungle Princess* was widely copied. In 1951 she created a strapless evening dress with a fitted BODICE covered with white violets and a skirt made of white tulle over green satin. This dress, which Elizabeth Taylor wore in *A Place in the Sun*, was copied

Elizabeth Taylor and Montgomery Clift in *A Place in the Sun* (1951). Taylor wears a dress by Edith **Head** which became widely popular.

throughout the United States. Head helped to popularize South American clothes, in particular the Spanish *camisa* (shirt), *rebozo* (scarf), and PONCHO.

headband *See* BANDEAU.

headscarf Square piece of fabric, folded into a triangle, which is worn over the head and tied under the chin. It was popular for sporting activities from the 1920s until the 1960s, when it somewhat faded from fashion. *See* *HERMES.

Hechter, Daniel 1938–. Designer. Born in Paris, France. Hechter's father owned a ready-to-wear clothing company. Hechter worked for Pierre d'Alby from 1958 before opening his own house in 1962. His first designs were ready-to-wear separates for young girls. He produced RAINCOATS, SWEATERS, and military-style MAXI coats. In 1964 he showed PANTS SUITS and smoking jackets; in 1966 gabardine khaki raincoats; in 1967 boot-top-length divided skirts and fur coats with leather strips; in 1968 ribbed DUFFLE COATS; and in the 1970s jersey wool greatcoats. Hechter's skill lies in his outerwear—sporty yet sophisticated jackets, BLAZERS, and coats, for both men and women.

heel-less shoes First introduced in the late 1950s and early 1960s, the heel-less shoe was a sculptured wedge with a cutaway heel and extended sole.

Heim, Jacques 1899–1967. Designer. Born in Paris, France. In 1923 Heim took over the furrier business started by his parents in 1898. He designed women's clothing for the firm until the 1930s, when he established a new company. Heim is one of the designers who has been credited with the introduction and promotion of the BIKINI. He produced several beachwear collections, one featuring a draped BATHING SUIT. Heim popularized cotton for beachwear when he used the fabric for a couture collection. An original, inventive designer whose efforts are largely ignored today, Heim opened a chain of BOUTIQUES selling SPORTSWEAR between 1946 and 1966.

Helanca Tradename for a crimped stretch yarn of the Heberlein Patent Corporation, used since the mid-20th century in fabrics that are required to stretch.

helmet Close-fitting cap with sides that cover the ears. Popularized by André COURREGES in the 1960s. *See* *SPACE AGE.

Hepburn, Audrey 1929–. Actress. Born Edda Hepburn van Heemstra in Brussels, Belgium. Hepburn trained as a dancer in London in 1951 but achieved fame in the 1950s as an actress. Her GAMINE looks—small, slight figure and elfin haircut and face—were accentuated by her clothes: black TURTLENECK PULLOVER, PEDAL PUSHERS or CAPRI PANTS, and flat CAPEZIO PUMPS. She also popularized a mode of wearing a shirt (often over a SWEATER) with the ends unbuttoned and tied in the front at waist level. Her best-known films are *Funny Face* (1957), *Breakfast at Tiffany's* (1961), and *My Fair Lady* (1964).

Hepburn, Katharine 1907–. Actress. Born in Hartford, Connecticut, USA. After graduating from Bryn Mawr in 1928, Hepburn

The Kelly bag, made by **Hermès** and named after American actress Grace Kelly, who became Princess Grace of Monaco.

Hermès headscarf from 1969 (Le Débouché).

began her acting career playing on Broadway. In the 1930s she moved to Hollywood. Hepburn is a highly respected actress of both stage and screen. To many Americans she represents the ideal free-spirited woman, almost always wearing pants and little or no make up. Her casual, sporty elegance has been widely influential since the 1930s.

Herbert, Victor 1944–. Designer. Born in Leicester, England. Herbert studied at Loughborough College of Art from 1961 to 1965 before moving to London's Royal College of Art. He graduated in 1968 and began work as a freelance designer for a number of companies and designers, notably Bruce OLDFIELD. In 1977 he opened his own SPORTSWEAR company but continues to work freelance for manufacturers.

Hermès The Hermès company dates from 1837, when a saddler, Thierry Hermès, opened a shop in Paris selling moneybelts, GAUNTLETS, GLOVES, and BOOTS. In the 1920s his grandson, Emile, began designing garments made from deerskin. The company's main concern lies with the production of hand crafted leather goods, though it has become famous for two items: equestrian motif headscarves and the "Kelly" bag. The latter, based on a saddle bag, was first launched in 1935. In 1955, it was named after the actress Grace Kelly, who was frequently seen with one.

Herrera, Carolina 1939–. Designer. Born Maria Carolina Josefina Pacanins y Nino in Caracas, Venezuela. After years on the US list of Best-Dressed Women, Herrera established her first ready-to-wear collection in April 1981. A New York based designer, she produced a collection of layered clothes which used a variety of fabrics in different lengths. She made the transition with ease to the slimmer styles of the mid-1980s and has become known for her elegant day- and eveningwear.

herringbone Pattern which resembles the skeletal structure of a herring, its zigzag effect produced by a broken twill weave. Herringbone has been popular since the 19th century for outer garments, suits, coats, and skirts.

Diagonal stripes of silver and gold wrap around the sleek evening silhouette in a 1982 silk crêpe gown by Carolina **Herrera**.

The fashionable **hippy**, complete with bed roll, returns from a pop concert in 1970.

Bakst drawing of his own design for a **hobble skirt** made by Paquin and published in a 1913 edition of *La Gazette du bon ton*.

hippy Nineteen sixties successor to the beatnik. Hippies often grew their hair long, walked barefoot, and wore colorful (often old) clothes and accessories. In the 1970s many designers copied hippy fashions, such as PATCHWORK skirts and coats; long, flowing, flounced skirts; and PSYCHEDELIC patterns and prints.

hipster Style of skirt or pants first introduced in the 1960s. Hipsters were cut to fit snugly around the hips where they were often held in place by a large, wide belt.

H-line Introduced by Christian DIOR in 1954, this dress style pushed the bust up as high as possible and dropped the waist to hip-level, creating the cross bar of the letter H. It was most evident in Dior's designs for eveningwear.

hobble skirt Skirt style introduced by Paul POIRET in the pre-World War I years. The material was cut and draped to narrow severely at some point between the knee and the ankle. At its narrow section, it was often encircled by a band which stretched downward from the knee. The skirt allowed only the briefest of steps to be taken and was denounced by the Pope, satirized by cartoonists, and made the subject of fierce public debate.

Holah, David 1958–. Designer. Born in London, England. Holah took a foundation course at North Oxfordshire College of Art before studying at Middlesex Polytechnic from 1979 to 1982. After graduating he formed BODY MAP with designer Stevie STEWART.

homburg Tyrolean style felt hat made in Homburg in the early 19th century. Like the FEDORA, the homburg had a high crown with a deep crease across the middle. A dark band of fabric is sewn around the base of the crown.

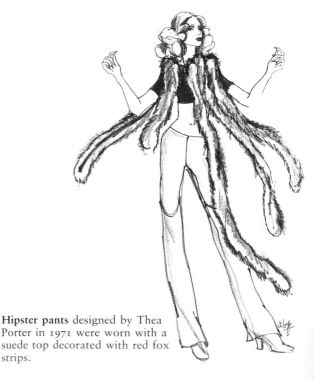

Hipster pants designed by Thea Porter in 1971 were worn with a suede top decorated with red fox strips.

Honiton lace Lace made in Honiton, Devon, England. The lace making industry was established in Honiton in the late 16th century. In 1839 Honiton lace was used for Queen Victoria's wedding dress and subsequently became fashionable for the remainder of the 19th century. It is adorned with motifs from nature, particularly flowers, and is made on a net background that is often spotted.

horseshoe collar Deep, U-shaped collar which appeared on blouses and suit jackets from the early 1950s. *See* DIOR *and* GALANOS.

Horst P(aul) Horst 1906–. Photographer. Born in Weissenfels, Germany. Horst studied architecture at the Kunstgewerbeschule in Hamburg from 1926 to 1928 and briefly with Le Corbusier in Paris in 1930. He posed for photographer George HOYNINGEN-HUENE and subsequently became his pupil. French VOGUE employed Horst as a photographer in 1932. Three years later, Horst emigrated to the USA. He served in the US Army in World War II and returned to a career in photography in 1946. Fashion pictures and portraits of society people are Horst's speciality. He uses elaborate settings and props, often taking pictures against blown-up backgrounds to create crowded but dramatic photographs. He is famous for the technical excellence of his lighting.

The timeless **homburg**, shown here in 1902.

hot-pants Very brief SHORTS, often made of velvet, which were sometimes trimmed with embroidery or beads. The name "hot-pants" was coined by WOMEN'S WEAR DAILY in 1970.

hound's-tooth Cloth with even, broken checks woven into it. Popular since the late 19th century for outerwear, jackets, skirts, and pants.

hourglass Shape associated with late 19th- and early 20th-century women, who wore constricting corsets which pulled in the waist and pushed out the hips and bust. The silhouette was revived in DIOR's NEW LOOK of 1947. *See also* S-BEND SILHOUETTE.

housecoat Loose, long-sleeved coat made of luxurious fabrics and worn around the house. It usually buttons or zips to a high neckline. The housecoat was popular between 1930 and the end of the 1960s.

Howell, Margaret 1946–. Designer. Born in Tadworth, Surrey, England. Howell attended Goldsmith's College, London, from 1966 to 1970. In 1971 she created a range of accessories followed in 1972 by a range of clothes. Two years later Howell established her own company and at the same time began working with Joseph. Shortly afterward she opened a retail outlet. Howell specializes in classic ready-to-wear garments created by adapting traditional styles and fabrics into fashion shapes. She favors pinstripes and suiting materials—wool, tweed, and melton—which she makes into up-to-the-minute riding jackets, TUXEDO suits, and tailored blouses. Her silhouettes are usually elongated and soft.

Hoyningen-Huene, George 1900–68. Photographer. Born in St. Petersburg, Russia. Hoyningen-Huene was educated in St. Petersburg and Yalta before attending an art course at the Académie de la Grande Chaumière, Paris, from 1919 to 1920. He studied with Cubist painter André Lhote from 1922 to 1924. In the early 1920s Hoyningen-Huene worked in Paris as a sketcher for many magazines, including HARPER'S BAZAAR, JARDIN DES MODES, and

High collared velvet cloak and leather gauntlets designed by Barbara **Hulanicki** for Biba, 1970.

VOGUE. In 1926 he became chief photographer of French *Vogue* but he worked for other Condé NAST publications in Europe and New York before emigrating to the USA in 1935. For the next ten years he was a staff fashion photographer at *Harper's Bazaar*, under editor Carmel SNOW and art director Alexey BRODOVITCH. In 1946 he moved to Hollywood to work in the film industry as a color coordinator. Hoyningen-Huene was influenced by Classical Greek art, posing statuesque models in sophisticated settings to resemble a tableau or frieze. He created rich, tonal effects, was famous for his clear, ethereal lighting, and was one of the first photographers to take pictures of models from above, arranging their skirts about them like an open fan. Hoyningen-Huene was among the 20th-century's most prolific chroniclers of fashion and society.

Hulanicki, Barbara 1936–. Designer. Born in Palestine of Polish parents. Hulanicki moved to England in 1948, attended school in

Worthing, Sussex, and later went to Brighton Art College. In 1955 she won a beachwear design competition in the *Evening Standard*, a London newspaper. Hulanicki left college during her second year and joined a London company of commercial artists. She illustrated fashions for major newspapers and for women's magazines, including VOGUE and the *Tatler*, and also worked for the London office of WOMEN'S WEAR DAILY. In 1961 she married Stephen Fitz-Simon. Two years later the couple started Biba's mail-order boutique with an offer for a skirt in the *Daily Express*. A more successful offer of a pink gingham dress in the *Daily Mirror* a year later, in 1964, prompted the opening of Biba, a BOUTIQUE in London's Kensington. Here Hulanicki sold her own designs— brown SMOCKS with KERCHIEFS, MINI skirts and dresses, and T-SHIRTS dyed in many different colors. Her tight-sleeved, high-fashion, inexpensive clothes were attractive to a wide, predominantly young, market. So successful was the venture that Hulanicki and her husband opened two more stores. The name Biba became synonymous with floppy, felt cut-out hats, vamp dresses, PANTS SUITS, T-SHIRTS with SWEETHEART NECKLINES, billowing crêpe dresses, MOB CAPS and ankle-length SMOCKS, JERKIN suits in ribbed rayon, and cotton BIKINIS with matching jackets. The most famous Biba store, in Kensington High Street, was decorated in nostalgic 1930s style, with dim lighting, black walls, velvet couches, and bowls of feather plumes. As part of the London youth trend of the 1960s, it attracted visitors from all over the world who bought and copied the clothes and accessories. In 1973 Biba took over an entire department store in Kensington, but the Biba style failed to make a successful transition into the 1970s. *See* col. pl.

husky Sleeved or sleeveless, padded, usually nylon jacket which closes at the front with snap fasteners or a zipper. Worn by SLOANE RANGERS.

I

ikat Silk fabrics which are made in Java and Sumatra, Indonesia.

I. Magnin In 1870 Mary Ann Magnin left London for San Francisco with her husband and eight children. She began working as a seamstress and her husband, Isaac, sold the clothes she made from a backpack. In 1876 Magnin opened a store, which she named after her late husband, selling blouses, dresses, and bridal trousseau. The first I. Magnin branch was opened in Los Angeles in 1893. I. Magnin stores have continued to sell clothing on the West Coast of the USA.

intarsia Design fitted into certain parts of a SWEATER, such as the neckline or cuffs. *See* FAIR ISLE.

Irene 1907–62. Costume designer. Born Irene Lentz in Brookings, South Dakota, USA. Irene studied at the Wolfe School of Design in Los Angeles, California, and then opened a dress shop which was

Detail of **ikat** textile.

patronized by Hollywood stars. In 1933 she became head of the Bullocks Wilshire Costume Design Salon in Hollywood, where she created on- and off-screen clothes for actresses. Irene designed freelance from 1938 to 1942, when she was appointed head designer for Metro-Goldwyn-Mayer. Throughout her career Irene produced costumes for more than 260 films made by Metro-Goldwyn-Mayer, Paramount, RKO, United Artists, and Columbia Pictures. Her clients included Judy Garland, Greer Garson, Hedy Lamarr, and Lana Turner. Irene was particularly noted for her softly tailored suits.

Iribe, Paul 1883–1935. Illustrator. Born Paul Iribarnegaray in Angoulême, France. Iribe was educated in Paris where, in his early twenties, he became an apprentice printer at *Le Temps* newspaper. From 1900 Iribe submitted illustrations to such French satirical papers as *Rire, Sourire,* and *L'Assiette au beurre.* He became a celebrated fashion illustrator in 1908 when Paul POIRET, who was looking for an artist to present his clothes in an original manner, asked him to compile a promotional brochure. The resulting *Les Robes de Paul Poiret* was widely influential both in terms of fashion and of illustrative style. Iribe's illustrations were clean, crisp, and balanced. He kept background objects to a minimum and concentrated on the stylish outline and witty detail of the garments. A contributor to VOGUE and FEMINA, Iribe also designed advertisements for PAQUIN and the house of CALLOT, perfume bottles, fabrics for BIANCHINI-FERIER, and furniture and interiors. Iribe spent six years in Hollywood working on film costumes and theatrical interiors for Paramount. Returning to Paris in 1928, he divided his time between contributing satirical illustrations to the weekly political paper *Le Témoin* and designing jewelry for CHANEL.

Iris *See* PEDLAR.

Ivy League Style of dress worn by students and graduates of US East Coast colleges. For men, the outfit usually comprises a grey flannel suit with a narrow-shouldered, loose-waisted jacket, a white shirt with a button-down collar, narrow striped TIE, CAMEL-HAIR coat or a CHESTERFIELD, and heavy-soled OXFORD shoes. Women wear a cashmere TWINSET with a KILT or tweed skirt, BLAZER, SHETLAND sweater, pearl necklace, and BROGUE shoes. In summer, woolens are replaced by LIBERTY print or madras blouses (often with PETER PAN collars), BERMUDA SHORTS or a flannel skirt, and PUMPS. *See also* BROOKS BROTHERS, LAUREN, *and* PREPPIE.

J

jabot Decorative frill of lace or other delicate fabric pinned at the chest or base of the neck. Originally a 16th-century item of male dress, the jabot was popular with women from the mid-19th century until the 1920s and 1930s.

Doucet's patron, the actress
Réjane, wearing an astrakhan and
sequin jacket and lace **jabot**.

Jackson, Betty 1940–. Designer. Born in Backup, Lancashire, England. Jackson attended Birmingham College of Art from 1968 to 1971. She then worked in London as a freelance illustrator until 1973, when she joined Wendy DAGWORTHY. In 1975 Jackson moved to the Quorum company, where she worked until 1979. The next two years she spent with Coopers. Since 1981 she has produced collections under her own name and has swiftly achieved an international reputation as a designer of young, up-to-the-minute clothes. She rescales separates into different, often larger, proportions and makes them up in boldly colored and patterned fabrics.

Jacob, Mary Phelps Better known as Caresse Crosby, who in 1914 patented a design for a *BRA, known as the Backless Bra. WARNERS bought the patent in the same year.

Jacobson, Jacqueline *See* DOROTHEE BIS.

jacquard Decorative weave created by a jacquard loom and used for brocades and damasks since the mid-19th century. *See* JACQUARD, Joseph-Marie.

Jacquard, Joseph-Marie 1752–1834. Frenchman who developed an attachment for machine powered looms which created elaborate weaves in fabric. *See* JACQUARD.

Jaeger In the 1880s Dr. Gustav Jaeger, Professor of Zoology and Physiology at the University of Stuttgart, campaigned for what he believed to be the benefits to health of wearing wool next to the skin. Inspired by Jaeger's studies and experiments, Lewis Tomalin, the London manager of a wholesale grocery firm, secured the rights,

Jaeger advertised jumpers like this one in its 1926 catalog.

patents, and Jaeger name. In 1884 Tomalin began manufacturing 100 percent wool sanitary underwear: CHEMISES, combinations, DRAWERS, and PETTICOATS in undyed sheep's wool or camel hair wool. In the 1900s Jaeger expanded its operations to include the manufacture of CARDIGANS, DRESSING GOWNS, gymnastic SWEATERS, knitted JUMPER suits, and laceknit SHAWLS. During the 1920s, fashion demanded lighter, more practical undergarments and Jaeger's lines were no longer popular. The company produced instead its own fashionable clothing line, including coats, skirts, SLACKS, and TWINSETS. Many of the garments were made of wool. In the second half of the 20th century Jaeger has been recognized as a fashion company selling good quality dresses, coats, suits, and knitwear to an international market.

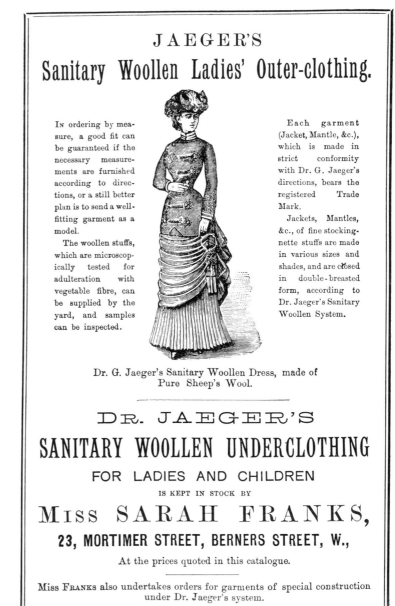

JAEGER'S
Sanitary Woollen Ladies' Outer-clothing.

IN ordering by measure, a good fit can be guaranteed if the necessary measurements are furnished according to directions, or a still better plan is to send a well-fitting garment as a model.

The woollen stuffs, which are microscopically tested for adulteration with vegetable fibre, can be supplied by the yard, and samples can be inspected.

Each garment (Jacket, Mantle, &c.), which is made in strict conformity with Dr. G. Jaeger's directions, bears the registered Trade Mark.

Jackets, Mantles, &c., of fine stockingnette stuffs are made in various sizes and shades, and are closed in double-breasted form, according to Dr. Jaeger's Sanitary Woollen System.

Dr. G. Jaeger's Sanitary Woollen Dress, made of Pure Sheep's Wool.

DR. JAEGER'S
SANITARY WOOLLEN UNDERCLOTHING
FOR LADIES AND CHILDREN
IS KEPT IN STOCK BY
MISS SARAH FRANKS,
23, MORTIMER STREET, BERNERS STREET, W.,
At the prices quoted in this catalogue.

MISS FRANKS also undertakes orders for garments of special construction under Dr. Jaeger's system.

In 1884, **Jaeger** was best known for its "sanitary" woolen clothing.

James, Charles (William Brega) 1906–78. Designer. Born in Sandhurst, England. James was educated at Harrow school and briefly attended the University of Bordeaux before being sent to Chicago by his family to work for a utilities magnate. James resigned almost immediately and in 1924 he opened a hat shop. Three years later he moved to New York and took up dress designing, showing his first collection in 1928. The following year James began commuting between London and New York. His designs are so timeless that his 1932 CULOTTES for the New York department store Lord & Taylor were still being sold in the 1950s. In 1934 and 1935 James worked in Paris under the patronage of Paul POIRET, designing fabrics for French textile manufacturers Colcombet. New York became James's base from 1939 until 1947 and during part of that period he designed clothes for Elizabeth Arden's salon. Returning to Europe at the end of the 1940s, James showed one of his most successful collections in Paris in 1947. He spent most of the 1950s in New York. James looked upon his dresses as works of art, as did many of his customers. Year after year he reworked original designs, ignoring the sacrosanct schedule of seasons. The components of the precisely constructed designs were interchangeable so that James had a never-ending fund of ideas from which to draw. He is most famous for his sculpted BALL GOWNS made in lavish fabrics and to exacting tailoring standards, but is also remembered for his CAPES and coats, often trimmed with fur and embroidery; his spiral zipped dresses; and his white satin quilted jackets. James retired in 1958.

A Cecil Beaton photograph of Charles **James** dresses in 1948. The tableau scene is one of Beaton's hallmarks. James's dresses suit the painterly quality of the photograph.

Japanese Since Japan opened its doors to the Western world in the 19th century, it has been a source of inspiration to many designers. The first major Japanese garment to be exported and widely copied was the KIMONO, though much is lost in the West of the symbolism and structure of the original. Japanese dress is concerned with ritual and tradition, with concealing rather than revealing the body, and with the dimensions between the body and the robe. By the early 1970s, several Japanese designers had established themselves in Paris. Hanae MORI used the traditional kimono as a basis for elegant eveningwear. Issey MIYAKE and KENZO concentrated on textiles and experimented with the relationship between Eastern and Western dress, mixing Japanese traditions with European ideas. In the late 1970s a different breed of designer came from Japan to Europe. Kansai YAMAMOTO, Yohji YAMAMOTO, and Rei KAWAKUBO of COMME DES GARCONS settled in Paris and proceeded to turn the fashion world upside down. Through their clothes they reflected an attitude toward dressing—almost an anti-fashion style—which was less concerned with dressing for occasion and season and more involved with constant adaptation of traditional Japanese dress. For the most part they ignored the Western stress on a sleek, proportioned body shape and focused on the creation of alternative dimensions and texture. Garments were cut away and slashed in strategic places to emphasize proportions and color; either drab, dark colors or boldly patterned mixtures dominated over the structure. Japanese influences on fashion, through these and other designers, have contributed to a greater flexibility in dressing. Western designers have begun to create more relaxed garments which, in Japanese style, concentrate on the flow and drape of the fabric.

Jardin des modes, Le Monthly magazine, with many supplements, first published in 1922 by Lucien VOGEL. It is one of the most prominent fashion journals in France.

Jeanmaire, Zizi (Renée) 1924–. Dancer. Born in Paris, France. Jeanmaire became famous with the Ballets de Paris company in 1949 in its production of *Carmen*. She starred in the film *Hans Christian Anderson* (1951) and in the Broadway musical *The Girl in Pink Tights* (1953). Throughout the 1950s Jeanmaire epitomized the GAMINE style, with her short, boyish haircut and slender figure.

jeans From *Gênes*, the French for Genoa, Italy, a port where sailors wore sturdy work pants. Jeans is a strong cotton cloth originally loomed in Nîmes, France, and is also the name for pants made from that cloth. During the 1850s, Levi *STRAUSS introduced denim jeans in San Francisco, California, as work wear for goldminers. They became fashionable in the 1950s in the USA. Since then jeans have been made in a variety of styles: narrow or baggy; HIPSTERS and BELL BOTTOMS; stitched with flowers or patched; tailored and stretch. Whatever the style or cut, the indigo blue fabric is still associated with casual wear. *See* DENIM.

Jenny House opened in Paris in 1911 by Jenny Sacerdote, who had trained at PAQUIN. The house was famous with Europeans and Americans for elegant, aristocratic outfits. Its popularity waned during the 1930s and it closed in 1938.

jerkin Hip-length garment, with or without sleeves, which fastens at the side or shoulders. It is often cut with slits at the sides. A popular garment in the mid-20th century. *See also* TABARD.

Spring 1922 design by **Jenny**, featuring the low waist of the period.

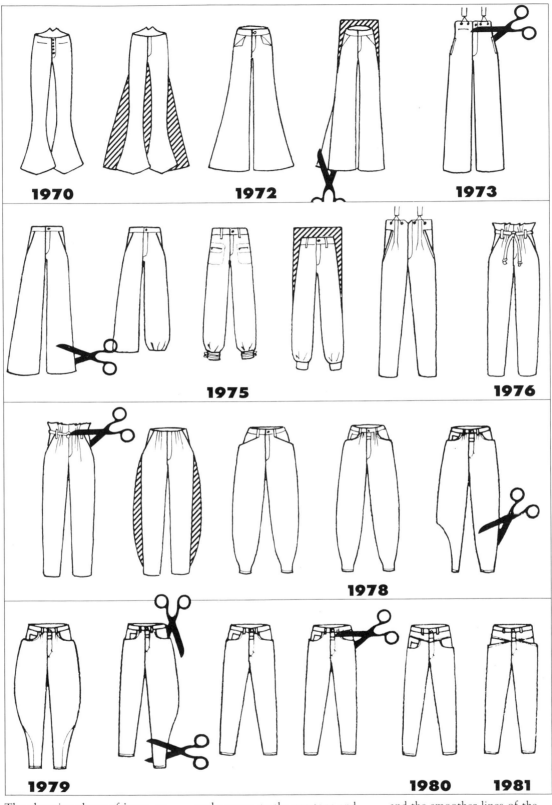

1970 **1972** **1973**

1975 **1976**

1978

1979 **1980** **1981**

The changing shape of **jeans**, as seen by the Girbauds: from the bell bottoms and flares of the early 1970s, to the peg tops and cuffed ankles of the mid 1970s, to the baggy jeans of the late 1970s and the smoother lines of the early 1980s.

jersey 1. Soft, stretchable knitted fabric first used on the Channel Island of Jersey in the late 19th century for sportswear and outer garments. Jersey is associated with the actress Lillie LANGTRY ("The Jersey Lily") who helped popularize its use. In the 1920s it was made up into dresses and two-piece suits and was the most fashionable fabric of the period. In the 20th century it is made of cotton, nylon, rayon, wool, and synthetic fibers. 2. Type of thick, knitted SWEATER originally worn by fishermen. *See* JERSEY COSTUME.

jersey costume In the 1870s, Lillie LANGTRY, the Edwardian actress, popularized a finely knitted silk or wool garment that clung to the figure to the mid-thigh, where it was swathed around the knees and worn over a flannel or serge skirt. Known as a jersey costume, it fastened at the back and was worn for sporting activities.

jet Dense form of black lignite coal obtained from decomposed driftwood found at Whitby on the Yorkshire coast of England. Although it has been known since Roman times, jet did not become popular until the 19th century, when it was associated with mourning jewelry. It was most fashionable in the 1870s and 1880s, at which time it was made into lockets, pendants, brooches, and bracelets, elaborately cut into fruit, flower, and animal designs.

Retail department of a **jet** workshop in England in the 19th century.

jodphurs Riding breeches, taking their name from a former state in north west India. Jodphurs are very full from the hip to the knee, billowing out at the sides in a semicircle, and skintight from knee to

ankle. They are finished either with a cuff or with a piece of fabric that goes under the foot. They were briefly fashionable during the 1950s.

jogging suit *See* TRACKSUIT.

John, Augustus 1878–1961. Painter. Born in Tenby, Wales. Portrait painter who inspired a Bohemian clothing style worn in London's Chelsea during the 1920s. John's long CLOAKS, wide black hats, and homespun garments were imitated by many young men, while women copied the SANDALS, GYPSY-like HEADSCARVES, and ankle-length flowing skirts of John's wife, Dorelia.

Johnson, Betsey (Lee) 1942–. Designer. Born in Hartford, Connecticut, USA. Johnson spent a year at the Pratt Institute in Brooklyn, New York, before graduating from Syracuse University in 1964. In that year she was guest editor on the summer college issue of *Mademoiselle* and was hired by the magazine for one year after graduation. During that year she made and sold clothing designs in her spare time and later became a freelance designer, retailing through Paraphernalia, a New York BOUTIQUE. In the 1960s Johnson gained a reputation as a radical young designer, producing chalk-striped "gangster" PANTS SUITS, a clear vinyl dress sold with paste-your-own star motifs, a "noise" dress made of jersey with loose grommets attached to the hem, silvery motorcycle suits, clinging T-SHIRT dresses, and a wrapped cowhide MINI SKIRT dress which was worn with thigh-high leather boots. In 1969 she opened a New York boutique called "Betsey, Bunky, and Mini." In the 1970s Johnson turned to DISCO wear and showed extravagant, body-conscious clothes for the dance floor, many made up in stretch jersey. She opened her own SPORTSWEAR business in 1978.

Jones, Stephen 1957–. Milliner. Born in West Kirby, Liverpool, England. Jones studied at High Wycombe School of Art, Buckinghamshire, from 1975 to 1976 before joining St. Martin's School of Art in London from which he graduated in 1979. After a brief period with the house of LACHASSE, Jones opened his own business in September 1980. He created hats for many stars in the pop music world. French designers Jean-Paul GAULTIER and Thierry MUGLER and British designers Benny ONG and Zandra RHODES have commissioned Jones to design millinery for their collections. Jones's hats are authoritatively executed, invariably witty, and often outrageous.

Journal des dames et des modes, Le Trimonthly journal published in Paris from 1912 to 1914, which contained copperplate fashion illustrations and articles on literature, the theater, fashion, and the arts. It was based on a journal of the same name which appeared from 1798 to 1839. Contributing artists included BAKST, BARBIER, Pierre Brissaud, BRUNELLESCHI, DRIAN, IRIBE, and MARTIN.

Jourdan, Charles Company started in 1921 as a shoe workshop by Charles Jourdan, at Romans, in the Drôme region of France. The business prospered, particularly in sales of women's shoes. After World War II Jourdan was joined by his three sons and in 1957 they opened a BOUTIQUE in Paris. In 1959 the House of DIOR granted the company a licence to design and manufacture Dior shoes. Jourdan's designs are up-to-the-minute. In the late 1960s and early 1970s the company created an avant-garde image for itself by using the

Riding breeches in 1921 became everyday wear **jodhpurs** in the 1980s.

The adventurous **jumpsuit** of 1979.

Right: Charles **Jourdan**'s hot favorite, Madly, for 1972.

Far right: Maxime, which became one of **Jourdan**'s most popular shoes, designed in 1958.

surrealist photographer Guy BOURDIN for its advertising campaign. During this period the company sold vast quantities of two notable styles: "Maxime," a low-heeled, square-toed COURT shoe with a satin bow, and "Madly," a thick-heeled PLATFORM SHOE with a high vamp in red or black patent leather. The firm also makes Pierre CARDIN and Xavier Danaud shoes, among others.

Juliet cap Small, round cap which fits snugly on top of the head, made of an open-weave fabric that is usually decorated with pearls or semi-precious stones. The cap was popularized by actress Norma Shearer in the film *Romeo and Juliet* (1930).

jumper 1. A short, sack-like coat with a narrow turn-down collar which buttoned to the neck, worn by men in the 19th century. 2. A 20th-century sleeveless dress with a low SCOOP or square-cut neck which is often worn over a blouse. 3. (Chiefly UK) A long-sleeved woolen sweater. *See* *JAEGER.

jumpsuit One-piece suit with long sleeves and legs, which zips from the waist or below to the collar. It has been worn by women since the early 20th century. Also known as a flying suit or boilersuit.

jute Glossy lustrous fiber obtained from the jute plant of East India. Since the 19th century it has been mixed with silk and wool to create fabrics for both indoor and outdoor garments.

K

kaftan *See* CAFTAN.

Kamali, Norma 1945–. Designer. Born Norma Arraez in New York, Kamali studied fashion illustration at the Fashion Institute of Technology in New York. She graduated in 1964 and worked in clerical jobs before opening a BOUTIQUE with her husband in 1967. Kamali's highly original clothes were popular among people from show business, the theater, and the music world. Gold lamé MAILLOTS and garments made of leopard print chamois were just some of her high fashion designs. After her divorce she started another business, OMO (On My Own), in 1978. Her weightless, fiber-filled nylon fabric coats made from the down of sleeping bags and her JUMPSUITS of parachute nylon received international attention. In the late 1970s Kamali began working with SWEATSHIRTING, a fabric previously used only for athletics and SPORTSWEAR. She made jackets, skirts, and narrow and baggy pants. Her RAH RAH SKIRTS were the first short skirts to sell in any volume since the MINI of the early 1960s. She uses jersey frequently to make broad-shouldered dresses and tops. Kamali's clothes are witty and dramatic enough to make accessories unnecessary. One of the most innovative designers of the 1970s and 1980s, Kamali shows boldness in her choice of fabric, making up skirts from Mexican tablecloths or remnants from the cutting room floor. In the 1980s she produced several successful collections of sportswear and one-piece BATHING SUITS which are remarkable for their cut-out sections and strong use of color.

Kangol Company established in 1938 by Frenchman Jacques Spreiregen at Cleator, Cumbria, England, to produce traditional *BERETS. Kangol provided British and overseas armed forces with military berets during World War II. Its berets and soft angora hats were particularly popular during the 1950s. *See also* *SMITH.

Kaplan, Jacques 1924–. Fur designer. Born in Paris, France. In 1941 Kaplan joined the New York branch of the furrier business established by his father in Paris in 1889. He became famous for his stenciled and colored furs; fun furs; and fur dresses, boots, and hats. He retired in 1971.

karacul Tightly curled, glossy, black fur of the young broadtail sheep found in Southern Russia. Karacul was a popular fur for coats and hats during the late 19th and early 20th centuries. It is also the name given to a fabric which imitates the fur. *See also* ASTRAKHAN.

Karan, Donna 1948–. Designer. Born Donna Faske in Forest Hills, New York, USA. Karan's father was a haberdasher and her mother a model and saleswoman. Karan attended Parsons School of Design in New York and during her second year was employed in the summer as a sketcher at Anne KLEIN. After graduating she spent almost a year at Anne Klein before joining manufacturer Addenda. In 1968 she rejoined Anne Klein and was appointed Klein's successor the following year. After Klein's death, Karan and Louis DELL'OLIO became codesigners for the company. Karan produced highly wearable, moderately priced SPORTSWEAR for the Anne Klein label until 1984, when she left to design under her own name.

kasha Soft, silky fabric made of a wool mixed with goat's hair. Kasha first became popular during the 1920s.

Kasper, Herbert 1926–. Designer. Born in New York, USA. Kasper studied English and advertising at New York University but left college prematurely to serve with the US Army in Europe. After demobilization he returned to New York where he studied at Parsons School of Design. In the following years he went to Paris, attended classes at the CHAMBRE SYNDICALE DE LA HAUTE COUTURE, and worked for Jacques FATH, Marcel ROCHAS, and *Elle* magazine. On his return to the USA in the early 1960s, Kasper joined John Fredericks as a millinery designer. In 1965 he moved to Joan Leslie, where he remains as vice president. Kasper's clothes have always been associated with couture garments at SPORTSWEAR prices. He is

Norma **Kamali**'s "sweats" collection of 1981, showing her favorite broad, padded shoulder, this time teamed with a basque-style waist and knickerbocker legs.

a master at translating an expensive, tailored cut to a mass market price tag and excels in knitwear, suedes, and silks.

Kawakubo, Rei 1942–. Designer. Born in Tokyo, Japan. Kawakubo studied literature at Tokyo's Keio University. After graduating in 1964 she joined the Japanese textile company Asahi Kasei. Two years later she became a freelance fashion designer and in 1969 formed the COMME DES GARCONS company. Kawakubo achieved her greatest attention in Paris during the late 1970s and early 1980s with her non-traditional clothing, which attempted to redefine accepted ideas of womenswear in both the East and the West. Her torn, crumpled garments, draped around the body with seemingly no acknowledgment of body shape, were initially viewed as ugly and ridiculous. Nonetheless, her somber shades and flat, sexless image had a considerable impact on dress styles of the 1980s in Japan, Europe, and the USA.

Kellerman, Annette Australian swimmer who made several attempts to swim the English Channel, the first in 1909. She moved to the USA in 1910 and became an exhibition swimmer. Kellerman helped to popularize the one-piece BATHING SUIT.

Kennedy, Jacqueline *See* ONASSIS.

Kenzo 1940–. Designer. Born Kenzo Takada in Kyoto, Japan. Kenzo studied art in Japan and after graduating he designed patterns for a Tokyo magazine. In 1964 he moved to Paris and for the remainder of the 1960s created freelance collections and sold designs to Louis FERAUD. In 1970 he opened his own shop, Jungle Jap. Success followed almost immediately. Kenzo's early clothes in cotton were very popular. By 1972 he was established, known initially for his audacious designs in either raucous Kabuki colors or austere shades. A master at mixing prints and layering, Kenzo produced Oriental style blouses, TUNICS, SMOCKS, wide-legged pants, and printed velvet garments. He also focused fashion attention on knitwear. His trendsetting approach to knitted fabrics ensured his position as a leading ready-to-wear knitwear designer, injecting color and new proportions into classic designs. Kenzo's ideas and influence have been far-reaching. He has been able successfully to blend Eastern and Western ideas, translating traditional designs into innovative contemporary garments. *See* col. pl.

kersey Thick, heavy, cotton and wool twill fabric which has a closely sheared surface and resembles melton. It was popular for coats during the 19th century.

kerseymere Closely woven twilled cloth similar to kersey, which was popular during the 19th century.

Khanh, Emanuelle 1937–. Designer. Born in Paris, France. Khanh worked as a model for BALENCIAGA in the mid-1950s and later for GIVENCHY. She began sketching, made up several garments, and in 1961 some of her clothes were featured in *Elle*. She joined DOROTHEE BIS for a brief period and then worked for CACHAREL from 1962 to 1967. In 1970 Khanh established her own business. She has continued to work freelance while pursuing her own lines. In the 1960s she became famous for her long, droopy collars on jackets, dresses, and blouses; highly cut armholes; low-slung skirts; tiny,

Kenzo's Spring and Summer collection for 1981 featured both short and long skirts.

Kenzo's silk taffeta "samurai" dress of 1973.

round collars on blouses; short, frilly skirts; linen outfits with lace trimming; and embroidered blouses. Her name is associated with the YE YE fashions of the 1960s.

Kiam, Omar 1894–1954. Costume designer. Born Alexander Kiam in Monterey, Mexico. Kiam attended the Poughkeepsie Military Academy in New York. By 1912 he was working for a department

Fashion designer Bill Gibb's version of the **kilt** for the mini-skirt years of the 1960s.

store in Houston, Texas, where he became head designer of the millinery department. He moved to New York to design clothes, furs, and theatrical costumes on a freelance basis. Kiam also spent some years working in Paris. By the 1930s he had returned to New York to create costumes for Broadway. In 1935 he was hired as head designer for Samuel Goldwyn's production company in Hollywood, designing specifically for actresses Merle Oberon and Loretta Young. In 1941 Kiam started producing a ready-to-wear line for a New York manufacturer.

kick pleat Short, inverted pleat which is inserted at the center back or side hem of a tightly fitting skirt to provide greater mobility. It was often used by designers in the 1940s and 1950s when a strictly tailored silhouette was fashionable.

kilt In early times the kilt was a long, toga-like garment, woven of vegetable-dyed yarns, which was gathered at the shoulders. It served as both clothing and a blanket. From the Middle Ages it was made from a plaid—a piece of fabric, usually 16′ × 5′, which was wrapped around the lower torso to make a calf-length skirt, with the other end draped across the chest and over the shoulder. By the 17th century the kilt had become identified with Scotland. It consisted of a skirt of $7\frac{1}{2}$ yards of TARTAN cloth, most of which was pleated, except for the last half yard at each end which was left unpleated. The unpleated ends were crossed over each other in the front and held in place by buckles or a large pin. By this time the plaid was a separate piece, worn over the shoulder. In Europe interest in kilts was promoted by Queen VICTORIA and her consort, Prince Albert, who, in the mid-19th century, spent a good deal of time at Balmoral, their Scottish estate. As fashion garments for women, kilts (usually the skirt without the plaid) have been popular since the 1940s. Modern versions are made from two yards of woolen material and do not conform to Scottish traditions. Fashion kilts were notably popular during the 1970s and formed part of IVY LEAGUE and PREPPIE dress for women.

kimono Loose, wide-sleeved JAPANESE robe which has a broad SASH that fastens around the waist. The kimono was introduced to Europe in the late 19th century. The shape, design, styling, and overall symbolism of the kimono inspired painters such as Toulouse Lautrec, MUCHA, and KLIMT. Toulouse Lautrec took to wearing the garment; others were satisfied to paint kimono-clad women. The kimono became the symbol of a general preoccupation with Japanese ideas, designs, and spatial concepts. In fashion terms, the kimono became popular in the late 19th and early 20th centuries, worn as an alternative to the TEA GOWN, and its long, flowing lines were frequently imitated in Hollywood film costumes of the 1930s. Throughout the 20th century, the kimono shape has been used for DRESSING GOWNS.

kimono sleeve Extra-large sleeve panel which is set into a deep armhole that reaches from shoulder to waist. The kimono sleeve has been used by designers since the late 19th century for coats, dresses, jackets, and SWEATERS.

King's Road Street in London's CHELSEA which has been the scene of many new trends in fashion since the proliferation of BOUTIQUES in the 1960s. The King's Road became the focus of fashion in the late 1970s as the favorite promenade of PUNKS.

Klein, Anne 1921–74. Designer. Born Hannah Golofski in New York, USA. In 1938 Golofski was working as a sketcher on New York's SEVENTH AVENUE. The following year she married Ben Klein and joined Varden Petites, where she was responsible for the junior lines. Shortly after, Klein formed Junior Sophisticates and made even more inroads on the fashion scene for young women. In 1968 Anne Klein and Co. was formed. Klein made young fashions sophisticated. She was one of the most popular SPORTSWEAR designers in the USA, famous for matching dresses and jackets, wasp-waisted dresses, BLAZERS and BATTLE JACKETS, hooded BLOUSON tops, and slinky jersey dresses. Her clothes were smart, practical, and fashionable. After her death Donna KARAN and Louis DELL'OLIO took over the design side of Anne Klein and Co.

Klein, Bernat 1922–. Textile designer and painter. Born in Senta, Yugoslavia. Klein attended the Bezalel Academy of Arts and Design in Jerusalem. After World War II he went to England where he studied textile technology at Leeds University. Klein then worked briefly for a large cotton mill in Lancashire and a woolen mill in Edinburgh before setting up on his own in Galashiels, Scotland, in 1951. Klein's work is based on continuous development and innovation in textile design. His personal contribution is associated with his approach to color. Klein has translated many of the color elements of his own paintings into fabrics with unusual color schemes.

Bernat **Klein**'s brown, sand, and white wool fabric designed into a coat by John Cavanagh, in 1963.

Klein, Calvin (Richard) 1942–. Designer. Born in New York, USA. Klein graduated from the Fashion Institute of Technology in 1962. He spent the following five years in New York working for various coat and suit manufacturers before starting his own business in 1968. For many years he specialized in designing coats and suits but during the mid-1970s he gained recognition for the softly tailored, clean lines of his SPORTSWEAR collections. PEA JACKETS, fur-collared melton overcoats, TURTLENECK sweaters, and long-line SLACKS in muted shades were as much Klein hallmarks as silk crêpe de chine shirt-style jackets, striped silk blouses, and velvet daytime separates. In the late 1970s Klein's designs became increasingly sophisticated. His collections featured long, slim lines on coats, loose unfussy jackets that hung straight from broadened shoulders, and carefully proportioned BLAZERS and blouses. Klein favors linen, silks, and woolen fabrics. In the mid-1970s his "designer" JEANS were widely copied yet managed to remain one of the most respected brands. Klein's clothes are immediately identifiable by their smooth, understated look.

Klein, Roland 1938–. Designer. Born in Rouen, France. Klein studied at the Ecole de la Chambre Syndicale de la Haute Couture in Paris from 1955 to 1957. After two years with DIOR, he moved in 1962 to PATOU, where he worked as Karl LAGERFELD's assistant. Klein traveled to London in 1965 to join the firm of Marcel Fenez. In 1973 he became managing director and in 1979 he opened his own shop, Roland Klein. Klein creates well-proportioned clothes along restrained lines.

Klimt, Gustav 1862–1918. Painter. Born in Vienna, Austria. Artist who became closely associated with ART NOUVEAU. Klimt's female figures of the early 1880s wore soft, flowing gowns. He designed dresses for a Viennese couture house and also worked on theater and poster design.

Elements of a man's wardrobe tailored for women. Double-breasted plaid coat, double-breasted plaid blazer, and gray flannel pants. The sleek lines of Calvin **Klein** for Fall 1983.

Knife-pleated skirt from the 1890s.

knickerbockers Loose, full breeches which are gathered below the knee and fastened by a button or buckle. Worn by men since the 18th century, they became an integral part of sporting attire for women in the 1890s, teamed with a NORFOLK JACKET. In the late 1960s and early 1970s knickerbockers became fashionable once again, promoted by *SAINT LAURENT.

knife pleats Narrow pleats pressed to form regular, sharp edges on a skirt or dress. Popular during both the late 19th and the 20th centuries, particularly from the 1920s to the 1950s.

knitting A craft that can be traced back to the ancient Egyptians, knitting is the interlocking of one loop of thread or yarn through another, using two needles. In the past hand knitting was popular for both functional and decorative garments in country areas where wool was readily available. By the 19th century knitting machines had come into use but it was not until the wool-related health cult of the late 19th century that woolen garments achieved a wide popularity. Sport also helped to promote wool. By the turn of the century fashionable outdoor knitted garments were being made up for women by both hand and machine. Sweaters, previously worn only as sportswear, became the vogue in the 1920s and continued to be popular through the 1930s. During both world wars women knitted garments for soldiers, some of which (the BALACLAVA, for example) became fashion items. In the 1950s knitwear became more fashion conscious: new and more flexible fibers were blended with wool to create a far wider range in design, color, texture, and wearability. The 1960s saw knitwear firmly established as a fashion force and in the late 1960s and early 1970s a revival took place of homeknitting, due in large part to the availability of brightly colored yarns and up-to-date patterns. This revival, particularly in the 1970s, was associated with ETHNIC fashions. *See also* ARAN, FAIR ISLE, ROBERTS, SWEATER, TROMPE L'OEIL, *and* TWINSET.

Koshino, Hiroko 1938–. Designer. Born in Tokyo, Japan. One of many Japanese designers who went to Paris in the early 1980s, Koshino formed her own company and shows separates in designs which draw on the basic kimono shape. Her confidently scaled garments have earned her a wide reputation.

Krizia Company—Kriziamaglia—founded in Milan, Italy, in 1954 by Mariuccia Mandelli. Mandelli, who had trained as a teacher, began by selling skirts and dresses. In 1967 she branched out into knitwear design and later into complete ranges of ready-to-wear clothes. Krizia's designs are always distinctive. Clever, lighthearted, and often witty, they manage nonetheless to retain considerable grace and glamour. In the 1970s an animal motif featured each season on many garments. Krizia has become a giant of the Milanese fashion scene, charting its own course with panache.

Kumagai, Tokio 1947–. Shoe designer. Born in Sendai, Japan. After graduating in 1970 from the Bunka Fukoso Gakuin, the Japanese college of design, Kumagai went to Paris. Throughout the 1970s he designed for a number of companies, notably CASTELBAJAC, Rodier, and Pierre d'Alby in France and FIORUCCI in Italy. In 1979 he began hand-painting shoes. He opened his first BOUTIQUE in 1980. Inspired by SURREALISM, abstract and expressionist styles, and artists such as Kandinsky, Pollock, and MONDRIAN, Kumagai hand-paints his shoes in a manner reminiscent of a particular artist's style. He often alters the structure of the shoe to accommodate his painting.

L

lace From the Latin *laqueus*, "knot, snare or noose," lace is a textile patterned with holes and designs created by hand or machine. The two most common kinds of lace are bobbin lace and needlepoint lace. Bobbin lace is created by the manipulation of numerous threads, each attached to a bobbin, and is usually worked on a pillow. Needlepoint lace is made by looping yarn—one end of it threaded through a needle, the other fixed to a base—in simple or elaborate stitches to create a preset pattern or design. Bobbin lace is believed to have originated in Flanders and needlepoint lace in Italy. In the 18th and 19th centuries the centers for bobbin lace were Chantilly and Valenciennes, both of which had distinctive designs. Alençon, Argentan, and Venice are centers associated with needlepoint lace. Early use of lace was restricted to the robes of ecclesiastics and royalty, usually in the form of ornamental gold and silver braid, but by the 17th and 18th centuries lace was in general use for headdresses, FLOUNCES, APRONS, and dress trimmings. In the early part of the 19th century lace was used extensively, for dresses, VEILS, TEA GOWNS, jackets, GLOVES, and trimmings on PARASOLS and MUFFS. BERTHAS, FICHUS, handkerchiefs, and SHAWLS have also been made of lace. Before the 19th century lace was commonly made from linen thread but cotton became more usual during the 1800s. Machine made lace came into use during the late 18th century, though it was not patented until the mid-19th century. The popularity of lace decreased during the latter part of the 19th century and the early 20th century. Since that time it has rarely been used, except on lingerie.

Lachasse Fashion house founded in London in the late 1920s by Frederick Singleton. Digby MORTON was its first designer, from 1928 to 1933, followed by Hardy AMIES from 1933 to 1939. MICHAEL succeeded Amies after World War II until 1953. The house specializes in tailored dresses, coats, and suits, many of which are supplied to members of the British aristocracy.

Lacoste French tennis star René Lacoste (1905–.) was nicknamed "Le Crocodile" because of his aggressive nature on court. When he retired in 1933 he launched a white, short-sleeved tennis shirt which had a collar and small buttons to the neck and a small crocodile emblem on the chest. This shirt has been popular as leisurewear since the 1930s. Lacoste crocodiles are no longer restricted to the traditional white tennis shirt: they have appeared since the 1970s on many other items of clothing in a variety of colors.

Lagerfeld, Karl (Otto) 1938–. Designer. Born in Hamburg, Germany. At fourteen Lagerfeld was sent to Paris to further his studies. Three years later, after winning first prize in a coat design competition sponsored by the International Wool Secretariat, he was hired by BALMAIN, who put the coat into production. Lagerfeld stayed with Balmain for three years before joining PATOU at the age of twenty. In 1964, disillusioned with the world of *haute couture*, Lagerfeld left Paris to study art history in Italy. But the lure of fashion was such that the following year he was back, working as a freelance designer for CHLOE, KRIZIA, and shoe manufacturer Charles JOURDAN. In 1967 he joined FENDI as a consultant designer.

The **Lacoste** crocodile—named after the famous tennis player of the 1920s.

These examples of Karl **Lagerfeld's** designs for 1986/87 show his impecable draftsmanship, as well as his flirtation with the hourglass shape. Note the fan trademark.

For Fendi, Lagerfeld created some truly innovative work in fur jackets and coats. He took mole, rabbit, and squirrel—furs previously considered unfashionable or unsuitable for coats—and dyed them in vibrant colors. He launched a reversible fur-lined coat and a KIMONO-style coat and also mixed fur with leather and various fabrics. Lagerfeld's name is equally associated with the firm of Chloé, where he became famous for his top quality ready-to-wear garments. Every collection was expressed in positive, unhesitant terms, whether Lagerfeld showed shepherdess dresses with scarves tied as BODICES, SHAWLS, or about the waist (1975); MINI skirts (1980), or layered skirts over pants (1981). An exacting, confident stylist, Lagerfeld's clothes are imaginatively accessorized. His ideas are sophisticated, often impudent but always stylishly executed. In 1983 he became design director of CHANEL for both the couture and ready-to-wear lines. The following year he launched his first collection under his own name. From the mid-1970s Lagerfeld has been a major force on the fashion scene, a designer who is not only able to move with the times but to move the times.

Lalique, René (Jules) 1860–1945. Jeweler, glass designer. Born in Ay, Marne, France. Lalique studied drawing in Paris from 1876 to 1881. He worked as a goldsmith and spent several years in London before returning to Paris. After a period as a freelance designer specializing in jewelry, textiles, and fans, Lalique opened his own company in 1885, designing and manufacturing jewelry which he sold to Boucheron, CARTIER, and other French jewelry companies. In 1891 Lalique created stage jewelry for actress Sarah Bernhardt. At the Paris Exhibition of 1900 he achieved considerable success with his ART NOUVEAU jewelry designs. From about 1895 Lalique's distinctive, sinuous style usually incorporated human forms with natural and symbolic motifs. Famous for both his glass and jewelry, Lalique was a prolific worker, crafting lavish designs on to rich materials. He was widely influential.

lambswool Wool from young sheep, used in the 20th century to make CARDIGANS and SWEATERS.

lamé From the French word for trimmings of gold or silver, lamé is the name given to fabrics woven with flat, metallic threads. Lamé has been popular for eveningwear since the 1930s.

Lamour, Dorothy 1914–. Actress. Born Mary Leta Dorothy Kaumeyer in New Orleans, Louisiana, USA. Lamour's major contribution to fashion was her popularization of the *SARONG, which she wore in her first film, *The Jungle Princess* (1936), and in many subsequent films. *See* HEAD.

Lancetti, Pino 1932–. Designer. Born in Perugia, Italy. Lancetti studied at the Art Institute of Perugia. In the 1950s he moved to Rome where he sold sketches to designers such as SIMONETTA and FONTANA and worked freelance for several companies, including CAROSA, before establishing his own business in 1961. Lancetti is a well known Roman designer who concentrates on cut and color, producing many sophisticated silk and chiffon creations.

Lane, Kenneth Jay 1932–. Jewelry designer. Born in Detroit, Michigan, USA. Lane studied at the University of Michigan and Rhode Island School of Design. Graduating with a degree in advertising design, he joined the art department of VOGUE in New York in 1954. Two years later, he left to become VIVIER's assistant, designing shoes for DELMAN. From 1956 to 1963 Lane also worked with Vivier in Paris, producing shoes for DIOR. In 1963, as an experiment, Lane started making jewelry from the RHINESTONES used to decorate evening shoes. One year later his part-time jewelry business had become a successful full-time operation. Lane's talent lay in his unashamed copying of valuable pieces and his inventive manner of mixing plastics or semi-precious stones. His strange and original creations have influenced many young jewelry designers.

Langtry, Lillie 1852–1929. Born Emilie Charlotte le Breton on the Channel Island of Jersey. After marriage to the diplomat Edward Langtry in 1874, Lillie Langtry achieved notoriety as the mistress of the Prince of Wales (later Edward VII) and in 1881 went on the stage. Known as the "Jersey Lily," Langtry was famous for her beauty. She popularized jersey and gave her name to a BUSTLE and a shoe style.

Lanvin, Jeanne 1867–1946. Designer. Born in Brittany, France. Lanvin trained first as a dressmaker and then as a milliner. In 1890 she opened a millinery shop in Paris. During the early years of the

Model Paulene Stone decked out in Kenneth J. **Lane**'s opulent costume jewelry in 1967.

Jeanne **Lanvin** and (*below*) an
example of the mother-and-
daughter ensembles that made her
famous, illustrated for *La Gazette
du bon ton* by André Marty.

20th century the clothes she made for her younger sister and later for
her small daughter attracted so much attention from customers that
Lanvin created copies and introduced new lines to sell in her store.
Over the following years demand by young women persuaded
Lanvin to open a couture house selling matching mother-and-
daughter garments. Shortly before World War I she created her
famous "robes de style," based on 18th-century designs. These
waisted, full-skirted dresses remained popular until the early 1920s
with only slight adjustments. She also designed romantic "picture"
dresses based on softened Victorian shapes and lavishly trimmed
with embroidery. Influenced by Orientalism from around 1910,
Lanvin turned to exotic eveningwear in Eastern style velvets and
satins. At the beginning of World War I she made a simple CHEMISE
dress which later became the basic outline for the 1920s. Lanvin's
postwar clothes were in the spirit of the age. In 1921 a Riviera
collection introduced Aztec embroideries. The following year the
Lanvin Breton suit was a short, braided jacket with lots of small
buttons, and a big white organdy collar turning down over a red
satin bow. A sailor hat or round straw hat topped the outfit. Lanvin
also sold beaded dance dresses, a wool jersey sportsdress patterned
in CHECK of gold and silver thread, dinner PAJAMAS, and CAPES. Her
work was easily recognizable by her skilful use of embroidery and
her fine craftsmanship. She used a particular shade of blue so often
that it came to be called "Lanvin blue." *See also* CASTILLO, CRAHAY,
and col. pl.

lapel Part of the front neckline of a blouse, coat, dress, or jacket which turns back or folds over.

Lapidus, Ted (Edmond) 1929–. Designer. Born in Paris, France. Lapidus is the son of a tailor. He attended schools in France and also studied technical engineering in Tokyo, Japan. In the early 1950s Lapidus opened a BOUTIQUE in Paris. He designed his clothes as a technician, concerned as much with cut as with design, and his precise garments soon earned him recognition. During the 1960s he produced a SAFARI JACKET which became widely popular. Lapidus's ideas were perfectly in tune with the UNISEX styles of that decade and he made his name in both menswear and womenswear. Since the mid-1970s his clothes have become far more classic in style.

Laroche, Guy 1923–. Designer. Born in La Rochelle, near Bordeaux, France. Laroche went to Paris at an early age and worked with a milliner. After World War II he spent two years in New York as a milliner on SEVENTH AVENUE. On his return to Paris he was given a job with Jean DESSES. He worked with Dessès for eight years before establishing his own business in 1957. At first Laroche produced couture lines but in 1960 he launched his ready-to-wear collection. He is famed for his skilful cutting and tailoring.

Lastex US Rubber Company's trade name for elastic yarn made of a rubber combined with silk, cotton, or rayon. Lastex was used in

Left: Jeanne **Lanvin**'s version of the New Look, 1947.

Center: **Lanvin**'s design for 1947 retains some of the "picture dress" style for which she was famous.

Right: The sleek lines of a 1931 **Lanvin** evening gown.

The man who created the "prairie
look" and "frontier fashions" in
the USA, Ralph **Lauren** also
tailors Englishwomen in 1982 with
a Norfolk jacket, lace jabot
blouse, and houndstooth skirt.

Leg-of-mutton sleeves were stylish
for riding habits of 1896.

foundation garments and underwear, particularly CORSETS and GIRDLES, during the early part of the 20th century.

Lauren, Ralph 1939–. Designer. Born Ralph Lipschitz in New York, USA. Lauren worked in New York at BROOKS BROTHERS, Allied Stores, and as a glove salesman while attending nightschool for business studies at City College. In 1967 he joined Beau Brummel Neckwear, where he created the Polo division to produce wide, handmade expensive neckties. The following year Lauren established the Polo range of men's clothing, featuring the natural shoulder line of the IVY LEAGUE style. In 1971 he turned his attention to womenswear and produced a collection of tailored shirts. The "Ralph Lauren" label was launched the following year with a complete range of garments for women in cashmere, cotton, and tweed. HACKING JACKETS, FAIR ISLE sweaters, pleated skirts, CREW NECK shirts, lace-collared velvet dresses, flannel pants and flannel skirts all featured in Lauren's subsequent collections. In 1978 he introduced the casual/sophisticated "prairie look": denim skirts worn over layers of white cotton PETTICOATS, fringed buckskin jackets, leather belts, and full-sleeved, soft blouses. In 1980 he showed hooded CAPES, linen ruffled blouses, madras shirts and full skirts as part of his American frontier fashions. Lauren upholds tradition with his choice of quality fabrics for menswear and womenswear.

lawn Named after the French town of Laon, lawn is a fine, lightweight sheer cotton or linen fabric which is plain woven and given a crisp finish. It was a popular choice for underwear and delicate blouses in the 19th and early 20th centuries.

leather Hide or skin of an animal which is tanned or chemically preserved. Used for accessories until the 20th century, when it was made up, notably during the 1960s, into dresses, suits, PANTS SUITS, jackets, and coats. *See* BATES, MONTANA, *and* VERSACE.

leggings Fitted leg covering which extends from the foot to the waist, thigh, or knee and is often fastened under the instep. Leggings or leg bindings have been worn since the Middle Ages as protection against the cold. They were worn by children and young girls from the mid-19th century until the early 20th century. In the 1980s they emerged as fashion items, notably in London.

leg-of-mutton sleeve Tight-fitting from wrist to elbow, the leg-of-mutton sleeve balloons out from the elbow to the shoulder, where it is gathered or pleated into the BODICE of a dress or blouse. A popular sleeve-style in the late 19th century and during the EDWARDIAN revivals of the late 1960s and early 1970s.

Legroux Two sisters, Germaine and Héloïse, who opened a millinery store in 1913 in Roubaix, near the French border with Belgium. They became known as Parisian milliners during the 1920s and in the following decade exported their hats to the USA. In the 1940s one of their nieces took over the business.

legwarmers Traditionally worn by ballet dancers, legwarmers are long, woolen, footless socks worn around the calves and ankles to maintain body heat before, during, and after exercising. During the health cult of the 1970s, legwarmers became fashionable worn over pants and tucked into BOOTS, or under long skirts. They were made up in a spectrum of shades.

Glamorous cocktail dress,
designed by Lucien **Lelong**, *c*.1936.

Lelong, Lucien 1889–1958. Designer. Born in Paris, France. Lelong's father founded a textile house three years before Lelong's birth. Lelong trained for a business career at the Hautes Etudes des Commerciales, Paris, from 1911 to 1913. His first collection was prepared for 1914 but was postponed because of Lelong's mobilization. After the war Lelong established his own business. Noted more for the skill and workmanship of beautiful fabrics than for innovative design, Lelong was one of the earliest designers to diversify into lingerie and STOCKINGS. He introduced a line of ready-to-wear in 1934 which he labeled "editions." In 1939, just before the outbreak of World War II, Lelong showed tightly waisted, full skirts—a style which became the NEW LOOK in DIOR's hands in 1947. President of the CHAMBRE SYNDICALE DE LA HAUTE COUTURE from 1937 until 1947, Lelong persuaded the occupying Germans to permit French couture houses to remain in Paris and not transfer to Berlin. Largely due to his efforts, ninety-two houses stayed open during the war. After World War II, in 1947, Lelong showed pencil-slim dresses; pleated, tiered, harem hemlines; and suits with wasp waists, cutaway fronts, and square shoulders. His second wife, Princess Natalie Paley, daughter of Grand Duke Paul of Russia, was a noted beauty who wore her husband's designs.

Lenglen, Suzanne 1899–1938. Tennis player. Born in France. Lenglen won the Wimbledon women's final from 1919 to 1926. Her impact as a tennis player was almost matched by her impact on the fashion world. She dispensed with the traditional tennis outfit: blouse, tie, and long skirt, and wore instead a thin, one-piece, loose-fitting dress or a SWEATER and skirt. She replaced her garter belt with knee garters and discarded her CORSET and PETTICOAT. Jean PATOU designed many of Lenglen's clothes: a pleated silk skirt reaching just to the knee and a straight, white, sleeveless CARDIGAN teamed with a bright orange HEADBAND. This outfit was widely copied off the tennis court.

leotard One-piece long-sleeved garment first worn by the 19th-century French trapeze artist, Jules Léotard. The leotard is cut low at the neck and fitted between the legs. It was adopted by dancers and gymnasts and until the 1950s it was invariably black. In 1965 André

Suzanne **Lenglen** in action, wearing a sleeveless, knee-length dress and a headband.

COURREGES and Jacques HEIM were just two French designers who experimented with the shape of the leotard. Leotards of strong, flexible, man-made fabrics became fashionable during the 1970s, in association with DISCO fashions and the general interest in exercise and dance. They have been made in various fabrics, many of which contain Spandex, and in many different styles of sleeve, neckline, and general body cut. *See also* CAPEZIO, DANSKIN, JOHNSON, *and* KAMALI.

Lepape, Georges 1887–1971. Illustrator. Born in Paris, France. Lepape studied at the Ecole des Beaux Arts in Paris. In 1909 he began working for Paul POIRET and two years later he illustrated Poiret's famous catalog, *Les Choses de Paul Poiret*. Lepape moved to Jean PATOU in 1912, to illustrate Patou's collections. He also worked freelance for many journals, including LA GAZETTE DU BON TON, FEMINA, VOGUE, HARPER'S BAZAAR, and LES FEUILLETS D'ART. Lepape was strongly influenced by Orientalism and the Ballets Russes. His work showed a distinctive, curvilinear style. He was better known than many other illustrators of the period, chiefly through his designs of posters and books and his work as a print-maker.

American *Vogue* cover, March 1927, designed by Georges Lepape.

Leser, Tina 1910–. Designer. Born Christine Wetherill Shillard-Smith in Philadelphia, Pennsylvania, USA. Leser studied at the Philadelphia Academy of Fine Arts and the Sorbonne in Paris. In 1953, she opened a small dress store in Honolulu, Hawaii, in which she sold Chinese brocade items as well as garments made of cotton, sailcloth, and silk, on to which she had hand-blocked prints. Specializing in SPORTSWEAR and PLAYSUITS (beach outfits of dress and matching SHORTS), Leser gained a reputation as an innovative designer. In 1940 she visited New York, where her playsuits were shown to fashion editors. Leser was subsequently introduced to the Saks Fifth Avenue department store which ordered five hundred playsuits. Two years later Leser moved to the city and designed for a clothing manufacturer until 1953 when she opened her own business. Leser produced RESORTWEAR during the 1950s: Lastex BATHING SUITS, SARONG-style skirts, TOREADOR PANTS, and Lurex PAJAMAS. Many garments featured bold ETHNIC prints and patterns. Leser is also noted for cashmere dresses, PLAID blanket dresses, SWEATERS cut like jackets, and at-home clothes.

levi's *See* STRAUSS.

Leyendecker, Joseph (Christian) 1874–1951. Painter, illustrator. Born in Montabour, Germany. Leyendecker moved to Chicago, USA, at the age of seven. He studied at the Art Institute of Chicago and later at the Académie Julian in Paris. It was in Paris at the 1897 Salon Champ de Mars that his first major exhibition of paintings was held. Leyendecker then worked as a commercial artist in Chicago and Philadelphia, before finally moving to New York in 1900. Throughout the early 1900s Leyendecker illustrated covers for the *Saturday Evening Post*, *Collier's Weekly*, and other magazines. After achieving fame through the crisp, angular strokes of his Chesterfield cigarette advertisements, he was hired by the *ARROW shirt and collar company to illustrate their publicity material. Leyendecker's work was so true to life that women were convinced that his characters (clean-cut, upstanding young American men) were portraits of real people.

Liberman, Alexander 1912–. Magazine editorial director. Born in Kiev, Russia. Liberman studied mathematics, architecture, and philosophy in Moscow and England. He emigrated to France and was hired at the age of twenty by Lucien VOGEL to work on *Vu*, a photo-journalism magazine published in Paris. Within one year Liberman became art director and eventually managing editor. He then spent several years painting in the South of France before moving in 1941 to New York, where he became art director of VOGUE in 1943. In 1962 he was appointed editorial director of Condé NAST publications. Liberman's influence on the world of fashion is considerable. An internationally recognized artist, he has encouraged and promoted all forms of art through the pages of Condé Nast publications.

Liberty Store established in London in 1874 by Arthur Lasenby LIBERTY which became fashionable during the 1890s for promoting the ART NOUVEAU style. It sells fabrics, furnishings, and garments.

Liberty, Arthur Lasenby 1843–1917. Storeowner. Born in Chesham, Buckinghamshire, England. Liberty's father was a draper. At the age of fifteen Liberty worked in the lace warehouse of his uncle's Nottingham based company. In 1861 he moved to London and soon joined Farmer and Roger's Great *SHAWL and Cloak Emporium where he was eventually put in charge of the Oriental warehouse. Liberty set up on his own in 1874 selling Eastern silks and Orientally-inspired household goods and costumes. He specialized in the importation of handwoven silks from Mysore and Nagpur in India, cashmere from Persia, Shantung and Shanghai silks from China, and crêpes and satins from Japan. Silk was promoted by a series of exhibitions in the Regent Street store. At the turn of the century Liberty was selling hand-blocked paisley designs and machine-made lawns, linens, and wools. He commissioned designers to produce Grecian- and Medieval-style gowns, metalwork, and furnishing fabrics. The Liberty store was patronized by supporters of the *AESTHETIC DRESS movement and also by admirers of ART NOUVEAU.

liberty bodice Undergarment introduced in the early 20th century by a British CORSET manufacturing company. It is a front-buttoning BODICE constructed of taped bands and made of a soft, knitted fabric. Lightweight versions were produced during the 1920s and 1930s. The bodice was manufactured until the 1950s.

linen Name given to any fabric made from flax fiber, obtained from the flax plant. Strong and smooth-surfaced, linen varies in weight and texture. Depending on the weave, it is possible to manufacture linen to be as fine as cambric or as coarse as canvas. It was used throughout the 19th century for underwear and became popular during the 20th century for blouses, jackets, skirts, and outerwear.

Linton Tweeds Distinctive tweed used for summer and winter coating produced by Linton Tweed Ltd of Carlisle, England. The company was founded in 1919 by William Linton. Until the outbreak of World War II it supplied international designers such as CHANEL, HARTNELL, MOLYNEUX, SCHIAPARELLI, and STIEBEL. After the war the company also supplied BALENCIAGA, BALMAIN, AMIES, COURREGES, DIOR, and SAINT LAURENT.

This **Linton Tweeds** woolen overcoat was designed in 1949 by Hardy Amies.

lisle Hardspun two-ply cotton yarn twisted to compact the fibers. Named after the French town of Lille, where it originated, lisle was chiefly used until the mid-1940s for STOCKINGS.

little black dress Emerging in the 1920s, the little black dress was based on the simple lines of the CHEMISE. It became a staple of the cocktail hour and an essential ingredient of every woman's wardrobe. Heavily promoted by CHANEL and MOLYNEUX in the 1920s and 1930s, the little black dress has been popular at some point in almost every decade. *See* *OLDFIELD.

Little Lord Fauntleroy Hero of a children's book of the same name by Frances Hodgson Burnett published in New York and London in 1886. The book's illustrations by Reginald Birch showed Little Lord Fauntleroy dressed in a black or dark blue velvet suit (jacket and KNICKERBOCKERS), a white blouse with a VANDYKE collar, a colored SASH, silk STOCKINGS, buckled PUMPS, and an oversize BERET. This outfit resembled male AESTHETIC DRESS of the period. Little Lord Fauntleroy clothes for women became fashionable in the 1970s.

Little Lord Fauntleroy outfit, popular during the late 19th century, has a long lace collar, lace cuffs, and a lace-trimmed shirt tucked into buttoned knee breeches. Leggings and Cromwell shoes finish off the outfit.

loafer Low-heeled shoe, resembling a leather MOCCASIN, which originated in Norway. It was introduced in the USA in the 1940s. Like the moccasin, the loafer is a slip-on shoe with a laced front panel. Traditionally worn by men, it is also used as casual footwear by women.

loden 1. Sturdy fabric originating in the Tyrol region of Austria. Loden was once made of sheep's wool but in the 20th century alpaca, camel, and mohair came into use. At the turn of the century, the traditional colors—red, black, or white—were succeeded by a shade of green which came to be permanently associated with the fabric. 2. Dark green, coarse woolen jacket trimmed with BRAID and with a PRUSSIAN COLLAR, which was popular for casual wear during the mid-20th century.

Lopez, Antonio *See* ANTONIO.

louis heel The louis heel was first named in the reign of the French King Louis XIV (1643–1715), when it described the method of making the sole and heel in one section. In the second half of the 19th century the term louis heel referred to a thick, often covered heel, which is tapered at the mid-section before flaring outward, first worn in the reign of Louis XV of France (1715–74).

Louis, Jean 1907–. Costume designer. Born Jean Louis Berthault in Paris, France. After studying at the Arts Décoratifs in Paris, Louis went to work for Agnès DRECOLL. In the early 1930s he moved to New York where he presented sketches to Hattie CARNEGIE, who subsequently employed him for seven years. In 1943 he was appointed head designer at Columbia Pictures in Hollywood. For Rita Hayworth in the film *Gilda* (1946) Louis created a strapless evening dress, designed to give the actress sufficient mobility for an energetic dance scene. The dress was widely copied. In 1958 Louis moved to Universal Studios. Since 1961 he has operated a ready-to-wear business, specializing in eveningwear, while continuing to create for the screen on a freelance basis.

Louiseboulanger 1900–. Designer. Born Louise Boulanger in France. At thirteen Boulanger became an apprentice at a

Lucile (Lady Duff Gordon) created soft, delicate evening dresses in the early 20th century. This one, designed with a décolleté neckline, Empire waistline, and handkerchief skirt, is topped off with an aigrette.

dressmaking establishment. Later she worked with Madeleine CHERUIT until in 1923 she opened her own establishment. For the next twenty years Louiseboulanger was a successful designer of graceful, elegant clothes often cut on the BIAS. She showed evening skirts which were knee-length in front but fell to the ankles at the back. Bold colors and heavy fabrics such as taffeta were her trademarks.

Lucas, Otto 1903–71. Milliner. Born in Germany. Lucas opened a London salon in 1932 after studying in Paris and Berlin. He became a highly successful milliner, popular on both sides of the Atlantic. Lucas supplied hats to stores and dress designers in addition to creating styles for his private clientele and for the cinema.

Lucile 1863–1935. Designer. Born Lucy Sutherland in London, England. After a divorce in 1890 Lucile started dressmaking for her friends and in 1891 she opened her own house. She married Sir Cosmo Duff Gordon in 1900. For the first twenty years of the 20th century Lucile was a well known designer with branches in London, New York (1909), Chicago (1911), and Paris (1911). She was most famous for her TEA GOWNS, made in flimsy gauzes, taffetas, poplins, and silks. Her clients included Irene CASTLE, Sarah Bernhardt, film stars, and royalty. Lucile claimed to have revolutionized women's underwear by refining the CORSET to make it less restrictive. In 1907 she created the costumes for Lily Elsie, star of *The Merry Widow*, a London stage production. Copies of these clothes were briefly fashionable in Britain. Lucile is also associated with the promotion of colored underwear; the use of models, whom she took with her to the USA; subtle, soft color schemes of predominantly pastel shades; and Orientally inspired, romantic dresses which were particularly well-suited for eveningwear. She was also a noted designer of formal BALL GOWNS covered in lace and beads. During World War I Lucile designed costumes for the Ziegfeld Follies. She sold her business in 1918. *See* MERRY WIDOW HAT *and* col. pl.

lumberjack shirt Thick, PLAID shirt with front buttons, worn by lumberjacks in Canada. Shirts based on these have been popular for male casual attire since the 1940s, usually made of printed cotton or wool.

Lurex Trademark of the Dow Badische Company for its metallic fiber yarn which was introduced during the 1940s. Woven or knitted with cotton, nylon, rayon, silk, or wool fibers, Lurex is made into dresses, CARDIGANS, and SWEATERS. It is particularly suitable for eveningwear and was popular until the 1970s.

Lycra Man-made fiber introduced in 1958 by DU PONT of Delaware, USA. Lycra is elastic, abrasion resistant, and has stretch and recovery powers. Since its introduction, Lycra has been an essential component of underwear, particularly GIRDLES and ROLL-ONS. During the 1970s it was incorporated into pantiehose, swimwear, and exercise clothes.

M

Macintosh, Charles 1766–1843. Scottish chemist who, in 1823, took out a patent to waterproof fabrics by cementing together two layers of woolen material with indiarubber dissolved in naptha. In 1830 Thomas Hancock, who had been in competition with Macintosh vulcanizing rubber to develop waterproof clothing, joined Charles Macintosh and Co. *See* MACKINTOSH.

Mackie, Bob 1940–. Born in Los Angeles, California, USA. Mackie studied at Chouinard Art Institute in Los Angeles before beginning his design career as a sketch artist for Jean LOUIS. He also worked for Edith HEAD at Paramount. While continuing his work in films, Mackie gained further design experience by creating costumes for the Judy Garland television show (1963) and later for the Carol Burnett show. He is best known for his glamorous clothes, swimwear, and fur lines.

mackintosh Waterproof coat developed in stages during the 19th century. In 1823 the Scottish chemist Charles MACINTOSH patented a waterproof woolen fabric. Sixteen years later Charles Goodyear of the USA introduced vulcanized rubber. Joseph Mandleburg of Lancashire, England, tackled the problem of the rubber smell in woolen waterproof garments and in 1851 launched the first odor-free waterproof coat. The first "macs" of the late 19th century were voluminous, neck-to-ankle garments, designed to keep the wearer completely dry. In the 20th century, fashion adapted the mackintosh into a number of styles, including the civilian TRENCHCOAT and the RAINCOAT. Cotton blends and, later in the century, synthetic blends were used to make waterproof coats. *See also* AQUASCUTUM *and* BURBERRY.

macramé Decorative knotting originating in Arabia. Macramé was used for fringes in home furnishings during the 19th century but did not become associated with costume until the 1960s when a revival of macramé included its use in the construction of dresses and tops.

Mad Carpentier Composite name for two of Madeleine VIONNET's protegées, Mad Maltezos and Suzie Carpentier, who continued to direct Vionnet's business after her retirement in 1939.

Madonna 1960–. Rock singer. Born Madonna Louise Ciccone in Bay City, Michigan, USA. Madonna spent one year at the University of Michigan and then left for New York City, where she earned money working as a model and became a singer with a band. In 1983 she began to launch her own records and to appear on MTV. Madonna has had an enormous impact on fashion, especially among teenagers. She popularized the wearing of lingerie (particularly BRAS) as outerwear; tube skirts that rolled down onto the hips, exposing the navel; black elbow length gloves; tight skirts and spiked heels; lace TANK TOPS, and strings of beads and pearls. Her first film, *Desperately Seeking Susan* (1984), further increased her influence. In the same year a clothing company, Madonna-Wanna-Be, was launched, aimed at the teenage market.

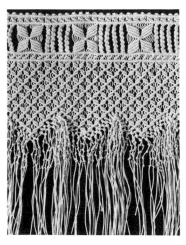

Turn-of-the-century cotton **macramé** border.

madras Fabric of vegetable dyed cotton yarns handwoven in large bold CHECKS which originated in India in the late 19th century. Machine-made madras is produced in a variety of weaves. It is used for SPORTSWEAR and summer attire.

Magyar dress Derived from traditional Hungarian costume, Magyar dress consists of brightly colored clothes: flounced skirts and blouses with fitted BODICES and very full sleeves that are gathered at the wrist. Variations on Magyar dress have entered the fashion picture in the late 19th century, the 1930s, the late 1960s, and the early 1970s.

Magyar sleeve *See* MAGYAR DRESS.

maillot *1.* Dancer's or gymnast's TIGHTS which take their name from a Monsieur Maillot, a French costume and hosiery maker for the Paris Opéra, who, during the 1800s, designed knitted tights and matching LEOTARD which were known as "fleshings." 2. Modern word for a one-piece, tight-fitting BATHING SUIT.

Mainbocher 1891–1976. Designer. Born Main Rousseau Bocher in Chicago, USA. Mainbocher attended the University of Chicago, the Chicago Academy of Fine Arts, and the Art Students League in New York. From 1911 to 1917 he studied and worked in Munich, Paris, and London. In 1917 Mainbocher served with the American hospital unit en route to France and at the end of the war he stayed on in Paris, intending to study singing. The loss of his voice forced him to seek an alternative career and in 1922 he joined HARPER'S BAZAAR as a fashion artist. The following year he was invited by Condé NAST to become fashion editor, and later editor-in-chief of French VOGUE, a position he held until 1929. In 1930 Mainbocher became the first American to open a successful couture salon in Paris. His success continued throughout the 1930s. Mainbocher was famous for his eveningwear: decorated evening SWEATERS, embroidered APRON-style evening dresses, BIAS-CUT dresses, and theater dinner suits that were worn with blouses. His wedding gown for Mrs. Wallis Simpson on her marriage to the Duke of Windsor created a vogue for "Wallis blue." Mainbocher's dresses were often described as "well-bred," elegant, and refined. Several times he revamped the LITTLE BLACK DRESS. A memorable collection, in 1939, previewed the NEW LOOK of 1947, with small waists and tightly laced CORSET-like garments. In 1940 Mainbocher returned to New York and opened a salon. He closed in 1971.

mandarin collar Stand-up collar on jackets, dresses, and blouses. Adapted from a close-fitting Asian collar. *See* MANDARIN JACKET.

mandarin jacket Straight, loose jacket or coat traditionally worn by Chinese officials. Often richly embroidered, the jacket had a small, standing collar and fastened in front or across the shoulder. *See also* MANDARIN COLLAR.

Mandelli, Mariuccia *See* KRIZIA.

mantle Hooded cloak with silk tassels worn by women as an outer garment in the mid- and late 19th century. It was usually waist- or hip-length and made of light woolen materials. *See* BURNOUS.

Mao suit Simple suit named after Mao Zedong (1893–1976), founder of the People's Republic of China. Made in black crêpe and designed along straight lines, the suit consists of a pair of pants and a jacket with long sleeves, a high-standing collar, and front buttons. It appeared in London in the mid-1960s as a man's suit but Paris soon adapted it to womenswear. The popularity of the Mao suit in the 1960s was associated both with UNISEX experimentation in dress and with the support from many students and young people of the period for left-wing politics.

marabou Feathers from a species of stork, used in the 19th and early 20th centuries to decorate hats and to trim evening gowns.

Marcel wave Wavy hairstyle created in 1872 by a French hairdresser, Marcel Grateau, who reversed curling tongs to produce a curl rather than a crimp. Marceling was popular until the 1930s, when the PERMANENT WAVE was introduced.

Marimekko Company founded in 1951 by Armi RATIA specializing in bright and cheerful prints for dresses and home furnishings.

Marks & Spencer Company founded as a market stall business in 1884 in Leeds, England, by Michael Marks, a Lithuanian immigrant. He was joined in 1894 by Tom Spencer and the company went public in 1926. After Spencer's death in 1905 and Marks's death two years later, the firm prospered under Marks's son Simon, and Israel Sieff. By the 1980s there were over 260 Marks & Spencer stores in the United Kingdom. The chain accounts for 15 percent of the UK clothing market. Over the years it has employed many notable British designers to contribute to its womenswear sections.

Marcel Grateau, creator of the **Marcel wave**, 1922.

By 1900 **Marks & Spencer** had 12 shops and 24 market stalls around the UK, this one in Cardiff, Wales.

1110

1110

Jacket Tweed

plain

Play

1935

Blue Suit

Tweed

Vera **Maxwell**'s weekend
wardrobe of 1935.

Martin, Charles 1848–1934. French artist who illustrated fashion for many magazines, including *Le Journal des dames et des modes, Modes et manierès d'aujourd'hui*, and LA GAZETTE DU BON TON.

Marty, André (Eduard) 1882–1974. French artist who illustrated fashion for many magazines, including LA GAZETTE DU BON TON, LE GOÛT DU JOUR, FEMINA, VOGUE, LES FEUILLETS D'ART, HARPER'S BAZAAR, and *Modes et manières d'aujourd'hui. See* *LANVIN.

mary janes Ankle-strap, button shoes, either flat or with small heels, which were originally designed for children. During the 1920s they became a popular style for women.

matinée hat Large-brimmed picture hat worn in the early 20th century for teas and afternoon excursions.

Matsuda, Mitsuhiro 1934–. Designer. Born in Tokyo, Japan. Matsuda attended the Japanese college of fashion, Bunka Fukùso Gakuin, from which he graduated in 1962. In 1965 he spent six months in Paris. He opened his own company, Nicole, in Tokyo in 1967. Throughout the 1970s Matsuda started both menswear and womenswear BOUTIQUES in Japan and in 1982 he expanded to the USA and Hong Kong. Matsuda's collections are carefully planned with an international clientèle in mind. He pays special attention to fabric and is sometimes whimsical in design.

Mattli, Giuseppe (Gustavo) 1907–82. Designer. Born in Locarno, Switzerland. After a period in London, learning English, Mattli moved to Paris and worked for the couture house of Premet. Returning to London in 1934, he opened his own house, producing both couture and ready-to-wear lines. Mattli was known to the fashion world on both sides of the English Channel. In 1955 he dropped his couture line, though he continued with other lines until the early 1970s. He was famous during the 1960s for his COCKTAIL DRESSES and theater coats, which he designed to be worn over low-cut dresses.

Maxfield Parrish Company established in London in 1974 by Nigel Preston (b.1946), who made clothes for pop stars. Maxfield Parrish is associated with suede and leather garments that are classically styled along fluid, sensitive lines.

maxi skirt Ankle- or floor-length, often full, skirt which became popular during the late 1960s. The maxi skirt was often worn with BOOTS. *See* EDWARDIAN *and* *MINI.

Maxwell, Vera 1901–. Designer. Born Vera Huppé in New York, USA. Maxwell's parents were Viennese. She trained as a ballet dancer, joining the Metropolitan Opera Ballet in 1919. In 1924, after her marriage, while working as a model for a wholesale company, she started to sketch, design, and model her own clothes. Influenced by numerous European childhood tours and a brief period in London studying tailoring, Maxwell produced classic styles made of the finest fabrics: silks, tweeds, and wools. By the mid-1930s her collections received attention in New York. She designed a "weekend wardrobe" in 1935 and a collarless tweed "Einstein" jacket in 1936—two of many innovative dressing ideas. In 1947 Maxwell opened her own business. She became known for classic separates and suits, dresses teamed with jackets, print dresses with matching print-lined coats, riding jacket suits, PRINCESS-LINE COAT

La Parisienne en tournée de Visites

André **Marty**'s 1922 depiction of an emancipated Parisienne driving herself about town in her Citroën. From *Fémina*.

Mattli's vivid lime green wool toreador cloak, with decorative frogging, for evening wear in 1949.

Mary **McFadden** in 1982, wearing one of her hallmark designs, a pleated top with long, pleated sleeves that wrap around the wrist.

DRESSES, CHESTERFIELD coats, and WRAP-AROUND jersey dresses. In 1970 the Smithsonian Institution held a retrospective of her work.

McCardell, Claire 1905–58. Designer. Born in Frederick, Maryland, USA. McCardell studied for two years at Hood College in Frederick before transferring in 1927 to Parsons School of Design in New York and later to Parsons' Paris branch. Back in New York at the end of the 1920s she worked as a sketcher for a dress shop. In 1929 McCardell joined designer Richard Turk, moving with him in 1931 to manufacturers Townley Frocks. Turk died shortly afterwards and McCardell took over his job as designer. In 1938 she introduced her "monastic dress," a highly successful, free-flowing garment, waistless and cut on the BIAS. The focus of attention, McCardell moved to Hattie CARNEGIE, where she stayed for two years. In 1940 she returned to Townley Frocks to design under her own label. Over the following years McCardell drew up the blueprint for American SPORTSWEAR. She designed practical clothing for women with practical lives. Taking simple fabrics—cotton, denim, mattress ticking, gingham, and jersey—she created clean, purposeful shapes, often using detail as a fashion focus. McCardell hallmarked her clothes with large PATCH POCKETS, metal rivets, top stitching, visible hooks, deep armholes, SHIRTWAIST sleeves, and shoestring ties over the shoulder. She launched many fashions throughout the 1940s and 1950s, notably the "popover" (1942), an unstructured WRAP-AROUND DRESS which became an American classic; and a diaper (nappy)-style one-piece BATHING SUIT (1943). In 1944 she persuaded CAPEZIO to produce PUMPS based on BALLET SHOES. Other innovations were soft, EMPIRE-LINE dresses; bloomer-like PLAYSUITS; DIRNDL skirts; elasticated, strapless tube tops; and bareback summer dresses. Many of McCardell's ideas have endured for almost forty years and she is considered to have been one of the USA's most influential designers.

McFadden, Mary (Josephine) 1938–. Designer. Born in New York, USA. McFadden was brought up on a cotton plantation near Memphis, Tennessee, and educated at Foxcroft, Virginia. After graduation she went to Paris to study at the Ecole Lubec and the Sorbonne. In 1957 she attended New York's Traphagen School of Design before taking a sociology degree at Columbia University. McFadden's first job was in public relations for DIOR, followed by a position as South African VOGUE's merchandising editor. In 1970 McFadden returned to the USA and worked as a special projects editor for *Vogue*. Her first designs, in 1973, for which she used African and Oriental fabrics, attracted a great deal of attention. McFadden formed her own company in 1976 and gained a reputation as a designer of individual, original jackets, coats, and dresses based on PEASANT designs of the Middle East and Asia. She uses lavish fabrics, especially hand-printed silks, and has experimented with pleating fabrics which, when made into dresses, resemble FORTUNY gowns. McFadden has been acclaimed for her evening gowns and intricately quilted and decorated jackets.

medici collar Collar used on gowns worn by the women of the Medici family, rulers of Florence in the 15th century. Made of stiffened lace, the collar was raised across the shoulders away from the neck. It was popular during the late 19th century on BALL GOWNS.

melton Thick, wool fabric in twill or satin weave which has a smooth surface. A popular choice of cloth for men's, and later women's, coats in the 19th century.

mercerization Process developed in 1884 by a calico dyer, John Mercer of Lancashire, England, whereby cotton is treated with caustic soda to give a silky, lustrous finish which helps to increase the strength of the fabric.

merino Thin, woolen, twilled cloth developed during the 19th century from the wool of the Merino sheep, for outdoor garments.

Merry Widow hat In 1907 actress Lily Elsie starred in the operetta *The Merry Widow* on the London stage. Her high-waisted chiffon and crêpe-de-chine dresses were designed by LUCILE, who was also responsible for her extremely large, plume-laden hat. Merry Widow hats were fashionable for several years. They were usually made of straw, with a deep crown swathed in black tulle and ostrich FEATHERS.

metal dress *See* RABANNE.

Michael (of Carlos Place) Company founded in 1953 by the Irish designer Michael Donellan after he had spent several years with LACHASSE. Michael was successful until the demise of couture in the 1960s.

Michiko, Koshino 1950–. Designer. Born in Osaka, Japan. Michiko graduated from Bunka Fukuso Gakuin, the Tokyo college of fashion, in 1974. The following year she went to London and soon established herself as a confident, successful designer, able to merge Oriental and Occidental ideas in a modern manner. Michiko's attention to detail can be observed particularly in her seaming and in the positioning of pockets on her clothes.

micro skirt Very short skirt, just covering the behind, which was briefly popular in the 1960s.

midi skirt In the late 1960s a calf-length skirt was introduced. Between *MINI and MAXI length, it was often worn with knee-high boots. Although the style was not widely popular at the time, ten years later it evolved, untitled, as an acceptable fashion length for skirts and dresses.

military Style of dress based on garments worn by servicemen. Military-style jackets and coats are severely cut and usually have EPAULETS, stiff collars, brass buttons, and belts. This style of clothing was popular during the late 1930s and also in the 1960s, when ARMY SURPLUS gear was worn.

mini skirt Skirt that ended well above the knee, popular from 1962 to 1970. Considered daring at its introduction, it was later generally adopted by younger women. *See* BATES, COURREGES, *and* *QUANT.

mink Either of two species of semi-aquatic weasel found originally in Eurasia and North America. Mink was not trapped in any quantity until the 19th century and did not become fashionable for coats until the mid-20th century. It is a short-napped, thick, glossy, and hard-wearing fur. There are two types of mink: wild and ranched. Wild mink is naturally dark in color whereas ranched mink is dyed various shades. Mink was first ranched in *c.* 1940 and careful genetic development has produced different strains. Mink is an expensive fur. Most of it comes from North America.

By the end of the 1960s it was possible to see **minis**, midis, and maxis on the street as women continued to experiment with skirt lengths before settling down to the more uniform lengths of the 1970s.

One of milliner Simone **Mirman**'s hat styles during the swinging sixties.

Mirman, Simone c. 1920–. Milliner. Born Simone Parmentier in Paris, France. As a very young woman, Mirman worked with milliner Rose Valois and for SCHIAPARELLI. After eloping to London in 1937, she found work at Schiaparelli's London salon. In 1947 she set up her own millinery establishment. Five years later Princess Margaret ordered several models and introduced the milliner to the rest of the British Royal Family. Mirman's hats were in great demand throughout the 1950s and 1960s. She designed collections for the London house of DIOR and SAINT LAURENT and for Norman HARTNELL. Noted for her MOB CAPS and BERETS, Mirman has produced every kind of hat for every occasion. She is a craftswoman with fabric and remains a respected milliner.

Miroir des modes, Le Magazine published monthly by the BUTTERICK Publishing Company from 1897 to 1934.

Missoni (Tai and Rosita) Italian husband-and-wife team who met in London at the 1948 Olympic Games, married, and in 1953 founded the Missoni company. Tai had previously owned a firm that made tracksuits and Rosita had worked for her family's bedding company, so the couple combined forces and, starting with a few knitting machines, began to produce knitwear which they sold to other designers. By the 1970s they were manufacturing under their own label highly individual knitwear in bold patterns and designs and cleverly blended colors. They made SWEATERS, suits, jackets, coats, and dresses. The company did much to alter the fashion world's rather condescending attitude to knitwear. Missoni is most famous for its long CARDIGAN-jackets and sweaters, but all its garments have become status symbols. *See* col. pl.

mitten In 1850 a mitten was a GLOVE of net or lace with the thumb and fingers cut off from the first row of knuckles. Gradually, the word has come to mean a glove that covers the fingers together in one part and the thumb in another. In this shape it is worn as casual attire, particularly for sportswear, and is usually made of wool or sheepskin. *See* *SCHIAPARELLI.

Miyake, Issey 1935–. Designer. Born in Hiroshima, Japan. Miyake graduated from Tama University in 1964 and went to Paris the following year to study fashion. He joined LAROCHE in 1966, leaving in 1968 to work for GIVENCHY. In 1969 Miyake traveled to New York and spent two years with Geoffrey BEENE. Miyake held his first show in New York in 1971 and a second in Paris two years later. At this time he developed the layered and wrapped look that was to become his hallmark. His fascination with texture expresses itself in his attitude toward design; he creates his linear and geometric shapes from the drape and flow of fabric. He works on a bold scale, often with his own fabrics, to produce inspired clothes, a balance of the influences of East and West. Miyake is an uncompromising and innovative creator who has helped turn the world's attention to the skill and ability of Japanese designers in general. *See* col. pl.

mob cap Larger, fuller, and less decorated than a BOUDOIR CAP, the mob cap was worn indoors during the 19th century to protect the hair. It was briefly popular in the 1960s.

moccasin Traditionally a piece of leather which wrapped the foot from underneath. Surplus material was gathered and seamed along the uppers. The origins of the moccasin are believed to lie in the

Issey **Miyake**'s sculptured bodice from his 1984 Bodyworks show at the Victoria & Albert Museum in London.

American Indians. Moccasins were adapted to casual footwear for men and women during the 20th century.

Mod UK term generally applied in the late 1950s and 1960s to teenage boys who wore long PARKAS, with ZIPPERS and hoods, and who rode about on motor scooters. Mods favored a neat appearance, with short haircuts.

Modes et manières d'aujourd'hui Fashion review published irregularly in France between 1912 and 1920 by Pierre Corrard and printed by the *pochoir* method—a time-consuming and laborious process where the image was built up with numerous hand-colored metal stencils. The journal featured the work of many notable artists, including BARBIER, LEPAPE, MARTIN, and MARTY.

mohair Fabric made from the long, lustrous hair of the angora goat which is loose woven with cotton, silk, or wool to produce a fuzzy texture. Popular for jackets, coats, skirts, and SWEATERS since the 1950s. *See also* CASHIN.

moiré Watered effect on fabric, usually silk, achieved by applying heated and engraved copper rollers. Watered silk was a popular fabric during the late 19th century. During the 20th century it has frequently been used for eveningwear.

Molyneux, Edward (Captain) 1894–1974. Designer. Born in London, England. Molyneux studied art and began to earn his living sketching for advertisements and magazines. In 1911 his sketch for an evening dress won him first prize in a competition set by LUCILE, who subsequently engaged him as a sketcher in her London salon. Over the following years Molyneux traveled with Lucile to her salons in New York and Chicago. After serving as a captain in the army during World War I, Molyneux opened a dressmaking salon in Paris in 1919. Between 1925 and 1932 he established branches in Monte Carlo, Cannes, Biarritz, and London. He was based in London from the mid-1930s until the end of World War II, when he returned to Paris. In 1950 Molyneux closed all but one of his houses and retired to Jamaica, handing over to Jacques GRIFFE. Fifteen years later, in an attempt at a comeback, Molyneux reopened and

The pleated neckline is complemented by the sleek lines of the skirt in this 1933 evening outfit by **Molyneux**.

Claude **Montana**'s clever blend of linen, leather, and silk for 1983.

took a ready-to-wear collection to the USA. Unfortunately for him, his particular design skills were not attractive to the 1960s public and he retired once again, this time handing over to a South African designer, John Tullis. Molyneux's reputation was based on the purity of line and cut of his tailored suits, pleated skirts, and discreet matching ensembles. The aristocratic elegance of his clothes made him a fashionable designer for film stars and society women. Gertrude Lawrence wore many of his garments on stage. During the 1930s he promoted the LITTLE BLACK DRESS, Orientally inspired clothes with bamboo motifs, DIRNDL skirts, and BIAS-CUT dresses. He was a well-respected designer throughout his career.

Mondrian, Piet 1872–1944. Artist. Born in Holland. In 1911 Mondrian went to Paris where he abandoned his realistic landscape painting to take up CUBISM. His work from 1917 on—colored shapes divided by a grid of black bands—was to inspire Yves SAINT LAURENT to produce in 1965 a line of dresses based on Mondrian's paintings. *See* col. pl.

monkey Long, silky, black hair of the Ethiopian monkey, which was highly fashionable as a trimming during the early 20th century.

Montana, Claude 1949–. Designer. Born in Paris, France. After taking his baccalaureate Montana went to London. At the end of the 1960s he began designing Mexican papier-mâché jewelry which he decorated with RHINESTONES and sold in London street markets. He returned to Paris in 1972 and two years later started to work for MacDouglas, a large leather manufacturer. He launched his first clothing collection under his own name in 1977. Montana is a forceful, influential designer with an international reputation. He works best in leather, creating strong silhouettes with hard, fairly masculine, lines. His broad-shouldered jackets and coats of the late 1970s appeared tough and aggressive. Montana makes his fashion statements through a mix of detail and bold color; brilliant hues of leather adorned with chains and buckles, for example. His SPORTSWEAR collections are authoritatively designed and well executed.

Moon, Sarah 1940–. Photographer. Born Marielle Hadengue in England of French parents. Moon studied drawing and taught herself photography. In the 1960s she worked as a fashion model in Paris before becoming a freelance photographer hired by CACHAREL for the company's advertising campaigns. Moon also took pictures for magazines such as *Elle*, *Marie-Claire*, VOGUE, and HARPER'S BAZAAR. Biba employed her to photograph advertisements for its cosmetics range. Moon's models are soft, dreamy, and mysterious, promoting a completely feminine, soft-focus, close-range image. Her color photography is muted, subtly blended, and verges on the surreal.

Moreni, Popy (Anne-Lise) 1949–. Designer. Born in Turin, Italy. The daughter of a painter and a sculptor, Moreni studied costume design in Turin. At the age of seventeen she went to Paris. She joined the Promostyl company in 1967 and worked for them and the Italian firm, Timmi, until 1972, when she opened her own business. Moreni is an inventive SPORTSWEAR designer who combines a predominantly French style with a color sense that lies in the strong Italian traditions. She opened her own BOUTIQUE in 1976. Moreni's clothes are often witty and lighthearted. She was one of the first designers to dye plastic shoes bright colors.

Mori, Hanae 1926–. Designer. Born in Tokyo, Japan. Mori studied at the Tokyo Christian University. She returned to college some years later to study fashion design and then began dressmaking for the Japanese film industry. She opened her first shop in Shinjuku and in 1955 moved to the Ginza, the smart shopping area of Tokyo. Her appeal to an international audience began in the early 1970s when she opened a salon in New York, and was extended by her first couture showing in Paris in 1977. Many of Mori's designs are based on the KIMONO. She adapts the style to eveningwear, in soft silky fabrics, belting her garments with the traditional OBI. Her ready-to-wear and couture lines, especially her COCKTAIL and evening dresses, are popular throughout the world.

morocain Heavy, crêpe fabric made of silk, rayon, or wool mixtures and used in the 19th and 20th centuries for dresses and outerwear.

Morton, Digby 1906–83. Designer. Born in Dublin, Ireland. Morton studied art and architecture in Ireland before moving to London where, in 1928, he joined the house of LACHASSE. Five years later he opened his own business. Morton was largely responsible for transforming the severe, tailor-made suit into a fashionable garment. Using delicately shaded tweeds, which he teamed with silk blouses, Morton added grace and flow to the classic outfit. He also favored ARAN knits and Donegal tweeds. In 1939 he designed uniforms for the Women's Voluntary Service in the United Kingdom. After the war, Morton created several collections for US manufacturers, notably between 1953 and 1957. A skilled designer of both day and eveningwear, and a British classicist, Morton was highly successful until the late 1950s. He closed his house in 1957.

Mosca, Bianca dates unknown. Italian designer who moved to London after spending fifteen years with SCHIAPARELLI in Paris. During World War II Mosca worked for Jacqmar. In 1946 she opened her own house, specializing in soft, romantic dresses.

mourning dress In the 19th century strict rules were observed for mourning dress. For close relatives black was worn for months, even years. For distant relatives, outfits would be trimmed in black. On the death of Prince Albert in 1861, Queen VICTORIA went into mourning and helped promote a huge vogue for black garments, particularly of crape. Caps, hats, coats, dresses, STOCKINGS, VEILS, MANTLES, gloves, and blouses were available in black crape muslin, gauze, cotton, and wool. JET jewelry was worn. Mourning wear was discarded gradually: black changed to purple, then to lavender and white for summer. The fashion for mourning clothes had almost disappeared by the end of the 19th century.

mousseline Fine, lightweight, plain woven fabric, usually cotton, silk, or wool, which has a slight stiffness. *Mousseline de soie* is the most popular version, used particularly during the 19th century for dresses, blouses, and skirts.

Mr. John 1906–. Milliner. Born Hansi Harburger in Vienna, Austria. Mr. John's mother opened a millinery shop on New York's Madison Avenue when the family emigrated to the USA after World War I. Sent to study medicine at the University of Lucerne, Mr. John

Digby **Morton**'s striped organza and chenille dinner dress of the 1950s.

Mourning dress, from *Harper's Bazar*, 10 May 1888.

transferred to the Sorbonne in Paris to study art. He eventually returned to New York and started a millinery business which later, with a partner, became the company John Fredericks. In 1948 the business partnership dissolved and Mr. John continued on his own. For over thirty years he was famous for his glamorous confections of chiffon, georgette, and tulle. He also created hats made of crochet and permanently pleated collapsible straw. He trimmed felt hats with pearls and jet and dressed tailored hats with tulle.

MTV Abbreviated form of Music Television, a company started in the USA in 1981 by Warner Amex Satellite Entertainment Company, through the national cable television network. MTV is a hugely popular twenty-four-hour television station featuring rock videos and contemporary music and appealing to the under-40 age group. It has had an impact on fashion both through the highly stylized dress of its rock video performers and through its publicization of singers such as MADONNA.

Mucha, Alphonse (Marie) 1860–1939. Decorative artist. Born in Moravia (now part of Czechoslovakia). Mucha was a prominent and prolific designer who worked in Paris, Berlin, and Prague. He turned his hand to most things, from biscuit tin labels to posters for Sarah Bernhardt and jewelry for Georges FOUQUET. His flowing, curvilinear designs are the epitome of *ART NOUVEAU.

muff Cylindrical accessory, popular in the late 19th century, into which the hands could be slipped for warmth. Muffs were also used to carry personal items and as a form of decoration. They varied in size and shape; by the early 1900s many resembled a small pillow. Muffs were made of silk, satin, taffeta, and FEATHERS as well as of sturdier materials such as wool, gabardine, and fur. Many were elaborately lined with satin and trimmed with tulle and artificial flowers. The PURSE/handbag began to replace the muff in the early 20th century.

muffler Long piece of fabric, usually hand or machine knitted wool, which is wound around the neck in cold weather.

Mugler, Thierry 1948–. Designer. Born in Strasbourg, France. Mugler made clothing as a teenager. He joined a ballet company and later worked as a window dresser in a Parisian store. In 1968 he visited London and Amsterdam, returning to Paris in 1971 to design a collection under the name Café de Paris. By 1973 he was designing under his own name. Mugler is a confident stylist, aware that his garments demand admiration as well as being both shocking and amusing. He is strongly influenced by 1940s and 1950s fashions, adapting their figure-hugging theatricality to the fashions of the 1980s. Beneath their glamorous, often sexy, exterior, Mugler's outfits are well designed and engineered. Top-stitching is often used as a design detail.

Muir, Jean c. 1933–. Designer. Born in London, England. Muir joined LIBERTY in 1950, first working in the stockroom, then selling in the made-to-measure department, and finally sketching at the London store. She was employed by JAEGER from 1956 until 1961, when she began to produce her own clothing line under the name Jane & Jane. In 1966 Muir went on to found her own company, Jean Muir. Working with the fabrics that she knows so well—jersey and suede—Muir manipulates the material by cutting, stitching, and

Actress Joanna Lumley wears Jean **Muir**'s fluid jersey tunic and culottes, from the designer's Autumn 1975 collection. Hat by Graham Smith.

seaming to create garments that carry her distinctive hallmark: fluidity achieved by discipline. Highly conscious of weight and balance, she tailors matte and rayon jersey into restrained and mannered dresses, skirts, and tops which are always subtle and never stiff or rigid. She punches, prints, and stitches suede into equally fluid shapes. In the 1960s she designed SMOCKS, PEASANT dresses, SHAWLS, draw-string-waist dresses, and two-piece suits. Muir is a craftswoman of the highest caliber who has gained an international reputation for her timeless, classic garments.

Mulberry Company established in 1971 by twenty-one-year-old Roger Saul and his mother, Joan. They began producing BELTS in top quality leathers, followed by bags in the saddlery traditions. Mulberry stores, within department stores, are now established internationally. They sell traditional PURSES/handbags, belts, and fashion accessories which are designed with the modern woman in mind.

mule Heeled, backless bedroom slipper which has been popular since the 1940s.

Munkacsi, Martin 1896–1963 Photographer. Born Martin Marmorstein in Kolozsvar, in the Munkacsi district of Hungary. In 1902 the family name was changed to Munkacsi. Munkacsi was educated in Hungary and after serving in the army he rapidly became one of that country's top photojournalists. Periods in Berlin and New York working for various magazines were followed in 1934 by his emigration to the USA, where he was placed under contract to Hearst Newspapers Inc., taking fashion photographs for HARPER'S BAZAAR and *Town and Country*, among others. Munkacsi's first pictures for Carmel SNOW of *Harper's Bazaar* show the influence of his early work as a sports photographer and they broke new ground in fashion magazine photography. His work concentrated on movement and spontaneity—a new feature at the time. He shot action pictures in the open air from previously inconceivable angles and was an inspiration to many later photographers. Munkacsi's work set the photographic fashion climate of the following thirty years.

muslin Fabric originally made in the city of Mosul (now in Iraq) and imported to Europe in the 17th century. By the 18th century, muslin was manufactured in both England and France. A plain-woven fabric which can be made in a wide range of weights, it was used extensively in the 19th century for undergarments, blouses, and summer dresses. In the 20th century its popularity was at its greatest in the 1960s, when there was a vogue for printed muslins imported from India.

musquash Fur of the musk rat, a water rodent found particularly in the Soviet Union, Canada, and the USA. Musquash is soft but hard-wearing, the natural fur is a dark blackish brown in color but fur from mutations is often dyed beige or gray. Musquash has rarely been considered a high fashion fur though its popularity has spanned well over a hundred years.

N

nainsook Fine, soft, plain-weave cotton made in various weights. Heavier than lawn, nainsook often resembles cambric. Nainsook was popular during the 19th century for lingerie and undergarments.

nankeen Yellow or buff-colored cotton cloth, originally hand-woven in Nanking, China, which was popular in the mid-19th century for summer wear.

Nast, (William) **Condé** 1873–1942. Publisher. Born in New York, USA. Nast was brought up in St. Louis, Missouri, and attended Georgetown University in Washington, DC. In 1897 he joined *Collier's Weekly* and was appointed advertising manager three years later. In 1904, as a personal venture, Nast became vice-president of the Home Pattern Company, a firm which manufactured and distributed women's dress patterns. When, a year later, he was promoted to business manager of *Collier's Weekly*, he divided the USA into different marketing areas to increase sales and also promoted the use of double-page spreads. It was Nast who encouraged Charles Dana GIBSON's work in the magazine. Nast left *Collier's Weekly* in 1907 and two years later bought VOGUE—a society periodical at that time. Several years later he acquired *Vanity Fair* and *House and Garden*. Nast raised magazine publishing to new heights. He sought out the best talents in photography, art, fashion, illustration, typography, and writing. He mixed society with business, art, the theater, and show business. Every one of his magazines adopted a strong editorial voice. In 1914 Nast established *Vogue Patterns* and later introduced foreign editions of the magazine.

needlepoint lace *See* LACE.

Nainsook's softness made it an ideal fabric for undergarments. This camisole was advertised in 1911. Note the slim-line petticoat of the period.

negligée Light, loose robe trimmed with lace and ruffles worn as informal attire at home during the 19th century. The negligée allowed women to loosen or remove their CORSETS between changes of dress. Its nearest relative is the PEIGNOIR. At the turn of the century the negligée was replaced by the TEA GOWN. In the 20th century, it is usually a luxurious, lightweight DRESSING GOWN, often made of a sheer fabric.

Nehru jacket Straight, slim, hip-length jacket, buttoned in front to a straight, standing collar, worn by Jawaharlal Nehru (1889–1964), Prime Minister of India from 1947 to 1964. American VOGUE promoted the Nehru jacket, which was often white, in the late 1960s.

New Look Style of dress generally attributed to Christian DIOR who, in 1947, introduced the COROLLE LINE, which became known as the New Look. Although other designers—BALENCIAGA, BALMAIN, and FATH—had already been working toward this shape by 1939, their efforts had been interrupted by the outbreak of World War II. Two years after the war Dior's show created an international sensation. The New Look was the exact opposite of the pared-down, economical garments demanded by rationing. One dress could use up to twenty-five yards of material and the style accentuated and exaggerated the female form with the aid of boned underwear and stiffened fabrics. The New Look caused controversy throughout the Western World. Although many women adopted the style, others reacted against it, deploring what they saw as its extravagance and artificiality. The House of Dior was picketed by indignant women and the resulting publicity made Dior a household name overnight. The New Look continued in various forms until the mid-1950s.

Newton, Helmut 1920–. Photographer. Born in Berlin, Germany. Newton was educated at the Heinrich Von Treitschke Real-gymnasium in Berlin from 1928 to 1932 and the American School in Berlin from 1933 to 1935. He worked as an apprentice to Eva, a Berlin fashion photographer, before emigrating to Australia, where he served in the army during World War II. After the war Newton worked in Sydney as a freelance photographer, also spending some time in Paris taking fashion pictures for *Elle*, *Marie-Claire*, JARDIN DES MODES, and VOGUE. In the 1960s he moved to Paris and became a regular contributor to the German magazine *Stern* and to French and American *Vogue*. His fine fashion photographs are often shocking, hinting at a decadence in society. Carefully posed models are tense, often aggressive; they seem to be playing out a secret drama hidden just beyond the range of the camera lens. Newton's work also contains elements of voyeurism and fantasy.

ninon Smooth, closely woven, semi-transparent voile, which was a popular dress fabric in the 19th century.

Nippon, Albert and **Pearl** Albert Nippon 1927–. Manufacturer. Born in Philadelphia, Pennsylvania, USA. Nippon graduated from Temple University in Philadelphia in 1951 and worked as an accountant for DU PONT until he took over his wife's small business venture. Pearl Nippon. 1927–. Designer. Born Pearl Schluger in Philadelphia, Pennsylvania, USA. After marrying Albert Nippon in 1953, Pearl Nippon began making one-piece maternity clothes the following year. The success of these dresses at the New York department store Saks Fifth Avenue led to the establishment of Ma Mère, a chain of retail stores opened and run by the Nippons. The Nippon line included a complete range of maternity wear. In 1973 the couple formed Albert Nippon Inc., which specializes in producing neat, classical SPORTSWEAR with an emphasis on tucking, pleating, and small bows.

Norell, Norman 1900–72. Designer. Born Norman Levinson in Noblesville, Indiana, USA. During World War I Norell spent a brief period at military school. In 1918 he attended Parsons School of Design in New York but returned home after one year to open a small dress fabric shop. Back in New York in 1920, Norell studied design at the Pratt Institute in Brooklyn. In 1922 he joined the New York studio of Paramount Pictures where he designed clothes for Gloria Swanson and other stars of silent movies. Norell then worked as a costume designer on Broadway, for the Brooks Costume Company, and for wholesale dress manufacturer Charles Armour. Shortly after leaving Armour in 1928, he was employed by Hattie CARNEGIE and remained with her until 1941. Anthony Traina then invited him to form Traina-Norell, with Traina as businessman and Norell as designer. By 1944 Norell had launched CHEMISE dresses, evening shirt dresses, fur TRENCHCOATS, sequinned evening SHEATHS, fur SLACKS, and EMPIRE-LINE dresses. In 1960 he opened his own company. His first collection featured CULOTTES for day and eveningwear, HAREM PANTS, and DECOLLETE evening dresses. In the 1960s Norell was acclaimed for his well-proportioned suits and clean, precisely tailored silhouettes. He used fabric flamboyantly, trimming garments in fur and feathers. Considered to be one of the foremost US designers, on a par with the French couturiers, Norell is best remembered for his sequin-covered sheath dresses.

Norfolk jacket Originally worn by men in the second half of the 19th century, the Norfolk jacket, named after the Duke of Norfolk, was a hip-length garment made of wool tweed, with large PATCH POCKETS, BOX PLEATS front and back, and a self-material belt. It was adopted by women in the 1890s for sporting activities, worn with KNICKERBOCKERS.

nylon Generic term for a manufactured fiber in which the fiber-forming substance is any long chain synthetic polyamide having recurring amide groups. Nylon was the result of a research program started in 1927 by Dr. Wallace H. Carothers at the DU PONT Company of Delaware, USA. The company first introduced nylon in 1938 and it was tested in knitted hosiery the following year. Nylon STOCKINGS were launched in 1940. Since then nylon has been used extensively in underwear and dress manufacture.

nylons *See* STOCKINGS.

The **Norfolk jacket**, illustrated in the April 1905 issue of the *Tailor & Cutter* and, some 20 years later, worn by the center figure in the photograph.

O

obi Wide, stiffened Japanese sash made of brocaded silk and lined with a contrasting color. The obi usually measures fifteen inches wide by four to six feet long. It is tied around the waist into a large bow at the back. In the 1980s it was adapted to fashion by Japanese designers working in Paris.

Oldfield, Bruce 1950–. Designer. Born in London, England. Oldfield taught art before studying fashion at Ravensbourne College of Art in Kent from 1968 to 1971. He furthered his studies at St. Martin's School of Art in London from 1972 to 1973 and then became a freelance designer. Oldfield created a line for the Henri Bendel department store in New York and sold sketches to Yves SAINT LAURENT. In 1975 he showed his first collection. Oldfield later produced ready-to-wear lines. He is most famous for his eveningwear, which is exciting, lavish, and sometimes zany. He is a popular designer among film stars and socialites.

Onassis, Jacqueline (Kennedy) 1929–. First Lady in the USA 1961–63. Born Jacqueline Lee Bouvier in East Hampton, New York, USA. In 1953, Bouvier married John Fitzgerald Kennedy, who was elected President of the USA in 1961. When Jacqueline Kennedy was First Lady, her clothes were widely copied. From 1960 onward, she often wore clothes of her own design, created for her by Oleg CASSINI. Her famous PILLBOX HATS were made by HALSTON. Kennedy frequently wore a two-piece outfit: a dress and a waistlength, semi-fitted jacket. She favored round or oval necklines or BOAT NECKS. Her sleeves reached just to the elbow, while her slimline, A-shaped skirts grazed the knee. Kennedy was often seen wearing PUMPS and fur-trimmed garments. She carried a gilt chain PURSE/handbag which became very popular. Her bouffant hairstyle was also imitated.

Ong, Benny 1949–. Designer. Born in Singapore. Ong was brought up and educated in Singapore. In 1968 he moved to London and studied at St. Martin's School of Art. After graduating he worked freelance for various companies before establishing his own business in 1974. Ong designs pretty clothes, graceful, flattering, and quite often loose. He is well known for his eveningwear, in which he handles beautiful fabrics in a sensitive manner.

Op Art Art form which emerged in the 1920s but became fashionable, printed on to fabrics, in the 1960s. The American dress manufacturer Larry Aldrich commissioned textile designer Julian Tomchin to create fabric based on paintings by Bridget *RILEY. The resulting spirals, circles, and squares are arranged in such a manner that they give an illusion of movement.

opossum Marsupial species found in the USA, Australia, and New Zealand. The opossum has dense, long hair in various shades of brown, gray, and black. The fur was used extensively at the turn of the century for lining coats and as a trimming.

The little black dress of 1986, made in silk crêpe and chiffon by Bruce **Oldfield**.

Orry-Kelly's glamorous and provocative designs for Marilyn Monroe in *Some Like It Hot* (1959).

organdy From the French *organdi*, meaning a book muslin, organdy is a very lightweight, fine, sheer, transparent cotton fabric which is stiffened by chemical treatment. It was popular in the late 19th and early 20th centuries for dress trimmings, particularly eveningwear. Since World War II, organdy has been made from rayon, silk, and other fibers.

Orlon Acrylic fiber produced by the US firm of DU PONT during World War II. Full-scale production for consumer use began in 1950. Orlon is a regular component of knitwear fabrics, where it acts as a substitute for wool.

Orry-Kelly 1897–1964. Costume designer. Born John Kelly in Kiama, Australia. Orry-Kelly studied art in Australia. In the early 1920s he moved to the USA and was hired to paint murals in a New York night club. Fox studios then employed him to illustrate film titles and he was soon able to turn his hand to scenery and costume design. Orry-Kelly joined Warner Brothers in Hollywood in 1932 as a costume designer and stayed for eleven years. He returned to Fox

Fashions for feathers prompted the London store of Debenham & Freebody to put out this 1906 advertisement announcing sales of **ostrich feather** stoles in assorted colors.

NEW FEATHER NECKWEAR

THERE is every indication that Feather Wraps will again be extremely fashionable. The reasons for their popularity are not far to seek. They are graceful and becoming, they take the place of every kind of outdoor wrap, they are both light and comfortable, and finally they are extremely moderate in price.

We are specialists in Feather Goods. Since the commencement of this fashion we have sold between 40,000 and 50,000 Feather Stoles, Boas, and Wraps. We have always had the largest and best assorted stock, and consequently have sold more than any other retail firm in the country.

Our prices are extremely moderate, as we buy in large quantities direct from the largest manufacturers. We are therefore enabled to sell our feather goods at exceptionally low prices.

Sent on Approval.

No. 1.   No. 2.   No. 3.

AMAZON OSTRICH FEATHER BOAS.
(As sketch.)

In long full selected feather, very rich effect, in white, black, grey and white, natural and white and black and white, 72 to 80 inches long.

No 1 Price 29/6.   No. 2 Price 49/6.   No. 3 Price 69/6.

Debenham & Freebody
WIGMORE STREET, LONDON, W.

to work on Bette Davis movies, and also worked as a freelance for Universal, RKO, and Metro-Goldwyn-Mayer. He designed costumes for hundreds of films from 1932 to 1964, notably for Marilyn Monroe in *Some Like It Hot* (1959).

ostrich feather Plume-like feather from the wing or tail of the African ostrich, a flightless bird. The white feathers were used extensively in the late 19th and early 20th centuries for millinery, feather BOAS, and exotic trimmings.

overalls Complete cover garment with long sleeves and legs, worn by women in the munitions factories and for agricultural labor during World War II. Overalls have also featured as part of American workwear. They were particularly popular for womens-wear during the 1960s, made of cotton and trimmed with pockets, flaps, and buckles. *See also* SIREN SUIT.

oxford Originally a half-boot worn in England during the 17th century. By the 20th century, the oxford had become a man's, woman's, or child's low-cut shoe, laced over the instep. *See* BROGUE.

Oxford bags Pants worn by undergraduates at Oxford University, England, in the 1920s. The hem measured approximately 20 inches wide and was cuffed. Oxford bags were a popular pants style for women during the 1930s and 1970s.

Oxford bags were the object of much ridicule. This cartoon is from the *Bystander,*

P

page boy Hairstyle in which hair of shoulder length or longer is rolled under on either side, from the top of the ears to the nape of the neck. It was popular during World War II and in the 1960s and 1970s.

pagoda sleeve Three-quarter or half length sleeve style which was frilled to the elbow where it widened into either several tiers of FLOUNCES or one large flounce seamed to curve in a shape resembling a pagoda. A popular style in the mid-19th century. The flounces were often trimmed with ribbons and bows.

In its report on Paris Fashions for April, the *Illustrated London News* of March 1856 shows a dress (*left*) with sleeves made of "four flounces of similar pattern only smaller." This was to be known as the **pagoda sleeve.**

Pajama style loungewear in the 1920s, typically made of satin and lace-trimmed.

Paisley Scottish town, famous for the production of a worsted fabric during the 19th century. As cashmere SHAWLS from India became popular, Paisley firms adapted the Kashmiri cone motif, weaving it onto large, square shawls in shades of red and brown. This particular pattern became known as Paisley and featured mainly on shawls and DRESSING GOWNS in the 19th and early 20th centuries. In the 1980s Paisley enjoyed a revival in fashionable clothing, including TIGHTS, skirts, dresses, shawls, and PURSES.

pajamas From the Hindi "paejama," meaning leg clothing. In the 19th century pajamas consisted of loose-fitting pants and sashed jacket tops. By the turn of the century various forms of pajamas existed, including lounging pajamas, worn by men as elegant early evening attire. In the 1920s and 1930s women wore decorative evening pajamas and beachwear versions. The film *It Happened One Night* (1934), starring Claudette Colbert and Clark Gable, helped to popularize pajamas for women. Modern nightwear pajamas evolved during the 1920s. *See also* *GALITZINE.

paletot From the English "pall coat." The word paletot has been used for many different garments in the 19th and 20th centuries. In the early 19th century the paletot was a single-breasted man's frock coat which had the skirt sections sewn on, and in early versions it was similar to a riding coat. By the mid-19th century it had become a heavy three-quarter-length overcoat which was slightly waisted. The paletot in the second half of the 19th century was a woman's partially or completely fitted three-quarter- or waist-length coat, often made of cashmere or wool cloth and decoratively embroidered. By the early 20th century the paletot had become an outdoor jacket.

panama hat Light-colored hat of various shapes, made from tightly woven straw of the plant *Carloduvica palmata*, found in Ecuador and neighboring countries. It is called a panama because US President Theodore Roosevelt wore one during a tour of the Panama Canal in 1906. Panama hats remained popular summer wear, mainly for men, until World War II.

The Kashmiri cone or "boteh," the most popular motif on late-19th-century **Paisley** shawls.

The 1904 style of **panama hat**.

The drama of Issey **Miyake**'s creations for 1985–86 is underlined by the theatricality of their presentation.

Missoni's subtle knits for Spring and Summer 1982.

Norman **Parkinson** photographed this Zandra Rhodes dress in Florida, USA, in 1971. The dress is in "Indian Feather Sunspray" print on silk chiffon; cut to the shape of the print, with handrolled edges.

panne Velvet-like fabric with the pile pressed flat in one direction.

pantiehose *See* TIGHTS.

pants (UK: trousers) Outer garment which covers the body from the waist to the ankles in two separate leg sections. Pants have been worn by men, in one form or another, since ancient times. Early-19th-century breeches, KNICKERBOCKERS, and pantaloons are the closest relations to modern pants. Straight, ankle-length pants began to emerge in the 1800s but they were not considered acceptable attire for men until the late 19th century. Although actress Sarah Bernhardt appeared in pants during the same period, pants were not commonly worn by women until the 1920s. In the 1920s and 1930s CHANEL introduced "yachting pants," and pants—mostly baggy—were worn for the beach and leisure acitivities. In the same period eveningwear pants in elaborate fabric became popular and there was a fashion for men to wear wide-legged OXFORD BAGS. During World War II women taking over men's work wore pants in the factories and fields but after the war the only pants that were fashionable were BERMUDA SHORTS, PEDAL PUSHERS, and TOREADOR PANTS, all worn as part of casual dress. The real pants revolution came in the 1960s, with UNISEX fashions, though even at this time women wearing pants were often refused entry to restaurants and the whole subject was one of heated debate. By the 1970s rules and social attitudes had relaxed and pants of many lengths and styles had become an acceptable part of female dress for both casual and formal attire. In the 1980s the women-in-pants battle has been almost entirely won, though there is still resistance in some quarters to the idea of women wearing pants to the office. *See also* BELL BOTTOMS *and* PANTS SUIT.

pants stockings *See* POP SOCKS.

pants suit (UK: trouser suit) Women's two-piece suit of tailored pants and jacket, a copy of the suit worn by men since the late 19th century. Although various women have worn men's suits since the early 1930s—the actress Marlene Dietrich, for example—pants suits for women did not become fashionable until the UNISEX vogue of the 1960s.

paper clothes Paper clothing enjoyed a brief vogue in the 1960s. Paper suits and underwear for men and women were inexpensive and disposable.

Paquin, Mme. ?–1936. Mme. Paquin, as she was usually known, trained at Maison ROUFF and founded her own house in Paris in 1891. In 1900 she was appointed president of the Fashion Section of the Paris Exposition and two years later she opened branches in London, Buenos Aires, and Madrid. Paquin was noted for her rich, glamorous, romantic clothes and fine workmanship. Her gowns, described as "from fairyland," were popular with actresses and socialites. Herself a woman of considerable elegance, Paquin was a skilful publicist and paraded her models at race meetings. She accepted dress designs by Paul IRIBE and Léon BAKST which she made up into garments. In 1913 she created day dresses that could also be worn into the evening. Many of Paquin's gowns were a blend of drapery and tailoring, suitable for the more active woman of the early 20th century, and her tailored suits were cut to facilitate walking. She was also famous for her TANGO DRESSES, lingerie, and an extensive fur department. Paquin retired in 1920, though her house remained open until 1956. *See* *HOBBLE SKIRT.

In the 19th century, **parasols** were the height of fashion and many were made in fabrics which matched outfits.

parasol Parasols were used from the mid-16th century as functional and fashionable accessories. In the 18th century, they were heavily decorated and sometimes trimmed with gold lace. In the 18th and 19th centuries, many parasols had elaborately carved ivory handles and silk linings, and were deeply fringed and ruffled. They were rarely carried after World War I. *See* UMBRELLA.

pardessus From the French for "passed over." In the 19th century the word pardessus described various fitted overcoats for men and women.

pareo Polynesian skirt or loincloth printed with bold flower patterns. Pareos have been used since the 1960s as beach attire.

Paris élégant Bimonthly fashion magazine published in France from 1836 to 1881. A monthly magazine of the same name was brought out by a different publisher between 1909 and 1936.

parka Hooded garment similar to an ANORAK but usually longer and more loosely cut. It was a popular casual jacket in the 1950s and 1960s. *See also* WINDCHEATER.

Parkinson, Norman 1913–. Photographer. Born Roland William Parkinson Smith in Roehampton, Surrey, England. Parkinson was educated at Westminster School in London. He became an apprentice at Speaight Ltd, a London photographic company which specialized in portraits of debutantes. In the mid 1930s, Parkinson embarked on a photographic career working for magazines such as *Life*, *Look*, and VOGUE, while pursuing interests in farming. During World War II he worked as both a military photographer and a farmer. After the war Parkinson achieved great success as a fashion photographer for *Vogue* and other fashion magazines and advertising agencies in London, New York, and Paris. In the 1950s he became a royal portrait photographer. Parkinson's work is usually vigorous and vivacious in style, often humorous in content. He manages successfully to merge the rustic with the sophisticated. His clean-cut images are overlaid with gentle wit. *See* col. pl.

Parnis, Mollie 1905–. Designer. Born Sara Rosen Parnis in New York, USA. Parnis graduated from Wadleigh High School, New York, in 1923. She started her fashion career as an assistant saleswoman in the showroom of a blouse manufacturer but soon turned to designing. Parnis worked briefly for another dress manufacturing company, David Westheim, before her marriage to a textile specialist in 1930. Three years later, she opened her own business with her husband, making smart, mannered, ready-to-wear suits and dresses. A popular American designer from the 1930s to the 1960s, Parnis turned out reliably fashion-conscious garments which were often understated, always well-tailored, and which reached a wide, appreciative audience. She was noted as a designer for several American First Ladies.

Partos, Emeric 1905–75. Fur designer. Born in Budapest, Hungary. Partos studied in Budapest and Paris and then traveled to Switzerland where he became interested in jewelry design. In the 1930s he took French citizenship and served in the army during World War II. After the war, in 1947, Partos joined DIOR as a designer of coats and suits. In 1950 he moved to Maximilian in New York as a fur consultant and five years later became head fur designer for the New York store Bergdorf Goodman. Partos tailored furs, working vertically and horizontally with skins, to create fine coats, jackets, CARDIGANS, and even dresses. He was well known for his patterns: bold stripes and flowers were two of his hallmarks. A first-class craftsman, Partos was one of the USA's foremost fur designers.

parure Matching set of jewelry, consisting of a necklace, earrings, bracelet, brooch, rings, and sometimes a head ornament, worn on formal evening occasions during the 19th century.

Pasquali, Guido 1946–. Shoe designer. Born in Verona, Italy. The Pasquali company was founded in 1918 by Guido Pasquali's grandfather. After studying mechanics and engineering at Bocconi University in Milan, Pasquali took over the company in 1967. During the 1970s he supplied shoes to Italian designers such as ALBINI, ARMANI, and MISSONI.

paste Compound of potash, glass, and white oxide of lead used to make artificial gemstones. Developed in the 15th century in Italy, paste became popular in jewelry design and manufacture in the 18th century in France and England. Demand for inexpensive but genuine-looking jewelry resulted in innumerable items made of colorless glass compounds often backed with a piece of colored foil. Paste continued to be popular until the 1950s. It was revived in the 1980s, made into elaborate settings. *See* COSTUME JEWELRY.

patch pocket Twentieth-century pocket, large and square, which is sewn on to the exterior of coats, jackets, and dresses.

patchwork The sewing together of small pieces of different materials has flourished since ancient times as a thrifty form of needlework for the household. In the 1960s patchwork coats, pants, dresses, and jackets made of square, round, or hexagonal pieces became fashionable.

patent leather Popular, high-gloss waterproof material used for many shoe styles since the 1930s, when it was developed by leather varnishers or japanners.

Mollie **Parnis**'s navy wool dress and jacket for Spring 1961, teamed with a hat by Lilly Daché.

Louise Brooks was one of many actresses to wear **Patou**'s gowns in the 1920s.

Patou, Jean 1880–1936. Designer. Born in Normandy, France. Patou's father was a leading tanner and his uncle owned a fur business which Patou joined in 1907. Five years later Patou opened Maison Parry, a small dressmaking establishment in Paris, and sold his entire 1914 collection to an American buyer. His career was then interrupted by the war, which he spent as a captain in the Zouaves. In 1919 Patou reopened his salon, this time under his own name. From the start, his collections were successful. He showed bell-skirted, high-waisted shepherdess-style dresses, many embroidered in the RUSSIAN style. He designed for actresses such as Constance Bennett and Louise Brooks but his finest achievements were in the field of SPORTSWEAR, which always occupied an important position in his collection. In the early 1920s his inspired work in this field gave fashion another dimension. He dressed tennis star Suzanne LENGLEN in styles that she wore on and off the court. These garments—calf-length pleated skirts and sleeveless CARDIGANS—endure today. Like Chanel, Patou created clothes for modern women, those who were active and those who wanted to look as if they were active. His branches in Monte Carlo, Biarritz, Deauville, and Venice sold to the international café society. The key to his design philosophy was simplicity. He promoted the natural waistline and an uncluttered silhouette. SWEATERS were always heavily featured and in the early 1920s he showed Cubistic sweaters which were highly successful. He was also famous for his BATHING SUITS. In 1924 Patou put his monogram on his clothing and in the same year brought six tall

Jean **Patou** counsels his American models in the mid-1920s.

American model girls to Paris to show his new collections. Patou worked with the French textile companies BIANCHINI-FERIER and Rodier, constantly searching for fabrics that would adapt to his sporting garments and bathing suits. In 1929 he showed a PRINCESS LINE, a dress which was molded from a high waist, giving the impression that the hips were level with the waistline. From 1919 until his death Patou was a giant of the fashion world, dominating both couture and ready-to-wear. The house continued after his death, run by family members, with BOHAN, GOMA, LAGERFELD, and PIPART as designers. *See* col. pl.

Paulette, Mme. dates unknown. Milliner. Born Paulette de la Bruyère in France. Paulette opened her millinery salon in 1939 and became famous in 1942 for her draped wool TURBANS. She created styles for many actresses, including Rita Hayworth and Gloria Swanson, and had branches in both London and Paris. Scarves and draped fabrics were predominant features of her hats, which were also noted for their lightness. During the 1960s she produced various fur hats. In the 1970s and 1980s she provided millinery for Claude MONTANA, among other designers. Mme. Paulette is one of the most famous names in French millinery. *See* *UNGARO.

Paulin, Guy 1945–. Designer. Born in Lorraine, France. While working as an elevator boy in the Parisian department store Printemps, Paulin sold the company some sketches. He moved

Patou specialized in sportswear for women and was one of the first designers to sign his outfits with his monogram.

Patou tea gown in white silk with drawn threadwork, *c.* 1922.

Patou evening ensemble in velvet and satin, *c.* 1922.

1962
Pea Jacket
gold buttons
white shantung
pants

Navy leather
sandal

The ever popular **pea jacket**, this one designed by Yves Saint Laurent in 1962.

Nylon printed tricot nightdress by Sylvia **Pedlar** for Iris in 1964.

briefly to rival store Prisunic, and later to manufacturer Jimper, DOROTHEE BIS, and the US firm of Paraphernalia. Paulin's extensive freelance experience has taken him to Italy and France, working for Georges Edelman, Mic Mac, Byblos, and others. He opened his own business at the end of the 1970s, only to close it in 1984 when he joined CHLOE, stepping into Karl LAGERFELD's shoes. Paulin is essentially a knitwear designer. His creations are gentle and serenely elegant.

pea jacket The Dutch word *pij* describes a rough, warm, woolen fabric. In the 19th century the pea jacket was a heavy, double-breasted, hip-length jacket worn by sailors, fishermen, and workmen. In the 1920s CHANEL popularized the shape.

pearls Pearls were popular throughout antiquity as decorative items sewn onto robes. They are created in the salt or freshwater mollusc—abalone, mussel, or oyster—when an irritant gets into (or is placed in) the shell and causes the mollusc to secrete nacre, a calcium carbonate crystalline substance. In the 18th century, the discovery of diamonds in Brazil resulted in a decrease in the interest in pearls. Interest was revived in the late 19th century with the commercial production of cultured pearls, developed mainly by Kokichi Mikimoto of Japan. Cultured pearls are created when a tiny bead made from the shell of a mussel and a piece of mother-of-pearl, or other substance, are placed into the pearl oyster. The oyster is returned to salt or fresh water for several years until nacre is secreted. Nacre accounts for 10 percent of a cultured pearl. Pearls are often dyed. In the early 1920s pearl SAUTOIRS became popular. Since the 1950s, a short necklace of pearls has symbolized conservative dressing and taste. *See* ALEXANDRA.

peasant Style of dress that refers to rural costumes of many countries, usually interpreted into fashionable attire with calf-length full skirts; full, PUFF-SLEEVED blouses, smocked or embroidered across the chest; and HEADSCARVES. An unsophisticated style of dress, it has nonetheless been fashionable on many occasions during the 20th century, notably in the 1930s, 1960s, and 1970s. *See* FOLKLORIC.

pedal pushers Loose, calf-length pants, often made with cuffs, which became popular during the 1950s.

Pedlar, Sylvia 1901–1972. Designer. Born Sylvia Schlang in New York, USA. Pedlar studied at Cooper Union and the Art Students League in New York. She started her own firm in 1929 and for many years designed mass-produced lingerie under the name Iris. Pedlar was famous for gracious nightgowns and PEIGNOIRS and she popularized a short, CHEMISE-style nightdress. She used LACE to trim and decorate many of her garments. Pedlar's lingerie designs were considered to be innovative and artistic. Christian DIOR and Hubert de GIVENCHY were just two couturiers who purchased her lines. She closed her business in 1970.

peep-toe Shoe style where the fabric of the shoe is cut away to expose the toe. Peep-toes have been popular since their introduction during the 1930s. *See* *SLING BACK.

peg-top skirt Skirt that is cut to be very full over the hips and narrow at the ankle. A popular style during the 1920s. It was revived in the late 1960s and early 1970s as a style for eveningwear.

peg-top trousers UK term for pants which are cut to be very full over the hips and narrowing toward the ankle. A fashionable style for men during most of the 19th century, peg-top trousers were adopted by women during the 1970s. The material is gathered into a series of folds at the waist for a narrow fit, which contrasts with the full hips and narrow ankles.

peignoir From the French *peigner*, "to comb," the peignoir dates from the 16th century. It is worn by women in their private rooms before dressing. It has always been a loose gown, sometimes worn with a SHIFT underneath, with long or short sleeves, and generally falling to the ankles. In the 19th century, peignoirs were usually made of cotton or other lightweight fabrics and trimmed with lace and ribbons.

pelerine Fashionable cloak worn by women in the mid-19th century. The pelerine, based on an old pilgrim's cloak, had long ends at the front and a short back, usually waist-length. Worn as an outdoor garment, it was made of wool and other warm fabrics.

pelisse Nineteenth-century coat, CLOAK, or MANTLE which was often fur lined or padded. It was usually worn open, to reveal a dress or gown beneath, and made of cambric, cashmere, kerseymere, merino, muslin, nankeen, plush, satin, or silk.

pencil skirt Skirt cut in one straight line from the hips to the hem. It has been popular since the 1940s, when economical cloth measurements were in use, though it was not named until the 1950s.

The long-sleeved **pelisse** was usually worn three-quarter length over a dress or skirt and trimmed in a variety of simple or elaborate ways. Fashion plate from the *Courier des Dames*, 5 November, 1845.

Elsa **Peretti**'s famous heart pendants in gold and diamond for Tiffany & Co.

Manuel **Pertegaz** designed this cotton brocade evening dress with matching sleeveless jacket for 1964.

Penn, Irving 1917–. Photographer. Born in Plainfield, New Jersey, USA. From 1934 to 1938 Penn studied under Alexey BRODOVITCH at the Philadelphia Museum School of Industrial Art. During the summers of 1937 and 1938 he worked as a graphic artist for Brodovitch, who was then art director of HARPER'S BAZAAR. During World War II Penn served with both the US and British armies and in 1943 was hired by Alex LIBERMAN to work in the art department of VOGUE in New York. Penn's job included creating covers for the magazine but he soon began to produce his own photographs. In 1944 he turned freelance, though he continued to work for *Vogue*. Penn's pictures are strong. Although they give the appearance of simplicity, they are often formal collections of something more complex. To fashion photography Penn has contributed a sober, sculptural quality. An artist whose brush is the camera, Penn is famous for his still-lifes, portraits, and female nudes.

peplum *See* BASQUE.

Peretti, Elsa 1940–. Jewelry designer. Born in Florence, Italy. Peretti studied interior design in Rome and worked as a model in London and New York before turning to jewelry design in 1969. Her first success came when HALSTON and Giorgio SANT'ANGELO featured her jewelry in their shows. Using horn, ebony, ivory, and silver, Peretti creates simple, striking shapes. TIFFANY of New York has carried her lines since 1974.

permanent wave In 1904 a German hairdresser, Karl Nessler (later known as Charles Nestlé), working in London, pioneered the use of an electric machine which permanently waved women's hair. Permanents did not become popular until the 1920s, when a steam process was invented. "Home perms" came into use after World War II. The first home perm solutions created tight, crinkly curls. In the years following World War II, a looser, softer style was preferred.

Persian lamb *See* ASTRAKHAN.

Pertegaz, Manuel 1918–. Designer. Born in Aragon, Spain. At the age of twelve Pertegaz became a tailor's apprentice. After his family moved to Barcelona, Pertegaz began making clothes for his sister and eventually, in the early 1940s, he established a salon. Over the following twenty years Pertegaz became one of Spain's great couturiers. In 1968 he opened a house in Madrid. Pertegaz is a classic designer of elegant clothes in the Spanish tradition of grand and stately garments. He was famous throughout Spain for his couture and ready-to-wear lines, despite the austerity of some of his designs.

Perugia, André dates unknown. Shoe designer. Born in Nice, France. Perugia trained in his father's workshop and at the age of eighteen opened a shop in Paris where he sold hand-made shoes. During the 1920s he made shoes for POIRET and later for FATH and GIVENCHY. His work was always associated with a high level of craftsmanship. Perugia retired in 1970.

peter pan collar Flat, round collar, about two or three inches deep, sometimes stiffly starched, named after Peter Pan, the boy hero of J. M. Barrie's play (1904) and children's book of the same name (1911). The peter pan collar was extremely popular with women during the

The **permanent wave** of 1921: *above*, the process; *below*, the result.

1920s, contributing to the boyish silhouettes of the decade. It has enjoyed revivals in subsequent decades.

petticoat From the Old French, *petite cote*, a petticoat was originally a man's undershirt. By the Middle Ages it had become a woman's garment resembling a padded WAISTCOAT or undercoat. As fashion replaced the undercoat with the CHEMISE, the petticoat became an under-skirt, tied around the waist with ribbons or tapes. In the early 19th century, the slim lines of the DIRECTOIRE necessitated the temporary abandonment of the petticoat, but by the 1840s it was again being worn, sometimes on view below skirts. In the 1860s support for Garibaldi's "redshirts" created a vogue for red flannel petticoats. Throughout the 19th century, petticoats were generally made of linen, cotton, muslin, or other fine fabrics. Warmer, heavier fabrics were worn in winter beneath dresses. By the early 20th century, petticoats were rarely visible. They became briefly popular in the 1970s when Ralph LAUREN showed cotton versions under denim skirts as part of his "prairie look."

Paloma **Picasso**'s multi-colored necklace of pearl with a rare hiddenite pendant, designed for Tiffany & Co.

Pfister, Andrea 1942–. Shoe designer. Born in Pesaro, Italy. At the age of three Pfister moved to Switzerland, where he was educated. Later, he returned to Italy to study art and languages. In 1961 he took a course in shoe design in Milan and two years later moved to Paris and established himself as a designer for LANVIN and PATOU. Pfister showed his first collection of shoes in 1965 and in 1967 opened his first shoe shop. His shoes are colorful, stylish, and amusing and have earned him an international reputation.

Picasso, Pablo (Ruiz y) 1881–1973. Painter. Born in Malaga, Spain. The 20th century's most famous artist, Picasso influenced fashion mainly through the work he did after meeting Georges BRAQUE in Paris in 1907. Their Cubist paintings inspired designs of SWEATERS and other garments in later years.

Picasso, Paloma 1949–. Jewelry designer. Born in Paris, France, the daughter of Pablo PICASSO and Françoise Gilot. Picasso was educated in Paris and attended the University of Nanterre. After completing her formal training in jewelry design in 1969, she became involved in theater and costume design. Using jeweled bikini strings from the Folies-Bergère, she fashioned exotic costume jewelry which attracted a great deal of attention. In the same year, Yves SAINT LAURENT showed her jewelry with his collections. In 1972 and 1973, Picasso was commissioned by the Greek jewelry company Zolotas to make jewelry in gold. She launched her first collection of semi-precious and precious stones designed exclusively for TIFFANY in 1980. Picasso's designs are vibrant and imaginative. She is fond of unusual colour combinations and highly polished surfaces.

Picken, Mary Brooks 1886–? Teacher, writer. Born in Arcadia, Kansas, USA. Picken was taught to sew, spin, and weave at an early age. After taking a dressmaking course in Kansas City, she studied design, tailoring, and cutting in Boston and then became an instructor at the American College of Dressmaking in Kansas City, Missouri. From 1914 Picken wrote numerous books and articles, many under pseudonyms, on the practicalities of fashion: dressmaking, styling, tailoring, and fabrics. In 1928 she opened her own studio where she offered classes in fashion and fabric styling for employees of department stores and for garment manufacturers.

pierrot collar Smaller version of the large, stiff, ruffled collar of Pierrot, the French pantomime character, used on blouses during the 20th century.

Piguet, Robert 1901–53. Designer. Born in Yverdon, Switzerland. Piguet was trained as a banker. In 1918 he went to Paris where he worked with REDFERN and POIRET. Piguet founded his own house in 1933. From 1933 to 1951, when he retired, Piguet hired or used designs by BALMAIN, BOHAN, DIOR, GALANOS, and GIVENCHY. He favored dramatic gowns in a romantic style and created many costumes for the theater. He was famous for his well-cut suits and softly tailored dresses.

pillbox hat Small, oval hat with straight sides and a flat top, usually worn perched on the head at an angle. ADRIAN helped to popularize the pillbox with a design made for Greta GARBO in *As You Desire Me* (1932) and it remained in fashion into the 1940s. In the 1960s HALSTON's designs for Jacqueline Kennedy (ONASSIS) brought the pillbox hat back into vogue. It was seen again briefly in the 1970s. *See* *CASSINI.

A 1960s version of the **pierrot collar**.

pinafore *1.* Form of APRON with a bib front, HALTER NECK, and long skirt, that ties behind the waist. *2. See* JUMPER.

pinchbeck Alloy of copper and zinc invented in 1732 by Christopher Pinchbeck, a London clockmaker, to imitate gold. Pinchbeck was a popular choice for jewelry in the 19th century.

Pinky and Dianne Company formed by Pinky Wolman and Dianne Beaudry (both born in 1946) of Indianapolis, USA. Both women studied fashion at Washington University in Missouri and graduated in 1967. In 1974 they moved to Milan where they worked freelance for FIORUCCI and later spent a few months as designers in Hong Kong. In 1975 they returned to New York and established their own label. Their humorous, often androgynous, sleekly styled clothes sell worldwide.

Pipart, Gérard 1933–. Designer. Born in Paris, France. At the age of sixteen, Pipart began working for BALMAIN. He also worked for FATH, PATOU, and BOHAN. After completing his military service he spent a short period as a freelance designer before being appointed chief designer at Nina RICCI, where he has continued the house's style of sophisticated clothes for all occasions.

plaid *1. See* KILT. *2.* TARTAN or CHECK cloth.

plastics Resin-like substances which are molded by pressure and heat to create jewelry such as beads, stones, and different settings. Plastics have been in use since the 1930s. They have also been employed to make garments. PVC, for example, was used for rainwear and outerwear in the 1960s.

platform soles Thick shoe sole introduced during the 1930s. Platform soles have been fashionable at some point in almost every decade, notably the 1940s and 1960s.

Plattry, Greta dates unknown. Place of birth unknown. Plattry was educated in Switzerland and Berlin. She was a popular American designer of knitwear, particularly after-six SWEATERS. In 1948 she designed knits for the American Olympic Association. She created several lines for manufacturer Teal Traina. Plattry closed her business in 1960, though she continued designing freelance for several years.

playsuit Two-piece outfit of BLOOMERS and top, popular for beach attire during the 1950s.

Platform shoes reached new heights in 1934.

plimsolls British term for a rubber-soled canvas shoe popular since the 1870s for beach and sportswear. The name was suggested by the introduction of the Merchant Shipping Act of 1876, sponsored by Samuel Plimsoll (1824–98), which required ships to display a line along their sides above which no vessel must sink into the water, thereby making overloading illegal.

Plunkett, Walter 1902–. Costume designer. Born in Oakland, California, USA. Plunkett studied law at the University of California although he intended to be an actor. Later, working in Hollywood, he turned his skills to costume design and in 1926 became head of the wardrobe department of FBO (later RKO) Studios. Apart from two years freelance work, he remained with the company until 1935. Then followed twelve years as a freelance until in 1947 Plunkett joined Metro-Goldwyn-Mayer, where he stayed until 1965. A respected costume designer, Plunkett contributed to hundreds of films, the most famous of which were *Gone with the Wind* (1938) and *Singin' in the Rain* (1951).

plus-fours KNICKERBOCKERS made of tweed or worsted, worn by Englishmen during the 1920s for sporting activities. The full cut permitted the fabric to fall four inches below the knee band, where it was gathered. Designers revived this garment as a fashion item for women during the 1970s.

plush Cotton fabric with a velvet-like pile which was popular as dress material in the 19th century.

pocketbook Small, flat PURSE/handbag which became popular during the late 19th century. In the 20th century the word can describe any small purse.

Mme. **Poiret** in 1913 in a gray tailored outfit with pink boots.

Poiret, Paul 1879–1944. Designer. Born in Paris, France. Poiret's father was a cloth merchant. In his teens Poiret became an umbrella maker's apprentice but his interests lay in fashion and he eventually sold some of his sketches to Madeleine CHERUIT at the house of Raudnitz Soeurs. In 1896 Poiret joined DOUCET, where his first design—a red cape—was extremely popular. In 1900 he moved to WORTH. Four years later Poiret decided to open his own house and was assisted in this by Doucet, who sent him Réjane, a famous actress of the period. Under her patronage, Poiret was launched. In 1906 Poiret was responsible for loosening the formal silhouette of fashion and achieving a more relaxed shape by extending the CORSET to the hips and reducing the number of underclothes. In 1908 he published a brochure illustrated by Paul IRIBE entitled *Les Robes de Paul Poiret*. The drawings showed simple, elegant, softly fitted gowns, quite unlike the tightly corseted, over-festooned dresses of the period. Poiret actually flirted with the basic shape created by the corset for many years, despite his claim to have freed women from its shackles. Nevertheless, this claim was not unfounded. He promoted the KIMONO shape in the early 1900s and was patronized by Isadora DUNCAN for his exotic, flowing garments. In 1909 Poiret featured TURBANS, AIGRETTES, and HAREM PANTS—all inspired by the BALLETS RUSSES, which had provoked enormous interest in Eastern and Oriental dress. Poiret fashioned garments of boldly colored silks, brocades, velvets, and lamé, simply constructed but rich in texture. In 1911 he commissioned another brochure, *Les Choses de Paul Poiret*, illustrated by Georges LEPAPE. In the same year he introduced a HOBBLE SKIRT which, while it freed the hips, confined the ankles. This fashion was not widely adopted though it attracted a great deal of attention and criticism. Poiret also established the Ecole Martine, where he employed untrained girls to design textiles and furnishings which were later made up by skilled craftsmen. DUFY worked with Poiret on many fabric designs for the textile company BIANCHINI-FERIER. Around this time Poiret produced one of his most famous shapes, "the lampshade," created by wiring a tunic so that the hem stood out in a circle around the body. In 1912 he toured Europe with a group of models and followed this with a tour of the USA in 1913. Poiret made several attempts to promote the wearing of harem-type pants below tunics. He was also noted for fur trimmings, scarves, and hair ornaments. In 1914 Poiret was instrumental in the creation of Le Syndicat de Défense de la Grande Couture Française, an attempt to protect member designers from piracy. At the outbreak of World War I, Poiret closed his business and joined the French Army. Although he was active after the war, Poiret could not regain his former status. Postwar fashions were far more straightforward than his exotic garments. *See* col. pl. BARBIER.

poke bonnet Hood-shaped bonnet with a small crown at the back of the head and a wide brim at the front. It was tied under the chin so that the brim shielded the side of the face. Poke bonnets were popular in the 19th century, reaching such exaggerated proportions that it was impossible to see the face except from the front. The vogue lasted until *c.* 1860.

Paul **Poiret**'s mannequins in his garden, showing their employer's talents. From this marvelous back view we can see the exotic lines of Poiret's designs, his interest in fabric and silhouette. The headdresses range from a Greek-like bandeau to a large matinée hat.

Polka dot sheer voile blouse, *c.* 1950.

polka dot Pattern of evenly spaced dots printed on cotton, linen, silk, voile, and mixed-fiber fabrics which has been popular for summer attire since the second half of the 20th century.

polo coat Coat first worn by attendants at sporting events, such as cricket and polo. Dating from the 20th century, the polo coat is a camel-hair or pale colored light wool coat with a full skirt at the back, intended for casual wear. *See also* BROOKS BROTHERS.

polo collar White, round, starched shirt collar for men which was popular at the turn of the century. Gradually, the name came to describe a soft, high, circular collar that turns down around the neck. Also known as a polo neck, it is often used on SWEATERS and casual attire for sportswear.

polo neck *See* POLO COLLAR.

polyester In 1941 J. F. Winfield and J. T. Dickson of the Calico Printer's Association introduced a polyester fiber composed mainly of ethylene glycol and terephthalic acid. By 1946 polyester fibers were used in home furnishings. In 1963 the DU PONT company launched Dacron to the US public. Polyester fiber was used to make all kinds of fashion garments throughout the 1950s and it has continued to be one of the most frequently used man-made fibers in the manufacture of clothing. Polyester is crease-resistant, dries quickly, and keeps its shape.

poncho Square or rectangular piece of woolen fabric with an opening in the center for the head. Ponchos are worn straight or diagonally. They originate in South America and are often woven with bright patterns and designs. They became popular in the US during the late 1940s and the fashion spread to Europe shortly after. The late 1960s fashions for ETHNIC clothes brought ponchos into vogue once again. *See* *CASHIN.

pongee From the Chinese word *pen-chi*, "home loom," pongee is a plain-woven fabric characterized by irregular cross-wise ribs and a dark écru color. It was originally a silk, but the 20th-century version is man-made, usually of a cotton mix. Both versions have been used for dresses and lingerie.

poodle haircut Hairstyle in which the hair is cut to about an inch and a half all over the head and curled. A popular style in the late 1940s and 1950s.

Three popular hair styles from the 1920s. *Left*, the sleek bob; *center*, the **poodle cut**; and *right*, the crinkled lines of a marcel wave. The dress or jacket of the girl on the left has a deep peter pan collar, while the center girl appears to be wearing a dress whose front section is patterned to resemble Egyptian hieroglyphics.

poorboy Ribbed sweater with a slightly BATEAU NECKLINE and elbow-length sleeves. The poorboy became popular during the 1960s, when it was worn with skirts and pants in summer and over blouses in winter.

poplin Strong, plain-woven fabric characterized by cross-wise ribs that give it a corded effect. Originally made of a silk warp and wool weft, the name comes from the fabric *papalino*, made in the Papal town of Avignon in France, and the French fabric *popeline*, which was used for clerical vestments. The name poplin was common in England by the 18th century. Today poplin is made of combinations of silk, cotton, wool, and man-made fibers. It is hard-wearing and is used mostly for summer outerwear, such as jackets and coats.

pop over *See* MCCARDELL.

pop socks Also known as pants stockings in the USA. Calf or knee-length nylon STOCKINGS worn under pants since the late 1960s.

Porter, Thea 1927–. Born in Damascus, Syria, of English parents. Porter studied English and French at London University from 1949 to 1950. Living in Beirut in 1953, she began painting. At the beginning of the 1960s Porter moved to London, where she opened a shop selling antique Turkish and Arabian carpets and silk textiles. By 1964 she was designing clothes, mainly based on Eastern and Middle-Eastern textiles. Porter's elegant CAFTANS attracted enormous attention. In 1968 she opened a store in New York, followed some six years later by one in Paris. She specialized in evening clothes of chiffon, crêpe de chine, brocade, silk, and velvet which were richly embroidered and decorated. Porter promoted the 1970s' *GYPSY styles with flounced chiffon dresses. Her clothes are sold worldwide, mostly in the Middle East. *See* *HIPSTER.

Thea **Porter** sketch of a keyhole gypsy design in two voiles with flat gold braid trim. Note the clumpy shoes of the early 1970s.

Poynter, Charles In 1881 Charles Poynter took over the Parisian couture house established by John REDFERN. There he continued to promote the firm's TROTTEUR as a fashionable outfit.

prairie dress The prairie dress was described in early SEARS ROEBUCK catalogs in the late 1880s. It was a long-sleeved calico or gingham dress with a frilled hem, reminiscent of the simple styles worn by the first women settlers in North America. In the 1970s, Ralph LAUREN produced a successful "prairie look" which featured flounced white PETTICOATS worn beneath denim skirts and cotton blouses trimmed with broderie anglaise.

Premet French fashion house which opened in 1911 and was successful into the 1920s. GRÈS trained at Premet.

Preppie Style popular in North America in the late 1970s which imitated the dress of the IVY LEAGUE student. Essential ingredients of the Preppie look were the KILT or PLAID skirt, BLAZER, tweeds, and SHETLAND or FAIR-ISLE sweaters. These were worn with white blouses with short, frilly collars. Pastel shades were popular and the combination of red, white, and blue was particularly fashionable. For men, the dress was corduroy pants, madras pants or shirts, and seersucker jackets. *See also* BROOKS BROTHERS.

prêt-a-porter French term for READY-TO-WEAR.

Margot Fonteyn models a **Pringle** cardigan in the early 1960s.

Princess-line dress for summer in the 1870s, showing the vertical seams that create the waist. Drawing by Jules David.

Price, Antony 1945–. Designer. Born in Bradford, England. Price attended Bradford School of Art and then studied fashion at the Royal College of Art, London, from 1965 to 1968. His first job was with manufacturer Stirling Cooper, with whom he remained until 1974 when he moved to Plaza. Price began designing under his own name in 1979, by which time he had already achieved a reputation as a designer on the rock music scene. His clothes were often theatrical and sexy, many of his designs harking back to Hollywood of the 1940s. Body-conscious, glamorous, and often aggressive fashions are Price's hallmark. In the 1980s he has become known. for his positive, shapely COCKTAIL DRESSES and party dresses.

princess line Sleek-fitting dress line achieved by making a garment without a waist seam. A popular style from the mid-19th century, the princess line was fitted over CRINOLINES and BUSTLES, with a gored skirt to create sufficient fullness. It was popular during the 1930s, 1950s, and 1960s, in varying lengths. The princess line has often been designed to button up the front. Also known as fourreau style.

Pringle of Scotland Sock, hosiery, and underwear company founded in 1815 by Robert Pringle. One of the largest companies specializing in the production of cashmere, lambswool, merino, and SHETLAND, Pringle is a subsidiary of Dawson International, the world's biggest processor of raw cashmere. During the 1920s and 1930s the name Pringle became synonymous with cashmere TWINSETS, CARDIGANS, and SWEATERS. The company is also known for traditional INTARSIA sweaters, hand inlaid with flower motifs and patterns.

Prussian collar High-standing, turn-down collar featured on the military greatcoats of Prussian officers in the 19th century. The Prussian collar has frequently been adapted to fashion garments.

Sweaters played a large part in **Patou**'s collections. His Cubistic designs of the 1920s were especially popular.

The influence of art on fashion has perhaps its most direct expression in this Mondrian-inspired cocktail dress designed by Yves **Saint Laurent** in 1965.

The superbly tailored lines of a 1970s pants suit from Mila **Schön**.

psychedelic Irregularly patterned, brilliantly colored clothes, often made of luminous cloth, which were popular in the 1960s. The colors and patterns were intended to represent the effects of taking hallucinogenic drugs.

Pucci (Marchese di Barsento), **Emilio** 1914–. Designer. Born in Naples, Italy. Pucci spent two years at Milan University before moving to the University of Georgia in Athens, Georgia, USA, for a further two years study. In 1937, Pucci enrolled at Reed College, Portland, Oregon, where he majored in the social sciences and received his MA two years later. Returning to Italy, Pucci studied at the University of Florence and was awarded a doctorate in political science in 1941. Pucci was a keen sportsman and as a highschool student had been a member of the Italian Olympic ski team. After World War II, he was photographed by Toni FRISSELL of HARPER'S BAZAAR on the Italian ski slopes, wearing ski pants of his own design. The magazine asked him to create some winter clothes for women which it subsequently published and which were put on sale in various New York stores. During the 1950s Pucci gained a reputation as a SPORTSWEAR designer and contributed to the success of post World War II Italian fashion design. He produced tapered pants, CAPRI PANTS, SHORTS, resort dresses, brilliantly printed silk blouses and shirts, SLACKS, and casual suits. His clothes were always boldly patterned and colored. Pucci also designed ranges of underwear, SWEATERS, and swimwear for US clothing manufacturers.

puff sleeves Short sleeves, gathered and set into the shoulders of garments to create a puffed effect. Used since the 19th century on evening gowns, puff sleeves were also used on children's dresses and blouses. In the 20th century they have been a popular feature of summer clothes for women.

Pulitzer, Lilly dates unknown. Place of birth unknown. In 1958 Pulitzer founded a company in Palm Beach, Florida, USA. She could not sew, but was able to translate her ideas to seamstresses who made up her designs. She popularized a one-piece cotton housedress known as a "Lilly." The company sold A-LINE skirts and dresses in unusual color combinations, such as pink and green. Colors like these and bold floral prints were Pulitzer's trademarks. Her clothes were popular with society women and she opened BOUTIQUES throughout the USA. Pulitzer closed in 1984.

pullover Long-sleeved waist- or hip-length knitted SWEATER worn at the turn of the century for sports activities. During World War I women knitted pullovers for the troops. They became fashionable in the 1920s in plain and patterned knitting, with various necklines, and trimmed with contrasting fabrics—often fur. *See also* CHANEL *and* JUMPER.

pumps Lightweight, flat, plain shoes originally worn by servants in the 18th century. In the late 19th century, black PATENT pumps became proper attire for men attending evening dances. In the 20th century, women adopted pumps made of plastic and leather for day, evening, and leisurewear. *See also* BALLET SHOES *and* CAPEZIO.

Punk Style of dress which first emerged in London, England, during the mid-1970s among teenagers, the unemployed and students. Hairstyles for both sexes included cropped hair, often shaved into strips, or longer hair, glued and back-combed to stick out at sharp angles and dyed red, green, purple, or yellow. Faces were painted pasty white and eyes ringed in black. Punk dress was intended both to attract attention and to frighten. Torn pants exposed dirty flesh; skirts were short and split. Black leather jackets, often studded, dominated the scene. Chains were used to tie one leg loosely to another or were worn around the neck. T-SHIRTS were daubed with slogans. Other popular accessories included STRING VESTS and steel armlets. Safety pins were used to hold clothing together or worn through the nose or ears. Pink and orange were favorite colors and often worn together. Many punk dress ideas found their way, in a more refined manner, into ready-to-wear fashions of the 1980s.

purse (UK: handbag) Bag which is carried in the hand, of any shape, size, or fabric, according to fashion trends, with flat or rounded sides, zipper or clasp fastenings on top, gussets inside, and pockets outside and in. From the Latin, *bursa*, "purse," the first purses were the RETICULES of the 18th and 19th centuries. By the mid-1850s travel created a demand for bags which could be carried by hand and which were roomy and strong enough to hold personal effects. Toward the end of the century, small, flat POCKETBOOKS became fashionable, followed by oversize bags which were the subject of much derision. The flowing fashions of the early 20th century left little or no room for bulky items to be carried about the person and since that time purses have been an important fashion accessory. Every decade has seen recurring fashions in shape and style, and the design of purses, in common with that of other accessories, has been influenced by art movements such as CUBISM and SURREALISM. Shoulder bags became popular after World War II, and from the 1960s photographer's bags, airline bags, and tote bags came into use as purses. The 1970s and 1980s have seen fashions for satchels, DUFFLE BAGS, and imitations of the classic, doctor's Gladstone bag.

PVC (polyvinyl chloride) Fabric originally developed in 1844 during experiments with oilcloth. A chemical relation to linoleum, PVC became fashionable during the 1960s when it was dyed bright colors and made up into outerwear, particularly hip-length "scooter coats."

Q

Quant, Mary 1934–. Designer. Born in London, England. Quant attended Goldsmith's College of Art in London from 1950 to 1953. In 1955 she spent several months with Erik, a London milliner, before leaving to open Bazaar, a shop on the KING'S ROAD, with her future husband, Alexander Plunket Greene, and Archie McNair. Quant began by selling clothes but soon began to design. Her low-priced, young fashions were an instant success. *Harper's & Queen*, a London magazine, featured her spotted PAJAMAS. Quant's clothes were in perfect tune with the 1960s. Bright, simple, and well-

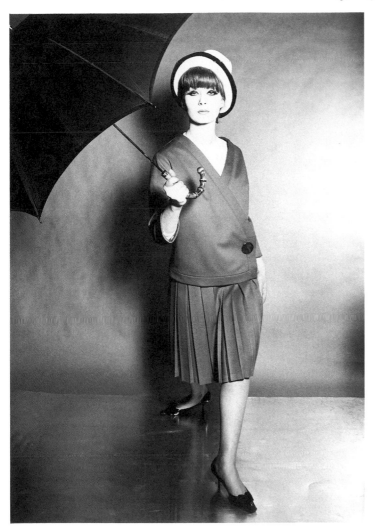

Mary Quant suit, not yet the mini, photographed by Terence Donovan in 1959.

Dramatically simple day dress by Mary Quant, 1964.

Mary Quant, quintessential 1960s designer, wearing one of her own designs, photographed by David Bailey.

coordinated, they epitomized young British fashion. She popularized MINI skirts, colored TIGHTS, SKINNY RIBS, and low-slung hipster belts. She created a "wet" collection of PVC garments and sold vast numbers of waist-length, sleeveless crochet tops. Quant's clothes were classless and appealed to young and old alike. She turned her hand to every kind of garment from underwear and STOCKINGS to all-year-round fashions. In 1963 she formed Ginger Group. Quant was also a success in the USA, where she designed lines for the J. C. Penney store chain and the Puritan fashion group. Although she has continued to design, notably knitwear lines for the Japanese market, Quant's name will always be linked with the 1960s.

Quiana Nylon introduced by DU PONT in the late 1960s. Light and wrinkle-resistant, Quiana was knitted or woven into fabrics that were subsequently promoted as high-fashion materials.

quilting Cotton filling enclosed by two layers of fabric and held in place by stitching of regular or irregular decorative pattern. Quilting was popular for coats and jackets in the early 1920s and again in the 1970s. *See also* KAMALI.

R

Rabanne, Paco 1934–. Designer. Born Francisco de Rabaneda-Cuervo in San Sebastian, Spain. Rabanne's mother was the chief seamstress at BALENCIAGA's Spanish branch. During the Spanish Civil War the family moved to France, where Rabanne was educated. He became a student of architecture at the Ecole des Beaux Arts in Paris from 1952 to 1964. Rabanne's earliest contributions to fashion were his bold plastic jewelry and buttons which he sold to Balenciaga, DIOR, and GIVENCHY. In 1965 he made his first plastic dress. A pioneer in the use of alternative materials for inventive fashions, Rabanne made dresses using pliers instead of needles and thread; metal discs and chains instead of fabric. His chainmail garments, constructed from small, geometric pieces, attracted a great deal of attention. Rabanne also designed dresses of crinkled paper, aluminum, and jersey toweling seamed with Scotch tape. He attached chain links to knitwear and furs. Rabanne was in demand as a costume designer for the cinema, theater, and ballet. In 1966 he opened his own house, where he has earned an international reputation with his unusual jewelry, accessories, and garments.

rabbit Long-haired fur of a rodent found in Europe, North and South America, China, Japan, and Australia. Different kinds of rabbit fur are dyed or marked to resemble other furs. Rabbit is usually inexpensive although it is seldom fashionable.

raccoon Small, carnivorous American mammal. Raccoon fur is hard-wearing and long-haired, varying from silver and iron gray to blackish-brown tones with a dark stripe. Raccoon was a very popular fur during the 1920s and 1930s and had a further vogue in the 1970s.

raglan Coat and sleeve named after Lord Raglan (1788–1855), British Commander during the Crimean War. A raglan sleeve extends from the neckline to the wrist. It is joined to the BODICE of a coat or dress by diagonal seams from the neck to under the arms, allowing for greater mobility of the arms and the body. Initially this sleeve was a feature of the short, woolen, raglan coat, but since the late 19th century it has been adapted to numerous other garments.

rah-rah skirt Short, frilly skirt worn by North American college cheerleaders in the 20th century. *See also* KAMALI.

Rahvis, Raemonde 1918–. Designer. Born in Cape Town, South Africa. Rahvis worked as a freelance designer in London from 1935 until 1941, when she opened a fashion house with her sister Dorothy, selling luxurious evening clothes and tailored daywear. Rahvis also designed costumes for a number of films.

raincoat Devised from the late-19th-century TRENCHCOAT, the raincoat was developed as a waterproof garment in the 20th century and is worn by both men and women. Military-style versions with EPAULETS and double YOKE at the shoulders were worn, collar turned up and looosely belted, by Hollywood film stars of the 1930s. This fashion endured into the 1980s. *See also* *AQUASCUTUM *and* BURBERRY.

Paco **Rabanne**'s innovative look for Fall/Winter 1968/69 is constructed of South African ostrich plumes and aluminum panels.

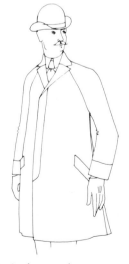

Man's short **raglan** coat, 1898.

Ratia, Armi 1912–. Born in Finland. Trained as a textile designer, Ratia began working with her husband, who produced fabric. She founded MARIMEKKO in 1951 to create simple house dresses. The Jokapoika, a plain Finnish farmer's shirt, was first introduced in the late 1950s. It has been produced in 450 colorways but in the 1980s the design remains unchanged. Marimekko was a great success, particularly in the USA. The brightly colored, simply designed SHIFT dresses featured huge checks and nonfigurative prints. Marimekko extended its cotton lines and introduced jersey dresses in the 1960s. In the 1980s the company produces mainly household furnishings.

Rational Dress Society Founded in London in 1881 with Viscountess Haberton as President, the society endorsed Mrs. BLOOMER's view of utilitarian fashions. Its members took to wearing TURKISH TROUSERS and resisted on the grounds of health any attempt by fashion to restrict or deform the body. Active in dress reform, the society sold boneless STAYS and what it considered to be practical garments. Its publication, *The Gazette* (1888–89), condemned high heels and advocated the wearing of no more than seven pounds of underwear.

Ray, Man 1890–1976. Artist, photographer. Born in Philadelphia, Pennsylvania, USA. Man Ray's family moved to Brooklyn, New York, in 1897. He graduated from school with a scholarship to study architecture but decided instead to take up painting. To finance his art, Man Ray opened a painting and photography portraiture studio. In 1921 he left for Paris and the following year was commissioned by Paul POIRET to photograph the latter's designs. Man Ray is best known for his work as a Surrealist and for his invention in the early 1920s of a photographic technique

The vogue for hygienic garments appealed to those women who favored **Rational dress** styles over the more stylized S-bend.

Madame **Récamier**, wearing the
Empire-line style of dress that she
popularized in the early 19th
century.

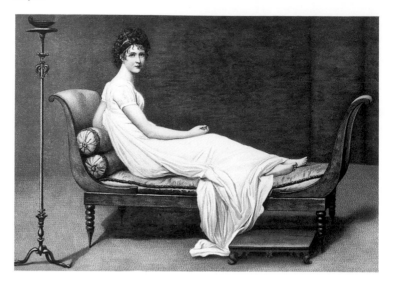

(solarization) which has the effect of surrounding the subject with a
thick outline of shadow. He worked as a fashion photographer for
various magazines and his photographs had a considerable impact
on the world of fashion photography.

Rayne, Edward 1922–. Shoe manufacturer. Born in London,
England. The firm H. & M. Rayne was founded by Edward Rayne's
grandparents in 1889. At the end of the century, H. & M. Rayne
made shoes primarily for the theater and counted numerous
actresses among its private customers. In 1920, to provide
interesting, decorative, and fashionable shoes for a nontheatrical
clientele, the company opened a shop in London's Bond Street which
became highly successful. Edward Rayne joined the firm in 1940 and
in 1951, after the death of his father, he took over as chairman and
managing director. For some time H. & M. Rayne had been closely
associated with Herman DELMAN of Delman Shoes in the USA but in
1961 it was acquired by Debenhams Ltd, one of the largest
department store groups in the UK. Rayne shoes are famous
worldwide and have extensive outlets in the UK and USA. Edward
Rayne has been responsible for finding and encouraging numerous
shoe designers. He has worked with couturiers such as AMIES,
CAVANAGH, MORTON, and MUIR, and for VIVIER, the shoe designer.
H. & M. Rayne have also made shoes for DIOR and MARKS &
SPENCER. *See* *SLING BACK.

rayon Named in 1924 by Kenneth Lord, Sn., after a competition to
find a new name for artificial silk. Rayon is made from cellulose. It
drapes well and has a high absorbency which allows it to dye well. In
1912 the first rayon "silk" STOCKINGS were produced. In 1916 the
first knitwear made of rayon came on to the market, and rayon
outerwear soon followed. Rayon production increased dramatically
in the 1920s and has continued at a high level. *See also* VISCOSE
RAYON.

ready-to-wear Clothes which carry a designer's label but which can
be bought ready-made off the peg.

Reboux, Caroline 1837–1927. Milliner. Born in Paris, France. In the
1860s Reboux's work came to the attention of Princess Metternich.

By 1870 she was installed in a shop in Paris and by the 1920s she was one of the city's leading milliners. Reboux is associated with the popularization of the CLOCHE hat of the period. She worked with most of the major designers, providing hats for their collections.

Récamier, Juliette (Jeanne Françoise Jule Adelaide Bernard) 1777–1849. Born in Paris, France. Daughter and wife of bankers, Madame Récamier was a noted leader of French fashion in the early 19th century. She wore the high-waisted DIRECTOIRE line— also known in France as the RECAMIER—styled in soft, clinging fabrics.

Redfern, John dates unknown. Born in England. In the 1850s Redfern worked as a tailor in the Isle of Wight. By 1871 he had extended his business to sell silk and mourning garments. When the town of Cowes became the center of the yachting world at the end of the 19th century, Redfern began designing sports clothes for women. In 1879 he created a costume worn by Lillie LANGTRY—the Jersey Lily—and tailored serge outfits. In 1881 he established businesses in London and Paris, followed later by branches in Edinburgh and New York. His son, Ernest, took charge of the London and New York branches while Charles POYNTER looked after the Paris salon. By 1885 Redfern was producing yachting suits, traveling suits, and riding habits. In 1888 he was appointed dressmaker to Queen VICTORIA. Redfern helped popularize the high-waisted, so-called Grecian style of 1908. In 1916 he created the first women's uniform for the Red Cross. Redfern closed his houses in the 1920s.

redingote From the English "riding coat," worn by men in the 18th century, the redingote of the mid-19th century was a long-sleeved gown with a large, turn-down collar, worn by women. Toward the end of the century it evolved into a tailored outdoor garment, cut in a

The **redingote** took a variety of forms in the 19th century, cut and adorned in different ways from decade to decade.

Janet **Reger**'s 1980s design for bras, mini slip, briefs, and garter belt.

PRINCESS style with a large, flat collar and a full skirt which was worn open to reveal the dress beneath.

reefer Single- or double-breasted, thigh-length top coat worn by sailors during the 19th century. The semi-fitted garment was often trimmed with EPAULETS, pockets, and brass buttons. In the second half of the 20th century the reefer became popular for casual wear.

Reger, Janet *c.* 1935–. Lingerie designer. Born in London, England. Reger attended Leicester College of Art and Technology. She worked in Zürich as a freelance beachwear designer for some years before returning to London in the late 1960s, when she showed her lingerie designs to the London store of Fenwick, which placed a large order. Throughout the 1970s Reger made a name for herself as a designer of glamorous, sexy underwear. In 1970 she produced TABARD style nightdresses with slits at the sides. Silky nightdresses, satin PAJAMAS, and bra-and-pantie sets in black, white, or pink with dyed lace inserts were popular selling items. In 1978 she created a beribboned WASPIE. Five years later her company was bought by BERLEI, but Reger returned to designing under her own name in 1984.

Rentner, Maurice 1889–1958. Manufacturer. Born in Poland. Rentner emigrated to the USA at the age of thirteen. He became a children's wear salesman and eventually bought a glove manufacturing company. In the 1920s Rentner began selling ready-to-wear clothing. He bought Paris models, notably by MOLYNEUX, which he copied and made up into off-the-peg clothes. Rentner was one of the first manufacturers to hire and promote designers. *See* BLASS.

Simone de Beauvoir in **resortwear** by Hermès in 1938.

resortwear Term for fashions worn in the fashionable resort areas of France during the 1920s and 1930s. SHORTS, beach PAJAMAS,

WRAP-AROUND skirts, and PLAYSUITS all fall in to this category. In the 1980s the word covers all kinds of lightweight garments for summer and cruisewear.

reticule Also known as a ridicule, this dainty 19th-century PURSE was originally made of network and served the function of a pocket. A cord was threaded through its neck and pulled tight and the reticule was carried around the wrist. Versions of the reticule were made in silk, velvet, and other soft fabrics.

retro Word used in France in the second half of the 20th century to describe clothes from another era, usually pre-World War II, which are enjoying a revival.

revers Wide LAPEL on jacket or coat.

Reville and Rossiter Couture house founded in London in 1906 by Mr. William Reville, a designer, and Miss Rossiter, who was in charge of running the business. Both founders had previously worked for the London department store of Jay's. In 1910 the company was appointed court dressmaker to Queen Mary and the following year it made the Queen's Coronation robe. Reville and Rossiter specialized in formal gowns in an EDWARDIAN tradition and were patronized by members of the aristocracy. In 1936 the house merged with WORTH.

rhinestones Glass or PASTE imitation stones, usually colorless or silvered. Rock crystal is also known as rhinestone. Rhinestones have been popular since the 1930s as dress and shoe decorations and jewelry.

Rhodes, Zandra 1940–. Designer. Born in Chatham, Kent, England. Rhodes studied textile printing and lithography at Medway College of Art from 1959 until 1961, when she went to London to attend the Royal College of Art. She graduated in 1966. Rhodes began by designing and printing highly individual textiles, which she sold, made up into dresses, from a London shop. In 1968 she formed her own house. Rhodes' clothes cannot be mistaken for those of any other designer. One of the most original talents to emerge since the 1960s, she has a unique way of mixing texture and pattern, handscreening many of her garments on chiffon and silks. Her exotic evening dresses often have uneven HANDKERCHIEF HEMS. Rhodes has produced felt coats with pinked edges, quilted TUNICS, and embroidered satin garments. Her signatures are Art Deco motifs, zigzags, lipsticks, cacti plants, etc. In the late 1970s she added jersey to her collections and revived the CRINOLINE. Rhodes' fantastic creations are found worldwide. Her chiffon dresses, floating and feminine, are worn by many movie stars. *See* col. pl. PARKINSON.

rhodophane Mixture of cellophane and other synthetics developed in the 1920s by the French fabric company Colcombet. SCHIAPARELLI created several glass-like tunics of rhodophane in the 1930s.

Ricci, Nina 1883–1970. Designer. Born Maria Nielli in Turin, Italy. The Nielli family moved to Florence when Maria was five. She married a jeweler, Louis Ricci. After an apprenticeship with a couturier, Ricci opened her own house in Paris in 1932. Working directly from bolts of cloth, she created elegant, sophisticated

An afternoon suit by **Reville** in the 1920s featuring a cardigan jacket—a graphic fabric design on the sleeves matching that of the dress. The model carries an envelope bag and wears a slouch hat.

Zandra **Rhodes'** "primavera" look for the summer of 1970 in hand-painted silk chiffon trimmed with feather fronds.

A doll dressed in Nina **Ricci** for 1937.

The kind of Op Art design that made Bridget **Riley** famous in the 1960s and attracted the attention of the fashion world.

clothes in classic styles. Ricci was noted for her high standard of workmanship and became a popular designer for older women. Her son took over the management of her house in 1945. Jules François CRAHAY worked at Ricci and Gérard PIPART was chief designer in the 1980s.

Riley, Bridget 1932–. Artist. Born in London, England. Riley studied at Goldsmith's College of Art and the Royal College of Art in London. Her early work was influenced by Impressionism but in the 1960s, after an extensive visit to Italy, she became a noted figure in the OP ART movement. Although her mostly black and white paintings are static, the optic nerve reacts to give an impression of dazzle and movement. In the 1960s Op Art designs became popular for fabrics and Riley's paintings were used as the basis for dress fabric designs.

Rive Gauche *See* SAINT LAURENT.

Robb *c.* 1907–. Illustrator. Born Andrew Robb in Leith, Edinburgh, Scotland. Robb graduated from Edinburgh College of Art in 1926. After some years traveling, he joined a commercial art studio in London and worked during the 1930s for VOGUE and the *Daily Express*. He returned to the *Express* after the war, to cover the Paris fashion shows. Robb was known for the boldness and economy of his illustrations. He worked often with Norman HARTNELL, making sketches of Hartnell's clothes for Queen Elizabeth II.

robe de style Dress style of the 20th century associated with Jeanne LANVIN. A *robe de style* has a close-fitting BODICE, a natural or lower waistline, and a full, bouffant skirt reaching to the calf or ankle.

Roberts, Patricia 1945–. Designer. Born in Barnard Castle, County Durham, England. Roberts studied at Leicester College of Art from 1963 until 1967, when she joined the knitting department of IPC Magazines in London. She became a freelance knitting pattern designer in 1972. Demand for her chunky, brightly colored SWEATERS, jackets, and CARDIGANS kept her busy. In 1976 she opened her first knitting shop selling handknitted clothes. Roberts' new, lively, and exciting ideas contributed to the revolution in knitwear fashions during the 1970s.

Rochas, Marcel 1902–55. Designer. Born in Paris, France. Rochas opened his house in 1924. He was a strong, influential designer with an international reputation who anticipated many of the most prominent fashions of the 20th century. In 1933 his collection featured wide shoulders—a style generally attributed to SCHIAPAR-ELLI. He favored HOURGLASS silhouettes and foreshadowed the NEW LOOK by showing longer skirts in 1941, and BUSTIERS and guêpières in 1943 and 1946. Rochas often worked with flower patterned fabrics. He promoted the three-quarter-length coat and was one of the first designers to feature pockets in skirts. Rochas also specialized in separates and accessories which he sold from a BOUTIQUE in his salon.

Roehm, Carolyne 1951–. Designer. Born in St. Louis, Missouri. Roehm graduated from Washington University, Missouri. In 1973 she began designing polyester fashions for SEARS, ROEBUCK. The following year she joined Oscar DE LA RENTA and progressed to designing for his younger BOUTIQUE collection. In 1948 Roehm established her own company. She is noted for her use of imported fabrics and embroideries to create pretty, luxurious day- and eveningwear.

roll on 1. GIRDLE. 2. Tightly elasticated girdle without GARTERS (UK: suspenders), worn in the 1960s when the popularity of pants demanded unobtrusive underwear.

Ronay, Edina 1943–. Designer. Born in Budapest, Hungary. Ronay studied at St. Martin's School of Art, London, from 1962 to 1964 and then worked as an actress and model, building a collection of antique clothes in her spare time. Inspired by knitwear of the 1930s and 1940s, she began producing a range of handknitted SWEATERS which she sold through London markets. Shortly after, Ronay was joined by Lena Stengard and by the late 1970s the firm of Edina and Lena was exporting sweaters worldwide. Ronay made her name with traditional FAIR ISLE patterns, motifs, and bead decorations. With her numerous outworkers, she is one of the biggest UK handknit designers. In the 1980s she is producing a clothing line.

Rosenstein, Nettie dates unknown. Born in the USA. Rosenstein established her own business in 1917. She retired in 1927 but returned to work in 1931. Until the outbreak of World War II Rosenstein was well known both for her LITTLE BLACK DRESSES and for her evening gowns. She was one of the first designers to use knitted jersey.

Rouff, Maggie 1896–1971. Designer. Born Maggie Besançon de Wagner in Paris, France. Rouff's parents were directors of the house

Edina **Ronay** models one of her own Fair Isle sweaters in 1981.

Known for her sportswear, Maggy **Rouff** was able to design evening gowns equally well. This early 1950s design is in black tulle with a sheer organdy long jacket— rather like a negligée—and silver choker necklace.

of DRECOLL and it was there that Rouff began her design career. She opened her own house in 1929. Known for her lingerie and SPORTSWEAR, Rouff created wearable fashions in the *haute couture* tradition, though she achieved considerable success with her ready-to-wear lines. She retired during World War II.

rouleau Piece of material cut on the cross and made into a thin tube which acts as a belt or piping on hats and coats.

Russian In the fashion world, the term Russian describes several styles of dress, the overall image of each being a full-skirted, layered look, with fur often used as a trimming. After the Russian Revolution Russian embroidery became popular in Paris. Grand Duchess Marie Pavlovna, daughter of Grand Duke Paul, organized a business which employed expatriate women to embroider traditional Russian peasant designs onto garments. The business was patronized by CHANEL and PATOU. There was a revival of Russian costume during the 1970s, when the COSSACK look included full, calf-length skirts; tall, baggy BOOTS; high-collared jackets trimmed with braid; HEADSCARVES and SHAWLS; and hats and circlets of fur.

Rykiel, Sonia 1930–. Designer. Born in Paris, France. In 1962 Rykiel started making her own maternity dresses. Shortly after, she designed clothes for her husband's company, "Laura." In 1968 Rykiel opened her first BOUTIQUE in the Galeries Lafayette department store in Paris. Rykiel is a first-rate designer specializing in knitwear. She creates elegant, fluid garments in soft wools, angoras, and mohair. In particular she favors long, figure-hugging SWEATERS or small, clinging PULLOVERS, large rolled-back cuffs and long SWAWLS and MUFFLERS. Her colors are predominantly beige, gray, dark blue, and charcoal. Rykiel gave knitwear a new sophistication during the 1970s.

S

sable Lustrous fur from a member of the weasel family native to Canada and Russia. Lighter than mink, sable was popular in the 19th and early 20th centuries before it became prohibitively expensive.

sack Loose dress shape which tapered to below the knees, introduced by BALENCIAGA in the 1950s but popularized by DIOR. Although the dress was loosely shaped, careful cutting was required to achieve the correct line. The sack created enormous controversy during the 1950s.

sacque *1.* Short, loose, sleeveless jacket worn with a PETTICOAT or slip as a NEGLIGEE in the early 19th century. *2.* Deep back pleats that fall from the neck to the heels on 18th-century dresses, which were briefly popular again during the 19th century.

safari jacket *See* *SAINT LAURENT *and* SAFARI SUIT.

safari suit Made from heavy, waterproof material, the hip-length safari jacket had large PATCH POCKETS with buttoned flaps and a waist belt. Worn with short pants, it was originally used in the African bush in the late 19th century. During the 20th century the style has been worn as summer attire with long or short pants or a skirt.

sailcloth Heavy, plain-woven cotton, jute, or linen which was originally used to make sails. Since the 1940s it has been made up into casual attire and clothes for sporting activities.

sailor collar Collar made of two thicknesses of a heavy fabric, sewn together and cut into a square which falls down the back and narrows to a point in front, where a bow is tied. It was a popular style for women in the 1920s. *See* SAILOR SUIT.

sailor suit Children's fashion first popular for boys in the 1840s when WINTERHALTER painted five-year-old Prince Edward (who became EDWARD VII) in a naval uniform of a white suit with BELL BOTTOMS, SAILOR COLLAR, neckerchief, and hat. The fashion was later adapted for girls and then for adults. It took various forms, the bell bottoms replaced by KNICKERBOCKERS, SHORTS, or pants. Usual fabrics were cotton or serge. In the 1920s and 1940s sailor suits for women became popular, consisting of pleated skirts, sailor-collar blouses, BOATERS, and REEFER jackets. Navy and white are the traditional colors.

Deep back pleats formed the 18th- and later the 19th-century **sacque**.

The 1984 version of the **sailor collar**, reversed on to the back, extra long, and finished with the kind of bow never seen on a sailor's suit. From the Emanuel 1984 daywear collection.

The young Edward VIII of England wearing a **sailor suit**, a popular outfit for young boys at the turn of the century.

Above: Yves **Saint Laurent** at Christian Dior in 1953.

Right: **Saint Laurent** design for Dior in 1959: a wool and taffeta afternoon dress worn with a pearl choker.

Saint Laurent, Yves (Henri Donat Mathieu) 1936–. Designer. Born in Oran, Algeria. Studying in Paris at the age of seventeen, Saint Laurent entered a competition sponsored by the International Wool Secretariat and won first prize for a COCKTAIL DRESS. Shortly afterward he was hired by DIOR. When DIOR died four years later, Saint Laurent took over the house. The collections of this precocious designer created considerable controversy; they were defiant and not what people had come to expect of the house of Dior. Saint Laurent's TRAPEZE of 1958 was a "little girl" look: a narrow-shouldered dress with a semi-fitted BODICE and short, flared skirt. The following year he revived a shorter version of the HOBBLE SKIRT. In 1960 he showed black leather jackets, TURTLENECK sweaters, and fur-trimmed hems. The audience watched modern, street fashion redesigned in the hands of a couturier. In that same year Saint Laurent was called up to serve in the Algerian war. Several months later, discharged because of illness, he returned to Paris to find that Marc BOHAN had taken over as head designer at Dior. With business partner Pierre Bergé, Saint Laurent opened his own house in 1962. His first collection featured a successful gold-buttoned navy wool *PEA JACKET and workmen's SMOCKS in jersey, silk, and satin. Year after year he made contributions to fashion. In 1963 his thigh-high BOOTS were widely copied. In 1965 he welded art to fashion in his MONDRIAN dresses. He launched in 1966 the "smoking" or *TUXEDO jacket for women—one of his most successful innovations. In the same year Saint Laurent opened a string of Rive Gauche ready-to-wear shops. Velvet KNICKERBOCKERS were an important feature of the 1967 collections. Nineteen-sixty-eight was the year he showed SEE-THROUGH blouses and the classic SAFARI JACKET; 1969 the year of the PANTS SUIT; 1971, the year of the BLAZER. Throughout the 1970s Saint Laurent continued to reign in Paris. One of his most

Yves **Saint Laurent**'s influences: the famous knickerbocker suit of 1967 (*above left*), the culottes of the following year (*center*); and the safari jacket of 1969 (*right*).

memorable collections of the decade, in 1976, variously nicknamed COSSACK or Russian, featured exotic PEASANT costumes. The long, full skirts, BODICES, and boots were widely influential, while the show made scarves and SHAWLS permanent fashion fixtures. Saint Laurent is one of the most important post-World War II designers. From his early days at Dior where he was part of the movement to rethink fashion without couture, Saint Laurent has been a leader. Until 1964 his outfits were basically for the young or young at heart but in the mid-1960s his designs became increasingly sophisticated. He put large numbers of women into pants, adapted many garments from the male wardrobe—blazers, RAINCOATS, and overcoats—into fashion items for women, and promoted black velvet to such an extent that it came to be associated with him. Strict, tailored, yet tactfully cut, Saint Laurent's inspired garments were ideal for the EXECUTIVE woman emerging in the 1970s. Smart, stylish, and casual, they reflected the feelings of the time. Yet Saint Laurent also showed considerable softness with his black COCKTAIL DRESSES, SWEATERS, and billowing skirts. He is hailed today as the father of a whole new way of dressing.

salopettes The French for OVERALLS, salopettes are long pants with a sleeveless bib top and shoulder straps. In the second half of the 20th century, the garment has been adopted for casual wear and sports activities, particularly skiing.

Sanchez, Fernando 1930s–. Designer. Born in Spain. After studying at L'Ecole Chambre Syndicale de la Haute Couture in Paris and winning a prize in the International Wool Secretariat competition of 1954, Sanchez worked for DIOR, creating most of the lines for the

Dior BOUTIQUES, notably the SWEATER collections. He spent a brief period with the fur company Revillion before starting his own company in 1974, specializing in lingerie and loungewear. In the early 1980s Sanchez produced his own ready-to-wear line, but it is for his sexy, glamorous lingerie that he is chiefly remembered.

Sant' Angelo, Giorgio 1936–. Designer. Born in Florence, Italy. Sant' Angelo was brought up in Argentina and educated in Italy, where he studied law and architecture. He moved in 1962 to Hollywood to work as an animator for Walt Disney. He also worked as a freelance textile designer and made jewelry from Lucite for the DU PONT company. In 1966 Sant' Angelo founded his own ready-to-wear business, helping to popularize the GYPSY styles of the late 1960s and early 1970s. During the latter decade Sant' Angelo began designing more sophisticated clothes, appealing to the executive woman. He is well known in the 1980s for his eveningwear and has been instrumental in the popularization of beaded SWEATERS.

sari Length of fabric, forty inches wide by five to seven yards long, made of brilliantly colored silk or cotton cloth, which constitutes the main outer garment of Indian women. The sari is worn over a short blouse and PETTICOAT into which it is tucked and folded at the waist to form a skirt. The remaining end is draped over the shoulder.

sarong Piece of fabric, usually about five to seven yards long, which is wrapped around the body and tied at the waist or over the chest. The traditional dress of Balinese and Tahitian women, the sarong became popular in the 1940s for beach attire, a trend started by Dorothy LAMOUR, who wore sarongs in many of her films, including *The Jungle Princess* (1936) and *Road to Singapore* (1940). Sarongs emerged again in the early 1980s when the basic wrapped and knotted shape was adapted for summer fashions.

Dorothy Lamour in one of many roles as heroine of the Tropics, wearing a tailored version of the **sarong**. She helped promote the garment's popularity as beachwear.

sash Long, wide piece of fabric worn around either the waist or the hips. Sashes made of luxurious fabrics were used on the waists of BALL GOWNS during the 19th century. In the 20th century, they have been used formally and informally, around both waist and hips.

Sassoon, David Sassoon attended the Royal College of Art, London, until 1958, when he joined Belinda BELLVILLE. *See* BELLVILLE SASSOON.

Sassoon, Vidal 1929–. Hairdresser. Born in London, England. Sassoon was brought up in an orphanage. He trained under Raymond (Mr. Teasie-Weasie) in the early 1950s and was soon patronized by pop stars and models. In 1959 he created "The Shape," a layered cut that was tailored to the bone structure and designed for movement. It was a radical change from the BEEHIVE haircuts of the 1950s. In 1963 he cut the "Nancy Kwan," a graduated bob, shorter at the back than in front. The following year he created the geometric "Five-point Cut," in which the hair was cut into points at the nape of the neck and in front and back of the ears. In 1972, in an effortless move from the 1960s to the 1970s, Sassoon and his partner, Christopher Brooker, launched the "brush cut," a soft style with the hair cut into a sphere and then brushed against the shape. The "Feather Cut" of 1977, with its wispy strands falling around the face, was extremely popular. Sassoon stopped cutting hair in 1974 but his salons continued to promote fashionable, up-to-the-minute hairstyles in tune with fashion's shapes.

Vidal **Sassoon**'s 1964 geometric "5-point cut," so different from the bouffant hairstyles of the 1950s.

sateen Strong, lustrous fabric which is usually made of cotton with a satin weave. Sateen has been used for coat linings and, in the 20th century, for eveningwear.

satin Named after Zaytoun, China, where it was first made, satin was originally a glossy, lustrous fabric of closely woven silk. In the 20th century rayon and other synthetic fibers have taken the place of silk. A luxurious fabric, satin is mostly used for eveningwear.

sautoir Long chain or string of pearls. The sautoir became enormously popular and fashionable in the 1920s for evening wear.

S-bend silhouette Toward the end of the 19th century the S-bend shape became fashionable. It was achieved by wearing restrictive underwear which produced a large, over-hanging, heavily-padded bust, and a small, flat waist, which were balanced at the back by a projecting behind, culminating in full, flowing skirts, often gathered and raised on to a BUSTLE. The device which created the shape was a CORSET, cut to be worn low down on the bust and extended over the hips. When tightly laced, it narrowed the waist and pushed the body out at the bust and bottom. This style of dress was worn until the early 1900s. *See also* *BEATON.

The crippling curves of the **S-bend**, the fashionable silhouette from the late 19th to the early 20th century.

Scassi, Arnold 1931–. Designer. Born Arnold Issacs in Montreal, Canada. ("Issacs" is "Scassi" spelled backwards.) Scassi attended the Montreal Design School and in the early 1950s went to New York to sketch for Charles JAMES. In 1957 he opened a wholesale business and after six years began to specialize in *haute couture*. He is noted in the USA for his tailored suits and glamorous eveningwear—often trimmed with feathers and fur.

Scavullo, Francesco 1929–. Photographer. Born in Staten Island, New York, USA. Fascinated by the cinema and photography from an early age, Scavullo was making home movies by the age of nine. On leaving school, he joined VOGUE for three years and was then apprenticed for a further three years to HORST. In 1948 Scavullo met the fashion editor of *Seventeen*, a new magazine aimed at teenagers. For two years, Scavullo traveled and photographed for *Seventeen*, often taking it upon himself to create the hairstyle and make-up of the models, as he preferred a natural look generally considered unfashionable at the time. Scavullo also took covers and fashion spreads for magazines such as *The Ladies' Home Journal*, HARPER'S BAZAAR, *Good Housekeeping*, and *Town & Country*. During the 1950s Scavullo became famous for his techniques using diffused lighting. Since 1965 his covers for *Cosmopolitan* have given the magazine its hallmark of attractive, unapologetic sexuality. Scavullo is also known as a portrait photographer.

Jean-Louis **Scherrer**'s dramatic approach to design is seen in 1985/86 in a taffeta and brocade evening dress and cape.

Scherrer, Jean-Louis 1936–. Designer. Born in Paris, France. Unable to continue his dancing career after a fall at the age of twenty, Scherrer began to sketch. His talent took him to the House of DIOR, where he worked with Yves SAINT LAURENT. When Saint Laurent took over after Dior's death, Scherrer set up his own house. Scherrer produces both a couture and a ready-to-wear line. He creates classic, restrained, and sometimes somber clothes and is known for his sophisticated eveningwear.

Elsa **Schiaparelli** in jazzy woolen mittens, scarf, and hat, contrasting with the plainness of the coat in 1935.

Below: Elsa **Schiaparelli**'s clear plastic necklace crawling with metal colored bugs.

Schiaparelli, Elsa 1890–1973. Designer. Born in Rome, Italy. Schiaparelli studied philosophy. She spent her early married life in Boston and New York and in 1920 moved to Paris. One of her first designs—a black SWEATER knitted with a white bow to give a TROMPE L'OEIL effect—was seen by a store buyer and subsequent orders put Schiaparelli in business. In 1928 she opened a shop called Pour le Sport. Her own salon followed a year later. Schiaparelli liked nothing better than to amuse, either by wit or shock. Her clothes were smart, sophisticated, and often wildly eccentric, but she had a huge following. Her ideas, coupled with those she commissioned from famous artists, were carried out with considerable skill. She hired DALI, BERARD, and COCTEAU to design fabric and accessories. Jean SCHLUMBERGER produced COSTUME JEWELRY and *BUTTONS. CUBISM and SURREALISM influenced her designs. In 1933 she introduced the PAGODA SLEEVE or EGYPTIAN look, a broad-shouldered sleeve which determined the basic fashion silhouette until the NEW LOOK. Schiaparelli used tweed to make eveningwear and hessian for dresses. Her thick sweaters had padded shoulders. She dyed furs, put padlocks on suits, and created a vogue for Tyrolean PEASANT costume. In 1935 she dyed the new plastic *ZIPPERS the same colors as her fabrics and positioned them in exposed places rather than concealing them as dress closings, making their use both decorative and functional. She showed phosphorescent brooches and buttons like paperweights. The French firm Colcombet developed for her a fabric printed with newsprint, from which she made scarves. In 1938 her Circus collection featured buttons in the shape of acrobats diving down the front of a silk brocade jacket decorated with carousel horses. Schiaparelli embroidered zodiac signs onto her clothes and sold PURSES/handbags that lit up or played a tune when opened. Two of her most famous hats were made in the shapes of ice cream cones and lamb cutlets. Schiaparelli's outrageous, irreverent chic was a great success. A brilliant colorist, she took one of Bérard's pinks, which she called "Shocking Pink," and promoted it vigorously. In merging art with fashion, Schiaparelli gave women yet another option in dressing. During World War II she lectured throughout the USA and in 1949 opened a branch in New York. Schiaparelli held her last show in 1954. *See also* *VERTES.

Above: A selection of **Schiaparelli** hats, designed by Salvador Dali.

Above right: A **Schiaparelli** suit, inspired by Jean Cocteau.

Right: **Schiaparelli**'s famous shoe hat designed with Salvador Dali. Dali was also the inspiration for the lips as pockets.

A Jean **Schlumberger** seabird, designed for Tiffany & Co. in gold-trimmed platinum, diamonds, and enamel, and with a tiny ruby eye.

Schlumberger, Jean 1907–. Jewelry designer. Born in Mulhouse, Alsace, France. Schlumberger studied in Berlin for a career in banking. In the 1920s he went to Paris where he began designing jewelry, notable BUTTONS and COSTUME JEWELRY for SCHIAPARELLI. He spent some time in the French Army before emigrating to New York in 1940. Shortly afterward, he opened his own business. Throughout the 1940s and 1950s Schlumberger became well known for his designs of flowers, shells, starfish, birds, and angels. In 1956 he joined TIFFANY & CO. as designer and vice-president. Over the following years he has remained faithful to his early designs of natural imagery. Seahorses are Schlumberger's personal hallmark.

Schnurer, Carolyn 1908–. Designer. Born Carolyn Goldsand in New York, USA. Schnurer trained as a teacher before turning to designing SPORTSWEAR in 1940 when she worked for her husband's BATHING SUIT manufacturing company. In 1944 she introduced a "cholo" coat. Based on an ancient garment worn by South American shepherds, it was a loose-fitting, hip-length jacket with a high neck. Schnurer is noted for innovations with fabric and uses many textiles of her own design. In the 1950s she produced a wrinkle-resistant cotton tweed. She also used cotton for bathing suits and helped promote form-fitting, one-piece swimwear.

Schön, Mila dates unknown. Schön's parents were Yugoslavs who settled in Italy. Schön opened a couture and ready-to-wear house in Milan in 1958. She is one of Italy's most respected designers, known for her skilfully tailored clothes and the couture-like appearance of her ready-to-wear, especially her long, beaded evening gowns. *See* col. pl.

scoop neck Low, U-shaped neckline, popular throughout the 20th century for dresses, BODICES, and T-SHIRTS.

Scott, Ken 1918–. Designer. Born in Fort Wayne, Indiana, USA. After studying at Parsons School of Design in New York, Scott went to Guatemala to paint. He moved to Europe and at the end of the 1950s opened a salon in Milan, Italy. Scott is known for his highly colored, boldly patterned flower printed fabrics which in the 1960s were made up into CAFTANS and TUNICS. Scott has also produced silky jersey BODYSTOCKINGS and is famous for his printed scarves.

seal Aquatic mammal found in colder regions of the world. Hair seals are hunted for their skins, and fur seals, found in the North Pacific, for their fur. Huge demand for the dense, shiny, but durable fur during the second half of the 19th century seriously depleted the seal herds. Seal fur was made into coats and hats. The fur of seal pups is considered particularly valuable.

Sears Roebuck In the 1880s, Richard Warren Sears, a station master and telegraphic agent in Redwood, Minnesota, USA, started R. W. Sears Watch Company. In 1887 he went to Chicago where he hired Alvah Roebuck of Indiana as a watch assembler and repairman. Later that year the company produced a mail order catalog featuring mostly watches, diamonds, and other jewelry. The catalog soon expanded to include supplies for the home, fashions, and some equipment. By 1905 it had reached a circulation of two million. Sears Roebuck is one of the largest mail order companies in the USA. It has traditionally supplied remote towns with household items and clothing by mail, though the company has established numerous retail outlets in the 20th century.

seersucker Lightweight cotton, rayon, or silk fabric with a crinkly striped surface created by weaving together fibers of different shrinkage capabilities. A popular fabric for summer attire during the second half of the 20th century.

see-through In 1968 Yves SAINT LAURENT introduced a blouse so sheer that the body was visible underneath it. See-through fashions appear periodically. They are seldom popular and always controversial.

Selincourt & Colman Wholesale MANTLE makers established in London by Charles de Selincourt in 1857. Joined by F. Colman, the company expanded to produce CLOAKS, SHAWLS, and children's wear. By the 1880s it had become one of Europe's leading wholesale furriers. It has exported worldwide since the 19th century and manufactures clothing for many stores.

sequin French form of the Italian word *zecchino*, a Venetian gold coin. Sequins are small, shiny discs which used to be made of metal. In the 20th century they are made of plastic and used as trimmings. Sequin dresses first became popular in the 1940s and were revived in the 1960s.

serge Even-sided twill weave worsted fabric originally made of silk and/or wool which takes its name from the Italian word for silk, *serica*. By the 19th century serge was used to make military uniforms and, in the latter part of the century, it was made up in various weights into dresses, BATHING SUITS, and outer garments. In the 20th century serge is usually made of wool blends and man-made fibers. It is most often used for suiting material.

The front cover of a **Sears Roebuck** catalog, published for the Fall of 1897.

Seventh Avenue Street in New York which has been the traditional base for the ready-to-wear industry of the USA since the early 20th century.

shantung Hand-loomed silk originally produced in the Shantung province of China. Shantung is thin and soft, woven with uneven yarns to produce an irregular surface. Twentieth-century shantung is usually made of silk mixed with cotton or rayon, which creates a heavier fabric than the original shantung, which is now rarely seen. Both fabrics have been traditionally used for eveningwear.

Sharaff, Irene dates unknown. Costume designer. Born in Boston, USA. Sharaff is known for her costume designs for *The King and I* (1956) and *Funny Girl* (1968).

shawl Square or rectangular piece of cloth worn around the shoulders, loosely tied in front, over the bust. The first shawls worn as high fashion items reached Europe in the 18th century with British and French soldiers returning from the Indian wars. The patterns and designs of these shawls influenced European versions for the following one hundred years. In the UK, the weaving centers of Norwich and PAISLEY produced numerous shawls throughout the 19th century. In the early 1800s shawls were small, silk squares but from the 1830s they emerged as major fashion items. Skirts increased in width at this time and CAPES and MANTLES became unsatisfactory because they could not adequately cover the bulging silhouette. Shawls were the alternative, both for indoor and outdoor attire. They varied from the long, narrow STOLES of the 1830s and 1840s to the massive shawls of the 1850s and 1860s which were designed to

The **shawl** was an integral part of fashionable wear in the second half of the 19th century. Arthur Lasenby Liberty, who founded Liberty of London, started his career at Farmer and Rogers' shawl shop on London's Regent Street. This is an 1866 advertisement for the store.

envelope the CRINOLINE. Indian shawls, especially those with the Kashmiri "cone" motif (*boteh*) were particularly popular throughout the 19th century. Stores specialized in selling shawls made of cotton, lace, silk, or wool; plain, printed, embroidered, and often fringed. In the 20th century, shawls have continued to be fashionable for both day and eveningwear.

shawl collar Coat or dress collar which is turned down to form a continuous line around the back of the neck to the front. It was popular in the 1930s, and again in the 1950s, when its shape was greatly exaggerated.

sheath Figure-hugging dress, usually with long sleeves, which has a tight, straight, ankle-length skirt. It was popularized by film actresses of the 1930s. The 1950s version was often made with a KICK PLEAT at the back. *See also* NORELL.

sheepskin Skin and wool of sheep found in Europe, North and South America, South Africa, and Australia, which is shorn, combed, tanned, ironed, and dyed before it is made into jackets and coats. Hard-wearing and warm, sheepskin outer garments are traditionally worn in cooler climates. They became fashionable for a brief period in the 1960s.

Sherard, Michael dates unknown. Place of birth unknown. London couturier who opened his house in 1946. Sherard was well known for tweed day dresses and eveningwear. In 1964, after the demise of *haute couture*, he closed his salon.

Shetlands Islands off the coast of Scotland, famous for the production of wool yarn and fabrics. In the 19th century, the Shetlands produced underwear, SHAWLS, and SPENCERS. Fabric for suiting, overcoats, and general outerwear was exported from the turn of the century. Shetland SWEATERS, popular during the 1960s, are long-sleeved, round-neck garments made in brightly colored wool which is slightly harsh in texture.

shift The 19th-century shift was a white linen CHEMISE, smocked at the shoulders for fullness. Its simple shape was adopted as nightwear and by agricultural workers. In the 20th century, the word shift describes a simple, unstructured dress which opens at the front and which was popular in various lengths in the 1950s and 1960s.

Shilling, David 1953–. Milliner. Born in London, England. At the age of twelve Shilling designed a hat for his mother to wear to the annual race meeting at Ascot. Over the following years Mrs. Shilling has continued to amuse and outrage race crowds by wearing her son's creations. In 1969 Shilling joined an insurance brokers in London but left shortly afterward to work as a wholesale designer of blouses, dresses, and scarves. At the same time he began making hats for private buyers. In 1975 Shilling opened a hat shop in London. His early hats were often pretty, highly trimmed affairs. They were widely copied to meet the demand created by a reawakened interest in hats. Later, Shilling concentrated on dramatic shapes and silhouettes. During the 1970s he produced the first "disco hats." He hand-prints many of his fabrics and trimmings in color combinations which are both startling and cohesive. Shilling's skill lies in his ability to produce hats which are not only appealing but also light to wear: an essential qualification for 20th-century dress. *See* col. pls.

The **shawl** was an essential component of the "granny style" of the 1970s.

Shawl collar, forming the bodice of a 1950s dress.

Shirtwaist with starched front from *Harper's Bazar*, 28 April 1894.

Ski-ing in 1963 in a quilted nylon coat, **ski pants**, and a striped hooded sweater with the cowl neck.

shingle Short hair cut popular during the 1920s which was shaped to a point at the nape of the neck. *See also* ANTOINE.

shirring Two or more rows of GATHERS used to decorate parts of garments, usually the sleeves, BODICE, or YOKE.

shirtwaister "Shirtwaist" was originally the word for a blouse, the feminine version of a man's shirt. By the 1940s the shirtwaister described a tailored, knee-length shirtdress which had long sleeves (buttoned at the cuff), a collar, and buttons to the waist, where it was often belted.

shorts Short pants, originally part of male dress, worn by women since the 1920s in various lengths. They were associated with sports attire and casual wear until the late 1970s when several suits appeared consisting of shorts and smart, tailored jackets.

shoulder pads Three-sided pads sewn into the shoulders of dresses, jackets, blouses, and coats to give a broad-shouldered appearance. ADRIAN's use of the wide, padded shoulder in his designs for actress Joan Crawford in the early 1930s started a vogue which continued into the 1940s. Shoulder pads were also employed by ROCHAS and SCHIAPARELLI in the late 1930s. They were briefly revived in the 1970s and used extensively in the early 1980s.

silk Natural fiber produced by the silkworm, a grub of the silkmoth (*Bombyx mori*), which feeds on mulberry leaves. The worms spin cocoons, exuding fine filaments which form a thread. Silk originated in China and was brought to Europe around the 12th century. It has always been considered a luxury because it is an expensive fabric. In the 20th century massive silk production in Japan has considerably reduced prices. Silk has been used throughout the 19th and 20th centuries for underwear, STOCKINGS, lingerie, blouses, dresses, and eveningwear.

Simonetta 1922–. Designer. Born Duchesa Simonetta Colonna di Cesaro in Rome, Italy. In 1946 Simonetta opened a studio in Rome and signed her first collection as Simonetta Visconti, the name of her first husband. In 1953 she married Alberto FABIANI. The two designers had separate careers until they tried a joint venture in Paris in 1962. Three years later Simonetta moved back to Rome, where she continued to design for several years. She was a popular international designer, famous for bouffant skirts and sprightly JUMPSUITS. She dressed many film stars in the late 1940s. Simonetta was also known for her knitwear and elegant COCKTAIL DRESSES.

Simpson, Adele 1908–. Designer. Born Adele Smithline in New York, USA. At the age of seventeen Simpson went to work at Ben Gershel's ready-to-wear company where she earned sufficient money to enable her to study at the Pratt Institute. In 1927 she was made head designer at Gershel's. Shortly afterward she moved to Mary Lee Fashions where she designed clothes under her own name. Simpson bought the business in 1949 and changed its name to Adele Simpson Inc. In 1964 the company made GIVENCHY's special collection for Bloomingdales. Simpson designed practical clothes for women who traveled—outfits which could be worn in layers and discarded to reveal eveningwear under daywear. In the 1950s she produced a CHEMISE dress with belts attached which could be tied at the front or back. During the 1960s she designed a collection based on Indian SARI fabrics. She worked directly with the fabric and co-ordinated dresses with accessories: her blouse-and-suit, dress-and-jacket, or coat-and-suit ensembles were extremely popular. Simpson designed for the wives of several leading US politicians.

siren suit One-piece OVERALL widely used during World War II. Based on the boilersuits worn in the munitions factories of World War I, the siren suit had ample pockets and a large hood. It was zipped or buttoned from waist to neck. The siren suit was popularized by Winston Churchill, who was the British Prime Minister from 1940 to 1945.

A 1965 version of the **skinny rib** sweater.

ski pants Until *c.* 1918 women had worn long skirts or breeches on ski slopes. In the 1920s, PLUS FOURS became fashionable. After World War II, when women became used to wearing pants, ski pants were worn. Made of wool, wool mixes, and synthetic fibers, ski pants were ankle-length and tapered, secured by an elasticated strap under the instep. In 1952 stretch ski pants of wool and nylon mix were introduced. These were worn with brightly colored poplin PARKAS. The ski pants shape was adopted in the 1950s as a casual pants style and was popular again in the early 1980s.

skinny rib UK name for a tight, figure-hugging, finely ribbed SWEATER worn in the 1960s.

slacks General name for sports PANTS which were first worn by women in the 1920s.

sling backs Shoe with an enclosed front but exposed heel, supported by a strap around the heel. Introduced during the 1920s, sling backs have been fashionable at some point in every decade. *See also* CHANEL.

Sloane Ranger Term first used by *Harpers & Queen* magazine in 1979 to describe a section of its readership. Sloane Rangers, who shopped or lived in the area around London's Sloane Street and Sloane Square, wear white, ruffled cotton shirts with pleated skirts or sprigged cotton skirts from Laura ASHLEY, round-neck SWEATERS of cashmere or lambswool, dark navy blue or pale TIGHTS, low-heeled PUMPS, a short PEARL necklace, and a HUSKY. The men wear CREW-NECK SHETLAND sweaters, huskies, and green rubber boots.

White calf and antelope **sling-back** peep-toe shoe designed by Rayne for 1960.

sloppy joe Hip-length, long-sleeved, loose-fitting knitted wool sweater with a round or V-neck, worn in the 1940s and 1950s, when it was often teamed with tight pants. The sloppy joe was so voluminous that it gave the impression of being several sizes too large for the wearer.

slouch hat Hat associated with Greta GARBO, who wore it in *A Woman of Affairs* (1928). Based on but slightly larger than the popular CLOCHE hat of the 1920s, the slouch hat was worn slanted at an angle and pulled down over the forehead. *See* ADRIAN.

Smith, Graham 1938–. Milliner. Born in Bexley, Kent, England. Smith attended Bromley College of Art from 1956 to 1957 and spent the following year at London's Royal College of Art. In 1959 he went to Paris, where he worked in the millinery salon of LANVIN-CASTILLO. Smith returned to London in 1960 to work for MICHAEL of Carlos Place and his work was promoted by the London store of

Graham **Smith**'s silk pillbox with a dramatic "S" pheasant curl, designed in 1985 for Kangol.

Fortnum & Mason. In 1967 Smith set up on his own, making hats for *MUIR and other designers. He joined KANGOL in 1981 and has successfully blended the company's traditional BERETS and CAPS with creations of his own.

Smith, Willi 1948–. Designer. Born in Philadelphia, Pennsylvania, USA. Smith studied fashion at the Philadelphia Museum College of Art and in 1964 he won a scholarship to Parsons School of Design in New York. After graduating in 1968, Smith became a freelance knitwear designer. He spent time in India and the USA and in 1976 opened Willi Wear Ltd., a ready-to-wear company specializing in casual SPORTSWEAR. The fabrics in Smith's designs show the influence of his frequent trips to India.

smock In medieval times a smock was a loose, knee- or calf-length garment with a YOKE, made of cotton or linen and worn by women under their gowns. It was also known as a CHEMISE. In the 18th and 19th centuries the smock became a loose, yoked, shirt-like outer garment worn by agricultural workers. Most versions had long sleeves and some had a large, flat collar. During the late 19th century women began wearing smock dresses made of fine cottons and lawn as an alternative to the rigid, corseted shapes of that period. Smock dresses sold by Liberty in its London store from the mid-1880s were adopted by advocates of AESTHETIC DRESS. Since that period, smocks have been worn by artists. In the 20th century the smock is a loose, usually lightweight, sleeved garment. It has been used as a fashion shape since the 1940s, especially in the 1970s, when it was promoted by Laura ASHLEY.

smocking Panel or integral piece of material which is tightly gathered with decorative stitching. Traditionally seen on the YOKE of a child's dress, smocking can also be applied to the waist, hips, or cuffs.

Smocking gone mad in 1881. The cut of the dress and the plainness of the bodice against the fussy smocking serve only to emphasize the hips, chest, arms and the narrow waist. The feather hat contributes further to the ruffled feeling of the outfit.

The **snood** could be worn with or without a hat.

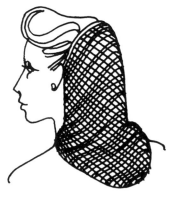

smoking jacket Man's silk, velvet, or brocade long-sleeved, short jacket, decorated with BUTTONS, which was worn at home in the second half of the 19th century. In the 20th century it describes a man's silk robe, similar to a DRESSING GOWN. *Un smoking* is French for a TUXEDO.

sneakers US term for a rubber-bottomed shoe with canvas uppers and laces worn for sportswear from the turn of the century. *See also* PLIMSOLL.

snood Knitted or openwork net which encases the hair at the back of the head. A snood can also be attached to a hat. An ADRIAN design for Hedy Lamarr in *I Take This Woman* (1939) helped popularize the snood. During the late 19th century and the 1930s and 1940s the snood was used to confine long hair.

Snow, Carmel 1887–1961. Magazine editor. Born Carmel White in Dublin, Ireland. In the 1890s, shortly after the death of Snow's father, Snow's mother moved the family to the USA, where she opened a dress-making establishment in Manhattan, New York. After studying in Brussels and New York, Snow joined the family business. In 1921 she became a fashion writer on VOGUE and two years later was appointed fashion editor. In 1932 Snow was made editor of American *Vogue* but in the same year moved as fashion editor to rival publication HARPER'S BAZAAR, where she succeeded in improving the magazine's editorial content. She had great skill in spotting and promoting talent. Snow worked with art director Alexey BRODOVITCH and with some of the most revered names in fashion photography: Irving PENN, Martin MUNKASCI, and Richard AVEDON. After her retirement in 1958, she continued to work as a fashion consultant in France and Italy.

sombrero Tall-crowned, wide-brimmed hat which has been worn for many centuries by men in Spain, Mexico, and South America. Rarely used as a fashion shape, the sombrero is nonetheless a popular choice for summer headgear in hot climates.

Soprani, Luciano 1946–. Designer. Born in Reggiolo, Italy. Soprani studied agriculture before he joined the ready-to-wear firm of Max Mara in 1967. He became a freelance designer in 1975, and in the 1980s designs for GUCCI and Nazareno Gabrielli, though he has been associated with BASILE since 1981. Soprani has a lively approach to fashion. Mixing disciplined tailoring with strong colors, he has emerged as a forceful Italian talent.

sou'wester Rubber or canvas waterproofed hat which has a wide brim and is longer at the back than at the front. In the second half of the 20th century, sou'westers were worn as rainwear.

Space Age Name given to André COURREGES' collection of 1964 which featured HIPSTER pants worn with sleeveless or short-sleeved dresses and jackets. Dresses were short and cut on clinically simple lines. Most outfits were worn with calf-length, square-toed BOOTS usually made of soft, white leather. A large, helmet-shaped hat topped the ensemble. Nearly all the clothes in this collection and subsequent derivative collections by other designers were made in white fabric with controlled use of color.

Space-Age outfit by Pierre Cardin for Fall 1966. The cut-out hole of the helmet is mirrored by those on the dress bodice.

Man's tan Russian calf and white buckskin **spectator** shoe, c. 1935.

The 18th-century **spencer** from which all other spencers derive.

This peach silk chiffon dress with its own capelet and scarf featured in George **Stavropoulos**'s 1985 collection.

Spandex Man-made fiber with high stretch qualities which was first introduced in 1958 by DU PONT. Lightweight yet strong, it is used in swimwear, lingerie, and hosiery.

Spanzelle Registered trademark for SPANDEX fiber made by the Firestone Tyre & Rubber Company.

spectator US name for a shoe popular in the 1920s. It was two-tone, usually black and white, and worn initially for casual attire. It continued to be popular throughout the 1930s and had a further vogue in the 1960s. In the UK, it is known as a co-respondent shoe.

spencer Emerging in England in the 18th century, the spencer was a short, waist-length jacket, single or double-breasted, worn by men. In the early 19th century it was adapted by women into either a short jacket reaching to just below the bust, worn as an outdoor garment, or an indoor evening jacket over a dress. At this time, it was sleeved or sleeveless, with a DECOLLETE neckline. In the late 19th century the spencer was a sleeveless garment made of wool or flannel which was usually worn under a jacket or coat for warmth.

Spook, Per 1939–. Designer. Born in Oslo, Norway. In 1957 Spook went to Paris, where he studied at the Ecole des Beaux Arts and the Ecole de la Chambre Syndicale de la Haute Couture. He joined DIOR for a number of years and also worked for FERAUD and SAINT LAURENT. Spook opened his own house in 1977. He has a lively approach to fashion, revealed in the bold clarity of his line and in his use of bright colors.

sportswear US term for daywear and separates.

Sprouse, Stephen 1953–. Designer. Born in Ohio, USA. After attending the Rhode Island School of Design for only three months, Sprouse spent three years working as an apprentice for Halston, followed by a short stay at Bill BLASS. Sprouse became known in the late 1970s and the 1980s for his stage clothes for rock and roll stars. In 1983 he launched his first collection. Sprouse's clothes were inspired by 1960s fashions, though his lines were far more deliberate. He specialized in bright, day-glo, fluorescent colors, especially "hot" pink and yellow. He made MINI dresses and mini skirts shown with bare midriffs, graffiti dresses, and stockings. Sprouse's clothes were unconventional and inspirational.

squirrel Lightweight, soft, fluffy, short-napped fur of the rodent of the same name found in almost every continent. Squirrel fur is naturally dark gray-blue or red but is frequently dyed pale brown. It is a serviceable fur, used since the late 19th century to make CAPES, coats, and STOLES.

Stavropoulos, George 1920–. Designer. Born in Tripolis, Greece. In 1949 Stavropoulos opened a salon in Athens, where he became known initially for his couture tailored suits and coats. His most popular designs, however, were those based on the classical draped Greek silhouette. In 1952 DIOR invited him to work in Paris but Stavropoulos declined. Nine years later he moved to New York and set up a ready-to-wear and couture business. His first ready-to-wear collections were less favorably received than his elegant, understated couture clothes. By the mid-1960s Stavropoulos's flowing chiffon evening gowns and coat-and-dress ensembles had become very popular, favored especially by Ladybird Johnson. The chiffon gowns were widely copied and as a result the designer created new, more innovative, styles using chiffon and lace or lamé. Stavropoulos's designs for daywear, cocktailwear, and eveningwear tend to be conservative, but his imaginative use of chiffon and his clever blending ensure his popularity.

stays Originally two pieces of stiffened fabric (a pair of stays) worn on the back and front of the body as foundationwear. The garment stems from the 17th century, when it was known as a "body" and made of heavy linen or cotton, usually stiffened with whalebone and short-waisted. In the 18th century stays were composed of rows of boned whalebone or cane sewn into a piece of fabric which was wrapped around the body and laced at the back. Fashions changed considerably in the early part of the 19th century but by the middle of the century the stiff, tightly laced shape was again popular and remained so until the early 20th century. During the second half of the 19th century the word CORSET began to replace the word stays.

Steichen, Edward (Jean) 1879–1973. Photographer. Born in Luxembourg. Steichen's family emigrated to the USA in 1881. He was brought up and educated in Milwaukee, Wisconsin. In 1894 he studied at the Milwaukee Arts Students League and shortly afterward he joined the American Fine Art Company as an apprentice photographer. Steichen went to Paris in 1900 and studied at the Académie Julian. From then until 1914 he moved between Europe and the USA, painting and taking pictures. In 1914 he joined the US Army and served as a commander of a photographic division. After the war, Steichen settled in New York, gave up painting, and concentrated on advertising and fashion photography, taking photographs for American VOGUE and *Vanity Fair*, among others. In 1923 his supreme craftsmanship earned him the post of chief photographer for Condé NAST publications. His work is striking, independent, and thoroughly modern in approach and content. His models confront the camera with their heads held high, posed in interiors and architectural settings which contribute texture and ambiance while providing a framework for fashion. Steichen worked best with one model, Marion Moorhouse, and used her frequently. In 1947 he left Condé Nast to become the Director of the Department of Photography at the Museum of Modern Art in New York.

Stewart, Stevie 1958–. Designer. Born in London, England. Stewart attended Barnet College in London and Middlesex Polytechnic from 1979 to 1982. She formed BODY MAP with David HOLAH in 1982.

Stiebel, Victor 1907–1976. Designer. Born in Durban, South Africa. Stiebel went to England in 1924 and as a student at Cambridge University he designed costumes and scenery for the Footlights revue. In 1929 he became an apprentice at REVILLE AND ROSSITER and in 1932 opened his own house. After serving in the British Army during World War II, Stiebel moved in 1946 to Jacqmar, reopening his own house in the 1950s. He was known for his romantic clothes, which were worn by many actresses both on and off the stage. A member of the Incorporated Society of London Fashion Designers, Stiebel dressed members of the British Royal Family and designed uniforms for the WRENS and the WRAF. He favored jersey and other soft fabrics and became famous for feminine evening dresses and for his outfits for the fashionable race meeting at Ascot.

Victor **Stiebel**'s 1933 plaid evening dress of red, white, and green, cut on the bias. The jacket has pleated sleeves and is lined in black chiffon.

English **stockings** *c.* 1900, with an interesting viper motif. Turn-of-the-century stockings would have been completely covered by the dresses of the period.

Seamed **stockings** like these were the only option in the 1940s. In the 1980s they were shown with the seams and heels colored bright red, a deliberate part of the design.

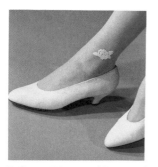

Delicate Dior **stockings** with a rose motif, popular in the 1980s.

Stile Liberty Italian term for ART NOUVEAU which derives from the association of the style with the London store of LIBERTY.

stiletto High, narrow heel which originated in Italy during the 1950s. It was made of nylon and plastic, which often covered a steel core.

stirrup pants Known as *fuseau* in France, stirrup pants are similar to SKI-PANTS. They taper towards the ankle and have a strap, often elasticated, around the instep and under the foot. Stirrup pants first became popular during the 1950s, when they were worn with large, baggy SWEATERS. They became fashionable again in the mid-1980s, made of lightweight knitted fabrics.

stockings Close-fitting coverings for the leg and foot which until the early 1600s were hand-knitted in silk, cotton, or wool. During the 1600s, stockings were generally knitted by machine. The 17th century saw both hand- and machine-knitted stockings but in the 18th century machine-knitted stockings became more and more popular—a trend which continued through to the 20th century. From the 1600s, stockings were made of silk, cotton, or wool, as well as mixtures of these fibers. Artificial silk stockings were popular from the end of the 19th century until 1940, when nylon stockings (NYLONS) were introduced. Nylons were classified into denier groups, a denier being the unit of weight by which the silk, rayon, or nylon yarns are measured. Fifteen denier is a light, very sheer stocking, while 40 denier is thicker and more durable. Throughout the 19th century colored stockings, largely knitted by machine, were popular. During the early 20th century, as skirt lengths began to rise, patterned stockings enjoyed a brief vogue; black stockings became fashionable in the 1920s, as did ribbed and patterned versions. Due to a shortage of materials during World War II, women were obliged to go without stockings and took to wearing ANKLE SOCKS. The flesh colors and sun-tan shades which had become essential before the war retained their popularity in the postwar years. In the 1950s seamless stockings became generally available and knee-high stockings and PANTIEHOSE were also launched. Ten years later there was a trend for stockings and pantiehose in stripes and lacy and geometric patterns, as well as stockings with ankle motifs. In the more sober 1970s, dark TIGHTS, especially heavy ribbed versions, were common. In the 1980s stockings regained some of their popularity and there was a great deal of fashion interest in legwear. It was fashionable to wear highly colored hose in PAISLEY patterns, CHECKS, hand-painted designs, and animal skin patterns.

stole Long, rectangular wrap which is usually worn around the shoulders and folded across the chest. It first became popular in the 1950s when it was worn in the evening over long dresses.

Strauss, Levi dates unknown. Born in Bavaria. Strauss arrived in San Francisco, California, during the goldmining boom of the 1850s. His first work pants for miners were cut from brown tent canvas but several years later he began using denim, a French fabric which he dyed blue with indigo. In 1872 Strauss took out a patent for his hardwearing pants. Jacob Davis, a tailor from Carson City, Nevada, joined Strauss in 1873 to patent a garment which had copper rivets at its stress points. Strauss died in 1902 but the business continues as a family concern. In the US the word "Levi's" is synonymous with denim JEANS.

Levi's from Levi **Strauss**:
the real thing: two miners wearing
their levi's. Levi's in 1982,
with the worn-in look rather than
the worn-out look of the 1960s.

string vest Loosely knit sleeveless vest of cotton based on an
undervest worn by men since the 19th century. It became popular as
outer attire for a brief period during the 1960s.

suede Suede is produced by buffing the flesh side of a tanned animal
hide. The result is a velvet-like surface on one side of the leather. In
the 20th century, especially after World War II, suede has been used
mainly for coats and jackets, though it is also made into skirts,
JERKINS, shoes, and PURSES/handbags.

suede fabric Man-made fabric made of knitted or woven cotton and
other fibers, which is finished to resemble suede. A popular material
in North America from the mid-20th century for dresses, coats,
skirts, and suits. *See also* HALSTON *and* ULTRASUEDE.

sunglasses First produced in lightly tinted glass in 1885, sunglasses
did not become a fashion accessory until the 1930s, when they were

The **sweetheart neckline** on a ruched bodice of 1943.

popularized by Hollywood's film stars. It was at this time that dark lenses became fashionable. The 1950s saw the appearance of sunglasses of outlandish design—star spangled versions, glasses designed to resemble flowers, and wrap-around glasses. This vogue continued into the 1960s. In the more sober, perhaps more status-conscious, 1970s, initialed "designer" glasses became popular. In the 1980s black sunglasses—both lenses and frame—became fashionable as the trend for less conservative sunglasses re-emerged.

sunray pleats Fine pleats which radiate out from a central point on the waistband of a skirt or dress. *See* DIOR.

surah The original surah, from Surat in India, was a soft, lustrous fabric made from twilled silk. In the 20th century surah is a man-made fiber used in the manufacture of blouses and dresses.

Surrealism Movement in art and literature between the two World Wars which reacted against the rationalization and formalism of prevailing trends and concentrated on fantasy and reconstruction of a dream-world. Painters who were influenced by Surrealism included René Magritte, Salvador DALI, Pablo PICASSO, and Joan Miró. In fashion, the term Surrealism emerged in the late 1920s and was most often used during the 1930s to describe weird or psychologically suggestive garments. *See* SCHIAPARELLI.

suspenders Designed to hold up men's breeches in the 18th century, suspenders were originally made of cord or webbing. By the late 19th century, canvas, cotton, rubber, and velvet were all used in the making of suspenders. Around 1900 suspenders became two bands joined at the back and attached to pants by buttons and, later, by metal clips. In the 20th century they are usually made of ELASTIC. Women appropriated suspenders during the 1960s and 1970s as part of the UNISEX trend. Known in the UK as "braces."

sweater Knitted woolen shirt worn by sportsmen in the late 19th century to encourage perspiration. In the 20th century the word sweater describes a sleeved, knitted woolen top reaching to the waist or longer. Evening sweaters trimmed with chiffon or crêpe and embroidered with jewels were fashionable in the late 1930s. In the 1940s, short, waist-length versions were all the rage. During the 1950s, there was a vogue for baggy, long sweaters, a look which some women achieved by wearing men's sweaters. In the following decade sweaters of all lengths and styles have been acceptable fashion wear and this trend has continued, though since the late 1970s sweater designs have become more sophisticated.

sweatshirt *See* SWEATSHIRTING.

sweatshirting Thick, fleecy, cotton fabric worn with the fleecy side against the skin. Made into casual SWEATERS and T-SHIRTS, called sweatshirts, they have been worn by 20th-century athletes for warm-up practice. In the 1960s sweatshirts printed with the name of various US universities became popular casual attire. *See* *KAMALI.

sweetheart neckline Neckline on dresses and blouses which is cut into two almost semicircular curves which resemble a heart. The sweetheart neckline has been popular throughout the 20th century.

swimsuit *See* BATHING SUIT.

David **Shilling**'s witty creations have brought him world renown. Best known for his confections for the fashionable race meeting at Ascot, he also turns his hand to frivolities such as these: *Above*, a 1976 disco hat and, *below*, a dotted crash helmet from a 1985 collection.

The **tailleur** belonged in every turn-of-the-century
wardrobe. This model dates from 1912.

Queen Victoria's fondness for the Scottish Highlands
was largely responsible for the popularity of **tartan**
garments in the second half of the 19th century. In
the 20th century tartan skirts and pants have made
their appearance on fashion runways. This is the
tartan of the MacInnes clan.

T

tabard Dating from the Middle Ages, when it was worn as a military or ceremonial garment, the tabard is a hip-length, rectangular, sleeveless top, with a hole cut out for the head. It was fashionable during the 1960s. *See also* TUNIC.

tablier French for apron. A gown or skirt, designed with a front portion which resembles a decorative apron. Tablier skirts were fashionable in the 1860s and 1870s.

taffeta Fine, stiff fabric woven from real or artificial silk, with a glossy, iridescent sheen. Taffeta is believed to be named after the Persian fabric "taftan." It has been popular for eveningwear since the 19th century.

tailleur Tailored suit or ensemble which became popular during the second half of the 19th century.

tam o'shanter Round woolen cap named after the hero of the poem of the same name by the Scottish poet Robert Burns. It has a tight headband and a full, soft crown and is usually decorated with a center pom-pon. During the late 19th century, women wore tam o'shanters for sporting activities. Also known as a Balmoral cap.

tango dress Dress worn to perform the tango, a South American dance popular in Europe between 1910 and the outbreak of World War II. An ankle-length dress, it was draped and split in the front to allow freedom of movement, and revealed part of the lower leg.

tango shoe Shoe which achieved popularity *c.* 1910 as a result of the craze for tango dancing. The tango shoe was often made in white satin, with ribbon ankle straps, and had a small, curved heel.

tank top Short, sleeveless top with wide armholes which was popular in the 1960s and 1970s for casual wear, made from brightly colored or patterned crochet or wool.

tapestry Originally an ornamental woven cloth in which the design tells a story. In the fashion world, the word tapestry describes a heavily flowered raised design on fabric. Tapestry garments were briefly popular during the 1960s.

Tarlazzi (Bayard de Volo), **Angelo** 1945–. Designer. Born in Ascoli Piceno, Italy. Tarlazzi studied political science in Rome but abandoned his studies in his last year, at the age of nineteen, to enter the house of CAROSA, where he spent four years designing BALL GOWNS. In 1966, Tarlazzi went to Paris as an assistant to Michel GOMA at PATOU. He left in 1969 to work freelance, work which took him to New York in 1971 and 1972. He eventually returned to Paris to take over the artistic direction of Patou. Tarlazzi opened his own house in Paris in 1978. He creates unconventional clothes for the conventional woman. His designs are generously cut but always neat, sculpted, and made of supple fabrics. Tarlazzi pays close attention to the body, which he swathes with long lines and highlights with asymmetrical drapes. He is famous for long, cashmere CARDIGANS and knitwear.

Who would have thought that 18th-century gentlemen's combinations would be the basic silhouette for a marvelously supple and fluid garment such as this? By Angelo **Tarlazzi** for his 1984/85 collection. Shoes designed by Guido Pasquali.

tartan Closely woven woolen cloth which originated in Scotland, where different patterns are used to identify individual clans. The fabric is cross-banded with colored stripes which create designs of various checked widths. In the 1840s Queen VICTORIA's frequent visits to her estate at Balmoral in Scotland stimulated a fashion for tartan garments. After World War II tartan KILTS and skirts became popular. In the 1980s tartan pants were introduced by various designers and many winter collections have featured tartan fabric. *See* PLAID *and* col. pl.

Tassell, Gustave 1926–. Designer. Born in Philadelphia, Pennsylvania, USA. Tassell studied at the Philadelphia Academy of Fine Arts. In the late 1940s he joined Hattie CARNEGIE in New York, working first as a window dresser and later as a designer. After spending 1952 to 1964 in Paris, selling sketches to couture houses, he set up his own business in California. The spare simplicity of his first collection made him famous. Tassell went on to design other clean, elegant garments until 1972, when he moved to New York to take over Norman NORELL's house after Norell's death. He later resumed designing under his own name.

T-bar Woman's heeled shoe with a T-shaped strap cut from the uppers. It was introduced at the turn of the century and has remained a popular style, notably in the first half of the 20th century.

tea gown In the mid-19th century women wore pre-dinner gowns which were simply structured to allow CORSETS to be loosened or removed underneath. By the 1870s the tea gown was an elaborate affair, often long-sleeved, high-waisted, and full at the back. It was

The **tea gown** of 1888, featured in *Queen*—a more relaxed version of the well-constructed day dress.

made of chiffon, muslin, silk, or satin and trimmed with lace ruffles and ribbons. Many tea gowns had elaborate TRAINS. In the 1920s, when women began to discard their corsets, and cut-away, slender COCKTAIL DRESSES became fashionable, the tea gown's popularity dwindled. It was replaced by the HOSTESS GOWN of the 1950s. *See* LUCILE *and* PEIGNOIR.

teddy One-piece undergarment of unstructured BODICE and knickers which originated in the 19th-century CAMISOLE and knickers. The teddy first became popular in the 1920s when that era's slender, boyish shapes required minimal underwear.

tent dress In 1951 Cristobal BALENCIAGA introduced a woolen coat which flared from a low-standing collar into a widening A shape. Known as the tent, it was used for both dresses and coats. It is similar to the A-LINE, although the tent is generally more exaggerated. *See also* MCCARDELL.

terry cloth Cotton cloth woven with uncut loops on one side. Usually used for towels, terry cloth has been made up into beachwear since the 1950s.

Terylene Man-made fiber developed by the Calico Printer's Association in 1941. It was produced by ICI and became the tradename for their fiber.

Thaarup, Aage 1907–. Milliner. Born in Copenhagen, Denmark. Thaarup left school at sixteen to work in the ladies' hat department of Fonnesbeck's, a Copenhagen fashion store. From 1926 to 1932 he traveled to Berlin, Paris, London, Bombay, and finally Delhi, where he set up a millinery business specializing in mourning hats. On his return to London in the early 1930s Thaarup's designs attracted great attention. One hat was decorated with tiny colored safety pins; another—a white felt PILLBOX called "Purl and Plain"—was trimmed with red and white knitting wool and two knitting needles. His other designs included peaked schoolboy caps; large "halo" hats which broke with the current trend of TURBANS and BRETONS that sat deep on the head; and straw hats trimmed with plastic vegetables. He made hats for the Queen Mother (then Duchess of York) and for numerous actresses. After World War II, Thaarup designed "Teen and Twenty" hats, a mass-produced line that sold worldwide. In 1955 he made Princess Elizabeth's bearskin plumed TRICORNE for the Trooping of the Colour. Thaarup continued to design millinery for Elizabeth after she became Queen.

Thomass, Chantal 1947–. Designer. Born in Paris, France. In 1967 Thomass sold dresses made from hand-painted scarves to DOROTHEE BIS. In the same year, with her husband, she established a company, Ter and Bantine, to sell young, off-beat clothes. The company was re-formed as Chantal Thomass in 1976. Since then Thomass has acquired a reputation for exotic underwear and theatrical, flirtatious clothes, many trimmed with frills and flounces, made in sophisticated fabrics. Her clothes are enchanting, highly individual, and distinctive.

ticking Heavy twill fabric, striped with colored yarns and used for covering mattresses. In the second half of the 20th century ticking has been used to make fashion garments. *See* BEENE.

A popular garment of the 1960s: the **tie-dye** mini-dress.

tie Originally "necktie," a wide band worn around the neck and elaborately draped or folded on the chest, worn by men in the 18th and 19th centuries. The tie, a narrow version of the above, usually worn under the collar of a shirt, evolved in the late 19th century and has been an essential item of formal menswear ever since. At the end of the 19th century women began wearing ties with blouses and skirts, though this was a trend rather than a longstanding fashion. Ties were again popular as part of the UNISEX fashions of the 1960s.

tie dye Method of dyeing fabric whereby tiny pockets of the material are tied with thread to prevent the color spreading to those areas, thus producing an irregular pattern. Tie-dye T-SHIRTS and casual shirts were popular in the 1960s.

Tiffany & Co. Company founded in New York City in 1837 by Charles Lewis Tiffany (1812–1902) and John B. Young (dates unknown) as a stationery and fancy goods store. A third partner, J. L. Ellis, was taken on in 1841 and in the same year the firm began to buy important European jewelry collections. In 1853 Tiffany bought out the company, thereafter known as Tiffany & Co. The company merged in 1868 with a silversmith, Edward C. Moore & Co., who had previously worked as a Tiffany designer. Louis Comfort Tiffany (1844–1933), son of the founder, joined the firm in 1900. Tiffany & Co. has an international reputation as a high class jewelers, dealing in gemstones and precious metals. *See also* PERETTI; PICASSO, PALOMA; *and* SCHLUMBERGER.

Tiffeau, Jacques 1927–. Designer. Born in Cheneuelles, France. Tiffeau studied men's tailoring in the provinces and in Paris. After military service, he worked with a Parisian tailor until 1951, when he emigrated to New York. Hired as a pattern cutter by Maz Pruzan at the firm of Monte-Sano, Tiffeau soon became the firm's designer. In 1958 he and Pruzan's daughter, Beverly Busch, formed Tiffeau-Busch, a company specializing in young SPORTSWEAR. The firm closed in the late 1960s and Tiffeau returned to Paris where he worked for SAINT LAURENT in the early 1970s. In 1976 he was back in New York, designing freelance for Bill BLASS, among others.

Jacques **Tiffeau**'s 1964 design in houndstooth, with a jacket and matching tight pants.

tights Stretchable garment covering the feet, legs, and body up to the waist. Associated with the theater for several centuries, tights and pantiehose (a combination of panties and STOCKINGS) were introduced onto the fashion market in the 1960s as an alternative to stockings. Although they were slow to catch on, by the 1970s most women wore them. Since then they have been made in almost every color and pattern and have become an indispensable part of dress in both summer and winter. In the 1980s highly decorated and patterned tights appeared on the market. Lacy patterns have been popular since the 1960s. Other designs include multicolors, stripes, dots, and even handpainted versions.

Tinling, Teddy 1910–. Designer. Born in Eastbourne, England. At the age of twenty-one, Tinling opened a fashion house in London and during the 1930s his innovative designs for tennis star Suzanne LENGLEN attracted many other tennis clients. He joined the British Army in 1939, reopening his house on his demobilization in 1947. Two years later his name became a household word when he designed a pair of frilly lace panties which were worn at Wimbledon by Gussie Moran. Tinling has always been involved in tennis, working for the Lawn Tennis Association and other tennis bodies, mostly in the field of public relations. From 1952 to the 1980s he dressed most of the internationally famous women tennis stars both on court and off, using bizarre fabrics, such as crush resistant tweed, for some of his designs. In 1975 he moved his business to the USA.

tippet Piece of fabric, usually lace or lawn, wound like a small SHAWL around the neck, with the ends left hanging. A fashionable accessory for day and eveningwear during the 19th century.

toggle Method of fastening a coat or jacket by looping a piece of cord or braid around a wooden or plastic peg.

topless The most celebrated topless garment was the topless BATHING SUIT, designed in 1964 in California, USA, by Rudi GERNREICH. In a decade of considerable experimentation with dress and undress, the topless bathing suit was important as a symbol of freedom, though it never gained popularity as costume. The suit covered the body from the thighs to a high waist, where two thin straps crossed between the breasts and over the back.

topper Generously cut hip-length coat, often with a SHAWL collar and large, turn-back cuffs, worn in the 1950s.

toque Close-fitting, brimless headdress made from light wool, jersey, or other fabrics with good draping qualities. An item of decoration, such as a FEATHER or jewel, adorned the center of the toque. It was a popular style during the 1920s and 1930s.

A 1960s advertisement for **tights** and pantiehose in the Sears Roebuck catalog.

The **topper** was an all-round coat shape during the 1950s.

toreador pants Tight pants which lace at the knee, copied from the pants worn by Spanish bullfighters. Toreador pants became popular during the mid-20th century.

tortoise-shell Translucent yellow and mottled brown material obtained from the carapace of the hawk's-bill turtle. Tortoise-shell has been used for making jewelry since Roman times. Piqué tortoise-shell, inlaid with gold, silver, or mother-of-pearl, was used from the 17th century for hair combs, brooches, and jewelry. The fashion for tortoise-shell peaked in the late 19th century and after World War I its popularity declined.

Toudouze, Anaïs 1822–99. Illustrator. Born in the Ukraine. Toudouze engraved fashion illustrations for more than thirty-five magazines, including *Monde élégant de 1850*, *Magazine des demoiselles*, *Modes de Paris de 1857*, and *Moniteur de la toilette*. Her daughter, Isabelle Desgrange (1850–1907), was also a prolific fashion illustrator.

tracksuit Two-piece outfit worn by athletes during the 20th century. Made of heavy cotton and/or synthetic fibers, the pants are elasticated at waist and ankle. The top has long sleeves and an elasticated or drawstring waist. In the 1970s the tracksuit became fashionable casual attire for women.

train Long, rectangular piece of fabric which is attached to the back of a dress at the shoulders or waist. During the 19th century, trains were popular for formal evening attire but they had almost disappeared from the fashion scene by the turn of the century. *See also* WORTH.

trapeze line Launched by Yves SAINT LAURENT in 1958, the trapeze—short for trapezium, a quadrilateral shape with two parallel sides—was a wide, full, tent shape which reached to the knees. The bust was high and the back of the dress was cut to fall free from the shoulders.

trenchcoat Nineteenth-century military-style coat with EPAULETS and a double YOKE at the shoulders. In the 20th century, the civilian version of a World War I soldier's coat became known as a trenchcoat. Made of lightweight wool or a cotton mix, it is worn as a RAINCOAT or topcoat.

Trevira Trademark of Hoechst Fibers. *See* POLYESTER.

tricorne Three-cornered hat with a turned up brim. Once part of military uniform, it was briefly popular with women in the 1930s.

tricot French for "knitting." Tricot is usually a woven or knitted cloth with fine lines on one side and cross ribs on the other. In the 20th century it has been used for a variety of garments, including SWEATERS, two-piece suits, and dresses.

Trigère, Pauline 1912–. Designer. Born in Paris, France. Trigère knew how to operate a sewing machine by the age of ten and assisted her dressmaker mother. Her father was a tailor. After leaving

A **tricorne** hat in straw, Spring 1939.

Just right for jogging: **tracksuits** advertised in 1982 by Sears Roebuck.

In the late 19th century, getting dressed to go out was a complicated process. One needed a hat as well as a muff and jacket, though it is unlikely that the wearer would feel cold in layers of bead-trimmed fabric and a long **train**.

Many women adopted **trilbies** in the 1940s.

The International Wool Secretariat commissioned these **trompe l'oeil** outfits in 1965. Schiaparelli first set the vogue in the early 1920s. Note the Tyrolean style hats in this picture, another Schiaparelli invention, this time of the 1930s.

school, Trigère was employed as a cutter at Martial et Armand in the Place Vendôme, Paris. In 1937 she moved to New York and became assistant designer to Travis BANTON at Hattie CARNEGIE. Five years later she started her own house. Trigère's first small collection of custom-made dresses was bought out by a group of US department store executives and she began producing ready-to-wear lines in the late 1940s. Trigère works by cutting and draping bolts of fabrics. She is known for her crisp, tailored cuts and innovative ideas, particularly with outerwear. Credited with the introduction of removable scarves and collars from dresses and coats, Trigère has also created dresses with jewelry attached, sleeveless coats, reversible coats, and opera CAPES. One of her capes is made from black blanket wool and angora reversible to a shocking pink. Many of her coats are designed to be worn with two interchangeable dresses. Fur trims are often seen in her collections. Trigère was one of the first designers to use wool for eveningwear.

trilby Soft felt hat with a plush-like texture, a dented crown, and a flexible brim. The same style, trimmed with a feather, is worn in the Austrian Tyrol. The trilby takes it name from the heroine of G. du Maurier's novel *Trilby* (1894), in the stage version of which a trilby was worn. It was a popular hat style in the 1930s and 1940s.

trompe l'oeil Optical illusion created by seaming or knitting a design into a garment. *Trompe l'oeil* is usually associated with painting and decoration. In the 1930s Elsa SCHIAPARELLI designed sweaters with *trompe l'oeil* collars knitted into the overall design.

trotteur French for "walking suit," an outfit introduced by John REDFERN in the 1890s. The trotteur consisted of a man's braid-trimmed jacket with buttons down the front and an ankle-length skirt which was flared at the back to permit easy walking. A highly popular suit, it was usually made of serge and wool.

trousers *See* PANTS.

T-shirt T-shaped, short sleeved, cotton shirts were worn by men under uniforms during World War I and were later adopted by laborers. Since the 1960s T-shirts have been widely popular in the West, printed with political slogans, logos, jokes, social comments, or brand names. Plain T-shirts, in cotton or cotton mix, are worn as summer attire.

Tuffin and Foale *See* FOALE *and* TUFFIN.

Tuffin, Sally 1938–. Designer. Born in England. Tuffin studied at Walthamstow School of Art and the Royal College of Art in London. She graduated in 1961 and the following year established Tuffin & Foale with Marion FOALE. Tuffin & Foale clothes were extremely popular in London during the 1960s, particularly the lace dresses and dresses with cut-outs under the arms. The firm was dissolved in 1972.

tulle Originally made of gauze or silk, tulle is a fine fabric of hexagonal mesh, used in dress trimmings, millinery, and bridal gowns. In the 20th century it is often made of nylon. Tulle is believed to have originated in Tulle or Toul in France in the 18th century.

tunic Originally a short dress worn by ancient Greeks and Romans. Usually sleeveless and tied about the waist or left untied, the tunic is a straight, tubular garment which has been adapted for many uses. In the 19th century it appeared as a coat-like garment worn over long skirts and dresses. In the early 20th century POIRET and other designers used the tunic as part of the long, slender lines of the prewar era. The tunic shape became fashionable again in the 1960s when short tunic dresses were worn over slightly longer versions. The tunic has also been worn belted and unbelted over pants.

turban Long scarf of fine linen, cotton, or silk worn wound around the head. Turbans are commonly worn by Muslim and Sikh men. In the early years of the 20th century, POIRET featured turbans with Orientally-inspired HAREM PANTS and TUNICS, made of lavish fabrics and exotically decorated and adorned. From 1910 to 1920 the turban became a popular hat style, preconstructed by milliners into the slightly pointed shape with which fashion is now familiar. In other decades, the turban became briefly popular for both day and eveningwear, notably in the 1930s, 1960s, and 1980s.

Turbeville, Deborah 1937–. Photographer. Born in Medford, Massachusetts, USA. Turbeville was educated in Boston from 1949 to 1954. She went to New York in 1956 and spent two years with Claire MCCARDELL, as a model and assistant designer. From 1960 to 1972, Turbeville worked as a fashion editor on the *Ladies' Home Journal*, and *Mademoiselle*. She then moved to London to work as a

Early-20th-century **tunic** dress of soft, fluid fabric, worn with a bandeau headdress of beads. For artistic effect, a garland of flowers is used as a boa.

freelance photographer and during the 1970s traveled between London, Paris, and New York, photographing for most of the major magazines. Turbeville's work is romantic and often eerie. Her women models look mysterious and elusive, as if they were acting out a scene in a play.

Turkish trousers *See* BLOOMERS *and* HAREM PANTS.

turtleneck High, close-fitting neckline on a knitted SWEATER or PULLOVER. Popular in the 1960s.

tuxedo Originally a semi-formal dinner jacket with silk lapels, generously cut in black or dark blue cloth, which took its name from the exclusive Tuxedo Club which opened in 1886 in Tuxedo Park, Orange County, New Jersey, USA. A similar dress coat without tails was popular in England at the same time. By the 1920s the tuxedo had become a double-breasted dinner jacket. It reverted to a single-breasted style after World War II. In France it is called a "smoking." Dinner jackets for women enjoyed a vogue in the late 1970s and 1980s.

tweed The word tweed is thought to be a misreading of "tweel," the Scottish pronunciation of twill. The fabric's association with the River Tweed, a large center for the weaving industry in the 19th century, has helped perpetuate the error. Tweed is a rough-textured fabric, woven from wool in a variety of colored patterns. It has been used since the end of the 19th century for coats and suits.

Twiggy 1949–. Model. Born Leslie Hornby in London, England. Under the guidance of entrepreneur Justin de Villeneuve, Twiggy was launched into the fashion scene in 1966. She was featured as a model in newspapers and magazines throughout the world, including *Elle* in France and VOGUE in the UK and USA. Dubbed "Face of 1966," she swiftly became the symbol of the decade and her waif-like figure and wide-eyed looks were eagerly copied.

The **tuxedo** of December 1919, and Saint Laurent's 1966 version for women.

twill Fabric woven with diagonal lines of WEFT threads passing alternatively under and over WARP threads.

twinset Matching knitted CARDIGAN and SWEATER introduced in the 1930s. *See* PRINGLE.

Tyrolean costume Costume worn by people in the Austrian Tyrol. Tyrolean garments were popularized by SCHIAPARELLI in the 1930s. Many are made of wool and embroidered. Male costume includes leather breeches with embroidered cloth SUSPENDERS, knitted woolen hose, and a black leather jacket. Women wear full skirts embroidered with motifs, PEASANT blouses, and short jackets. Both sexes wear a plush felt hat, similar to a TRILBY, trimmed with a feather. *See* *TROMPE L'OEIL.

U

ulster Long, loose-fitting, calf-length woolen overcoat with a full or half belt which originated in the Irish province of Ulster. It was a popular coat for men and women from the late 19th to the early 20th century.

Ultrasuede Synthetic fabric of POLYESTER and polyurethane which is crease resistant and machine washable. Ultrasuede is the trademark of the American Skinner Fabrics Division of Spring Mills Inc. *See also* SUEDE FABRIC.

umbrella From the Latin *umbraculum*, "a shady place," the umbrella was originally used as protection against both rain and sun. In the 16th century it was made of leather and then of increasingly lighter fabrics until the appearance of the soft lace and tulle confections of the 19th century. It was at this time that the distinction was made between the PARASOL, a light instrument used by women for protection against the sun, and the umbrella, a sturdier object carried by both men and women to shield them from rain. In the late 19th century light umbrellas specially designed for women began to appear. Umbrellas are usually functional items but they have been objects of fashion at certain points in most decades, made with carved or decorated handles. In the 1960s and 1970s they became a more prominent fashion accessory and were produced in bright colors.

Ungaro, Emanuel (Maffeolti) 1933–. Designer. Born in Aix-en-Provence, France, to Italian parents. Ungaro was trained initially to be a tailor in the family business but in 1955 he went to work in Paris and after a brief period with a small tailoring firm he joined BALENCIAGA. In 1961 Ungaro moved to COURREGES and four years later opened his own business. He specialized in futuristic, angular, tailored coats and suits; short, sharp A-LINE dresses; lace SEE-THROUGH dresses; deeply cut armholes on dresses and coats; SHORTS

The traveling **ulster**, featured in *Queen*, 1880.

Maggy Rouff's dinner dress, row of buttons as ornamentation only

Lelong's wool dress Double row rouleau at neck. Cuffs turned back

Molyneux suit. Turn-back cuffs and buttoned flap on pockets

Piguet. Wool dress shoulder buttons as ornament, not fastening

Lelong. One too many buttons and used as ornamentation only

Wartime designers ignoring the **Utility Scheme**'s guidelines get a dressing down from the British Board of Trade for wasteful use of fabric and buttons.

Emanuel **Ungaro**'s velvet panne dress, fabric from Abraham, from his Spring 1984 collection. The hat is by Maison Paulette.

and matching BLAZERS; thigh-high BOOTS; over-the-knee socks; and metal garments. Many of his clothes were made from special fabrics designed by Sonja Knapp. Ungaro produced his first ready-to-wear lines in 1968. During the 1970s his work became softer and less rigid. His clothes are most often made in the rich, boldly printed fabrics that have become his hallmark. Ungaro pays great attention to detail in order to enhance the colors, patterns, and texture of the cloth.

unisex Clothes designed to be worn by either sex, popular in the 1960s and 1970s. Unisex garments included pants, jackets, WAISTCOATS, and shirts. The unisex look emerged as men took to wearing floral patterns and women adopted men's garments. Although novel at the time, the idea has been accepted in fashion since the early 1980s.

Utility scheme In 1941, because of the exigencies of World War II, clothes were rationed in the UK. The following year Hardy AMIES, Norman HARTNELL, Edward MOLYNEUX, Digby MORTON, Victor STIEBEL, Bianca Mosca, and Peter Russell cooperated with the Board of Trade to design Utility clothes made of a prescribed yardage of material and number and manner of trimmings. The designers produced coats, suits, dresses, and OVERALLS to Board of Trade requirements. Rationing ceased after the war but fabrics remained in short supply until the end of the 1940s.

V

Valenciennes Lace-making town on the French/Flemish border, which gave its name to a type of bobbin lace characterized by a background of diamond-shaped mesh.

Valentina 1904–. Designer. Born Valentina Nicholaevna Sanina Schlee in Kiev, Russia. After a sojourn in Paris during the Russian Revolution, Valentina moved in 1922 to New York where, four years later, she started her own dressmaking business. Trained for the stage and interested in theater, she made costumes for many stage productions, and her clothes were popular with actresses for off-stage wear. Valentina designed along architectural lines, producing dramatic clothes, including TURBANS, VEILS, swirling CAPES, and evening gowns. She was a highly successful designer until her retirement in 1957.

Valentino 1933–. Designer. Born Valentino Garavani in Voghera, Italy. Valentino studied at the Accademia Dell'Arte in Milan and the Chambre Syndicale de la Haute Couture in Paris. He then spent almost ten years in Paris, working first with DESSES, from 1950 to 1955, and then with LAROCHE. Valentino returned to Italy in the late 1950s and in 1959 opened a couture house in Rome. He showed his first collection in 1960 but it was with his 1962 collection, shown in Florence, that his name became internationally known. Probably Italy's most famous designer, Valentino makes clothes that are elegant, glamorous, and gracefully cut. His dramatic yet tasteful touches and accessories have been widely copied: big bows, embroidered STOCKINGS, and the initial V worn as buttons and at the neckline. He is as well known for his daywear as for his eveningwear. Valentino's confident, stylish designs are made of quality fabrics. His clients include many international socialites and in Italy his name is a household word.

Valentino elegance for 1964.

van den Akker, Koos 1930s–. Designer. Born in The Hague, Holland. Van den Akker left home at fifteen and moved in with various artist and writer friends. In 1955, with no prior formal training, he enrolled at the Royal Academy of Art in The Hague. Van den Akker's first work in the fashion field was with Christian DIOR in Paris. After some years with Dior, van den Akker returned to The Hague and opened his first BOUTIQUE. In 1968, with a portable sewing machine in his luggage, he moved to the USA and set up shop on a Manhattan sidewalk, making quilted garments with inserts of lace. By 1970 he had opened the first of several stores in the city. Taking his inspiration from fabric, van den Akker creates clothes that are highly individual and boldly colored statements in collage and patchwork.

vandyke Large, white, lace-trimmed collar which fans out over the shoulders, named after Sir Anthony Van Dyck (1599–1641), the Flemish painter, in whose portraits the collar was often shown. *See* LITTLE LORD FAUNTLEROY.

Multi-fabric drop-waist dress with bright floral collage from Koos van den Akker, Fall 1985.

vareuse Fisherman's SMOCK from Breton, France. A loose garment with a standaway collar, which is cut to hang to the hips. In his 1957 collections, Christian DIOR included variations of the vareuse, made up in a variety of fabrics.

Varon, Jean *See* BATES.

Varty, Keith 1952–. Designer. Born in Darlington, England. Varty attended St. Martin's School of Art and the Royal College of Art in London until the early 1970s, when he joined DOROTHEE BIS in Paris. He spent over four years with the firm before moving to Milan to work for Complice and Byblos, two Italian design companies. Varty has a successful design career with a number of Italian firms.

Vass, Joan 1925–. Designer. Born in New York, USA. Vass was educated at Vassar College and studied philosophy at the University of Wisconsin, graduating in 1942. She worked in New York as an editor before joining the Museum of Modern Art, where she spent ten years as an assistant curator. In 1974 she began a non-profit-making company helping knitters market their skills. Vass created designs for hats, MUFFLERS, and SWEATERS, which she supplied to knitters. Two years later Vass was designing woven garments, adding coats and daywear to her collection. Known mostly for her sweaters knitted from chenille, alpaca, angora, and other fine quality wools, Vass has also established a reputation for her clothing lines, which are distinguished by their lack of both shoulder pads and applied decoration. Her most popular line is called Joan Vass USA.

veil Thin piece of fabric that falls over the eyes and/or face, partially concealing them. Tulle or lace veils attached to BONNETS were popular throughout the 19th century. Toward the end of that century, there was a vogue for motoring veils, worn over a hat and tied under the chin with a curtain at the back to keep out the dust.

Charming hat and **veil**, trimmed with a bird for late 1950s fashions.

Other versions resembled a bag with a slot for the eyes. Veils can be made in many lengths and fabrics. In the 1890s veils sprinkled with chenille dots enjoyed a brief vogue. Heavy crêpe mourning veils were in vogue throughout the 19th century. During the 20th century veils gradually declined in favor, though short veils which just covered the eyes and half the face were popular until the 1940s. The fashion for long, white, bridal veils has endured since the 19th century.

velour French for velvet. A smooth, soft, closely woven fabric with a short, thick pile, which can be made of cotton, mohair, wool, or synthetic fibers. Velour has been used in the 20th century for many garments, notably TRACKSUITS and leisurewear.

velvet From the latin *vellus*, meaning "fleece" or "tufted hair," velvet has been known in Europe since the Middle Ages. It is a closely woven fabric with a short, dense pile which produces a soft, rich texture. In the 19th century velvet was made in part or completely of silk but in the 20th century it is made from acetate and rayon. Commonly used in the 19th century for dresses and jackets, in the 20th century velvet is considered a luxury fabric and is usually reserved for eveningwear, though there was a vogue in the late 1960s and early 1970s for velvet skirts and pants for daywear.

velveteen Twill or plain weave cotton with a short weft pile made to imitate velvet. It has been in use since the early 20th century.

Venet, Philippe 1929–. Designer. Born in Lyon, France. At the age of fourteen, Venet became an apprentice to Pierre Court, a well-respected couturier based in Lyon. He moved to Paris in 1951, working first for SCHIAPARELLI and two years later for GIVENCHY. In 1962 Venet opened his own house, achieving fame with his finely tailored coats.

Venetian lace Needlepoint LACE with a distinctive circular pattern, which has been made in Venice since the 15th century.

vent Slit or open section in a jacket or coat which gives fullness and width, used by dressmakers since the 19th century.

Vernier, Rose ?–1975. Milliner. Place of birth unknown. Brought up in Vienna, Austria, Vernier established a millinery business in Poland before moving to London in 1939. After World War II, she became a popular London milliner, patronized by society figures and by the British Royal Family. She worked closely with AMIES, CREED, MORTON, and MATTLI, producing designs for their collections. Vernier retired in 1970.

Versace, Gianni 1946–. Designer. Born in Calabria, Italy. Versace worked with his dressmaker mother before moving to Milan. He swiftly established a reputation as a skilled designer and created suede and leather collections for Genny and evening clothes for the firm of Complice. In 1978 he opened his own business. Versace is famous for his strong color sense and clean lines. He likes to wrap the female form, often with BIAS CUT clothes and fluid silks. Many of his ideas are audacious but all are carried out to a high level of technical achievement. Versace enjoys experimenting with new fabrics and trimmings. His leather-trimmed knitwear was notably successful in the late 1970s. He also designs for the theater and ballet. *See* col. pl.

Vertès, Marcel 1895–1961. Illustrator. Born in Ujpest, near Budapest, Hungary. Vertès studied to become an aviation engineer, but turned instead to drawing and painting. His studies at the Academy of Fine Arts in Budapest were interrupted by World War I. Vertès served in the Hungarian Army and in 1919 went to Vienna, where he won a poster competition with an etching of war orphans. Two years later he arrived in Paris and in the same year the Salon des Humoristes Exhibition showed twenty-five of his watercolors. Subsequently, Vertès worked for the satirical magazine *Rire*, and for LA GAZETTE DU BON TON, studying in his spare time at the Académie Julian. Based in Paris, Vertès illustrated books and designed costumes and sets for films, the theater, and musicals. In 1935 Condé NAST invited him to work for *Vanity Fair* in New York. Returning to Europe a short time later, Vertès designed sets in London for *The Mikado*, planned the interior decor of Elizabeth Arden's Paris beauty salon, and worked as an advertising artist, notably for SCHIAPARELLI perfumes. At the outbreak of World War II he joined the French Army but fled to the USA during the German Occupation of France. In the following years he worked as a book and magazine illustrator and as an interior designer. He also produced more than eight hundred circus costumes. Vertès' hallmarks were his light, graceful, and witty watercolor sketches of high fashion and high society.

Victor, Sally 1905–. Milliner. Born Sally Josephs in Scranton, Pennsylvania, USA. Victor acquired her training as a milliner by working in her aunt's New York shop. At the age of eighteen she joined the millinery department of Macy's store and after two years moved to a New Jersey department store as head millinery buyer. In 1927 she married Sergiv Victor, the head of Serge, a wholesale millinery company, and soon became the company's chief designer.

Marcel **Vertès**'s drawing from a 1948 issue of *Fémina*, advertising "Shocking," Schiaparelli's famous perfume.

Gianni **Versace,** the master cutter of leather, displays his talents in this luminous and striking jacket, part of his Spring/Summer collection for 1982.

Diane **von Fürstenberg** created her best-selling jersey wrap dress
—a modern classic—in 1976.

In the early 1930s she sold hats under her own name and in 1934 opened her own millinery store. From the 1930s to the early 1950s, Victor was one of the most influential and innovative milliners in the USA. She wove and dyed fabric on her own premises, experimenting with felt and denim as well as more exotic fabrics. She produced chessmen-shaped PILLBOXES, collapsible BONNETS, a SAILOR HAT and hats based on Chinese lanterns, geisha bonnets, Ali Baba topknots, and American Indian headdresses. Victor was a popular designer with the wives of American political figures, as well as with stage and screen actresses, all of whom wore her less controversial hats. She retired in 1968.

Victoria (Alexandrina Victoria), **Queen** 1819–1901. Born at Kensington Palace, London, daughter of Edward, Duke of Kent, and Princess Victoria Mary Louisa of Saxe-Coburg-Gotha. Victoria became Queen in 1837. In 1840 she married Albert of Saxe-Coburg-Gotha, her cousin. Her wedding gown was made of Spitalfields silk and her veil of Honiton lace. Although Victoria was not herself a figure of fashion, she was responsible for many vogues. Her affection for her Scottish estate at Balmoral, for example, produced a trend for garments named after the house, and for TARTAN in general. Her adoption of MOURNING DRESS, on the death of her consort in 1861, made such dress *de rigueur* for widows and caused a dramatic increase in the production of suitable fabrics.

Madeleine **Vionnet** at work in 1935.

vicuna Wool from the vicuna, a small animal of the llama family found in the Andes mountain range of South America. One of the finest fibers, vicuna is soft, strong, and expensive to produce—a dozen animals make one piece of cloth. Naturally cinnamon brown or fawn in color, vicuna has been a popular material in the 20th century for coats, CAPES, jackets, and suits.

Vionnet, Madeleine 1876–1975. Designer. Born in Aubervilliers, France. Apprenticed to a seamstress at an early age, Vionnet worked in the Paris suburbs in her late teens before joining Kate O'Reilly, a London dressmaker, in *c.* 1897. In 1901 she returned to Paris and was employed by Mme. Gerber, the designing member of CALLOT SOEURS. Vionnet joined DOUCET in 1907 and remained with him for five years. In 1912 she opened her own house, closing during World War I and reopening shortly after. Greatly favored by pre-World War I actresses Eve Lavallière and Réjane, Vionnet was one of the most innovative designers of her day. She conceived her designs on a miniature model, draping the fabric in sinuous folds. Mistress of the BIAS CUT, Vionnet commissioned fabrics two yards wider than usual to accommodate her draping. She dispensed with the CORSET and used diagonal seaming and FAGGOTING to achieve her simple, fluid shapes. Many of Vionnet's clothes looked limp and shapeless until they were put on. In the late 1920s and early 1930s Vionnet reached the height of her fame. She was credited with the popularization of the COWL and HALTER NECK. She favored crêpe, crêpe de chine, gabardine, and satin for evening dresses and day dresses, which were often cut in one piece, without armholes. Suits had gored or bias-cut skirts, wrap-around coats were made with side fastenings, and many garments fastened at the back or were pulled on over the head without a fastening of any kind. Bands of grosgrain often acted as lining and support for the insides of fine crêpe dresses. Vionnet used striped fabrics but she was not a colorist. A smooth shape and fit were her main aims in achieving the ultimate in dress designs—a dress that fits sympathetically to the body. No other designer has

Madeleine **Vionnet**'s expertly cut dress of 1933.

Two shoes from Roger **Vivier**'s collection for Winter 1963/64. The upper shoe, in embroidered pink tulle trimmed with imitation pearls, has a heel that makes it easily identifiable as one of Vivier's designs.

equaled her enormous technical contribution to *haute couture*. Vionnet retired in 1939.

viscose Man-made cellulose fiber derived from wood pulp. In 1905 COURTAULD's began production of viscose rayon. Viscose is used in SWEATERS, dresses, coats, blouses, and leisurewear.

viscose rayon The most common of the various types of rayon production, viscose rayon was invented by three British chemists, Cross, Bevan, and Beadle, in the late 19th century. It was patented in 1892. Viscose rayon fibers have been used in most types of garments since the turn of the century, though major production did not begin until after World War II.

Vivier, Roger 1913–. Shoe designer. Born in Paris, France. Vivier studied sculpture at the Ecole des Beaux Arts in Paris until an invitation from friends to design a collection of shoes for their shoe factory interrupted his studies. In 1936 he worked for other shoemakers before opening his own house the following year. Vivier designed for many major shoe manufacturers: Pinet and Bally in France, Miller and DELMAN in the USA, RAYNE and Turner in the UK. Delman turned down one of his designs, a Chinese style platform shoe—which was subsequently taken up by SCHIAPARELLI. In 1938 Vivier agreed to work exclusively for Delman in the USA, but the completion of his contract was prevented by his mobilization in 1939. One year later he was out of the army and off to New York where he worked with Delman until 1941. In 1942, having studied millinery, Vivier opened a shop with Suzanne Remi, a well-respected Parisian milliner who was living in New York. In 1945, back with Delman, he produced several collections, one of which included his "crystal shoes." He returned to Paris in 1947 and worked freelance until Christian DIOR opened a shoe department in his salon in 1953 and appointed Vivier as designer. During his stay at Dior, Vivier designed some of the most influential shoes of the period. He translated 18th-century MULES into evening shoes, PUMPS, and day BOOTS. In 1957 he created a stacked, leather-heeled, chisel-toed shoe which became very popular. He made circular DIAMANTE heels, wedge shoes, and bead-embroidered shoes. In the 1960s he designed African sandals and a shoe with a mother-of-pearl, TORTOISE-SHELL, or silver buckle. A nonconformist master craftsman who rarely falters, Vivier is noted for his skill in positioning and balancing innovative heels and for his imaginative use of texture. He reopened his business in 1963 in Paris and continues to produce two collections a year.

Viyella Tradename established in 1894 by William Hollins & Company for its woven fabric of wool and cotton. Viyella was used in the late 19th century for men's nightshirts and underwear but in the 20th century it gradually became a popular fabric for all the family, made into PAJAMAS, nightgowns, and JUMPERS. Soft, warm, and hard-wearing, Viyella clothing has maintained its popularity. During the 1960s and 1970s Viyella shirts were popular, often printed with a Tattersall CHECK.

Vogel, Lucien Vogel founded LA GAZETTE DU BON TON in 1912 and encouraged such artists as Etienne DRIAN, Georges BARBIER, Georges LEPAPE, Paul IRIBE, André MARTY, and Charles MARTIN to produce elegant hand-colored plates. In 1922 he launched LE JARDIN DES MODES, which was purchased by Condé NAST, and edited the magazine until he died in 1954.

Vogue Magazine started in the USA in 1892 as a fashion weekly catering to society women. In 1909 *Vogue* was purchased by Condé NAST and became twice monthly in 1910. British *Vogue* was added to the American stable in 1916. French, Australian, Spanish, and German *Vogue* followed, though Spanish *Vogue* lasted only from 1918 to 1920 and German *Vogue* survived only a few issues in 1928. *Vogue* was transformed by Nast from a small weekly paper into the most influential fashion magazine of the 20th century. Devoted to fashion, society, and the arts, *Vogue* has successfully promoted art, photography, illustration, and literature through its pages. *See also* CHASE, *LEPAPE, *and* VREELAND.

voile Fine, sheer, semi-transparent plain woven fabric of tightly twisted yarns, made of cotton, silk, wool, or, in the 20th century, man-made fibers. Voile has been used since the 19th century for making blouses and dresses.

Volbracht, Michaele 1949–. Designer, illustrator. Born in Kansas City, Missouri, USA. Volbracht joined Parsons School of Design in New York at the age of seventeen. After graduation he worked for both Geoffrey BEENE and Donald BROOKS before joining Norman NORELL, with whom he stayed until 1972. Volbracht also created a number of illustrations for the New York store Bloomingdales. In the 1970s he started his own business, selling garments made of hand-printed silks. This company was closed down and a new one opened in 1981. Volbracht's figurative hand-painted designs are printed by Bellotti, an Italian company. He is known for his bold colors and dramatic designs.

Von Fürstenberg, Diane 1946–. Designer. Born Diane Michelle Halfin in Brussels, Belgium. Educated in Belgium, Switzerland, Spain, and England, Von Fürstenberg majored in economics at the University of Geneva. In 1969 she became an apprentice to Angelo Ferretti, an Italian textile manufacturer, and using silk jersey prints she produced a line of clothes, mostly TUNIC dresses in varying lengths and BIAS-CUT SHIRTWAISTERS. In 1972 Von Fürstenberg opened her own business in New York. In the 1970s she created a WRAP-AROUND DRESS which became a bestseller. It had long sleeves, a fitted top, and a skirt which wrapped around the body to tie at the waist. Von Fürstenberg favors jersey and often uses geometric prints. *See* col. pl.

Vreeland, Diana 1906–. Magazine editor. Born Diana Dalziel in Paris, France. Vreeland moved to New York at the age of eight. She spent her early married life in Albany, New York. In 1937 she joined HARPER'S BAZAAR in New York, becoming fashion editor in 1939. In 1962, after twenty-five years with *Harper's Bazaar*, Vreeland left and became associate editor of VOGUE the following year. Soon after, she was appointed editor-in-chief and stayed with *Vogue* until 1971. Since the late 1930s Vreeland has been an arbiter of fashion and style. Her keen eye for talent has promoted numerous models, photographers, and designers. Her own sense of personal style, which she never hesitates to reveal, has not only inspired others but has made her famous. She edited *Vogue* during the 1960s with flamboyance and flair. In 1971 Vreeland became a consultant to the Costume Institute of the Metropolitan Museum of New York and she has been responsible for many of the museum's memorable exhibitions on fashion and style.

Vuokko dates unknown. Designer. Born Nurmesniemi Vuokko in Finland. Vuokko studied dressmaking at the Ateneum in Helsinki and then took a course in ceramics at Helsinki's Institute of Industrial Design. She graduated in 1952 and worked for various textile companies, for MARIMEKKO, and in industrial and houseware design before forming Vuokko in 1965. Her fashion garments are based on simple shapes. She uses cotton and jersey in clear, bright colors and the patterns in her fabrics are an integral part of the overall design. During the late 1960s and early 1970s she produced various lines but was particularly noted for prints designed with swirling circles and stripes.

Vuokko's fresh and simple dresses for Scandinavian summers. The designs date from the mid-1970s, the fabrics from the early 1980s. An uncomplicated approach contributes to Vuokko's success.

W

Wainwright, Janice 1940–. Designer. Born in Chesterfield, England. Wainwright studied at Wimbledon School of Art, Kingston School of Art, and the Royal College of Art, London. From 1965 to 1968 she worked for the company Simon Massey, creating many lines under her own name. Then followed six years of freelance designing before Wainwright established her own company in 1974. Her interest in fabrics is evident from her long, lean shapes, sinuous seaming, and use of the BIAS-CUT. She favors matte jersey, crêpe, and soft wools, which she manipulates into swirling, spiraling outfits that are often full-shouldered.

waist cincher *See* WASPIE.

waistcoat Man's waist-length, sleeveless garment worn under a jacket and over a shirt. Often made from silk or heavily embroidered fabrics, the waistcoat buttoned at the front and usually had two small pockets. Women adopted waistcoats in the late 19th century and wore them with skirts and blouses into the early 20th century. In the 1960s, as part of the general fashion explosion, women often wore waistcoats borrowed directly from a man's wardrobe, favoring in particular pin-striped versions. During the 1970s and 1980s the waistcoat, made of many different fabrics, was absorbed as another item of female dress, often worn with tailored suits. *See* *BANKS *and* EXECUTIVE.

Warner Bros Co. In 1874 two Americans, Lucien G. Warner and I. de Ver Warner, who were brothers and both doctors, established a company to manufacture and promote health CORSETS. In 1914 they bought the patent to the backless BRA from Mary Phelps JACOB. The company expanded in the USA and in England. In 1932 it introduced ROLL-ONS and in 1935 cup fittings for bras. The Warner's Birthday Suit of 1961—a close-fitting, smoothly lined pantie-corselette made with Lycra—was an innovation in its field. Warner's has for many years been one of the largest producers of foundationwear.

warp Loom threads which stretch lengthwise and are interwoven with the weft or filling threads.

waspie Also known as a waist cincher or *guêpière*, the waspie is an abbreviated CORSET constructed of bone and elastic inserts, and laced back or front to draw in the waist. Marcel ROCHAS was one of the first designers to introduce the *guêpière* in 1946. It was worn under the NEW LOOK fashions of the post-World War II period. In the 1980s wide, laced belts, resembling the waspie, were briefly fashionable.

Watteau Name given to a dress style of the late 19th century that resembled dresses in paintings by Jean Antoine Watteau (1684–1721) in the early 18th century. A Watteau style dress has a SACQUE back and a tightly fitted front BODICE.

wedgies Shoe with a wedge-shaped sole. Wedgies have varied in height and style since their introduction during the 1930s.

weft Crosswise threads woven into fabric on a loom. *See* WARP.

Westwood, Vivienne 1941–. Designer. Born in England. Westwood spent one term at Harrow Art School before leaving to train as a teacher. In the late 1960s she and Malcolm McLaren opened a shop in the KING'S ROAD, London. During the 1970s both McClaren's pop group, the Sex Pistols, and Westwood's shop attracted a great deal of attention. Representing an anarchic urban youth culture, the shop, which was known by a variety of names, sold leather and rubber clothes to people with interests in PUNK, bondage, and fetishism. In the early 1980s Westwood launched her "Pirate" and "New Romanticism" looks, which brought her to the attention of the fashion world. Huge swirling PETTICOATS, buckles, ruffles, pirate hats and baggy BOOTS set a vogue. Westwood followed this with a "Witches" collection in 1983. She is a totally uncompromising designer who claims to have no interest in tailoring, but only in how and where the fabric touches the body. Nothing "fits" in the traditional sense of the word. She cuts extra armholes, makes sleeves

Janice **Wainwright**'s pagoda style dress of 1976. The bias cutting and clever appliqué trim earmarked this designer for success from an early age.

Promotion for **Warner**'s "Rust-Proof" corset on a showcard of 1902. Rust stains on underwear were the most troublesome corset problem of the late 19th century.

TROUSERS, black leather T-SHIRTS, and stove-pipe hats, and showed
BRAS worn over garments. She hired a graffiti artist to paint
SWEATSHIRTS. The ETHNIC hobo styles of Westwood's clothes have
had a wide influence on both the public and other designers.
Anarchic and perverse, her clothes are met with both outrage and
curiosity. Whether she uses bold patterns or drab colors, Westwood
continues to produce new dimensions in fashion.

wet look *See* CIRE.

whalebone Horny substance from the upper jaw of the whale. A
whaling industry was established in the Bay of Biscay in the 12th
century. By the 17th century demand had moved the industry to
Greenland. Whalebone was generally used for *CORSETS and STAYS.
In the years *c.* 1855 to 1866, when the CRINOLINE was popular, the
demand for whalebone was so great that whales were threatened
with extinction. In the late 19th century, ELASTIC fibers and metal
replaced whalebone as elements of body shaping and support.

windbreaker *See* WINDCHEATER.

windcheater Waist-length jacket with a fitted waistband which was
adapted from British Royal Air Force flying jackets in the late 1940s
and early 1950s. Made from wool, gabardine, or nylon, the
windcheater is usually waterproof and zips or buttons from waist to
neck. It is worn for sporting activities and casual attire. *See also*
ANORAK *and* PARKA.

wing collar High, stiff collar of a shirt or blouse with pointed end
corners which turn down. It was a popular shirt style for men's
formal wear in the late 19th and early 20th centuries. Women briefly
adopted the shirt style in the 1920s. Since the 1970s it has enjoyed a
revival for both men and women.

Winterhalter, Franz Xaver 1806–73. Painter. Born in the Black
Forest, Germany. Winterhalter became the court painter in
Karlsruhe in 1828. During the 1850s and 1860s he traveled and
worked in Paris and London, returning to Germany in 1870.
Winterhalter is known for his famous portraits of the Empress
EUGENIE and Queen VICTORIA. He painted their full-skirted, off-the-
shoulder gowns in such detail that this style of dress has been linked
with his name.

Women's Wear Daily Originally a journal for the clothing industry,
Women's Wear Daily was successfully converted to a popular

The **wing collar** of the 1890s was
worn almost exclusively by men
until the 1920s, when it was
briefly adopted by women (*left*).

magazine appealing both to the trade and to the public. The journal's new direction was masterminded by John FAIRCHILD, who became publisher of WWD in 1960. The magazine reported trade goings-on as well as fashion shows. It also covered parties and charity functions, describing the clothes of the guests and passing on gossip. Fairchild gave space to first-rate fashion artists. In 1973 he launched W, a bi-weekly journal printed on paper heavy enough to allow him to reproduce good quality photographs.

A **Winterhalter** portrait of the Empress Eugénie and her maids of honor, *c.* 1860.

wool Mass of strong and flexible fibers which makes up the fleece of sheep. The outer cells of the coiled fiber repel water while the inner cells absorb moisture, thus making the cloth very warm. Used since the Stone Age, wool has been made up into almost every kind of garment. In the late 19th century it was used for underwear and swimwear as well as indoor and outdoor clothes. The main areas of wool production are Australia, New Zealand, South Africa, and Argentina. Woolen yarns are pliable and less expensive than the harder, smoother, and stronger worsted yarns. *See* BOTANY, LAMBS-WOOL, MELTON, *and* WORSTED.

worsted Hardwearing woolen fabric made of smooth yarn, which takes its name from Worstead in Norfolk, England, where it was originally made. Serge and gabardine worsteds have been popular since the late 19th century for suits and outer garments.

Worth, Charles Frederick 1825–95. Designer. Born in Bourne, Lincolnshire, England. Worth started work at the age of twelve in a draper's shop in London and a year later began a seven-year apprenticeship at the haberdasher's Swan & Edgar's, selling

Top left: Charles Frederick **Worth,** the father of couture, who dominated the fashion scene from the mid-19th-century crinoline (*top right*), to the bustle (*below*), to the slender new lines of the 20th century (*center left*).

*SHAWLS and dress materials. After moving to the silk mercer's Lewis & Allenby for a brief period, Worth left for Paris in 1845. His first job in the French capital was at Maison Gagelin, where he sold MANTLES and shawls. Five years later he opened a dressmaking department at the store. In 1858 Worth went into partnership with a Swedish businessman, Otto Bobergh, and opened his own house. He was soon a favorite of the Empress EUGENIE, and her influence and patronage were instrumental in his success. In the 1860s he introduced the TUNIC dress, a knee-length gown worn with a long skirt. In 1864 he abolished the CRINOLINE and pulled skirts up and back into a train. Five years later he raised the waistline and created a BUSTLE behind. In 1870, when the Second Empire collapsed, Worth closed his business, only to reopen the following year. Although there was less demand for court trains and crinolines, Worth continued as the top Parisian couturier, dressing actresses Sarah Bernhardt and Eleonora Duse and patronized by European royalty and international society. He handled rich materials in a sensitive manner, using simple designs and creating clothing on flattering lines. Much of his work is associated with the movement to redefine the female form and fashionable shape by removing excessive RUFFLES and frills, altering BONNET shapes by pushing them back off the forehead, and reshaping the crinoline and the bustle. Worth's copious use of rich fabrics throughout the second half of the 19th century inspired the silk manufacturers of Lyon in France to weave more and more interesting textiles. For some of his clients he designed a complete collection of clothes for every occasion. Worth's customers enjoyed being "created" by the master and were happy to trust him to enhance their finer points by his skilful cutting of cloth. Although Worth designed restrained traveling clothes and walking garments, he was most famous for his evening gowns, often of white tulle. Worth was a gifted designer who, in retrospect, seems to have had a clear understanding of the times in which he lived. He was able to dress both society and the demi-monde with equal good, though obviously affluent, taste. After his death in 1895, Worth's two sons, Gaston and Jean-Philippe, continued the business, which passed through four generations before it was taken over by the house of PAQUIN in 1954.

Worth, Gaston 1853–1924. Born in Paris, France, son of Charles Frederick WORTH. With his brother, Jean Philippe, Gaston Worth took over the business after his father's death in 1895. He was the business administrator and commercial mind behind the company. He was also the first president of the CHAMBRE SYNDICALE DE LA HAUTE COUTURE, an organization set up to protect designers from piracy. *See also* WORTH, JEAN PHILIPPE.

Worth, Jean Philippe 1856–1926. Designer. Born in Paris, France, son of Charles Frederick WORTH. Jean Philippe Worth was instrumental in the House of Worth's smooth transition from the late 19th century to the early 20th century without altering the style set by its founder. Strongly influenced by his father, Jean Philippe Worth was particularly well known for his eveningwear. He designed until the late 1900s. *See also* WORTH, GASTON.

wrap-around dress/skirt Twentieth-century style originating with the SARONG. The skirt section, made of a rectangular piece of fabric, is wrapped once around the body, the front panel overlapping to fasten at the waist. Wrap-around garments are popular for casual wear, beach attire, and—in ankle-length versions—for eveningwear.

Y

Yamamoto, Kansai 1944–. Designer. Born in Yokohama, Japan. Yamamoto studied English at Nippon University. After working briefly for a designer, he opened his own house in 1971. The presentation of Yamamoto's shows made him famous: dramatic clothes shown in an exciting environment. By blending the vigorous, exotic, and powerful designs of traditional Japanese dress with Western sportswear, Yamamoto achieves a unique, abstract style.

Yamamoto, Yohji 1943–. Designer. Born in Japan. Yamamoto graduated from Keio University in 1966 and then attended the Bunka College of Fashion in Tokyo for two years. After working as a freelance designer, he formed his own company in 1972 and his first collection was shown in Japan in 1976. Yamamoto is an uncompromising, nontraditionalist designer. He swathes and wraps the body in unstructured, loose, voluminous garments, similar in style and philosophy to those of COMME DE GARCONS. Many of his clothes have additional flaps, pockets, and straps.

Yantony One of fashion's legends, about whom few facts are known, Yantony was an Asian shoemaker who created some of the world's most expensive and exquisite shoes in the early years of the 20th century. He had a shoe store in Paris and was known in his time for his high prices, the length of time it took him to make shoes—often several years for one pair—and the high-handed manner in which he treated his clients.

Yé Yé French version of the Beatles' "Yeah, Yeah, Yeah" refrain, used to describe the clothing of the early 1960s.

Y-line Line of Christian DIOR's 1955 collection which showed a slender body with a top-heavy look achieved by large collars that opened up into a V-shape. The Y could also be inverted in the form of long TUNICS with deep slits at either side.

yoke Traditionally an integral portion of a SMOCK, a yoke is the upper part of a garment, usually fitted across the bust and around the back between the shoulders. Pleated, gathered, or plain, it supports the rest of the garment. A yoke can also be the oversize waistband of a skirt, curved downward, from which the rest of the skirt hangs. Yoked skirts were particularly popular during the 1930s and again in the early 1970s when fashions based on rural dress and PEASANT costumes were in vogue.

yoked skirt See YOKE.

Yuki 1937–. Designer. Born Gnyuki Torimaru in Mizki-Ken, Japan. Yuki qualified as a textile engineer and was briefly involved in the production of animated films and cartoons before leaving Japan in 1969. He studied English in London for three years, took a one-year history of architecture course at the Art Institute of Chicago, and returned to London in 1964 to attend the London College of Fashion. After graduating in 1966 he worked briefly with Louis FERAUD before joining MICHAEL for two years. In 1968, Yuki

A rustic smock with **yoke** of 1860 is transformed in the 1970s to a yoked blouse and matching yoked skirt.

spent several months working for HARTNELL and in the following year he went to Paris to spend three years with CARDIN. In 1971 he designed a collection for Saga Furs which was followed in 1972 by a dress collection exclusive to the London department store Harvey Nichols. Yuki opened his own company in 1973. He became famous for his sculpted, one-size, draped jersey dresses which are designed to fall away from the body as it moves, then resume their intended shape and position.

Z

zazou suit Female version of the ZOOT SUIT, worn in the USA in the 1940s and 1950s. The zazou suit consisted of a jacket and tight skirt and was worn with high heels.

zip *See* ZIPPER.

zipper (UK: zip) In 1893 W. Litcomb Judson of Chicago, USA, patented a clasp locker system of fastening which was constructed of a series of hooks and eyes with a clasp lock for opening and closing. In 1913 Gideon Sundback, a Swede working in the USA, developed Judson's ideas and produced a hookless fastener with interlocking

On 4 September 1935, when this advertisement appeared, the word **zipper** was not yet in general use.

metal teeth. This fastener was first used on money belts and tobacco pouches and in 1917 members of the US Navy were issued with windproof jackets with clasp-lock fasteners at the front. It was B. G. Worth of B. F. Goodrich Co. who gave the name "zipper" to a fastener that was used at the time for closing shoes. In the early 1930s SCHIAPARELLI was one of the earliest designers to use zippers on fashion garments. By the mid-20th century the zipper had been further refined and was composed of two strips of metal or plastic on either side of an opening, to which are attached two rows of metal teeth which lock in one direction and open in the other.

zoot suit Smart outfit worn in the USA in the 1940s and 1950s. The jacket was wide at the shoulders with a drape which fell deep into the back. Often knee-length, the jacket tapered to baggy pants which were slightly narrowed at the bottom. The zoot suit was usually made of brightly colored fabric.

Zoran 1947–. Designer. Born Ladicorbic Zoran in Belgrade, Yugoslavia. Zoran graduated from the University of Belgrade with a degree in architecture. In 1971 he moved to New York. Zoran is a minimalist designer. His first collection in 1977 attracted a great deal of interest. He cuts luxurious fabrics into precise, simple shapes and avoids where possible the use of fastenings, accessories, and decorations. Zoran has produced a capsule wardrobe consisting of pants, a CARDIGAN, a top, four T-SHIRTS, and several skirts of different lengths, which is intended to answer all the travel requirements of his clients. Cashmere is one of his favorite fabrics. He restricts his use of color to a basic palette of red, black, gray, cream, and white.

zouave jacket Collarless, waist-length, braid-trimmed, BOLERO-style jacket with three-quarter-length sleeves. It is named after the Zouaves, a regiment of French soldiers attached to the Hussars, who in the 1830s adopted an Arab-style costume which incorporated such a jacket. During the 1860s women wore zouave-style jackets for indoor and outdoor wear.

The **zoot suit** found its way from South to North America in the early part of the 20th century. It was most popular in the 1940s and 1950s.

SOURCES OF ILLUSTRATIONS

Page numbers in italic refer to color illustrations.

David Arky, from *Art Plastic: Designed for Living* by Andrea di Noto (Abbeville Press). Collection: Tender Buttons, NYC: p. *51b*. David Bailey: p. 207br. David Bailey/*Sunday Times*: p. 27. BBC Hulton Picture Library: pp. 20, 23b, 26, 32b, 45, 46b, 47, 49b, 58t, 62t, 67t, 68t, 72, 73t, 74, 75b, 78r, 82t & c, 94, 99t, 117t, 134t, 135, 136, 146b, 159, 167t, 180, 182b, 184t, 187, 188, 195, 200b, 202r, 210, 213t, 233, 242t, 244b, 248l. Courtesy of Bill Blass, Ltd. Archives: pp. 42, 43. Bord Failte: p. 22t. Brooklyn Museum, Millicent Rogers Collection: p. 222b. Caisse Nationale des Monuments Historiques et des Sites: pp. 6, 44r, 87t, 139l, 245b, 247, 264tl. Camera Press: p. 16. Central Museum, Northampton: pp. 54, 197, 232t. Chateau Compiégne/Photographie Giraudon: p. 263. Stuart Cosgrove Collection: p. 268. European Silk Commission: p. 221b. Fotomas Index: pp. 28b, 29, 58b, 250t. *Illustrated London News* Picture Library: p. 17, 183t. Jaeger Archives: pp. 61t, 139r, 140. Kobal Collection: pp. 131b, 182t. Diana Korchien: pp. 36b, 80t, *101b*. Peter Lindbergh: p. *119*. Peter Hope Lumley: pp. 19, 62b, 80b, 106, 168b, 175t, 229b, 258b. Mansell Collection: pp. 40t, 63t, 129t, 163, 178, 209, 215b, 217br, 221t, 226, 230bl, 234c. Musée de la Mode et du Costume: pp. 69r, 160t, 173b, 257b. National Film Archive: p. 31b, 36t, 220t. Norman Parkinson: p. *186*. Drawings by John Peacock: 32t, 45, 95t, 103t & b, 129b, 152, 196b, 208b, 217t, 227b, 230b, 232c, 236, 244t, 262, 266. Philippe Peraldi: pp. 133bl & r. Photo Source: 171. Collection Poiret-de Wilde: pp. 198, 199. Popperfoto: p. *51t*. Rowan Gallery: p. 214b. Royal & Ancient Golf Club, St. Andrews/Colnaghi & Co. Ltd.: p. 98. Scottish Tourist Board: p. *238b*. Sears, Roebuck & Co.: pp. 74t, 104, 243, 245t. David Shilling: *jacket*, p. 237. Caroline Smith: pp. 200t, 252. *Sunday Times* Costume Research Institute: pp. 114b, 116, *118*, *128*, 151t, 192b, 194b, 213b, 218r, 228b, 229t, 242b, 246r, 251t. O. Toscani: p. 149t. By Courtesy of the Board of Trustees of the Victoria & Albert Museum: pp. 24, 35, 40b, 48, 49t, 59, 61b, 70t, 87b, 107, 137, 141, 184b, *203t*, 234t, 264b. Visual Arts Library: pp. 108, 134bl, 164, 212b, 222t, 223l. Weidenfeld & Nicolson Archives: pp. 18b, 78l, 96b, *120*, 150, 155, 264cl.

The publishers would like to thank all the designers and companies who generously made available original sketches and photographs from their archives, and in particular:

Aquascutum Ltd., Giorgio Armani, Laura Ashley, Jeff Banks, Geoffrey Beene, Lee Bender, Elio Berhanyer, Laura Biagotti, Manolo Blahnik, Bill Blass, Body Map, Tom Brigance, Brooks Bros., Burberry & Co., Cacharel, Calman Links, Cartier, Bonnie Cashin, Oleg Cassini, Nino Cerruti, Chanel, Caroline Charles, Cluett, Peabody & Co., Sybil Connolly, Courrèges, Wendy Dagworthy, Christian Dior, Edina & Lena, Perry Ellis, Emanuel, Ferragamo, Fontana, Frederick Fox, Gina Fratini, Jean-Paul Gaultier, Bill Gibb, Marithé & François Girbaud, Givenchy, Andrew Grima, Gucci, Norman Hartnell, Carolina Herrera, Hermès, Margaret Howell, Betsey Johnson, Jaeger, Charles Jourdan, Norma Kamali, Kangol, Kenzo, Calvin Klein, Lacoste, Karl Lagerfeld, Lanvin, Ralph Lauren, Liberty & Co., Marks & Spencer plc, Vera Maxwell, Mary McFadden, Simone Mirman, Missoni, Issey Miyake, Claude Montana, Jean Muir, Bruce Oldfield, Mollie Parnis, Jean Patou, Thea Porter, Pringle of Scotland, Mary Quant, Paco Rabanne, Janet Reger, Oscar de la Renta, Zandra Rhodes, Patricia Roberts, Nina Ricci, Vidal Sassoon, Mila Schön, Sears Roebuck & Co., David Shilling, George Stavropoulos, Yves Saint Laurent, Levi Strauss, Angelo Tarlazzi, Tiffany & Co., Pauline Trigère, Emanuel Ungaro, Koos van den Akker, Verdura Inc., Gianni Versace, Diane von Fürstenberg, Vuokko, Janice Wainwright, Warners, Whitmore-Thomas, Yuki.

BIBLIOGRAPHY

Plates and dates are, where known, those of first publication.

General fashion references

Arnold, Janet, *A Handbook of Costume*, London, 1973.
Batterberry, Michael and Ariane, *Mirror, Mirror: A Social History of Fashion*, New York, 1977.
Black, J. Anderson and Garland, Madge, *A History of Fashion*, London, 1953.
Boucher, François, *A History of Costume in the West*, London, 1967.
———, *20,000 Years of Fashion*, New York, 1982.
Bradfield, Nancy, *Costume in Detail, 1730–1930*, London, 1968.
Brooke, Iris, *A History of English Costume*, London, 1937.
Crawford, M. D. C., *The Ways of Fashion*, New York, 1941.
Cunnington, C. W. and Phillis, *Handbook of English Costume in the 19th Century*, London, 1959.
Cunnington, Phillis, *Costume*, London, 1966.
Davenport, M., *The Book of Costume*, 2 vols, New York, 1948.
Ewing, Elizabeth, *History of 20th Century Fashion*, London, 1974.
Garland, Madge, *Fashion*, London, 1962.
Glynn, Prudence, *In Fashion: Dress in the Twentieth Century*, London, 1978.

Godey's Lady's Book(s), Philadelphia, 1872.
Gurell, Lois M. and Beeson, Marianne S., *Dimensions of Dress and Adornment*, Iowa, 1977.
Kempner, Rachel H., *Costume*, New York, 1977.
Khornak, Lucille, *Fashion 2001*, New York, 1982.
Laver, James, *Taste and Fashion*, London, 1937.
———, *Costume*, New York and London, 1963.
———, *Fashion*, London, 1963.
———, *Style in Costume*, London, 1949.
———, *Modesty in Dress*, London and Boston, 1969.
———, *A Concise History of Costume*, London and New York, 1969.
Mansfield, Alan and Cunnington, Phillis, *Handbook of English Costume in the 20th Century, 1900–1950*, London, 1973.
Monserrat, Ann, *And The Bride Wore*, London, 1973.
Moore, Langley Doris, *The Woman in Fashion*, London, 1949.
Picken, Mary Brooks, *Dressmakers of France*, New York, 1956.
Rubin, Leonard G., *The World of Fashion*, San Francisco, 1976.
Russell, Douglas A., *Costume History and Style*, New Jersey, 1983.
Wilcox, R. Turner, *Mode in Costume*, New York, 1947.
Yarwood, Doreen, *English Costume*, London, 1952.

Bibliography

Fashion dictionaries and encyclopaedias

Anthony P. and Arnold, J., *Costume: A General Bibliography*, 2nd edition, London, 1974.

Calasibetta, Charlotte, *Fairchild's History of Fashion*, New York, 1975.

Houck, Catherine, *The Fashion Encyclopedia*, New York, 1982.

Ironside, Janey, *A Fashion Alphabet*, London, 1968.

Picken, Mary Brooks, *The Fashion Dictionary*, New York, 1939.

Stegemeyer, Anne, *Who's Who in Fashion*, New York, 1980.

Watkins, Josephine Ellis, *Who's Who in Fashion*, 2nd edition, New York, 1975.

Wilcox, R. Turner, *Dictionary of Costume*, New York, 1969.

Yarwood, Doreen, *Encylopedia of World Costume*, New York, 1978.

Books about fashion and costume designers

Baillen, Claude, *Chanel Solitaire*, London, 1973.

Brooklyn Institute of Arts and Sciences, *The Age of Worth*, New York, 1982.

Charles-Roux, Edmonde, *Chanel*, London, 1976.

————, *Chanel and Her World*, London, 1981.

Chierichetti, David, *Hollywood Costume Design*, New York, 1976.

De Graw, Imelda, *25 Years/25 Couturiers*, Denver, 1975.

de Marly, Diana, *Worth, Father of Haute Couture*, London, 1980.

Galante, Pierre, *Mademoiselle Chanel*, Chicago, 1973.

Haedrich, Marcel, *Coco Chanel, Her Life, Her Secrets*, London and Boston, 1972.

Keenan, Brigid, *Dior in Vogue*, London and New York, 1981.

Latour, Anny, *Kings of Fashion*, New York, 1956.

Laynam, Ruth, *Couture, An Illustrated History of the Great Paris Designers and their Creations*, New York, 1972.

Lee, Sarah Tomerlin, ed., *American Fashion: The Life and Lines of Adrian, Mainbocher, McCardell, Norell, Trigère*, New York, 1975.

Leese, Elizabeth, *Costume Design in the Movies*, London, 1976.

Madsen, Axel, *Living for Design: The Yves St. Laurent Story*, New York, 1979.

Mulassano, Adriana and Custaldi, Alfa, *The Who's Who of Italian Fashion*, Florence, 1979.

New York City Metropolitan Museum of Art, *The World of Balenciaga*, New York, 1973.

Osma, Guillermo de, *Fortuny, Mariano Fortuny: His Life and Work*, London, 1980.

Perkins, Alice K., *Paris Couturiers and Milliners*, New York, 1949.

Saunders, Edith, *The Age of Worth*, London, 1954.

White, Palmer, *Poiret*, London and New York, 1973.

Williams, Beryl, *Fashion Is Our Business: Careers of Famous American Designers*, Philadelphia, 1945.

Books by fashion designers, milliners, costume designers, etc.

Amies, Hardy, *Just So Far*, London, 1954.

————, *Still Here*, London, 1984.

Antoine, *Antoine by Antoine*, New York, 1945.

Balmain, Pierre, *My Years and Seasons*, London, 1964.

Creed, Charles, *Made to Measure*, London, 1961.

Daché, Lilly, *Talking Through My Hats*, London, 1946.

Dior, Christian, *Christian Dior and I*, New York, 1957.

————, *Dior by Dior*, London, 1957.

Ferragamo, Salvatore, *Shoemaker of Dreams*, London, 1957.

Gordon, Lady Duff, *Discretions and Indiscretions*, London, 1932.

Greer, Howard, *Designing Male*, New York, 1951.

Hartnell, Norman, *Royal Courts of Fashion*, London and New York, 1971.

————, *Silver and Gold*, London, 1955.

Head, Edith and Ardmore, Jane K., *The Dress Doctor*, Boston, 1959.

Hulanicki, Barbara, *From A to Biba*, London, 1984.

Klein, Bernat, *Eye for Colour*, London, 1965.

Links, J. G., *The Book of Fur*, London, 1956.

————, *How To Look At Furs*, London, 1962.

Poiret, Paul, *En Habillant l'Epoque*, Paris, 1930.

————, *My First Fifty Years*, London, 1934.

————, *Revenez-Y*, Paris, 1932.

————, *King of Fashion: The Autobiography of Paul Poiret*, Philadelphia, 1931.

Quant, Mary, *Quant By Quant*, London, 1965.

Schiaparelli, Elsa, *Shocking Life*, London and New York, 1954.

Sharaff, Irene, *Broadway and Hollywood: Costumes designed by Irene Sharaff*, New York, 1976.

Thaarup, Aage, *Heads and Tails*, London, 1956.

Tinling, Teddy, *White Ladies*, London, 1963.

————, *Sixty Years in Tennis*, London, 1983.

Worth, Jean-Philippe, *A Century of Fashion*, Boston, 1928.

Fashion illustrators and illustration

Barbier, Georges, *The Illustrations of Georges Barbier in Full Color*, New York, 1977.

Brunelleschi, Umberto: fashion stylist, illustrator, stage and costume designer, New York, 1979.

Delhaye, Jean, *Affiches Gravures Art Deco*, London, 1977.

Erté, *Things I Remember: An Autobiography*, London and New York, 1975.

Etherington-Smith, Meredith, *Patou*, London, 1983.

Gallo, Max, *L'Affiche miroir de l'histoire*, Paris, 1973.

Ginsburg, Madeleine, *A Introduction to Fashion Illustration*, London, 1980.

Kery, Patricia Franz, *Great Magazine Covers of the World*, New York, 1982.

Moore, Doris Langley, *Fashion Through Fashion Plates 1771–1970*, London, 1971.

Packer, William, *The Art of Vogue Covers*, New York, 1980.

————, *Fashion Drawing in Vogue*, London, 1984.

Petersen, Theodore, *Magazines in the Twentieth Century*, Chicago, 1965.

Schaw, Michael, *J. C. Leyendecker*, New York, 1974.

Spencer, Charles, *Erté*, London, 1970.

Vertès, Marcel, *Art and Fashion*, New York and London, 1944.

Fashion photographers and photography

Beaton, Cecil, *Photobiography*, New York, 1951.

————, *The Glass of Fashion*, London, 1954.

————, *Selected Diaries, 1926–54*, London, 1954; (*The Wandering Years: Diaries 1922–39*); (*The Years Between: Diaries 1939–44*); (*The Happy Years: Diaries 1944–48*); (*The Strenuous Years: Diaries 1948–55*); (*The Restless Years: Diaries 1955–63*).

Devlin, Polly, *Vogue Book of Fashion Photography*, New York, 1979.

Hall-Duncan, Nancy, *The History of Fashion Photography*, New York, 1979.

Kery, Patricia Franz, *Great Magazine Covers of the World*, New York, 1975.

Packer, William, *The Art of Vogue Covers*, New York, 1980.

Steichen, Edward, *A Life in Photography*, New York, 1963.
Vreeland, Diana and Penn, Irving, *Inventive Paris Clothes, 1909–1939*, London, 1977.

World of magazines

Ballard, Bettina, *In My Fashion*, New York and London, 1960.
Chase, Edna Woolman and Ilka, *Always in Vogue*, New York and London, 1954.
Garland, Ailsa, *Lion's Share*, London, 1970.
Kery, Patricia Franz, *Great Magazine Covers of the World*, New York, 1982.
Packer, William, *The Art of Vogue Covers*, New York, 1980.
———, *Fashion Drawing in Vogue*, London, 1984.
Petersen, Theodore, *Magazines in the Twentieth Century*, Chicago, 1965.
Seebohm, Caroline, *The Man Who Was Vogue*, New York, 1982.
Snow, Carmel, *The World of Carmel Snow*, New York, 1962.
White, Cynthia L., *Women's Magazines 1693–1968*, London, 1970.
Yoxall, H. W., *A Fashion of Life*, London, 1966.

Department stores and retailing

Adburgham, Alison, *Shops and Shopping*, London, 1964.
Brady, Maxine, *Bloomingdales*, New York, 1980.
Daves, Jessica, *Ready-Made Miracle: The American Story of Fashion for the Millions*, New York, 1967.
Jarnow, Jeanette and Judelle, Beatrice, *Inside the Fashion Business*, 2nd edition, New York, 1974.
Levin, Phyllis Lee, *The Wheels of Fashion*, New York, 1965.
Marcus, Stanley, *Minding the Store*, Boston, 1974.
Pope, Jesse, *The Clothing Industry in New York*, New York, 1970.
Rees, Goronwy, *St. Michael: A History of Marks and Spencer*, London, 1969.
Roscho, Bernard, *The Rag Race*, New York, 1963.

Haute-couture and ready-to-wear

Allen, Agnes, *The Story of Clothes*, London, 1955.
Bertin, Celia, *Paris à la mode*, London, 1956.
———, *La Couture, Terre Inconnue*, Paris, 1956.
Daves, Jessica, *Ready-Made Miracle: The American Story of Fashion for the Millions*, New York, 1967.
de Marly, Diana, *The History of Haute Couture 1850–1950*, London and New York, 1980.
Halliday, L., *The Makers of Our Clothes*, London, 1966.
Ley, Sandra, *Fashion for Everyone: The Story of Ready-to-Wear 1870s–1970s*, New York, 1976.
Lynam, Ruth, ed., *Couture*, New York, 1972.
Richards, Florence, *The Ready-to-Wear Industry, 1900–1950*, New York, 1951.
Riley, R. and Vecchio, W., *The Fashion Makers*, New York, 1967.

Accessories

Baynes, Ken and Kate, *The Shoe Show: British Shoes since 1790*, London, 1979.
Becker, Vivienne, *Antique and 20th-Century Jewellery*, London, 1980.
Braun, Ronsdorf M., *The History of the Handkerchief*, Leigh-on-Sea, England, 1967.
Buck, Anne, *Victorian Costume and Costume Accessories*, London, 1961.

Clabburn, Pamela, *Shawls*, Buckinghamshire, England, 1981.
Crawford, T. S., *A History of the Umbrella*, New York and Devon, 1970.
Epstein, Diana, *Buttons*, New York, 1968.
Foster, Vanda, *Bags and Purses*, London, 1982.
Grass, Milton E., *History of Hosiery*, New York, 1953.
Houart, V., *Buttons: A Collector's Guide*, London, 1977.
Irwin, John, *The Kashmir Shawl*, London, 1973.
Kennett, Frances, *The Collector's Book of Twentieth Century Fashion*, London, 1983.
Sallee, Lynn, *Old Costume Jewellery 1870–1945*, Alabama, 1979.
Swann, June, *Shoes*, London, 1982.

Underwear

Cunnington, C. W. and Phillis, *The History of Underclothes*, London, 1951.
Ewing, Elizabeth, *Dress and Undress*, London and New York, 1978.
St. Laurent, Cecil, *The History of Ladies' Underwear*, London, 1968.
Waugh, Norah, *Corsets and Crinolines*, London, 1954.
Willett, C. and Cunnington, Phillis, *The History of Underclothes*, London, 1981.
Yooll, Emily, *The History of the Corset*, London, 1946.

Textiles

American Fabrics Magazine, ed., *Encyclopedia of Textiles*, New York, 1972.
Earnshaw, Patricia, *The Identification of Lace*, Buckinghamshire, England, 1982.
———, *The Dictionary of Lace*, Buckinghamshire, England, 1981.
Kleeburg, Irene Cumming, *The Butterick Fabric Handbook*, New York, 1982.
Linton, George E., *The Modern Textile and Apparel Dictionary*, New Jersey, 1973.
Luscombe, S., *The Encyclopedia of Buttons*, New York, 1967.
Picken, Mary Brooks, *The Fashion Dictionary*, New York, 1939.
Simeon, Margaret, *The History of Lace*, London, 1979.

General history

Adburgham, Alison, *A Punch History of Manners*, London, 1961.
Howell, Georgina, *In Vogue*, London, 1975.
Keenan, Brigid, *The Women We Wanted to Look Like*, New York, 1977.

Period history

Arlen, Michael, *The Green Hat*, London, 1924.
Battersby, Martin, *The Decorative Twenties*, London, 1969.
———, *The Decorative Thirties*, London, 1971.
Belle, Jean-Michel, *Les Folles Années de Maurice Sachs*, Paris, 1979.
Bennett, Richard, *A Picture of the Twenties*, London, 1961.
Bernard, Barbara, *Fashion in the 60s*, London and New York, 1958.
Blythe, Ronald, *The Age of Illusion*, London, 1963.
Brough, James, *The Prince and the Lily*, London, 1975.
Brunhammer, Yvonne, *Lo Stile 1925*, Milan, 1966.
Dorner, Jane, *Fashion in the Forties and Fifties*, London, 1957.
Engen, Rodney, *Kate Greenaway*, London, 1981.
Garland, Madge, *The Indecisive Decade*, London, 1968.
Garrett, Richard, *Mrs Simpson*, London, 1979.

Bibliography

Goldring, Douglas, *The Nineteen Twenties*, London, 1945.
Haney, Lynn, *Naked At the Feast*, London, 1981.
Hillier, Bevis, *The World of Art Deco*, Minneapolis, 1971.
Jenkins, Alan, *The Twenties*, London, 1974.
Lardner, John, *The Aspirin Age 1914–1941*, London, n.d.
Laver, James, *Between The Wars*, London, 1961.
———, *The Jazz Age*, London, 1964.
Margueritte, Victor, *La Garçonne*, Paris, 1922.
Melinkoff, Ellen, *What We Wore*, New York, 1984.
Montgomery, James, *The Twenties*, London, 1957.
Ridley, Jasper, *Napoleon III and Eugénie*, London, 1979.
Roberts, Cecil, *The Bright Twenties*, London, 1970.
Robinson, Julian, *Fashion in the 40s*, London and New York, 1976.
———, *Fashion in the 30s*, London, 1978.
Sachs, Maurice, *La Décade de l'illusion*, Paris, 1932.
Seaman, C. C. B., *Life in Britain between the Wars*, London, 1970.
Stevenson, Pauline, *Edwardian Fashion*, London, 1980.

The fashion scene

Adburgham, Alison, *View of Fashion*, London, 1966.
Bender, Marilyn, *The Beautiful People*, New York, 1967.
Brady, James, *Super Chic*, Boston, 1974.
Carter, Ernestine, *20th Century Fashion, A Scrapbook 1900 to Today*, London, 1957.
———, *With Tongue in Chic*, London, 1974.
———, *The Changing World of Fashion*, London and New York, 1977.
———, *Magic Names of Fashion*, London, 1980.
de Wolfe, Elsie, *After All*, London, 1935.
Fairchild, John, *The Fashionable Savages*, New York, 1965.
Flanner, Janet, *Paris Was Yesterday*, New York, 1979.
Kelly, Katie, *The Wonderful World of Women's Wear Daily*, New York, 1972.
Lambert, Eleanor, *The World of Fashion, People, Places, Resources*, New York, 1976.
Morris, Bernadine and Walz, Barbara, *The Fashion Makers*, New York, 1978.
Spanier, Ginette, *It Isn't All Mink*, New York, 1960.
———, *And Now It's Sable*, London, 1970.
Wilcox, R. Turner, *The Mode in Hats and Headdresses*, New York, 1959.
Wilson, Eunice, *The History of Shoe Fashions*, New York, 1969.

Psychology and sociology of fashion

Anspach, Karlyne Alice, *The Why of Fashion*, Amos, Iowa, 1968.
Baines, Barbara, *Fashion Revivals*, London, 1981.
Bergler, Edmund, *Fashion and the Unconscious*, New York, 1953.
Delbourg-Delphis, Marylene, *Le Chic et le look*, Paris, 1981.
Dorner, Jane, *The Changing Shape of Fashion*, London, 1974.
Flugel, John C., *The Psychology of Clothes*, London and New York, 1966.
Garland, Madge, *The Changing Form of Fashion*, London, 1970.
Gernsheim, A., *Fashion and Reality 1840–1914*, London, 1963.
Hawes, Elizabeth, *Fashion is Spinach*, New York, 1938.
———, *It's Still Spinach*, Boston, 1954.
———, *Why Is a Dress?*, New York, 1954.
Hollander, Anne, *Seeing Through Clothes*, New York, 1978.
Horn, Marilyn J., *The Second Skin: An Interdisciplinary Study of Clothing*, 2nd edition, Boston, 1975.
Hurlock, Elizabeth B., *The Psychology of Dress*, New York, 1929.
Konig, Rene, *The Restless Image, a Sociology of Fashion*, London, 1973.
Laver, James, *How and why fashions in men's and women's clothes have changed during the past 200 years*, London, 1950.
Lurie, Alison, *The Language of Clothes*, New York, 1981.
Polhemus, Ted and Procter, Lyn, *Fashion and Anti-Fashion: An Anthropology of Clothing and Adornment*, London, 1978.
Pritchard, Mrs Eric, *The Cult of Chiffon*, New York, 1902.
Roach, Mary Ellen and Eicher, Joanne B., *Dress, Adornment and the Social Order*, New York, 1965.
Rosencrantz, Mary Lou, *Clothing Concepts: A Social-Psychological Approach*, London, 1972.
Ryan, Mary S., *Clothing: A Study in Human Behaviour*, New York, 1966.
Young, Agatha Brooks, *Recurring Cycles of Fashion*, New York, 1937.